Themes from the Ancient Near East BANEA Publication

FORCES OF TRANSFORMATION
THE END OF THE BRONZE AGE IN THE MEDITERRANEAN

*Proceedings of an international symposium
held at St. John's College, University of Oxford
25–6th March 2006*

Edited by

CHRISTOPH BACHHUBER AND R. GARETH ROBERTS

OXBOW BOOKS
British Association for Near Eastern Archaeology (BANEA)

First published in the United Kingdom in 2009. Reprinted in 2016 by
OXBOW BOOKS
The Old Music Hall, 106–108 Cowley Road, Oxford OX4 1JE

and in the United States by
OXBOW BOOKS
1950 Lawrence Road, Havertown, PA 19083

© Oxbow Books and the individual authors 2009

Paperback Edition: ISBN 978-1-84217-503-3
Digital Edition: ISBN 978-1-84217-960-4

A CIP record for this book is available from the British Library

For a complete list of Oxbow titles, please contact:

UNITED KINGDOM
Oxbow Books
Telephone (01865) 241249, Fax (01865) 794449
Email: oxbow@oxbowbooks.com
www.oxbowbooks.com

UNITED STATES OF AMERICA
Oxbow Books
Telephone (800) 791-9354, Fax (610) 853-9146
Email: queries@casemateacademic.com
www.casemateacademic.com/oxbow

Oxbow Books is part of the Casemate Group

Printed and bound in Great Britain by
Marston Book Services Ltd, Oxfordshire

Cover design drawn by Katharina Streit

CONTENTS

EDITORS' PREFACE

Christoph Bachhuber and R. Gareth Roberts

'Forces of Transformation: the end of the Bronze Age in the Mediterranean', was an international symposium held at St. John's College, University of Oxford, on 25–6 March 2006. The inspiration for the conference was found over a cup of coffee with Stephanie Dalley in the Oxford Playhouse. We, the editors, had been recently introduced and she suggested our respective research interests might benefit from a local (if casual) seminar addressing the end of the Bronze Age in the Mediterranean. This seemed like such a good idea that we extended an invitation to the international academic community.

Forces of Transformation continues in the footsteps of a series of highly influential symposia addressing this period in the greater Mediterranean and Western Asia. Readers of this volume will doubtless know of the conferences held at Brown University in 1990 (Ward and Joukowsky 1992), at the Hebrew University in 1995 (Gitin *et al.* 1998), and at the University of Pennsylvania also in 1995 (Oren 2000). All three meetings drew together some of the most esteemed scholars in their respective fields of ancient Mediterranean and Near Eastern studies. Subsequent symposia have addressed aspects of this period in wider chronological and related thematic forums (Karageorghis and Stampolidis 1998; Laffineur and Greco 2005), though Forces of Transformation is the first in over a decade to be devoted exclusively to the LBA–EIA transition (or transformation!). We hope to follow the example of the previous seminars and to offer a fresh and vital re-assessment of this compelling period.

We share the vision of the previous organizers and editors who outlined the global nature of the problem and the broad perspective required to address it. At risk of being overly diffuse, we invited into the mix archaeologists, paleo-climatologists, historians and iconographers with regional interests from Mesopotamia to Iberia. The response was enthusiastic and we wish here to briefly outline some of the aims of the symposium and some of the results.

The conference was dominated by archaeologists as the end of the Bronze Age continues to be a material problem more than any other. For much of the latter half of the last century archaeologists have had at their disposal only one methodological framework broad enough to address the global dynamic of the LBA–EIA transition – namely cultural-historical diffusionism, in which the movement or dislocation of social groups has been understood to be a fundamental agent of social and cultural change. This perspective has generally agreed with textual suggestions of mobile (seafaring) populations who were implicated in threatening and disrupting the interests of the Late Bronze Age interregional elite. Aspects of material culture change after the destruction and abandonment of many Late Bronze Age palatial centres have thus been outlined within a dramatic historical narrative of dislocation, migration, conflict and conquest.

The problem of the LBA–EIA transition has remained geographically too vast to interest or benefit much from the more micro-scale approaches that have since dominated archaeological enquiry – namely within processual and post-processual frameworks. New models to address this period have been necessarily rooted in a new global perspective, which have posed a direct challenge to the cultural-historical interpretations of the LBA–EIA transformation. The works of Andrew and Susan Sherratt (respectively and together) have been prominent in modernizing diffusionism in Mediterranean and European prehistory and proto-history. The Sherratts' well known adaptations of World Systems Theory to problems in the Bronze Age Mediterranean and Europe, which have included incorporating largely post-processual considerations like the embodiment of social meaning in objects and materials and implications for their consumption within networks of long distance exchange, have offered scholarship a unified model within which to outline social and economic interrelations and relationships between Europe (particularly the Aegean), the eastern Mediterranean, Egypt and Western Asia. The swift decline of an inherently unstable and unsustainable Bronze Age political economy would have complex and varying consequences for different social groups, in different regions, within different levels of social, political and economic organization.

The Sherratts' influence is tangible in this volume, as is the longer established paradigm. These need not be mutually exclusive bases of interpretation; a few papers appear to draw on the agency of both perspectives and neither are explicitly relevant in others, but most current approaches on the broader concerns of the period fall within this spectrum of interpretation. We have exposed our bias to some extent by choosing 'transformation' as the operative concept for the conference title, hoping some participants might highlight continuities as well as change in their material, or highlight rates or intensity of change that may have differed from the sudden collapse that guides the historical narrative of the LBA–EIA transition. We very much enjoyed seeing scholars working in regions from around the Mediterranean outline these variable patterns in their material.

We were nevertheless mostly interested in providing a comfortable arena for scholars from a wide range of regional, methodological and professional backgrounds to engage with one another. In this way the conference was much in the spirit of Andrew Sherratt, as was the global perspective. We have dedicated the conference and volume to the memory of this extraordinary man, who died on 24 February 2006, one month before the symposium. The event was also held in honour of his wife Susan Sherratt. Both have deeply influenced and inspired our respective careers.

We warmly thank the paper- and poster presenters who travelled from four continents to attend this meeting, including Trude Dothan for accepting our invitation to offer the keynote address. We enjoyed their stimulating presentations, their good company, and we thank them also for their patience and promptness through the editing process. Paper presenters who were unable to contribute to this volume include Naoise MacSweeney, Trude Dothan, Stephen J. Bourke and Christofilis Maggidis (read by Jessica Miller). The conference and publication both received generous financial and logistical support from the British Association for Near Eastern Archaeology (BANEA). We would particularly like to thank Wendy Matthews for her involvement and encouragement. The School of Archaeology at the University of Oxford also provided financial support, and we would like to thank the Ashmolean Museum and particularly the webmaster Jonathan Moffet for granting the conference web space and for his patience and humour through the barrage of updates. Thanks also go to Stephanie Dalley for the initial spark of inspiration for the conference and for her continued support and assistance through its formation. Many thanks go to the session chairs, including Elizabeth Frood, Rachael Sparks, Irene Lemos, Matthew Fitzjohn and Gideon Henderson, a few of whom travelled from other universities to participate. Thanks also to the staff of St. John's College, Oxford for creating a comfortable and tasteful venue for the event (and particularly to those who were understaffed one morning but nevertheless helped avert a coffee crisis). Lastly, we wish to thank the student volunteers from the School of Archaeology, Jessica Miller and Richard Bliaut, and also our significant other and sibling volunteers, Christine Khoo and Anika Bachhuber. The efforts of all the above individuals and institutions were joined to create a very enjoyable and inspiring seminar event.

LIST OF CONTRIBUTORS

CAROLYN CHABOT ASLAN
(Koç University)
caslan@ku.edu.tr

CHRISTOPH BACHHUBER
(St. John's College, Oxford)
christoph.bachhuber@arch.ox.ac.uk

MAUREEN BASEDOW
(Miami University)
basedow@muohio.edu

CAROL BELL
(British School at Athens)
carol.bell.pullan@btinternet.com

ELIZABETH FRENCH
(Newnham College, Cambridge)
lisacamb@aol.com

FRANCESCA FULMINANTE
(Magdelene College, Cambridge)
FF234@cam.ac.uk

MERCOURIOS GEORGIADIS
(University of Nottingham)
merkourisgeorgiadis@hotmail.com

JOHN D. M. GREEN
(Ashmolean Museum, Oxford)
jack.green@ashmus.ox.ac.uk

SABINE LAEMMEL
(Kings College, Cambridge)
sabinelaemmel@yahoo.fr

MICHAEL FRANKLIN LANE
(University of Maryland, Baltimore County)
mflane@umbc.edu

BARTŁOMIEJ LIS
(Polish Academy of Science)
blis79@o2.pl

JENNIFER MOODY
(University of Texas at Austin)
hogwildjam@mac.com

NAVA PANITZ-COHEN
(The Hebrew University of Jerusalem)
panitz@mscc.huji.ac.il

ANGELOS PAPADOPOULOS
(SACE, University of Liverpool)
a.papadopoulos@liv.ac.uk

KATIA PERNA
(Turin University)
katia.perna@libero.it

R. GARETH ROBERTS
(Greyfriars, Oxford)
r.gareth.roberts@googlemail.com

EELCO J. ROHLING
(National Oceanography Centre, Southampton),
ANGELA HAYES
(Mary Immaculate College, University of Limerick),
PAUL A. MAYEWSKI
(University of Maine) and
MICHAL KUCERA
(Eberhard Karls Universität Tübingen)
E. Rohling@noc.soton.ac.uk

BRUCE ROUTLEDGE
(SACE, University of Liverpool)
Bruce.Routledge@liverpool.ac.uk

and

KEVIN MCGEOUGH
(University of Lethridge)
mcgekm@uleth.ca

PHILIPP STOCKHAMMER
(Heidelberg University)
philippstockhammer@yahoo.de

DAVIDE TANASI
(Turin University)
davide.tanasi@tele2.it

ANDREA VIANELLO
(Intute, Oxford)
a_vianello@hotmail.com

SHARON ZUCKERMAN
(University of Jerusalem)
mssharon@mscc.huji.ac.il

PART 1

CONSIDERATIONS OF CLIMATE

HOLOCENE CLIMATE VARIABILITY IN THE EASTERN MEDITERRANEAN, AND THE END OF THE BRONZE AGE

Eelco J. Rohling, Angela Hayes, Paul A. Mayewski, and Michal Kucera

---

The Late Bronze Age/Early Iron Age transition in the eastern Mediterranean (about 1200–900 BCE) coincided with one of the current interglacial (Holocene) Rapid Climate Change events (RCC), as documented in about 50 globally distributed climate proxy records (Mayewski *et al.* 2004). That compilation study demonstrates that the RCC between 1500 and 500 BCE was characterised by glacier advances on a global scale (in Scandinavia, Central Asia, North America, and the Southern Hemisphere), similar to other RCCs in the intervals 4000–3000 and 2200–1800 BCE, and 800–1000 and 1400–1850 CE. It is evident, therefore, that the RCC at around the end of the Bronze Age was not unique, but part of a repeating pattern of global climate deteriorations during the Holocene.

The present contribution reviews previous studies to evaluate the severity of the impact of the Holocene RCCs in the eastern Mediterranean region with emphasis on the RCC of 1500–500 BCE. It also evaluates the constraints on the timing relationship between the end of the Bronze Age and expressions of the RCC of 1500–500 BCE in the eastern Mediterranean region.

Holocene RCCs and the eastern Mediterranean

Besides global glacier advances, the Holocene RCCs are also marked by distinct increases in the concentration of K^+ ions (*i.e.* [K^+]) in the GISP2 ice core from the Greenland summit (Fig. 1: O'Brien *et al.* 1995; Mayewski *et al.* 1997; Mayewski *et al.* 2004). Potassium transport to the Greenland ice sheet is strongly related to the late winter-spring intensity of the atmospheric high-pressure conditions over Siberia (Meeker and Mayewski 2002). Enhanced [K^+] within the RCCs therefore suggests an intensification of Eurasian winter conditions.

The Holocene RCCs are also characterized by peaks in the sea-salt [Na^+] series from the GISP2 ice core (Fig. 1.1). These sea-salt [Na^+] variations closely reflect the intensity of the Icelandic Low (Meeker and Mayewski 2002). An intensified (deeper) Icelandic Low causes intensification of onshore winds to Greenland, so that sea ice stays longer each season, and more persists from season to season. The inferred increase of North Atlantic sea-ice extent and duration during the Holocene RCCs is supported by concomitant increases in Holocene, most likely sea-ice transported, ice-rafted debris concentrations in North Atlantic sediments during the RCCs (Bond *et al.* 2001).

A key record for the identification of Holocene RCCs in the eastern Mediterranean region has been developed by investigation of marine microfossil assemblages in sediment core LC21 (Rohling *et al.* 2002b). LC21 was recovered from the SE Aegean Sea, on the boundary between the north-south extended Aegean Sea and the west-east extended Levantine Sea. This is a highly sensitive location for the recording of expansions and contractions of the cooler Aegean signature relative to the warmer Levantine signature.

Temperature changes in the region of sediment core LC21 have been deduced from changes in the assemblages of marine unicellular zooplankton microfossils (planktonic foraminifera Rohling *et al.* 2002b). These were grouped in species clusters according to affinities to warmer or cooler conditions, yielding a relative record of warming and cooling. Based on mapping of the same assemblages in core tops from the Aegean Sea, the relative changes were roughly calibrated to quantitative estimates of sea surface temperature change. This suggested that the RCCs were associated with temperature drops of the order of 2–3°C in the SE Aegean region, notably in winter. We corroborate this initial estimate by similar values from statistically more robust calibrations of the faunal changes using an Artificial

Neural Network approach (Fig. 1.1: for method, see Hayes *et al.* 2005). In central Aegean Sea core SL-11 (Casford *et al.* 2002; Casford *et al.* 2003), the ANN method suggests a magnitude of cooling of about 2.5°C for the Holocene RCCs (unpublished data). This may suggest that the impact of cooling was stronger in more northern sites, and somewhat weaker further to the south, which would agree with the inferred cause of the cooling events in the Aegean Sea (northerly outbreaks of cold air – see below).

The approximate 2°C magnitude of the Holocene RCCs in the Aegean compares well with the magnitude of contemporaneous cooling events in the western Mediterranean, which were quantified with organic geochemical techniques (Cacho *et al.* 2001). Oxygen isotope analyses from speleothems in southwest Romania (Poleva Cave) also provide evidence of climatic cooling within this time period. In that record, the oxygen isotope record is used as a relative temperature proxy, and the magnitude of the decrease was not quantified. However, the observed shift of about 1.5‰ in the isotope data implies a significant temperature decrease in the period between 1500 and 500 BCE (Constantin *et al.* 2007). Another

speleothem record, from Spannagel Cave in the central Alps, also shows a marked interval of relatively heavy oxygen isotope ratios (about 1500–800 BCE), which starts with a shift that implies around 3°C winter cooling (Mangini *et al.* 2007). The temporal structure of the Spannagel Cave record closely resembles that of records of North Atlantic hydrographic/sea-ice variations, as obtained from ice-rafted debris counts in marine sediment cores (Bond *et al.* 2001) and supported by the GISP2 ice-core [Na⁺] series (Fig. 1.1). The combined information demonstrates a significant correlation between terrestrial and marine palaeoclimate records at this time, with an emphasis on winter-time perturbations.

The cooling events in the Aegean Sea have been ascribed to intensification and frequency increase of wintertime northerly outbreaks of cold polar and continental air over the basin, relative to the present (Rohling *et al.* 2002b). Such outbreaks still occur today (for a summary and data of such an event in the year 2001, see Casford *et al.* 2003). These outbreaks are a consequence of the Mediterranean's latitudinal position and its mountainous northerly margin, which exert an important control on circulation and

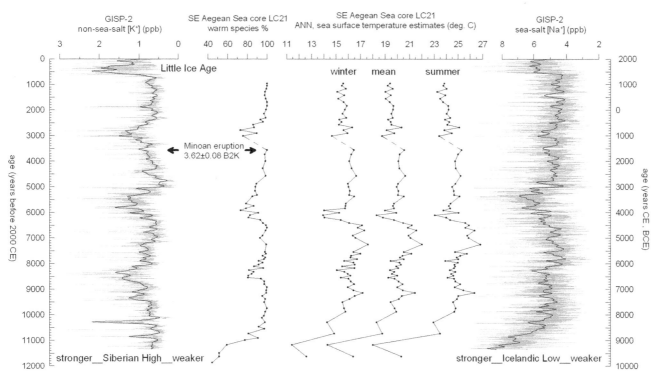

Fig. 1.1: Compilation of the Holocene non-sea-salt [K⁺] and sea-salt [Na⁺] series for the GISP2 ice core from Greenland (O'Brien et al. 1995; Mayewski et al. 1997), with 200-year bandpass filters, along with the sea surface reconstructions for the SE Aegean Sea from planktonic foraminiferal abundance data for sediment core LC21. The qualitative warm species percentage record is the same as that shown in Rohling et al. (2002b). An artificial neural network (ANN) technique is used to transform the faunal abundance data into records of winter, summer, and annual mean sea surface temperature. The technique and its core-top calibration set are fully explained in Hayes et al. (2005). Note that the records are presented on the left-hand side versus age in years Before 2000 CE (B2K), which is the conventionally used ice-core reference datum, as well as (right-hand side) versus age in years CE/BCE (as used throughout this volume). The age of the Minoan eruption is indicated after Bruins and Van Der Plicht (1996) and Kuniholm et al. (1996)

water-mass transformations in the Mediterranean Sea. Contemporaneous cooling events have been found in the Adriatic Sea and in the western Mediterranean (Rohling *et al.* 1997; Cacho *et al.* 1999; Cacho *et al.* 2000; Cacho *et al.* 2001; Casford *et al.* 2001; Rohling *et al.* 2002a; Frigola *et al.* 2007). To understand the relationship between the frequency and intensity of wintertime northerly outbreaks over the Mediterranean and the climatic patterns inferred from proxy records from the wider northern hemisphere (particularly the Greenland ice sheet), it is important to first consider the main drivers behind the general climatic conditions over the region.

During summer, climatic conditions over the Levantine Sea (the eastern sector of the eastern Mediterranean) are dominated by displacement of the North African subtropical high-pressure conditions to the north, causing widespread drought. The Aegean Sea then comes under the influence of northerly winds ('Etesians'), caused by extension of the deep monsoon low-pressure system of northwest India over the Iranian highlands and Anatolia. Although this semi-permanent extension of the monsoon low causes local depression formation around Cyprus and the Middle East, dry summer conditions prevail due to descent in the upper troposphere that is related to the intense Asian summer monsoon (Rodwell and Hoskins 1996; Trigo *et al.* 1999).

During winter, the North African subtropical conditions are displaced southward, and polar/continental conditions expand southward from the north. Low surface-pressure conditions over the central to eastern Mediterranean develop as a consequence of the high sea-surface temperatures relative to the surrounding land masses, fuelled by the high thermal capacity of the basin's water masses (Lolis *et al.* 2002). Interactions between this Mediterranean Low and north-eastward extension of the Azores High (over Iberia, France, and southern Britain), or westward ridging of the Siberian High towards northwest Europe and southern Scandinavia (Maheras *et al.* 1999; Lolis *et al.* 2002), drive intense northerly flows of cold and dry air masses towards the Mediterranean basin. These airflows are channelled (concentrated) through valleys in the mountainous topography of the northern Mediterranean margin. Channelling of polar and continental airflows through the lower Rhone Valley towards the Gulf of Lions gives rise to the 'Mistral', and similar flows towards the Adriatic and Aegean Seas cause the 'Bora' and 'Vardar'. These wintertime outbursts of polar and continental air cause intense evaporation and associated cooling of the sea surface (*e.g.* Leaman and Schott 1991; Saaroni *et al.* 1996; Poulos *et al.* 1997; Maheras *et al.* 1999; Casford *et al.* 2003 and the references therein).

As stated above, the enhanced potassium accumulation in the Greenland ice sheet during Holocene RCCs suggests an intensified late winter-early spring Siberian High. Given that expansion and westward ridging of the Siberian High is

an important processes controlling northerly outbreaks over the Mediterranean (Maheras *et al.* 1999; Lolis *et al.* 2002), we infer that the enhanced Siberian High intensity during RCCs led to an increase in the frequency and intensity of northerly air outbursts over the Mediterranean (notably the Aegean). This would offer a realistic mechanism to explain the observed episodes of about 2°C winter sea surface cooling (up to ~3°C further to the north).

Timing and extent

If, as argued, the enhanced Siberian High intensity at times of RCCs caused an increase in the frequency and intensity of northerly air outbursts over the Mediterranean (notably the Aegean), then it would follow that the Aegean cooling events were in phase with non-sea-salt [K⁺] maxima in Greenland. Within the constraints of the independent dating techniques for the Aegean sediment core (radiocarbon) and Greenland ice core (layer counting), this expectation was found to be valid for the RCC centred on about 6400 BCE, but for the younger RCCs this initial comparison appeared to suggest an older age for the RCCs in the Aegean region than in Greenland (Rohling *et al.* 2002b).

The apparent radiocarbon-based age 'offset' for the RCC of interest in Aegean Sea core LC21 could be evaluated using the presence in LC21 of a 10-cm thick ash-layer from the Minoan eruption of Santorini, which has been accurately dated at 1620 ± 80 BCE (Bruins and Van Der Plicht 1996; Kuniholm *et al.* 1996). The RCC in core LC21 followed sharply after the Minoan eruption. This comparison demonstrated that radiocarbon ages in the younger part of core LC21 were somehow biased towards 'too old' values by about a few centuries, and that the RCC actually started around 1500 BCE. This confirms that it is the temporal equivalent of cooling event TC2 (Cacho *et al.* 2001) and M3 (Frigola *et al.* 2007) in the western Mediterranean and, indeed, of the globally recognised RCC of 1500 to 500 BCE (Bond *et al.* 2001; Mayewski *et al.* 2004; Constantin *et al.* 2007; Mangini *et al.* 2007), which brackets the end of the Bronze Age and the Early Iron Age (about 1200–900 BCE). In Fig. 1.1, the chronology of the LC21 record has been adjusted to account for the correct age of the Minoan eruption (for details, see Rohling *et al.* 2002b).

The onset of the RCC shortly after the Minoan eruption is coincidental, and should not be interpreted to imply causality. David Pyle (1997) argued that an eruption similar to the Minoan eruption might cause a relatively cool period of only a couple of years, and it would be expected to be much more pronounced in proximal sites than in far-field sites. Hence, the multi-century duration and wide-spread (global) appearance of the RCC of 1500–500 BCE would not be consistent with the magnitude of the eruption, nor with the expected distribution pattern of any far-field impacts.

Also, other RCCs have been recognised within the Holocene without associations with major volcanic events (Mayewski *et al.* 2004). As yet, there is no comprehensive theory to explain the quasi-periodic recurrence of RCCs during the Holocene. The repeated pattern of Holocene RCCs appears to be truly global in extent, however, and comparisons with records of cosmogenic isotope (*e.g.* ^{14}C, ^{10}Be) production suggest that a relationship with small reductions in solar output should be considered (*e.g.* Bond *et al.* 2001; Mayewski *et al.* 2004, Maasch *et al.* 2005).

Globally, the RCC of 1500–500 BCE displays a distinct 'cool poles, dry tropics' configuration (Mayewski *et al.* 2004), and this character is obvious also in the eastern Mediterranean domain. A study of clay mineral ratios in SE Aegean sediment core SL123 – which is well dated and includes a clear Minoan ash layer – indicates a relatively high Nile River flow regime from 2200 to 1800 BCE, followed by a sharp decline that culminated in an arid episode from about 1600 BCE (at which level the Minoan ash layer anchors the absolute chronology) until about 800 BCE (Ehrman *et al.* 2007). The timing of the inferred 1600–800 BCE low Nile-flow period in core SL123 (Ehrman *et al.* 2007) agrees rather closely with that of the 1500–500 BCE northerly cold spell recognised in core LC21 (Rohling *et al.* 2002b, and Fig. 1.1). At the base of the interval, the chronologies of cores LC21 and SL123 are firmly anchored relative to one another (and Greenland) by the Minoan ash layer.

The onset of the northerly cold spell / low Nile flooding episode around 1600 to 1500 BCE coincides with a general shift to hyperaridity around 1500 BCE in the Sahara, which marks a culmination in the stepwise decline in moisture availability over that region since about 3500 BCE (Hassan 2002). In the Near East, stable isotope data from caves in Israel suggest a general aridification trend from 2500 to 500 BCE, with an especially arid culmination between 1000 and 500 BCE. During this arid culmination, estimated annual rainfall amounts over Israel may have reached only about 60% of modern values (Bar-Matthews *et al.* 2003).

Impacts

Relative to atmosphere, seawater holds an enormous amount of heat, so that a cooling of 2–3°C throughout the Aegean winter mixed layer (150 or more metres deep) would require a significant atmospheric forcing. Consequently, the impacts on land should be expected to have been much sharper and more pronounced, and to potentially consist of highly variable conditions with considerable extremes (which get 'smoothed out' by the long time-integration in the sea).

Today, occasional northerly outbreaks, with individual event durations of a week to several weeks, cause widespread sharp frosts and aridity (upwind of the water), and snowfall (downwind from the water) around the Aegean shores. During periods when northerly winter outbreaks were more intense and/or frequent – sufficient to cause a sea surface temperature drop of about 2°C – significantly intensified winter frosts and aridity might be expected upwind of the water, notably along the northern and northeastern sectors of the Aegean coast, with milder frosts and snowfalls downwind of the water. To evaluate whether these projected consequences were sufficiently severe during the event of 1500–500 BCE to affect the agricultural quality of the land and consequent food production, highly resolved continental records are needed that can be unambiguously correlated to the marine records.

Outside the Aegean Sea, the northerly cooling influences seem to have been dampened (probably by the vast heat reservoir of the open Levantine Sea) so as to become undetectable. However, records do reveal similarly dated events of enhanced aridity around the southern Levantine margin and in the Near East. From around 1600 BCE there was a period of substantially reduced Nile flooding that lasted about 800 years. In the critical setting of the Nile valley, reduced flooding would likely have affected the agricultural capacity, while the definitive step to hyperaridity in the wider Sahara around 1500 BCE would have finally rendered that environment incapable of any substantial food production. In the Near East, there was a sharply defined arid episode between 1000 and 500 BCE, which would appear to have been severe enough to influence the agricultural capacity of that region.

The question remains whether the listed changes in the Aegeo-Levantine climate would have been severe enough to have a lasting impact on societal structures. To answer that question, more highly resolved records will be needed from around the region, with carefully established correlations between sites (*e.g.* on the basis of volcanic ashes within the various sequences). In addition, any impacts of regional climate change would need to be considered within an appropriate context of potential adaptability to adverse conditions by means of trade within existing (seafaring) networks.

CHANGES IN VERNACULAR ARCHITECTURE AND CLIMATE AT THE END OF THE AEGEAN BRONZE AGE

Jennifer Moody

Most buildings are concerned with sheltering their contents, whether human, animal, foodstuffs, or otherwise, from the elements or weather. How this is done depends on the nature of the local climate, available building resources, topographic constraints, and socio-economic concerns and traditions. Because my interest is in climate change in antiquity and its impact on cultural development in Crete, this paper questions whether any of the architectural changes seen from Late Minoan I to the Early Iron Age could be interpreted as adaptations to a changing climate rather than entirely due to social, defensive or topographic conditions, as is often claimed (Nowicki 2000; 2002; Wallace in preparation).

The relationships between climate and architecture are well known, though not always taken into account by local architects (Table 2.1; Givoni 1969; Geva 1995; Oktay 2002). For example, buildings in hot and arid climates should endeavour to exclude outside air. Ventilation is undesirable as it brings the hot dry air inside raising indoor temperatures. Conversely, buildings in hot and humid climates function best if they are well ventilated, with the circulating air drying and cooling the interior. In Table 2.2 I show that by properly manipulating building materials and building design, a pleasant living environment, well within the range of most cultural definitions, can be achieved without

CLIMATE TYPE	GOALS FOR THE BUILT ENVIRONMENT
HOT-ARID	In hot and arid climates the main function of a building is to moderate the daytime heating effects of the external air (Givoni 1969, 290). In other words, it is important to design buildings whose structure and interior can **keep warm air out**.
HOT-HUMID	In hot and humid climates it is important for a building to **cool and dry the interior air** (Givoni 1969, 285). Ventilation keeps air moving through the environment, keeping the inhabitants cooler and drier.
MEDITERRANEAN CONTINENTAL	Conditions are similar to hot-arid climates: best to **keep warm air out**. Large openings are not desirable. Ventilation causes indoor temperatures to raise both day and night, increasing dust levels. Buildings requiring light will need good ventilation to keep indoor temperatures tolerable, but smaller the openings the better.
MEDITERRANEAN MARINE	Conditions are similar to hot-humid climates: the goal is to **cool and dry the interior air**. Good ventilation is critical. Tall buildings are better ventilated and a tower in a community can improve ventilation for lower structures. Balconies and verandas are effective features.
MEDITERRANEAN MONTANE	Colder winters are a distinguishing feature, necessitating a combination of goals, plus heating in winter. So provision for ventilations as well as a means of closing up the openings is desirable.
COLD	A building constructed in cold climates should ideally have healthy and comfortable indoor thermal conditions and a reasonable fuel economy with the heating methods locally employed. The goal is to **keep warm air in**.

Table 2.1: Climate and building design: the goals

CLIMATE VARIABLE		RANGE OF VARIATION	ARCHITECTURAL SOLUTION
RADIATION	Solar radiation absorbed in the walls.	15–90% of incident radiation.	External colour. Whitewashed surfaces absorb *c.* 15% radiation; cream or light grey absorb 40–50%; dark green, dark grey, red etc absorb 40–50%; black absorbs 80–90%.
	Solar radiation penetrating through windows/doors.	10–90% of incident radiation.	Size and shading of windows and doors. Dark external shading allow as little as 10% of radiation to enter a building; internal shades allow 40–70%; no shades allow 90%.
INDOOR AIR TEMPERATURE	Indoor air temperature amplitude.	10–150% outdoor amplitude.	External colour building materials, size and shading of windows and doors, ventilation.
	Indoor maximum air temperature.	-10 to +10°C from outdoor maximum.	See above.
	Indoor minimum air temperature.	0 to +7°C from outdoor minimum.	See above.
	Indoor surface temperature.	-8 to +30°C from outdoor maximum and minimum.	See above.
VENTILATION AND HUMIDITY	Average internal air speed (windows open).	15–60% of outdoor wind speed.	Effective cross-ventilation.
	Actual air speed at any point in any room.	10–120% of outdoor wind speed.	See above.
	Indoor vapour pressure.	0–7 mm Hg above outdoor level.	Effective cross-ventilation. Crowded buildings and in winter when windows are closed indoor vapour pressure can rise to 7 mm Hg+ above outdoor level.

Table 2.2: Climate variables and architectural solutions (derived from Givoni 1969)

recourse to modern high-tech, high-energy construction. Simple solutions such as thick walls built of an insulating material (mud-brick/adobe), combined with small, high windows or a vent in the roof to allow hot air to escape to the outside without exposing the interior to the outside heat, work especially well in hot and arid climates. Thick, light-colour roofs also insulate and reflect heat, such as the stucco that is often slathered on modern Cretan flat roofs today; according to Baruch Givoni (1969), whitewashing exterior walls alone can reduce absorption of thermal radiation by 85%. Similar structures also work well in cold-arid climates but are not at all suited to humid climates. Instead common architectural features seen in warm humid climates are large external openings, balconies and verandas, all of which promote cross-ventilation.

On the basis of this information five variables have been chosen to assess the climate suitability of Late Bronze- and Early Iron Age houses (Table 2.3), though the list is by no means exhaustive: ventilation, insulation, shade, artificial heating, and artificial cooling. Vernacular houses, *i.e.* non-elite, domestic dwellings, at a number of sites in Crete were then reviewed with these variables in mind (Fig. 2.1). One important caveat is that at most sites only the ground floor of a building is preserved and most walls stand less than one meter high, making the reconstruction of windows

problematic. A second is regional variation. Crete is by no means homogeneous environmentally (Rackham and Moody 1996) or culturally (McEnroe 1990) and it is possible that the sites chosen for this survey are not representative of the island as a whole.

Late Minoan I vernacular architecture

Over 25 years ago John McEnroe (1982) defined three major house plans in Late Minoan (hereafter LM) I architecture. Of interest to this study is his Type-3 house, which occurs all over the island and as of 1982 represented 70% of LM I houses (McEnroe 1982, 10), making it the vernacular dwelling of the time (Fig. 2.2). Type-3 houses were built with stone foundations (either dry or mortared with mud) and mud-brick upper walls. Stone sizes ranged from 'fist-sized' to megalithic boulders. Interior walls could be entirely of mud-brick. Roofs were flat and made of beams, brush and earth. Entry into the vestibule could be on any side, though there may have been a slight preference for the south. Most houses are believed to have had two stories as evidenced by stairwells and debris fallen from upper floors (Michailidou 1990). Erik Hallager (1990) cautions, however, that stairs may have simply led to the roof which could have been used

	Hot temps	Cold temps	Humidity (wetness)	Aridity (dryness)
VENTILATION Windows and doors on multiple walls; roof (clear-story?); multi-storeyed; balconies and verandas; orientation.	x		x	
INSULATION Colour of exterior walls; minimal or no windows; balconies etc.; flat roofs of dense material; thick walls of dense material; party-walls; low to the ground.	x	x		x
SHADE Tall buildings; narrow paths or streets; large eaves; awnings; shutters; gardens.	x			
ARTIFICIAL HEAT Interior hearths; ovens; animals; small rooms.		x		
ARTIFICIAL COOLING Water channels; pools; fountains; gardens; large rooms.	x			

Table 2.3: Architectural variables as related to climate

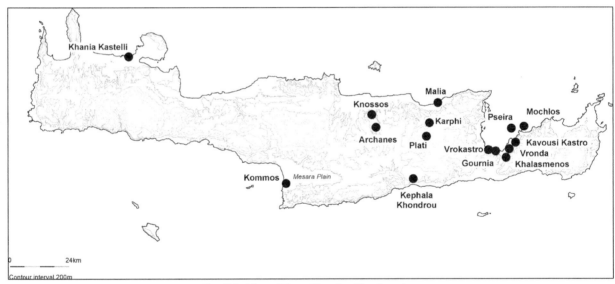

Fig. 2.1: Map of Crete Showing Site Locations

as a covered outdoor room for a variety of activities. Many LM I houses were built on top of a 'door-less' space which can only have been reached from an upper floor. Thomas Brogan and Kellee Barnard (in preparation) suggest that at Mochlos these spaces were not full height rooms and that in at least some cases served as underground storage cellars. Double entries and windows are common features of Type-3 houses. Fixed interior hearths and ovens are rare. The identification of indoor kitchens, except at 'palaces' or 'court buildings' (Schoep 2004) and a few other elite structures, is rare in LM I houses (Muhly 1984; Shaw 1990; Brogan and Barnard in preparation). Similar features can be seen in the LM I vernacular architecture at two recently published sites: Pseira and Kommos.

Pseira

Pseira town is organized along a northwest-southeast ridge on the southeast side of the island (Fig. 2.3). It includes a large square (40 × 25 m) and cobbled pathways which would have allowed air circulation through the village. Only one built hearth is reported from the settlement. According to McEnroe (2001) building materials were much more varied than had previously been supposed. Stone foundations were

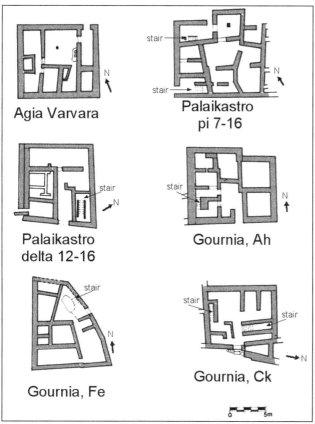

Fig. 2.2: Type-3 houses (after McEnroe 1982)

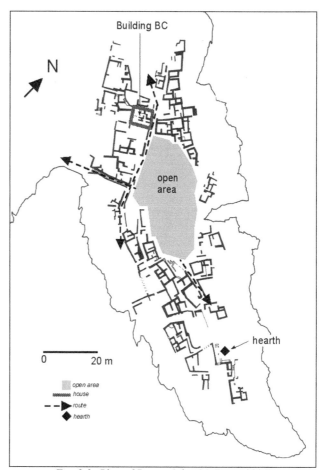

Fig. 2.3: Plan of Psiera (after McEnroe 2001)

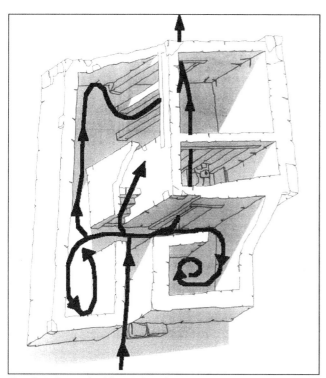

Fig. 2.4: Psiera building BC with reconstructed ventilation (after McEnroe 2001)

the norm, but the use of mud-brick, especially for internal walls, was fairly common. Roofs were probably flat, though there is little evidence for this. A detailed look at building BC shows that the placement of windows, doors and stairs encouraged cross-ventilation (Fig. 2.4).

Kommos

The excavated Minoan town at Kommos sprawls along a northwest-southeast ridge immediately above the beach. A close look at the hilltop houses shows that outdoor open areas were spacious and abundant (Fig. 2.5), and that the street plan was airy. There are three main structures: North House, Oblique House and the so-called 'House with the Press'. Two of the LM I buildings had fixed central hearths. The hearths all occur in large rooms and Maria Shaw (1990, 235) suggests that such centrally located fires were not exclusively, or perhaps even primarily, for cooking but instead were for lighting and heating a space that was 'the hub of life'. That notwithstanding, fixed hearths were rare in LM I vernacular houses.

Both hard and soft limestone was used for building

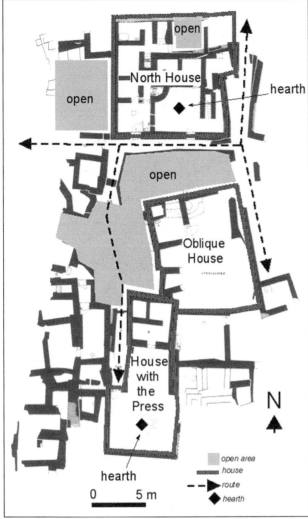

Fig. 2.5: Plan of the hilltop houses at Kommos in LM I (after Shaw and Shaw 1996)

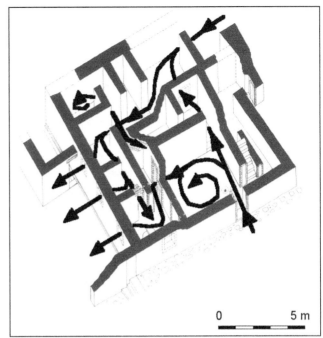

Fig. 2.6: Kommos North House with reconstructed ventilation (after Shaw and Shaw 1996)

stone at Kommos. Beachrock, aeolianite and beach cobbles were also incorporated into the walls. Curiously, there is no evidence for mud-brick in the Mesara (Shaw 1996b, 349), though mud mortar was used between stone courses. Plaster may have covered some exterior walls but evidence is ambiguous. Most plaster seems to have fallen from interior walls and was often painted solid colours: white, red and blue-grey. At Kommos wood is more apparent in LM constructions than in earlier ones, especially for stairs and door frames. As at Pseira, a close look at an individual house, in this case North House, also reveals ample evidence for cross-ventilation, again due to the placement of doors, windows and stairwells (Fig. 2.6).

LM I architectural imagery

In addition to structural remains at archaeological sites,

Minoan houses are well represented in Minoan art (Morgan 1988; Boulotis 1990). A well known, though slightly earlier, example is the so-called Town Mosaic (Warren 1975, 73; Morgan 1988, fig. 33). Features of interest include numerous large latticed or shuttered windows, 'clear-stories' or smaller rooms with doors on the tops of houses, and the fact that they all have a minimum of two stories. All these features would have encouraged interior air circulation. A house model from Archanes also has latticed windows on many walls and verandas which would have created tremendous cross-ventilation (Warren 1975, 94; Morgan 1988, 111).

Large latticed windows, and balconies or verandas are also clearly represented in Minoan fresco fragments, though the best examples come from LM IA Thera (see Morgan 1988, pl. C). In this and other frescoes exterior wall colours are red and blue, not white, which Lyvia Morgan (1988) interprets as a way to represent different building materials; red being mud-brick and blue being stone. Whether this is really the case, it is clear that exterior walls were not whitewashed. As noted above, having light colour exterior walls is one of the simplest and most efficient ways to reduce effective solar radiation and keep an interior space cool in a hot, dry climate. Apparently this was not a major concern in the Minoan Palatial period.

This brief review of LM I vernacular architecture shows it to have been designed for cross-ventilation and shade (Table 2.4). Cooling by devices other than those discussed above are not apparent, though water management in general seems to have been a Minoan *forte* (MacDonald and Driessen

FEATURES	*Late Minoan I houses, esp. Type 3*
TOPOGRAPHY	Usually gentle to moderate slopes.
ALTITUDE	Sea level to 1200 m.
ORIENTATION	Any direction?
BUILDING MATERIAL	
WALLS	Stone foundations with mud-brick and wood.
ROOFS	Beams packed with mud; overlain with split beams, cane, or brush; overlain with clay.
EXTERNAL COLOR	Not necessarily white.
ELEVATION	Usually 2 floors.
ROOFS	Flat with parapet?
INDOOR HEATING/COOLING DEVICES	
HEARTHS	Rare.
WATER	Drains.
VENTILATION	
WINDOWS	Common.
DOORS	Multiple.
ROOM ORGANIZATION	Semi-courtyard.
CLEAR-STORIES	Yes.
VERANDAS AND BALCONIES	Yes: multiple?
COURTYARDS AND PATIOS	Yes: large and public; light-wells?
PROXIMITY TO OTHER STRUCTURES	Close, but sometimes nearly free-standing. Divided into blocks with paved streets/paths.

Table 2.4: Summary Late Bronze I vernacular architecture

1990; Cadogan 2007). Insulation seems to have been a moderate concern, as demonstrated by the thick earthen roofs and perhaps by the partial use of mud-brick in wall construction. Regarding the latter, however, the absence of mud-brick in the Mesara, which then as now would probably have been the hottest part of the island, is puzzling. Also, not whitewashing house exteriors suggests that reflecting the heat of the day was not a prime concern, and heating interior spaces does not seem to have been important.

Late Minoan III A–B architecture

Barbara Hayden (1981) analyzed Late Bronze III architecture for her PhD dissertation and divided it into two major types: Axially Organized Buildings and Minoanizing/Mycenaean Buildings. Almost without exception the 'axially organized' buildings, which have a series of rooms linked in a linear fashion resulting in a long, narrow house, have poor ventilation (Fig. 2.7). Like many LM I houses, some LM III houses were constructed on top of 'door-less' spaces which can only have been reached from an upper floor. However, as noted previously, this feature cannot be reliably used to posit a multi-storied building as it is not clear if they represent full-height rooms.

Hayden's Minoanizing/Mycenaean plans, represented in Fig. 2.8 by houses at Plati and Gournia, have somewhat better ventilation, perhaps a relic of LM I architecture. The two outdoor entries in Building B at Plati dramatically improve cross-ventilation. Both these houses, however, were

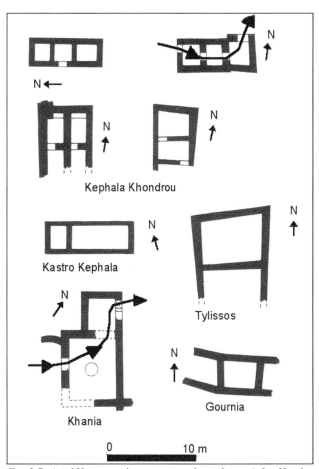

Kephala Khondrou

Kastro Kephala

Tylissos

Khania

Gournia

0   10 m

Fig. 2.7: Axial Houses with reconstructed ventilation (after Hayden 1987)

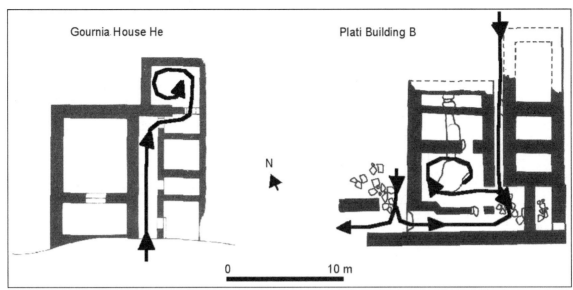

Fig. 2.8: Minoanizing/Mycenaean plans with reconstructed ventilation (after Hayden 1987)

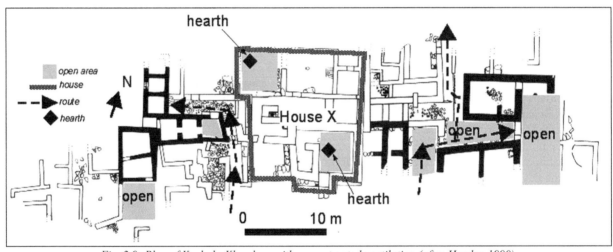

Fig. 2.9: Plan of Kephala Khondrou with reconstructed ventilation (after Hayden 1990)

probably elite residences and may not be representative of LM III vernacular architecture. In fact, most of Hayden's examples of Minoanizing/Mycenaean buildings seem to be of high-class houses. Overall, however, a decline in cross-ventilation can be seen in the LM III settlements at Kephala Khondrou and Kommos.

Kephala Khondrou

The published plan of Kephala Khondrou gives us some idea of what a newly founded settlement in LM III looked like near the south central coast (Fig. 2.9; Hayden 1990, 204–13). Located on a narrow north-south ridge, the LM III village included a number of open areas, but compared to those from LM I Pseira and Kommos, they are small and enclosed.

The paths through the settlement are winding and narrow and would have provided shade but little ventilation. Two hearths are reported, both located in enclosed courtyards associated with House X, a large central building. All the houses, except for House X, have 'axial' plans and poor ventilation.

The central structure at Kephala Khondrou has Minoanizing characteristics (Fig. 2.10). According to Hayden (1990) it was a single building built in 3 stages, though Nikolaos Platon (1962), the excavator, thought it was two distinctive structures. Whatever the case may be, ventilation in these rooms would have been minimal, but not as poor as in the axially organized structures which comprised the rest of the village. Hayden's reconstruction of a stair in room H also suggests the possibility of an upper floor, or at least

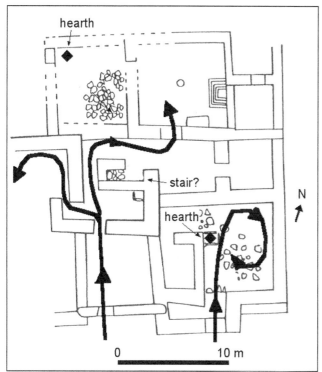

Fig. 2.10: House X at Kephala Khondrou with reconstructed ventilation (after Hayden 1990)

access to the roof in the last phase of construction, though this is conjectural.

Kommos

The large LM I residences on the hilltop at Kommos were subdivided into several smaller units in LM III (Fig. 2.11; Shaw 1996b). Numerous '*pi*' shaped hearths were installed in and around these units, and the central hearths were disused and paved over. As at Kephala Khondrou smaller, enclosed courtyards became a feature of the town. The previous large open areas were encroached upon and blocked. Although the main streets to the north and east survived these modifications, the one that connected to the so-called 'House with the Press' was blocked.

A closer look at North House in the earlier part of LM III shows that it was subdivided into two or three apartments, each with a separate outdoor entry (Fig. 2.12; Shaw 1996a). The stairs leading to what had probably been an upper floor in LM I were blocked, suggesting that it had become a single-story building in LM III. In a second building phase a new stair was installed in the north apartment, but it is thought to have lead to a roof terrace rather than to a second floor. Ventilation was substantially reduced.

The changes seen on the hilltop in LM III, and in North House in particular, characterise the site as a whole, involving the subdivision of living space, installation

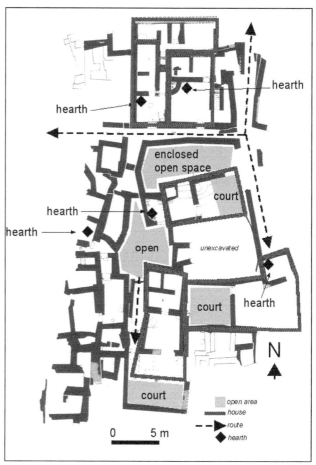

Fig. 2.11: Plan of hill top houses at Kommos in LM III (after Shaw and Shaw 1996)

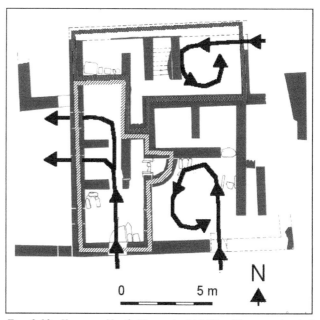

Fig. 2.12: Kommos North House in LM III with reconstructed ventilation (after Shaw and Shaw 1996)

FEATURES	LM III A–B houses: 'Minoanizing' and axial plans
TOPOGRAPHY	Mostly gentle to moderate slopes, but occasionally steep.
ALTITUDE	Sea level to height (maximum unknown).
ORIENTATION	Any direction?
BUILDING MATERIAL	
WALLS	No ashlar except reused.
ROOFS	Wooden support posts.
EXTERNAL COLOR	Unknown.
ELEVATION	Usually 1 floor.
ROOFS	Flat (?); earthen.
INDOOR HEATING/COOLING DEVICES	
HEARTHS	Common, but mostly in enclosed private courtyards.
WATER	Drains.
VENTILATION	
WINDOWS	Few?
DOORS	Single.
ROOM ORGANIZATION	Mixed.
CLEAR-STORIES	Unknown.
VERANDAS AND BALCONIES	No.
COURTYARDS AND PATIOS	Yes: smaller, enclosed.
PROXIMITY TO OTHER STRUCTURES	Party walls; streets blocked or narrowed.

Table 2.5: Summary Late Bronze III A–B vernacular architecture

of *pi*-shaped hearths both in indoor rooms and enclosed courtyards, gradual abandonment of upper floors and some ground floor rooms, the construction of 'crude' outdoor rooms that blocked streets and cluttered open spaces, and the enclosing, though not roofing, of outdoor spaces (Shaw 1996b, 371). The list of changes seen at Kommos can be applied to LM III settlements in general (Table 2.5). Houses became smaller and single-storied. Ventilation through the town and within a building was greatly reduced. Built hearths were more common than before and were found in indoor and outdoor spaces.

Early Iron Age (LM IIIC) architecture

A number of scholars have suggested that the features found in LM IIIC vernacular architecture were already present on the island in LM IIIA–B (*e.g.* Tsipopoulou 2005; Wallace in preparation).

Karphi

At 1147 m, Karphi is said to be the highest large Early Iron Age habitation in Crete. The settlement consists of four hamlets, the main one being Kera Karphi, which was excavated by John Devitt Stringfellow Pendlebury in the 1930s, and several studies of the site have been carried out more recently (Nowicki 1987; 2002; Day in preparation; Wallace in preparation). The new and improved site plan shows a large, open space and some enclosed unroofed

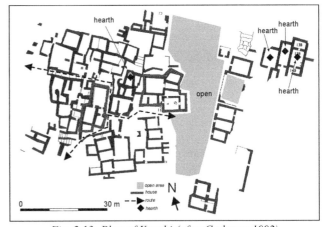

Fig. 2.13: Plan of Karphi (after Cadogan 1992)

spaces to the east (Fig. 2.13). Other courtyard areas are ambiguous. For the most part the cobbled paths are narrow and winding, though in a few places they widen out. The apparent concentration of fixed central hearths in the so-called Megara on the east side of the site is curious. Saro Wallace (in preparation) notes, however, that the excavators (Pendlebury *et al.* 1937–1938) suggested the presence of hearths elsewhere in the settlement though they were not recorded on the plan. 'Door-less' basements continue to be a feature of a number of the houses at Karphi, but as noted above cannot be interpreted as evidence for full two-storied buildings. Nevertheless, Krzysztof Nowicki (1987, fig. 6; Nowicki 2000, fig. 93) has restored a few two-story rooms

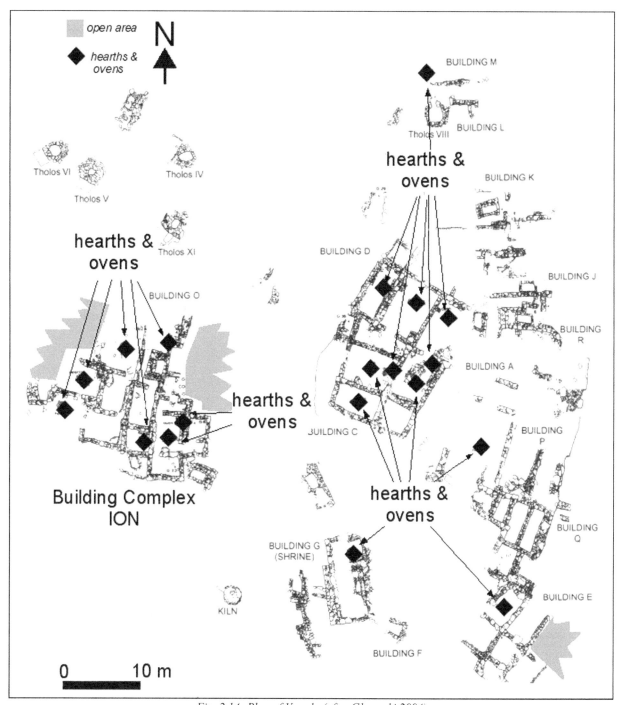

Fig. 2.14: Plan of Vronda (after Glowacki 2004)

in his reconstruction of the site, though on what evidence is unclear. Most houses are low, one-story constructions with flat roofs and party walls.

Vronda

The small Iron Age village of Vronda is less precipitous than Karphi and at a much lower elevation, 421–427 m.

What is so striking about this site is the number of indoor hearths and ovens (Fig. 2.14). Over-heating house interiors does not seem to have been a concern, suggesting that at this stage in LM IIIC conditions were colder. Erosion at the site makes it difficult to know where open areas would have been, and it is impossible to reconstruct the paths and streets that must have existed.

A close look at complex ION (Fig. 2.15) suggests that

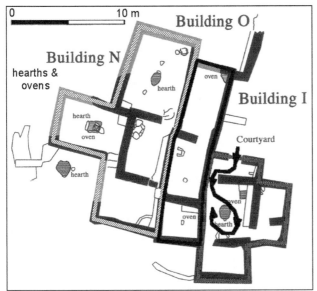

Fig. 2.15: Plan of block ION at Vronda (after Glowaki 2004)

it was a block of four households each with its own hearth and oven (Glowacki 2004). A large courtyard is proposed to the north of Building I with an entry into the house. None of the other houses have clearly preserved entries making it impossible to reconstruct ventilation. But the ventilation in Building I, the second oldest unit in the complex, appears to have been very poor. ION complex is one-story with party walls and a probable flat earthen roof, all of which would have provided good insulation against heat and cold.

Khalasmenos

The site of Khalasmenos is a few kilometres to the south-southwest of Vronda but at a lower elevation, 240 m. (Fig. 2.16). The large 'megara' with fixed central hearths relate the site to Karphi, while the proliferation of indoor hearths and ovens connects it to Vronda (Tsipopoulou 2005). Like Karphi and possibly Vronda, Khalasmenos includes a large, apparently unenclosed open space and well-ordered, rather

Fig. 2.16: Plan of Khalasmenos (after Tsipopoulou 2005)

FEATURES	*Early Iron Age settlements and houses*
TOPOGRAPHY	Topography can be steep, but many sites are gently rolling even in mountains with slopes of no more than 7–10 degrees.
ALTITUDE	Altitude ranges widely from coastal to 1200 m.
ORIENTATION	Any direction?
BUILDING MATERIAL	
WALLS	Usually built of smaller stones.
ROOFS	Wooden support posts.
EXTERNAL COLOR	Unknown.
ELEVATION	Usually one floor.
ROOFS	Flat? Earthen; some pitched?
INDOOR HEATING/COOLING DEVICES	
HEARTHS	Very common in interior, enclosed spaces.
WATER	Unknown.
VENTILATION	
WINDOWS	Few?
DOORS	Single.
ROOM ORGANIZATION	Axial.
CLEAR-STORIES	
VERANDAS AND BALCONIES	No.
COURTYARDS AND PATIOS	Yes: large, public. Small enclosed courtyards do not seem to be as prevalent as they were in LM III A–B.
PROXIMITY TO OTHER STRUCTURES	Semi-party walls are the norm, though some sort of block structure may have existed at Vronda and Khalasmenos.

Table 2.6: Summary of Early Iron Age vernacular architecture

wider paths through the site. Available publications do not make it clear whether enclosed courtyards were a feature of the settlement. The numerous hearths suggest an interest in indoor heating. The propensity for party walls and absence of opposed doors or windows indicate a general lack of concern for interior ventilation.

From the discussion above it seems that poorly ventilated, single-storied dwellings continue to be the norm for Early Iron Age houses, as they were in LM IIIA–B (Table 2.6). There are, however, two important changes: first, the tendency for fixed hearths and ovens to be moved indoors, suggesting an active interest in indoor heating, and second, the presence of moderate to large open areas within the village or town, suggesting large-scale, perhaps seasonal, outdoor activities.

Conclusions on the architecture

Three striking changes in Cretan vernacular architecture from LM I to the Early Iron Age have been revealed by this review: a tendency to axially organized, single-storied houses, a decline in interior ventilation, and an increase in interior built hearths and ovens (Table 2.7). These can all be seen as adaptations to a more arid, colder and probably more seasonal climate. There are, however, other explanations, and Table 2.8 assesses each of these three features in terms of topography, economy and defence, as well as climate.

It has been argued that single-storied 'axial' houses were adaptations to the steep topography of Early Iron Age sites (Hayden 1983; Wallace in preparation). However, not all EIA sites were built on steep slopes. Vronda and Khalasmenos, for example, have slopes of between just seven and ten degrees, and yet they too are composed of single-storied, poorly ventilated houses with indoor hearths and ovens. The poor ventilation of Early Iron Age houses is also difficult to attribute to topography, even on steep sites like Kavousi Kastro or Vrokastro (Hayden 1983; Mook 1993). The simple construction of doors, or a door and a window, at both ends of an axial, single-storied house would dramatically improve cross-ventilation, but this is seldom observed. It might be argued that wall preservation precludes us from knowing whether windows existed in the wall opposite the door, but that is not the case at Kavousi Kastro where some walls stand over 2 m and such constructions are unknown (Mook 1993). The only topographic consideration that might have led to an architectural change, specifically the proliferation of indoor built hearths and ovens in the Early Iron Age, is elevation. Systematic regional surveys suggest that about 18% of EIA sites occur between 400 and 800 m, while only 10–12% of Minoan Palatial period sites occur in that elevation range (Moody and Steele in preparation). But at least 50% of EIA sites are below 400 m. It can therefore be argued that topography was not the main reason for the change in house plans in LM III.

Single-storied dwellings might also be considered a

CHRONOLOGY	LM I	LM III A–B	Early Iron Age
VENTILATION	EXCELLENT Large windows and doors, on more than one side of a building, multi-storied, semi-detached.	POOR to GOOD The new axial 2–3 room structures appear poorly ventilated, while those built on Minoan foundations are better.	POOR Poorly ventilated. 'Axial' plan and lack of windows prevent cross-ventilation.
INSULATION	MODERATE Building materials would provide insulation, but exteriors colours were not always white allowing exterior walls to heat. Offset by windows and doors.	MODERATE to GOOD Building materials would provide insulation, Minoanizing structures less so than the 'axial' ones.	GOOD? Building materials would provide insulation, 'axial' plan and lack of windows.
SHADE	GOOD Tall structures would provide shade, possible gardens.	GOOD to MODERATE Shade would be provided by the narrow lanes and courtyards.	GOOD to MODERATE Shade would be provided by the narrow lanes and courtyards.
HEAT	MODERATE to POOR Portable braziers? Rare indoor hearths.	MODERATE Common hearths and ovens, but often in outdoor courtyard.	GOOD to VERY GOOD Common indoor hearths and ovens.

Table 2.7: Summary of Late Bronze and Early Iron Age vernacular architecture

FEATURES OF EIA HOUSES	Climate	Topography	Economy	Defence
SINGLE-STORIED	Easier to heat and cool. Less wind exposed. Greater flood risk (though probably not where EIA sites are located)	Work well in steep terrain, but so do 'split-level' houses.	Less labour-intensive to construct. Multi-storeyed houses can be associated with wealth.	Less visible from a distance, but easily accessed if attacked directly. A tower house would be much more defensible.
POORLY VENTILATED	Suitable for dry climates, whether warm or cool. Not suitable for humid, especially humid, warm climates. Also suitable for cold humid climates.	Steep topography does not constrain the construction of doors and windows except on the slope side. It would be easy to improve ventilation in an axial house by having a door at both ends.	Windows and doors are labour-intensive to build and maintain. In some cultures they indicate wealth.	Fewer or smaller windows and doors would make breaching the walls of the single storied house more difficult. And would make the light from interior hearths less visible.
INTERIOR HEARTHS AND OVENS	Suitable for cold climates.	Might expect more hearths at higher elevations? But most EIA settlements are below 450 m, including those with the most hearths!	No connection? (See Wallace forthcoming for a discussion of social considerations).	The movement of hearths to the interior would make it harder to see a settlement at night from a distance.

Table 2.8: Early Iron Age vernacular architecture: climate, topography, economy, and defence

sign of economic constraint, because they require less labour to build. The extra-wide foundations, floor supports and bracing for upper walls and stairwells would seem to offset the economy of a having a single, smaller roof. From an economic perspective, windows and doors might be considered 'expensive', because like second floors, they require extra labour to construct. The frequent construction of fixed hearths and ovens, however, also required extra labour and might have offset savings from the elimination of doors and windows.

As for defence, the single-story house has little to recommend it, except that it is harder to see from a distance, and the construction of fixed hearths in essentially window-less interior spaces also might have made the habitations less visible at night. Windows and doors also would make an already poorly defensible single-storied house less secure, so it could be argued that the lack of additional windows and doors, or of slit windows too high in the wall to be recognizable in the archaeological record, was for defence. However, if defence of an individual house was the main concern of Early Iron Age inhabitants, they might have built a tower house with blank, steep exterior walls.

From a climate perspective single-storied houses are less exposed to the elements, especially wind. More important, however, is that they are easier to heat and cool, especially if they have a well insulated roof. Although it is difficult to identify collapsed roofing in the archaeological record, ethno-archaeological work by Margaret Mook and Donald Haggis (1994; Mook 2000) on abandoned, traditional houses in the Kavousi area has allowed them to do so at the site of Kavousi Kastro. They suggest that EIA roofs were constructed like those of historic traditional houses and made of reeds, brush and thick layers of silt and clay. Such roofing would have been excellent insulation against heat and cold. Poor ventilation, or lack of cross-ventilation, is desirable only in hot arid and cold arid climates; the goal being to keep the hot or cold outside air out, and works especially well when combined with well insulated roofs. The presence of interior hearths and ovens indicates that heating interior air was considered important, suggesting either seasonally or generally colder temperatures. It is, however, not clear whether Early Iron Age houses had attached courtyards, as they did in LM IIIA–B, where it would have been easy to construct an outdoor kitchen if heating the indoor air was undesirable.

The discussion above suggests that although all four phenomena – topography, economy, defence, and climate – probably impacted the development of vernacular housing in the Early Iron Age, defence and, particularly, climate may have been the more critical factors.

Reconciling the architectural data and climate data

The architectural changes documented from LM I to the Early Iron Age suggest a change in climate from warm and humid to cool and arid. A variety of climate proxy data support this, suggesting that the Eastern Mediterranean experienced warming winters and cooling summers between *c.* 1600 and 1300 BCE (Moody 2005a; 2005b). Around 1300 BCE a number of proxies, such as a dramatic drop in the level of the Dead Sea (Enzel *et al.* 2003), indicate a sudden increase in temperatures and aridity in the Eastern Mediterranean. This abruptly reversed in the late 12th to early 11th centuries BCE when winters became much colder, as indicated by a 25% drop in warm water foraminifera in the deep sea core LC21 (Rohling *et al.* 2002b, fig. 1d). Note, however, that a gap in the deep sea core data before this point means we cannot currently confirm whether this was a steady or a sudden decline in temperature. Conditions are likely to have been cold and dry rather than cold and wet, as suggested by hiatuses in two unpublished cores from western Crete beginning *c.* 1100 BCE. One from Limnes was analyzed by Clay Magill (2006) for his undergraduate honours thesis. The other from Lake Kournas was a collaboration by a number of scientists under the general direction of Harvey Weiss (Curtis *et al.* in preparation). Temperatures rose in the 11th century, evidenced by an 18% increase in warm water foraminifera in LC21, but it fell again in the 10th century and did not recover until the 6th to 5th centuries BCE. The persistence of the hiatuses in the two unpublished cores until the first century CE suggests that drier than normal conditions prevailed through these centuries.

It is apparent that from the 13th to the 10th centuries BCE climate conditions were unstable with wildly fluctuating temperatures, but on the whole significantly drier than previously (there is one short, wet period in the mid to late 12th century BCE recorded in tree-rings from Gordian in Anatolia; see Kuniholm *et al.* 1996; Moody 2005b). The single-storied, cosy houses of the Early Iron Age with their indoor hearths and ovens would have been better suited to such changes in temperature and humidity than the airy houses that characterized the Minoan Palatial periods. I would therefore argue that a changing climate played an important role in the development of Early Iron Age vernacular architecture on Crete.

Acknowledgements

I would like to thank Susan Sherratt and Lucia Nixon for their helpful comments on this paper.

PART 2

EXCHANGE AND INTERREGIONAL DYNAMICS

JUST WHAT COLLAPSED? A NETWORK PERSPECTIVE ON 'PALATIAL' AND 'PRIVATE' TRADE AT UGARIT

Bruce Routledge and Kevin McGeough

While the importance of international trade for our understanding of the Late Bronze to Iron Age transition in the eastern Mediterranean is hardly controversial, the same cannot be said for any specific proposition one might make about this trade. More than any other topic in the study of antiquity, trade has seen a sustained, energetic, and theoretically informed debate that encompasses not only issues of empirical interpretation, but also fundamental differences of opinion regarding the nature of human social life. It is true that, after more than a century, we may have grown tired of debating the relative merits of 'primitivist' versus 'modernist', or 'substantivist' versus 'formalist', understandings of ancient trade. However, most of the interim compromises meant to move us beyond these impasses have left untouched the underlying, and intransigent, conceptual issues. This is illustrated most clearly in discussions of palace administration versus private initiative in international trade in the eastern Mediterranean during the Late Bronze Age. Scholars now, almost universally, suggest that the question itself is misplaced, and that elements of both 'state' and 'private' initiatives can be seen in the archaeological record (*e.g.* Cline 1994; Knapp and Cherry 1994, 146). However, this open-minded pluralism glosses over the underlying framework by means of which categories such as 'state' and 'private' trade are defined. After all, the issue was never really about the conditions under which specific objects were exchanged or under which specific trading expeditions operated. Rather, the question has always been about social and economic totalities; what form did they take? How were they generated? Did they, in fact, exist (see Rowlands 1987; Sjöberg 1995; Liverani 2005)? Hence, when one comes to talk about the relationship between international trade and the dramatic changes that mark the end of the Late Bronze Age, in contrast to the more

polemic positions of the past, simple pluralism provides no tools for analysing and understanding these events in an historically dynamic manner.

An exception to this can be found in the slightly surprising convergence of recent work around a model of the place of long-distance trade in the Late Bronze to Iron Age transition, conducted by scholars beginning from rather different perspectives, most notably Susan Sherratt (1998; 1999; 2003; Sherratt and Sherratt 1991; 1998), Michal Artzy (1985; 1997; 1998) and Mario Liverani (2003). These scholars have characterised the transition from the Late Bronze to the Iron Ages in terms of a shift in the balance of international trade from palace to private dominance, emphasising in particular the initially marginal social position of private merchants, sailors, and caravan traders. To differing degrees, each scholar suggests that this 'privatisation' of trade began as a by-product of the routes, facilities, skills and demand engendered by state-sponsored trade, but that it went on to play a significant role in undermining these very same centralised palatial economies. Because this model manages both to accept the empirically attested co-existence of palace and private trade interests, and to construct a dynamic historical relationship between them, it has proven a popular and useful tool in recent analysis (*e.g.* White *et al.* 2002, 174–75).

While we do not deny either the attraction or the utility of this 'privatisation' model, reflection on empirical problems raised by the epigraphic evidence from Ugarit has led us back to those unresolved issues of how to conceptualise ancient societies lying at the heart of our old debates. Certainly, in the case of Ugarit, we would suggest that the palace was both more and less involved in Late Bronze Age international trade than the privatisation model implies. The palace was more involved in the sense that the range of exchange activities that came under the purview of the palace at Ugarit was not as strongly defined by 'high-level transfers of bodies of important commodities' (Sherratt and Sherratt 1998, 341) as the model seems to require. The palace was less involved in the sense that palatial exchange relations were not exclusively characterised by 'tightly controlled conditions of nominal gift-exchange and centralised redistribution' (Sherratt 1999, 195). As we shall argue below, the boundaries between palatial and non-palatial economic activity at Ugarit are very difficult to draw, either in terms of participants or commodities. While most of this textually documented activity could be broadly defined as elite-dominated (whether or not the individuals were specifically 'royal'), its dispersal and diversity raises many problems for the privatisation model. In particular, the central argument that it was the development of a decentralised private trade network independent of palatial control that undermined the social and political foundations of the Late Bronze Age palaces becomes difficult to maintain.

In empirical terms, what seems most problematic in the privatisation model is its tendency to cite markers of private, as opposed to royal, trade even as the traders themselves are held to move between each of these two circuits of exchange. In particular, with regards to cargoes, ships, and the production, distribution and consumption of so-called 'added-value' or 'sub-elite' commodities, we will show that evidence from Ugarit provides no easy or absolute basis for these divisions. Critique, however, is not an end in itself, and hence we also present an alternative 'critical network' approach to the issue of exchange relations at Ugarit. This approach attempts to account for the dominant position of the palace within Ugarit, without reifying the economy as a distinct sphere to be controlled by the palace, or presuming the easy separation of palatial and non-palatial economic activities. This approach will allow us to account for the shifts in trade already noted, but within a framework that rethinks, rather than sublimates, the difficult conceptual issues at the heart of our long-standing debates on the nature of ancient trade.

Beyond luxuries?

The international exchange of luxury items, especially by means of formal gifting, is a well-studied aspect of the Late Bronze Age, and rightly so (Zaccagnini 1987; Liverani 1990; Cochavi-Rainey and Lilyquist 1999; Feldman 2006). This striking feature of relations between various Late Bronze Age palaces must, of course, play a large role in our understanding of how such palaces were reproduced through time as social institutions. Our argument then is not about the importance of either luxury goods or international exchange in the Late Bronze Age. Rather, it is about the implications of isolating these issues from questions of internal exchange

relations and the production, distribution and consumption of bulk or utilitarian goods.

For Susan Sherratt (see Sherratt and Sherratt 1991; 1998; Sherratt 1998; 1999; 2003) luxury goods and raw materials have a particularly important catalytic role in the eastern Mediterranean; initially as objects of desire motivating long-distance trade, and later as marks of distinction, serving as social capital to be restricted and protected, thereby fuelling the market amongst sub-elites for substitute items like Mycenaean pottery. Both Artzy (1998) and Sherratt suggest that something approaching a dual-circuit developed between the 14th and 12th centuries BCE, with entrepreneurial 'private' traders dealing in 'value-added' sub-elite goods, often bypassing palace centres focused on the exchange of luxury goods and high-value raw materials. While seldom so clearly articulated, the presumption of something like a dual circuit would also seem to underlie attempts to identify the nature of given trading missions on the basis of the cargo recovered from Late Bronze Age shipwrecks (Muhly *et al.* 1977, 361; Knapp and Cherry 1994, 143; Pulak 1997, 256; Bachhuber 2006). This is most evident in the contrasts drawn between the apparently high-value cargo of the wreck at Uluburun and the more utilitarian cargo at Cape Gelidoniya (esp. scrap metal; Knapp and Cherry 1994, 143) or Point Iria (agricultural products; Vichos and Lolos 1997, 330–31).

What light might the epigraphic material from Ugarit shed on this question of 'dual circuits' of exchange? As is well-known, French excavations conducted at the site of Ras Shamra since 1928 have uncovered numerous clusters of clay tablets, written in both syllabic Akkadian and alphabetic Ugaritic, in contexts defined as both royal and 'private'. As in all cases of archaeologically derived texts, accidents of discovery and preservation play a large role in shaping what we know about Ugarit. Similarly, poorly attested languages such as these, recorded at times on poorly preserved texts, result in many uncertainties regarding the semantics and syntax of specific texts. Add to this the problem of the poor excavation and recording methods employed at Ras Shamra under the direction of Claude Schaeffer, and it soon becomes necessary to compose all interpretative statements based on these texts as interrogative sentences. Nevertheless, the content of these texts provides information on a wide-range of economic activities, including international trade. Additionally, the simple fact that certain people, things, and activities were being recorded provides often overlooked information on the relationship between those empowered to write and those who were the object of recording.

Cargo

There is no question that texts originating from the palace of Ugarit are concerned with the description (*e.g. KTU* 4.265) and movement of luxury goods, metals and valuable raw materials. This includes tribute (*e.g. KTU* 4.369; 4.610; see also *KTU* 2.36 for Hittite expectations) and gifts (*e.g.* EA 49), but also contexts where exchange values are given in silver (*e.g. KTU* 4.132). We also find the royal palace acquiring and distributing metals directly to smiths, presumably for the purpose of producing finished goods (*e.g. KTU* 4.310).

Not surprisingly, we also find an enormous concern for the acquisition, distribution and/or exchange of labour (*e.g. KTU* 4.125), agro-pastoral products (*e.g. RS* 16.125, *RS* 16.357, *RS* 17.37), tools (*e.g. RS* 19.23) and other equipment (*e.g. KTU* 4.92). What is more surprising is that the few texts providing information on the contents of ships refer more frequently to the shipment of grain then they do to any other commodity (*e.g. KTU* 2.38, *KTU* 2.46, *RS* 20.212, *RS* 26.158, *RIH* 78.3+30). This is of course influenced by Hittite demands for grain as tribute. However, we also have at least two cases of grain shipments between Egypt and Ugarit (*KTU* 2.38, *RIH* 78.3 + 30), one of which mentions silver (*RIH* 78.3 + 30). Additionally, the Akkadian letter from Takhulinu of Ugarit to Haya of Egypt, discovered at Tel Aphek in Israel, also deals with a large shipment of grain, perhaps 15 tons in total, although no ships are actually mentioned (see Owen 1981; Singer 1983). Minimally then, we can conclude that bulk commodities played a role in sea trade initiated by the palace at Ugarit.

Interestingly, in *RS* 16.238 + 254, the well-known declaration of tax-exemption for Sinaranu on the return of his ship to Ugarit from Crete, states that his grain, beer, and oil will not enter the palace, suggesting perhaps that this would be the content of his ship. Given that this wording suggests that Sinaranu is a person external to the palace, this could show that grain (as well as 'value-added' agricultural products) was shipped to Ugarit by both royal and non-royal interests.

Besides grain, Ugaritic texts are not overly informative on what commodities were being shipped. The king of Amurru, one of Ugarit's neighbours, enquires after an expected shipment of an uncertain type (*algamiššu*) of presumably high quality building stone for the construction of his palace (*RS* 34.135). While this is certainly a case of inter-elite exchange, the material involved is somewhere between a bulk and a high-value commodity. One text (*KTU* 4.394) does seem to meet archaeologists' expectations in recounting the loss of what seems likely to have been a load of copper ingots in a shipwreck. However, before we begin to correlate excavated shipwreck cargoes with Ugaritic texts, we need to look carefully at the range of cargoes represented in the textual record. George Bass (1967, 163–4), for example, suggested on the basis of the eclectic mix of bronze tools, scrap metal, and ingots that the Cape Gelidonya wreck represents a travelling tinker, while Bernard Knapp, James Muhly and Polymnia Muhly (1988)

suggested that it was a founder's hoard of scrap metal. Yet, as Elisha Linder (1972) noted, the fragmentary cargo list of a ship from Alashiya (Cyprus) recorded on *KTU* 4.390 has numerous parallels with the contents of the Cape Gelidoniya shipwreck, especially if the 'talents' mentioned in line 4 refer to copper as some suggest (Zaccagnini 1970, 317–24).

KTU 4.390
1. (Inventory of the) Cyp[riote] ship
2. that is in Atallig:
3. fifte[en]
4. talents of co[pper],
5. six shields,
6. 2 baskets,
7. 3 *ult*-tools,
8. *krk*-tools (?)[ ]
9. 5 jav[elins],
10. 6 sa[cks],
11. ele[ven]
12. purple [dye]
13. *krk*-tools[ ]

Minimally, this shows that the palace at Ugarit was aware of, and carefully documented, ships with cargoes like the Cape Gelidoniya wreck, whether the ship's content is to be interpreted as 'royal' cargo or 'private' *bricolage.*

Evidence for overland trade similarly demonstrates the impossibility of defining trade as 'private' or 'palace', not only in terms of what is traded but who is doing the trading. Akkadian letters, recovered from what is now called the House of Urtenu at Ugarit, attest to a caravan venture running (at least minimally) between Ugarit, Carcemish, and Emar. The head of the enterprise was Šipṭi-Baʿal, who was related to Queen Šarelli of Ugarit and acted as the manager of her commercial enterprises. In this venture, however, Šipṭi-Baʿal may have been using his official status as a means of inaugurating or facilitating regional exchange transactions but he does not seem to have been acting on behalf of any royal interest. The correspondence was retrieved from the house of one of the managers working beneath Šipṭi-Baʿal, Urtenu, and consists of letters from various other managers and economic actors within this venture. Given the small sample of texts that have been preserved from this venture, it is difficult to make generalisations. However, it is possible to make some suggestions about what was involved in this caravan venture, at the very least. At the end of *RS* 34.133, Tuna (another commercial agent) comments that purple wool, precious stone, and horse equipment is needed in 'Ḫatti-land' (presumably Carchemish and environs are included in this designation). *RS* 94.2284 similarly refers to purple wool as well as various manufactured garments. In addition, wine is discussed as a negotiable item and silver seems to be a major medium for exchange (although not the sole one). Wool, precious stone, and clothing are mentioned in *RS* 34.134; oil and clothes are the trade items in *RS* [Varia 26]; and tin and oil are the subjects of *RS* 34.141. While this was likely not the extent of goods traded, this combination is difficult to categorise as solely luxury or solely staple, solely 'private' or solely 'royal'. Indeed, these products come closest to the Sherratts' 'value-added' category. Grain is not mentioned but given the particular challenges grain poses for overland transportation, it is not unlikely that overland grain trade would have been limited to relatively short distances.

Ships

Michal Artzy (1985; 1988) has argued that depictions of ships in the eastern Mediterranean suggest the introduction of two new forms during the latter part of the Late Bronze Age, namely long-boats for war and round boats for trade. She suggests that these ships were distinct from the traditional multi-purpose sea-going vessels used by palaces for both warfare and trade. In particular, Artzy (1997) suggests that the round boats were merchantmen, used by what she terms 'nomads of the sea' for tramping and small-scale private trade shipping. Hence, for Artzy, such ships were a material correlate of the development of entrepreneurial trade out of an expedient 'sailors' trade', precisely the process held to be fatal to Bronze Age palaces in the privatisation model.

The texts from Ugarit, however, raise certain questions with regards to Artzy's correlation. Alphabetic Ugaritic texts use several different names for types of ship. Most common is *any*, which appears to be a general term and is frequently used in the headings of lists, but is also used to designate ships from a particular location (*e.g. KTU* 4.81; 4.390) and ships belonging to royalty (king of Byblos – *KTU* 4.338; king of Ugarit (?) – *KTU* 4.421). As *KTU* 4.81 illustrates, *br* and *thkt* are subdivisions that can be made within the category of *any*. A single text (KTU 4.421) seems to distinguish within the category of *any* between *br* and, otherwise unattested, *'tk* vessels. The meaning of this later term, however, remains unclear.

Both *br* and *thkt* occur in Egyptian (see Sasson 1966, 131; Jones 1988, 136–7, 145–6) and appear to refer to a larger and a smaller vessel respectively. *br* is clearly a loan word in Egyptian, appearing exclusively in the New Kingdom (Jones 1988, 136–7). Ships transporting timber from Byblos in the story of *Wenamun* are referred to as *br*, suggesting this was a large transport or multi-purpose ship. *thkt*, attested in Egyptian as *sktt* (Jones 1988, 145–6; *contra* Loretz 1996), already appears as a term in the Old Kingdom and may have referred to a smaller vessel (Sasson 1966, 131; Hoftijzer and Van Soldt 1998, 337), although use of the term in Egyptian does not indicate a specialised function. Interestingly, the Hebrew equivalent of *any* (*'oniyah*) and *thkt* (*sekiyah*) appear in parallelism in Isaiah 2.16 (Lipiński 1971, 87), where 'ships (*'oniyah*) of Tarshish' is paired with 'stately vessels' (*sekiyah*). Unfortunately, while 'ships of Tarshish' in the Hebrew Bible are certainly merchantmen, the conventions of Biblical Hebrew poetry mean that the two phrases could have been intended either as synonyms (for emphasis) or antonyms (to represent a category by its two extremes).

Both *br* and *thkt* vessels are associated with personal names (*e.g. KTU* 4.81, 4.366, 4.647) that could refer either to the ship's captain or its owner, although in one case (*KTU* 4.647) the captain and owner of a *br* vessel are carefully distinguished. Minimally, this shows that ownership of the larger, apparently multi-purpose, *br* vessels was not exclusively royal. It is, of course, rather difficult to say with confidence that these two sub-divisions of *any* equate directly with Artzy's vessel categories. *br*, for example, seems most like Artzy's traditional large multi-purpose vessel. *thkt* is more difficult to equate with Artzy's categories, but is perhaps closest to her 'round-boat' merchantmen. However, in terms of attestation in Egyptian, *br* is the name that appears to have been introduced in the Late Bronze Age (when distinct long- and round boats are said to have been introduced), while *thkt / sktt* is used from at least the third millennium BCE. What we can say is that, much as Artzy suggests, Ugaritic texts witness a categorical division between vessels that seem to differ in size and perhaps also function. However, ownership and use of these vessels does not seem to divide along these same lines in any straightforward manner and, perhaps more importantly, both sorts of boats are clearly recognised and documented in the palace archives. Of course, neither *br* or *thkt* may have referred to Artzy's 'round boats', nor for that matter were the referents of these terms necessarily consistent or their semantic fields necessarily defined on principles equivalent to those used by Artzy to classify Late Bronze Age representations of ships. At the very least, however, Ugaritic texts require us to recognise that types of ships, patterns of trade, ownership and palatial engagement were likely to be interrelated in relatively complex ways rather than by means of direct equations.

'Value-added' and 'sub-elite' commodities

Susan Sherratt's argument is, of course, not limited to either luxury cargoes or the nature of ships. She makes much of Mycenaean and Cypriot pottery as the hallmark of the commercially oriented, decentralised trade that she sees being driven forward by urban centres on Cyprus from the Late Cypriot IIC period on. As Sherratt notes (1999, 169, 173), this pottery is absent from Late Bronze Age texts (see also Liverani 1986), although this is not entirely surprising given the general lack of enthusiasm pottery seems to have generated amongst ancient Near Eastern scribes. Mycenaean pottery is also relatively under-represented in elite Egyptian and Hittite contexts, while it is widely distributed in the Levant. According to Sherratt, as a commodity that was easily imitated and hence difficult to control in terms of either raw materials or skilled craftsmen, Mycenaean pottery provided a sub-elite market with identity markers and consumption strategies independent of palatial control, ultimately undermining the ideological and economic basis of the palatial system itself. But is this really the case at Ugarit?

Archaeological find spots for Mycenaean pottery at Ras Shamra are infamously dicey, and it seems very likely that at least some of the Mycenaean and related pottery excavated by Shaeffer was not preserved or recorded (Yon *et al.* 2000, 1–3). This said, the published corpus of Mycenaean and related pottery from Ugarit continues to expand (Yon *et al.* 2000; Monchambert 2004b) and is now approximately twice as large as that analysed by Albert Leonard (1994) and Gert van Wijngaarden (2002). Most interesting for our purposes is the fact that 118 of the 414 previously unpublished vessels and sherds from the Louvre's collections catalogued by Marguerite Yon, Vassos Karageorghis, and Nicolle Hirschfeld (2000, 68) are said to come from contexts in the *Palais Royale*. This rather dramatically changes the previously published evidence, in which only 5 of 554 Mycenaean vessels and sherds from Ugarit were said to come from the *Palais Royale* (see van Wijngaarden 2002, table 5.1). Whether these contexts are funerary, domestic, or storage in nature is unfortunately unclear. However, as Yon notes, it is clear that 'la ceramique mycenienne faisait partie du mobilier normal des habitants Palais' (Yon *et al.* 2000, 9).

While stressing the general distribution of Mycenaean pottery across distinct contexts at Ugarit, van Wijngaarden was clearly influenced by Sherratt in labelling it as a sub-elite commodity (van Wijngaarden 2002, 73). Clearly the publication of the Louvre collection, which van Wijngaarden (2002, 40) was not able to include in his analysis, requires that we take seriously the consumption of Mycenaean and related pottery in the *Palais Royale*. Indeed, several of the finds from the palace have been classified as locally made Late Mycenaean IIIC1B and so-called 'derivative' styles (Yon *et al.* 2000, 159–60), key components of Sherratt's proposed phenomenon of 'import substitution' (Sherratt 1998; 1999).

Beyond this, van Wijngaarden (2002, 73) bases his argument for the 'sub-elite' status of Mycenaean pottery on the presumed connection between inhabitants of the city of Ugarit and the social category *bunušu malki* or 'Man of the King' in Ugaritic texts, as defined in the so-called 'two-sector' model of Ugaritic society and economy (*e.g.* Heltzer 1982; Liverani 1989). This model presumes a two-fold division in Ugarit between free peasantry and royal dependants, with the latter forming a 'public sector' of craftsmen, soldiers, and merchants concentrated most particularly within the city of Ugarit itself. As the critique of Ignacio Rowe (2002, 4)

points out, this argument rests on interpretations of the term *bunušu malki* or 'Man of the King', which occurs clearly in only eight texts at Ugarit, but is then extended by Heltzer to cover all uses of the term *bnš* ('man'). Both Rowe (2002) and David Schloen (2001, 246) have rather vigorously, and we feel successfully, questioned the suggestion that this term refers to a permanent status. Rowe (2002, 9) in particular has offered the compelling alternative that it refers to a temporary relation of dependence, such as debt-servitude. Hence, it is no longer necessary to imagine the entire city of Ugarit inhabited by royal dependants distinct from a largely unattached countryside. Taken together, this evidence suggests that at Ugarit Mycenaean pottery is not a sub-elite commodity but a generalised one. It may be that, as van Wijngaarden notes (1999), differences in the distribution of specific forms suggests that perhaps 'Mycenaean pottery' is too blunt an instrument for the interpretation of imported pottery consumption at Ugarit. Yet, this fact in itself suggests that in the case of Mycenaean pottery distinctions between 'elite' and 'sub-elite' lie within, rather than between, categories of material culture.

Sherratt also suggests that the distribution of Mycenaean pottery in the eastern Mediterranean is tied to decentralised trade activities based on Cyprus, which eventually subverted palatial monopolies over the consumption of semiotically charged commodities. Certainly, trade relations with Cyprus/Alašiya are well attested in Ugaritic texts. However, these are not subversively decentralised, but rather frequently involve the kings of Ugarit and Alašiya directly (see Knapp 1983). Indeed, in letters between Alašiya and Ugarit (*e.g.* RS 20.238) the king of Ugarit takes the role of subordinate partner, calling the king of Alašiya 'father' in keeping with the stereotypical language of Late Bronze Age international diplomacy. So, while Cyprus may well have played a key role in the distribution of Mycenaean pottery to the Levant, one is hard-pressed to see this Cypriot trade as particularly distinct or 'subversive' in the manner that Sherratt suggests.

Interestingly, Sherratt does set Ugarit aside as a special case of an increasingly commercial exchange economy constrained by 'a macro-regional hierarchical structure' (Sherratt 1998, 299, n. 14) constituted through Hittite and Egyptian imperial interests. This, however, ignores the parallels in trade activities between Ugarit and inland sites such as Carchemish and Emar, as well as the parallels in political and ideological activities between Alašiya and various Near Eastern polities besides Ugarit. In short, both the distribution of Mycenaean pottery at Ugarit and the nature of economic and political relations between Alašiya and various Near Eastern polities including Ugarit, make it difficult to maintain Sherratt's argument that Cyrpriot-organised trade in this commodity was peculiarly subversive and threatening to the palatial systems of the Eastern Mediterranean.

External consumption vs. internal production

In many ways, archaeological approaches to trade necessitate the elevation of luxury goods, restricted raw materials, and imported craft products to a primary explanatory role. After all, since at least the Early Bronze Age everyone in the Mediterranean has had wheat and barley, sheep and goats, even wine and olive oil. Where then, amongst this commonality, does the socially and historically dynamic aspect of economic activity lie?

Recent work that isolates and analyses the consumption (*e.g.* van Wijngaarden 1999a; Steel 2002) of imported commodities has certainly demonstrated the potential of such a perspective for generating new social insights, especially in relation to the constitution of individual and group identities. Indeed, Sturt Manning and Linda Hulin (2005, 280), in their review of Late Bronze Age trade, go so far as to suggest that consumption is 'the proper focus' of studying trade, especially as it relates to the formation and negotiation of personal identities.

We agree that consumption is an important, and heretofore understudied, aspect of Bronze Age trade, but this celebration of 'pure consumption' makes us uneasy. In particular, Manning and Hulin deploy the language of globalised capitalism, where choice is largely unconstrained and 'social forces' do no more than 'simply stake out an individual's room to manoeuvre by determining what is appropriate' (Manning and Hulin 2005, 288). To quote James Carrier and Josiah Heyman (1997, 361), 'Such an approach ignores the fact that the people who confront, use and respond to objects and their meanings do so in terms of the material, social and cultural constraints of their own personal situations.'

To be clear, it is both true and methodologically important to note that the meaning and significance of objects are not fixed in their production and can change as an object enters and is consumed within a new context. However, one cannot separate such acts of consumption from the acts of production that make consumption possible. In other words, while the meaning and significance of a Mycenaean pot might change between its point of origin in the Argolid, or Cyprus, and its point of consumption at Ugarit, at Ugarit the consumption of that vessel has to be understood in relation to those acts of production that created the resources necessary for the vessel's acquisition. Certainly, within the corpus of Ugaritic texts, foreign goods are not separated out from local products, and indeed circuits of production, exchange, and consumption resist analysis in such terms. This means that understanding trade at Ugarit requires some larger understanding of economic activity in general, and herein lays our final problem.

Networks and 'economies'

One might ask if, by evoking the need for a larger understanding of economic activity in general, we were proposing a return to the totalities that so often constrained explanations in the past; Karl Marx's 'Modes of Production', or Karl Polanyi's 'Modes of Integration', for example. Here we would note one fact often overlooked in discussions of Late Bronze Age trade, namely that Polanyi's central concern was not to define the evolution of different modes of exchange, but rather to demonstrate that the autonomy of the economy as a distinct social sphere was a necessary myth of capitalism (esp. Polanyi 1964). Reflecting even for a moment on issues such as the relationship between the labour market and the social and biological reproduction of labour in 21st century Britain illustrates that even in highly developed capitalist economies this thing we call 'the economy' has very fuzzy edges indeed. Polanyi's insight suggests that in antiquity we should not be looking for 'an economy' that the state or palace could control. Indeed, with no 'economy' in this autonomous sense, it is difficult to see how modes of exchange could define social formations in the kind of all-encompassing and epochal manner suggested by Polanyi himself.

If one looks systematically at the syllabic and alphabetic texts from Ugarit, what one finds is a dizzying variety of exchange relations recorded and administered in an apparently *ad hoc* manner. Indeed, characterising the Ugaritic 'economy' in terms of any single mode of production or exchange requires rather drastic reductions in the complexity and diversity of these texts. For example, while forms of labour service and redistribution are the most commonly attested exchange relations within texts from the *Palais Royale*, one also finds evidence for royal land grants to individuals, directly commissioned craft production, agricultural and pastoral production on royal farms, tax and duty collection, loans, the direct purchasing of commodities with silver, the delivery and receipt of gifts and tribute, and of course, foreign trade. Interestingly, texts found in the houses of apparently non-royal elites, such as Yabinu and Urtenu, show a similar range of economic activities on a smaller scale. Since these archives include texts, or copies of texts, clearly addressed to the king, one cannot be certain that all of the economic texts in these houses relate to the activities of the apparent owners. However, texts naming, or addressed directly to, both Yabinu and Urtenu indicate their involvement in foreign trade and foreign affairs under the auspices of the king and, apparently, also on their own initiative. Certainly, cases such as that of Sinaranu, point to the existence of non-royal merchants with ships conducting overseas trade. However, we only know about Sinaranu because of the favours shown to him by the palace. In short, the ways in which non-royal elites move in and out of direct royal service presents a particular problem in terms of characterising economic activity at Ugarit.

The Ugaritic evidence necessitates thinking about economic activities in terms of networks of social relations, rather than in terms of over-arching structures. In current economic analysis networks are understood as formal systems of organisation that lack a formal source of sovereign authority. Rather, the organisation stems from informal relationships that are related through vertical relationships (Fukuyama 1999, 199). The defining aspects of a network are the rules that govern the connections between different nodes and the transformations that these connections go through in the various movements of the network (Wolfram 2002, 193). Network theory provides a useful model for the study of ancient economy. It suggests that contacts between individuals in an economic relationship are worthwhile focal points of study. Moments of contact between agents are governed by many social norms and rules. These patterns of associations (*i.e.* networks) provide consistent social frameworks for economic interaction. Roger Friedland and Alexander F. Robertson (1990, 28) describe these social frameworks in these terms: 'The reality of economic life is that most actors interact repeatedly over time and thus form expectations about each other's behaviour, constructing patterns of behaviour that are not only valued in themselves but become mechanisms for the dissemination of information and for the control of each other's behaviour.'

At the same time, economic network theory remains problematically wedded to the individual decision-making models so dear to economists. It also confuses the absence of an overall hierarchy and organising intelligence in the relationship between nodes, with an absence of hierarchy and strategic agency within specific social relations, rendering the study of power and the perpetuation of inequality rather difficult. So, for example, it is very fruitful to imagine the diverse exchange relations witnessed in Ugaritic texts in terms of networks with different nodes shaped informally by norms and conventions that provide regularity to given relationships, indicating who gives tribute, who gives gifts, and who pays cash. However, it is not very fruitful to pretend that these relationships are all equal and free of compulsion, or to avoid asking how it is that the king stays king from one generation to the next. This is where the 'critical' part of 'critical network theory' comes into play. Fig. 3.1 is an attempt to represent graphically the various exchange relations reflected in Ugaritic texts. As one can see, the royal palace is marked by the particularly dense network of exchange relations within which it is embedded.

To be reproduced the nodal position of the palace had to be regularised, and to be regularised it had to be represented. As Schloen (2001) has shown in some detail, at Ugarit the palace was given substance (as a unity) and legitimacy through its representation as a household headed by the king. There is, in this sense, no public sector as the palace operated not as manager of a state-economy,

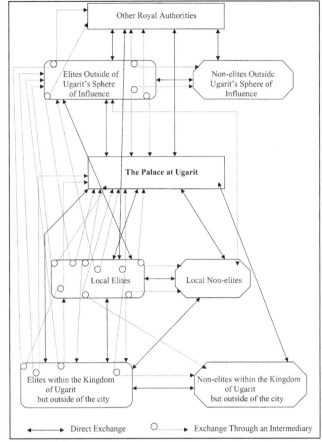

Fig. 3.1: A network-based model (NBM) of Ugaritic exchange relationships

but as the biggest household in a network of households. In this sense, as the supreme house, the palace could be represented as both encompassing and interacting with smaller households depending on the context and purpose of the representation.

The shared understanding of the palace as the supreme household of Ugarit provided the consistent social framework for economic interaction that network theory requires. However, it also provides a means of conceptualising the perpetual reproduction of inequalities central to political analysis and generally unaccounted for in the decision-making orientation of most network approaches within economics. In short, the political and strategic aspects of palatial power were not given in a structure, but were realised in the palace's nodal position between different networks of social relations. Because the palace was able to transfer resources and social capital between the networks of foreign, military, religious, judicial, and economic relations within which it was embedded, the palace was able to achieve things that others, less extensively connected, experienced as impossible.

Conclusion

Returning now to the question of the transition from the Late Bronze to Iron Ages, we can both assimilate and reject various aspects of the privatisation model. First, our critical network approach suggests that merchants and sailors could be embedded to different degrees and with different intensities in networks interacting with the palace. In this way, the palace at Ugarit could play a major role in stimulating, structuring and influencing long-distance trade without needing to directly manage or control all relevant aspects of this trade. There is certainly more than enough room in this reconstruction for Artzy's (1997) 'nomads of the sea', and on this issue we see little reason to differ with the privatisation model. Our objections begin when this loose network is said to develop into entrepreneurial trade that is largely independent of palaces while still contributing directly to the demise of such palaces by actively undermining their ability to control and monopolise socially significant modes of consumption.

To begin with, most of the evidence central to the arguments of Sherratt and Artzy in particular dates between the mid-fourteenth and twelfth centuries BCE. It is important to remember that the majority of our evidence from Ugarit dates from the last century or so of its existence (*c.* 1300–1185 BCE) and so cannot be treated as representing conditions prior to the emergence of this putative decentralised private trade network. Furthermore, Ugarit was clearly burned and abandoned. Prior to this, texts suggest that Ugarit was experiencing harassment from the sea and that its resources were being stressed by Hittite demands for food, ships, and military support, and by land-based threats on their own borders. Additionally, given the evidence of the Amarna letters, there is no reason to doubt that the extractive economic relations between Late Bronze Age palaces and subsistence farmers were such that 'peasant flight' was an endemic problem easily worsened by poor harvests and rural insecurity (Liverani 1987; Bunimovitz 1994). What we do not see is any sort of 'legitimacy crisis', Burberry-like devaluing of semiotically charged commodities, or notable evidence for an alienation from maritime activity. In other words, at Ugarit we see none of the symptoms one would expect if political collapse had been brought on by the undermining of state-controlled trade by decentralised entrepreneurial activity. This is principally because the initial conditions required by the privatisation model, a state-controlled trade economy, never obtained at Ugarit.

In addition to this critique of the 'palace economy', we believe that a critical network perspective provides a better explanation for one of the phenomena that stimulated the privatisation model in the first-place; namely the uneven decline of sea trade in the Early Iron Age. As Sherratt (1998, 304–6) well notes, Cyprus provides abundant evidence that long-distance trade did not cease everywhere in the twelfth century. Yet, if it was the growth and influence of decentralised, entrepreneurial trade that undermined the Late Bronze Age palaces of the eastern Mediterranean, why did this trade not go on from strength to strength across the region? Indeed, in the Early Iron Age why do we find only active fragments of the Late Bronze Age system, such as that between Cyprus and the Phoenician coast, rather than a pan-Mediterranean explosion in sub-elite consumption?

When viewed as informal networks linked to, rather than bypassing or undermining, key nodes like the palace at Ugarit, the fate of long-distance trade at the end of the Late Bronze Age can be understood somewhat differently. Even when such networks were built up initially on the back of palatial demand, the disappearance of palaces such as at Ugarit could very well have left certain segments of these networks intact. Cyprus and the Phoenician coast in the 12th and 11th centuries may represent one such segment. Notably, the Phoenician coast is one of the regions of the Levant that seems to witness social, political and economic continuity across the Late Bronze – Iron Age divide. Such fragmented networks are more in line with the actual scale and scope of international trade in the Early Iron Age.

In the end, just what separates our position from what we have termed the privatisation model? In terms of the sequence and nature of events, we agree that Late Bronze Age trade networks and agents were likely to have been diverse and dispersed and that in the Early Iron Age some segments of this Late Bronze Age network remained active despite the absence of anything resembling a palatial system. We differ most fundamentally, however, over the issue of causation. The argument that decentralised, entrepreneurial trade undermined the political and economic foundations of Late Bronze Age palaces contains within it a misunderstanding of the 'palace economy', at least insofar as it is manifested at Ugarit. Palaces were dominating, rather than managing or controlling institutions; the biggest house on the block, if you will. At Ugarit the palace was already diverse and at least partially decentralised in terms of the arrangements and relations by means of which it acquired, used and dispersed human and material resources.

Not surprisingly, the idea that free trade was threatening to aristocratic interests vested in the prebendal control of agricultural surplus carries the conviction of the familiar – it is, after all, the story of the emergence of middle class Europe. We would argue, however, that it is not the story of the end of the Bronze Age.

CONTINUITY AND CHANGE: THE DIVERGENT DESTINIES OF LATE BRONZE AGE PORTS IN SYRIA AND LEBANON ACROSS THE LBA/IRON AGE TRANSITION

Carol Bell

Ugarit was a strategic node between land and sea routes at the close of the Late Bronze Age and its entrepreneurial merchants, many of whom we know by name through the administrative documents found in their homes, engaged in transactions for economic gain. Why Ugarit was never meaningfully resettled again after its destruction in the early 12th century BCE is a question of regional importance with respect to gaining a better understanding of how and why the mechanisms of trade evolved at this critical time. That Phoenicia came to dominate maritime trade in the Mediterranean in the succeeding period is widely accepted, but the reasons behind this rise to pre-eminence are poorly understood.

To address these issues, this paper is divided into three parts, each of which concentrates on what evidence exists for specific maritime trading relationships at different ports on the Levantine coast. First, I will briefly summarise the results of the analysis I conducted during my doctoral research on the trade in fine-wares between the Aegean and Cyprus and the Levant during the LBA. I will then characterise the pre-eminent role of Ugarit in the trade of copper and tin and describe the international trading contacts of some of its wealthy merchants. Finally, I will suggest what may happened to long-distance trade networks after the destruction of Ugarit, and many other Levantine ports, in the early 12th century BCE.

The LBA trade in Mycenaean and Cypriot fine-wares in the eastern Mediterranean

By the end of the LBA, ceramics were moving from the Aegean and Cyprus to the Levantine coast in considerable quantities, not only as containers for trade goods, such as perfumed oils, but also as attractive dinner-wares. The range of Mycenaean vessel shapes found in domestic contexts in sites such as Ugarit and Sarepta is high, suggesting that they were available to ordinary citizens of these ports, not just the elite (Bell 2005). The ubiquity of Cypriot LBA wares at Levantine coastal sites, in conjunction with the presence of Mycenaean wares, provides a data set that can be used to examine intra-Levantine variation in the ceramic assemblages, and what this might mean for the routes by which these fine-wares arrived at their point of deposition.

The coast of Syro-Palestine varies considerably along its length in topography and in the availability of access routes into the interior. The first step in my analysis is to divide the Levant into four Zones (L1–L4) that reflect the realities of its topography. Splitting the region along topographical lines removes modern political boundaries and takes us closer to the challenges that faced long distance traders in the LBA (see Fig. 4.1).

Zone L1 centres on Ugarit and extends to the Euphrates sites of Emar and Carchemish, with which Ugarit had commercial and administrative links respectively (Lackenbacher 2000; Malbran-Labat 2000). This zone was part of the Hittite sphere at the close of the LBA whereas my other three zones were, to a greater or lesser extent, in the Egyptian sphere following the battle of Qadesh (c. 1278 BCE). The inclusion of Emar on the Euphrates and Ugarit within the Hittite sphere was important for the security of tin supplies that were arriving from the east (Macqueen 1996, 44), as the route between these two cities is the shortest from the Euphrates to the Mediterranean. Zone L2 is, essentially, the area that is understood to be Phoenicia in the Iron Age in which the only extensively excavated and published coastal site is Sarepta. This port is likely to have had important inland links via the Litani River valley to

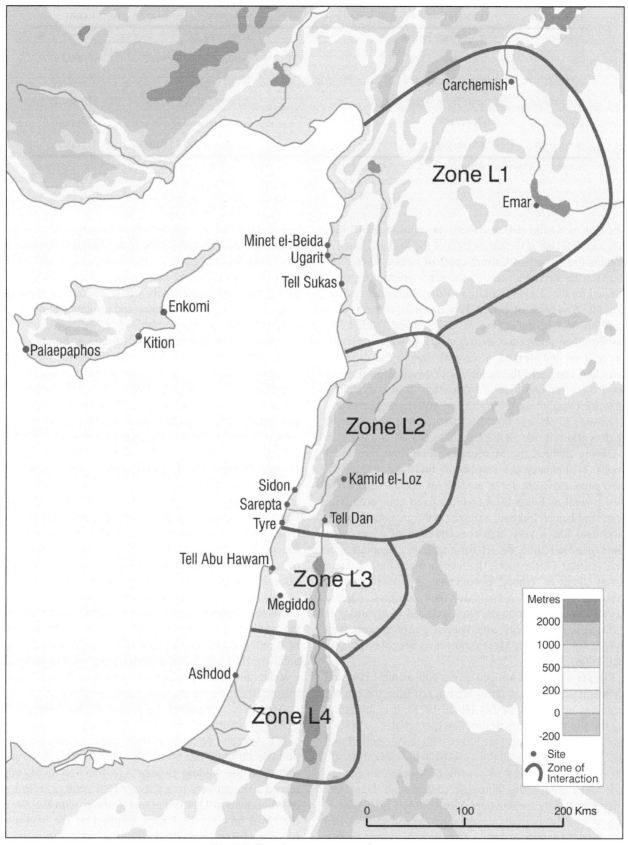

Fig. 4.1: Four Levantine zones of interaction

Ethnonym	Translation	Archive	From
pe-ri-ta	'man from Beirut'	Knossos	Zone L2
tu-ri-jo	'man from Tyre'	Knossos and Pylos	Zone L2
po-ni-ki-jo	'man (?) or spice (?) from Phoenicia'	Knossos	Zone L2
a-ra-da-jo	'man from Arad/Arvad'	Knossos	Zone L2
ku-pi-ri-jo	'Cypriot'	Knossos and Pylos	Cyprus
a-ra-si-jo	'Alashiyan'	Knossos and Mycenae	Cyprus

Source: Yasur-Landau (2002): Chapter 2, Section 2.3.3 (with references)

Table 4.1: Levantine and Cypriot ethnonyms in the Linear B texts

sites such as Kamid el-Loz in the Biqa valley (Koehl 1985, 144) and Tell Dan at the headwaters of the Jordan. Zone L3 contains the important Carmel coast of Israel, where Tell Abu Hawam served as one of the entry points for goods destined for the Jezreel and Jordan Valleys and sites such as Megiddo. The coast of Zone L4, meanwhile, contains Iron Age Philistia, with major ports at Ashkelon and Ashdod. My approach then selects domestic contexts, in which ordinary people lived and worked, at coastal sites in the different zones and compares the quantities of Mycenaean imports found there per unit area of excavation. It also examines the relative quantities of Cypriot and Mycenaean wares and endeavours to observe how this changed with time (where the data allowed; see Bell 2005; 2006, 30–60).

Having divided the Mycenaean wares into functional groups, I calculated the number of finds per 100 m² of excavation exposure for a number of coastal Levantine sites as well as Enkomi on Cyprus. Even compared with the assemblage at Enkomi, Sarepta (in the area that became Phoenicia) had a very high concentration of Mycenaean wares (see Bell 2006, fig. 21 for a graphic presentation of these results). Furthermore, the Sarepta assemblage, unlike that of Ugarit or Ashdod, is dominated by closed vessels, presumably acquired initially for their contents. Sarepta was also unusual among the sites included in my analysis in that it is he only site with fewer Cypriot imports than Mycenaean ones, once Mycenaean wares become available (Bell 2006, 58).

Sarepta was not destroyed at the end of the LBA, and nor was nearby Tyre as far as we can tell from the limited soundings made there to date (Bikai 1978). It is intriguing that the site that escapes destruction (perpetrated or at least catalysed by invaders that are linked with an Aegean cultural background elsewhere in the Levant) is the Levantine site that possessed the greatest density of Mycenaean pottery finds when comparable domestic contexts are examined. I have postulated elsewhere (Bell 2006, 110) that if Aegean merchants (and, presumably, Aegean sailors) had no personal contacts at Ugarit (which is discussed further in the context of textual evidence later in this paper) they

would have had few qualms about sacking and plundering its houses, palaces and tombs if conditions were such that they were forced to leave their homeland. Conversely, if these Aegean elements had traded directly with Sarepta during the LBA, surely this would encourage a peaceful request for refuge or assistance and militate against the use of force as an opening gambit?

No textual evidence has been found at Sarepta or any other port in Phoenicia that sheds light on international relations during the LBA. Looking at the Mycenaean Linear B archives, Assaf Yasur-Landau (2002) has examined the extent of knowledge of foreign lands, in terms of ethnonyms and toponyms. The sections of his analysis that pertain to the Levant and Cyprus cite Fernando Aura-Jorro (1985–93, I, 93; II, 112, 139–40, 378), Eric Cline (1994, 124, 129–30), Thomas Palaima (1991, 280–1) and Cynthia Shelmerdine (1998, 295) and the ethnonmyms and toponyms in question are summarised in Table 4.1. I am grateful to Dr Yasur-Landau for drawing my attention to the fact that that neither Ugarit nor any site in modern Israel is mentioned in the Linear B archives. Meanwhile, Cypriots are mentioned in more than one archive while four separate names in Phoenicia (coastal Zone L2), namely Beirut, Tyre, Arwad (Arvad) and Phoenicia itself, are represented in at least one archive. Simply the absence of reference to Ugarit and the southern Levantine coastal cities might be argued to be a reflection of the very partial nature of these Linear B archives. However, when taken together with the presence of Cypriots and four separate ethnonyms from Zone L2 therein, this pattern must surely have some significance.

Moreover, it matches the pattern Itamar Singer (1999, 676) has characterised for Ugarit, namely that not a single Aegean merchant is mentioned in the vast written documentation of that port. This contrasts with the situation portrayed the Middle Bronze Age Mari archives, which record a tin delivery to a Cretan (Bell 2006, 27). In terms of individuals at Ugarit that had dealings with the Aegean, the royal archives of Ugarit mention of the ship-owner Sinaranu being granted special privileges with respect to maritime trade with Crete by Ammistamru II, king of Ugarit

	Rapanu	Yabninu	Rašap-abu	Urtenu
Inland Syria	✓		✓	✓
Anatolia	✓	✓		✓
Upper Mesopotamia	✓			✓
Babylonia				✓
Phoenicia	✓	✓		✓
Coastal Israel		✓		
Egypt		✓		✓
Cyprus	CM	CM	CM	CM✓

CM = Cypro-Minoan document

Table 4.2: Interregional contacts of Ugaritic merchants

(Monroe 2000, 195). Overall, however, both the ceramic and philological evidence are consistent with the idea that Aegeans had more direct knowledge of the area that became Phoenicia than the remainder of the Syro-Palestinian coast during the LBA.

The pre-eminent role of Ugarit in the LBA trade in copper and tin

Turning to the trade in copper and tin, these metals, and particularly the latter, had a strategic value during the LBA not too dissimilar to that of crude oil today. Tin was absolutely vital for the maintenance of the status quo in LBA society. Bronze tools had become widely used in all manner of trades and the availability of enough tin to produce weapons made of high grade bronze must have exercised the minds of rulers much in the same way as keeping the oil flowing occupies our politicians today. Unlike copper, tin is rare in nature, and the best evidence we have for the source of tin used in the Levant during the LBA is that it came from Uzbekistan or Tajikistan, where mines of the appropriate age have been found by researchers from the Deutsches Bergbau-Museum in Bochum (Weisgerber and Cierny 1999; Cierny *et al.* 2001).

Bringing tin to the foundries of the Levant, Cyprus and beyond required both long-distance trade overland by donkey caravan as well as port facilities for onward maritime shipment. Ugarit was strategically placed to profit from this trade, at the nexus or '*Schnittpunkt*' of these routes (Stockfisch 1999). As already mentioned, a portion of the likely tin route, between the Euphrates at Emar and Ugarit, lay securely within Hittite-controlled territory in the closing years of the LBA. Furthermore, being only 160 km, or one day's sail, from the major copper export centre of Enkomi, no doubt, added to the value of the metal trade passing through Ugarit.

The stone oxhide ingot mould, discovered in 1982 at Ugarit's subsidiary palatial site of Ras Ibn Hani, supports the notion that this LBA port played an important role in the trade of Cypriot copper as it contained traces of Cypriot copper (based on lead isotope analysis; Lagarce and Lagarce 1997; Bounni *et al.* 1998, 43–4). This unique find suggests that copper was re-melted at Ras Ibn Hani to produce oxhide ingots for shipment to other consumption centres. Surely, if this copper had been destined for the furnaces of bronze smiths of Ugarit, effort and energy would not have been expended to cast the metal into this internationally recognised form?

Recent textual work by Christopher Monroe (2000) draws attention to the entrepreneurial activities of individual merchants in Ugarit. Benjamin Foster (1987) suggests that the palace establishment there extracted the majority of its wealth through taxation rather than direct control over long-distance trade. Buying and selling metals was one of the principal activities of the wealthy merchants of Ugarit. Individual merchants such as Rapanu, Yabninu, Urtenu and Rašap-abu conducted business on their own account on a profit motivated basis, but they did occasionally acquire goods for and provide services to the royal palace of Ugarit (Bell 2006, 65–7). Not one of these merchants is mentioned in the lists of those that were endowed directly by the royal palace, a group contractually obliged to carry out business on behalf of the king (Monroe 2000, 123). All four, however, did periodically engage in transactions with the palace. This calls to mind the activities of merchants in the British East India Company between 1600 and 1834 CE. By the end of the 18th century, company employees were able to conduct trade on their own account as a result of relationships they had established with merchants and ship owners across the region on official company business (Farrington 2002, 79).

Based on the currently available texts, Yabninu seems to have been the largest player in the tin trade of Ugarit. One of his shipments, documented in the text RS 11.799, amounted to 20 talents (approximately 600 kg; Courtois 1990). This is not quite on the scale of the Uluburun shipwreck which yielded a ton of tin ingots (Pulak 2000), but amounts to well over half of that ill-fated shipment. Yabninu had contacts along the length of the coast of Syro-Palestine, as well as in Cyprus, Egypt and Hittite Anatolia (see Table 4.2). The significance of the presence of four out of the total known corpus of nine Cypro-Minoan tablets in or near the houses of Rapanu, Yabninu, Urtenu and Rašap-abu at Ugarit (Ferrara 2005, 123) cannot be underestimated and must suggest that an important relationship existed between these merchants and Cyprus.

Among Levantine ports, therefore, Ugarit has the strongest claim to be the Eastern Mediterranean's principal LBA tin port as well as being a considerable importer of copper. Entrepreneurial merchants were responsible for some, if not the majority, of this trade at the end of the LBA. They traded tin and copper onwards, both by land and by ship to other Levantine destinations. This prosperous, peaceful world, rich in bronze and imported ceramics, came to an abrupt end in the early 12th century BCE. Different parts of the Levantine coast were affected to different extents: Ugarit in Zone L1 meets its final destruction, Zone L2 (the area that becomes known as Phoenicia) seemingly avoided hostilities, and coastal sites in Zones L3 and L4 (in modern Israel) rose from the ashes of their destruction with little delay.

Trade networks in the earliest Iron Age

As Colin Renfrew (2004) recently pointed out, one of the most profitable places to look for explanatory models on the nature of the economic restructuring that followed the end of the LBA is in the places were there appears to have been continuity. Consequently, the remainder of this paper will focus on the relationships between Cyprus, particularly the west of the island, and Phoenicia across the LBA/Iron Age transition.

But first, if Aegeans and Canaanites in my Zone L2 had the most direct trading relationships with each other during the LBA, what route might they have taken to achieve this? Sturt Manning and Linda Hulin (2005, 276, fig. 11.1) recently published a map that shows the areas of the Eastern Mediterranean sea from which landmasses are visible. Their analysis shows that a ship leaving Byblos on the coast of modern Lebanon for Cyprus would see its destination landmass before losing sight of its coast of origin. This would not be the case for a ship departing from Ashdod or Ashkelon on the lower relief coastline of the southernmost Levant. Patricia Bikai (1987) suggests that a Phoenician ship heading towards Rhodes or Crete in the Iron Age could well have made landfall on the west coast of Cyprus. As evidence of this, she cites the presence of the earliest Iron Age Phoenician ceramics in this part of Cyprus, and not in any other.

The two LBA shipwrecks at Cape Gelidonya and Uluburun are markers of shipping routes between the Levant and the Aegean (see Bell 2005, pl. lxxviii for a map of the hypothetical route about to be described). A vessel sailing east from the Aegean would probably need to stop somewhere on the west coast of Cyprus to take on fresh water and possibly provisions – perhaps around Palaepaphos, where several hundred Mycenaean ceramic finds have been excavated (Maier and Karageorghis 1984, 55). Such a vessel then might call in at Kition or Hala Sultan Tekke before reaching Enkomi. Alternatively, the Mycenaean goods might be landed at this first Cypriot port and re-loaded on to a Cypriot ship to continue their voyage to other Cypriot or Levantine ports. The lack of reference to Aegean traders in the texts of Ugarit, together with the Cypro-Minoan marks on some Mycenaean vessels found there might argue in favour of a Cypriot ship transporting the Mycenaean trade goods to Ugarit from, say, Enkomi (Hirschfeld 2000). Whereas Ugarit is hidden behind Cyprus from the Aegean perspective, Sarepta, and Phoenicia, lie straight ahead, with the same distance to sail as from Cape Gelidonya to the west coast of Cyprus.

To explore this hypothesis, I will now examine the degree of continuity of trade between Phoenicia and the west coast of Cyprus across the LBA/Iron Age I transition. Relatively few LBA/Iron Age settlements have been excavated on the western coast of Cyprus, the area one might expect LBA shipping from the Aegean to make landfall to pick up water and other supplies on a longer journey to the Levantine coast. The characteristics one would look for in such a way-station would be the availability a sheltered anchorage, fresh water supplies nearby and an easy position to defend. A way-station might begin life as a seasonal stop-off point, but if the level of traffic warranted it, a permanent establishment with a different architectural and material culture signature from that of the surrounding indigenous culture might well develop.

Maa-Palaeokastro (see Fig. 4.2) stands out as a site that matches the characteristics I have outlined. Located 10 km north of modern Paphos, it stands on a rocky peninsula between two natural harbours with fortifications defending it on the landward side Karageorghis' excavations between 1979 and 1986 demonstrated that the site was occupied during the LC II–LC IIIA periods (or LH IIIB–IIIC:1 in Mycenaean pottery styles; see Karageorghis and Demas 1988, I, 2). The material culture of Maa is interesting on two counts. First, Maa exhibits many Aegean cultural manifestations. Yasur-Landau (2003a) has recently commented on the predominantly Aegean material culture of this site, including hearth rooms, LH IIIB wares, locally made LH IIIC fine-wares, loom weights and cooking jugs. Second, it has also produced an unusually high number of Canaanite amphorae, attesting an intense relationship with the Levant.

The Mycenaean IIIC pottery at Maa-Palaeokastro is

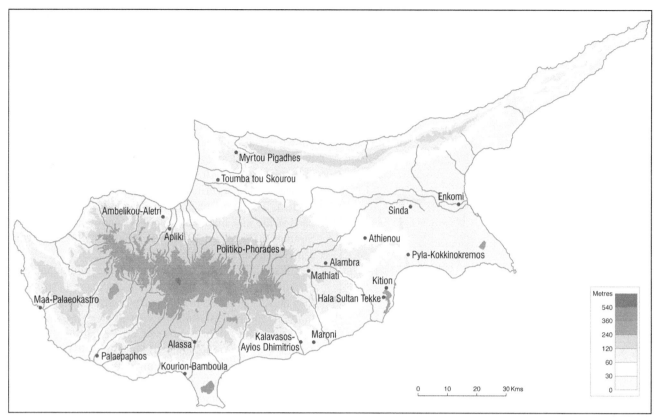

Fig. 4.2: Cypriot LBA sites

probably among the earliest in Cyprus (Karageorghis and Demas 1988, I, 261). One of the features of the Mycenaean IIIC:1 repertoire at Maa is a large number of skyphoi (drinking cups). Such vessels are also known at Palaepaphos but not in the eastern Cypriot sites, and comparanda also exist at Tarsus in Cilicia (Karageorghis and Demas 1988, I, 326). The presence of locally made versions of these wares at Maa surely suggests that individuals who were, at the very least, highly influenced by Aegean cultural preferences, manufactured them there. Taken together with the other archaeological evidence, including cooking jugs and loom weights, the balance of probability must be in favour of some Aegeans living at this short-lived settlement.

Turning to evidence of strong Levantine contact, it is clear that the large number of Canaanite jars found in LC IIC and LC IIIA contexts at Maa is diagnostic of regular trade with the Levant (Hadjicosti 1988, 360) that continues across the LBA/Iron Age transition. The finds represent at least 84 jars, the majority of which date to LC IIIA. Maria Hadjicosti (1988, 359) states that these do not form a large variety of types, suggesting trade with a limited number of Levantine production centres. The raises the possibility that Maa may have served as a distribution centre for these jars and/or their contents. This hypothesis is based on the

disproportionately large number found there, which suggests a direct link with Levantine ports (Hadjicosti 1988, 361). Chemical and petrographic studies on these jars (Jones and Vaughan 1988) prove that they were predominantly from the central Levant and southern Palestine, rather than being locally made. Tristan Barako (2000) has made the point that the absence of imports from Cyprus in Philistia in the earliest Iron Age, and the relative proximity of, for example, Tyre and Sarepta to Cyprus, makes it likely that the Canaanite imports to Cyprus during the LC IIIA period came from the major Phoenician centres.

Another interesting feature of the material culture of Maa is the corpus of balance weights found there, namely 37 weights dating to the LC IIC period (Courtois 1988). Balance weights are integral to mercantile trade, both within a culture and between individuals from different cultures (Petruso 1984). Jean-Claude Courtois (1988) noted that the excavations at Maa yielded a good number of weights for a small, fortified site of brief duration. This would support the view that this site was heavily engaged in commerce, as weights may be regarded as the most important tool in a merchant's assemblage (Hafford 2001, 156). The Maa weight repertoire contains a relatively high number of weights (six in total) that have correspondence with Aegean

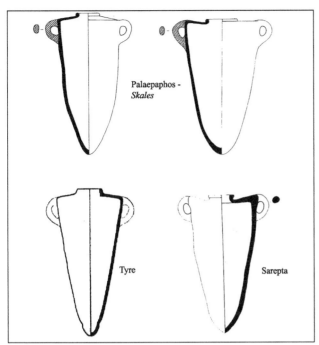

Fig. 4.3: Canaanite jars from Palaepaphos-Skales, Tyre and Sarepta (after Pritchard, 1975, fig. 24.6; Bikai, 1978, pl. XXXV.2; Bikai, 1983, 397)

weight systems, even if the majority (21 weights) correspond with Syro-Egyptian standards.

This contrasts strongly with the situation at Pyla-Kokkinokremos (see Fig. 4.2), another fortified site over-looking the southeast coast of the island, which Vassos Karageorghis excavated at about the same time as Maa (Karageorghis and Demas 1984). At Pyla, the weight system is characterised by a wide range of weight denominations, from half a shekel to a talent, within one standard, namely the Syro-Egyptian one (Courtois 1984). While the weights of Pyla appear to conform to eastern metrology, a significant number at Maa conformed to Aegean standards. One would expect this if the site had functioned as a way-station on the maritime route from the Aegean to the Levant.

Excavations at Palaepaphos-Skales, 26 km south of Maa, revealed tombs of the Iron Age Cypro-Geometric period. Patricia Bikai (1983) wrote the ceramic report for the eastern imports in these tombs. The most easily identified class of ceramic artefact found was the Iron Age version of the Canaanite storage jar (Bikai 1983, 396). Twelve of these were found in the tombs, which represented two types. The first type (of which there were ten examples) is described as being probably from IA I contexts based on comparanda from Bikai's (1978) own sounding at Tyre. They are also known at the Phoenician site of Tel Keisan in northern Israel (Bikai 1983, 396). This type of vessel continues until the 8th century BCE and its ascription here to the early part of the

Iron Age is due to the other items contained in the tombs, including the second group of Canaanite jars.

Two examples were found of the second type, which are more useful in determining specific trade connections (illustrated in Fig. 4.3). This type is characterised by flat shoulders and a triangular body and is heavy with thick walls. Here the parallels are very specific, namely one from each of Tyre and Sarepta. Only two intact examples are known that are comparable to these jars. The first was found in Stratum XIII at Tyre (Bikai 1978, pl. xxxv.2) dating to immediately after 1070/50 BCE (Bikai 1978, 66) and the second at Sarepta (Pritchard 1975, fig. 24.6) from an earlier context. The intact example from Sarepta was found in a part of the site that was a pottery manufacturing area in Stratum V (Pritchard 1978, 120; Khalifeh 1988, 27) which James Pritchard tentatively dated to 1200 BCE.

Bikai (Bikai 1983, 396) stresses the point that these Phoenician parallels from Tyre and Sarepta are so strong '… they must be products of the same workshop.' She concludes that the imports of Palaepaphos-Skales, are important because of the light they shed on Levantine – Cypriot relations in IA I. She adds (Bikai 1983, 404): '…it is a surprise to find such a large group of imports on the Western end of Cyprus; early pieces have appeared sporadically, particularly at Amathus, but there has been nothing to compare with this.' Karageorghis concluded (1983, 371) that the twelve Canaanite amphorae found together with other Levantine ceramics represent an unprecedented find compared with other early Cypro-Geometric sites on the island. He rationalises this as either being the result of Palaepaphos being the most important trading centre on the island in CGI–CGII (and, therefore, it was natural that the Phoenicians should trade there) or that the Phoenicians had started their westward expansion earlier than previously thought and used Palaepaphos as their trading base (as they did at Kition later in the Iron Age).

I would argue in favour of a third alternative. This evidence also supports the notion that contact between Phoenicia and the western part of Cyprus did not stop across the period of the Levantine LBA/Iron Age transition. The nature of the trade may have changed, but sites in both western Cyprus and Phoenicia that were not destroyed at this time and appear to have carried on trading with each other. Maria Iacovou (2006, 35) has pointed out that destructions on Cyprus were not as drastic as those suffered in the Aegean in the early 12th century BCE and both Palaepaphos and Kition saw monumental enhancement in this period. Franz Georg Maier has drawn attention to the unique position of Palaepaphos within the Cypriot archaeological record. This settlement is neither destroyed, abandoned nor transferred to another location in late LC III to early CG I (Maier 1999). He stresses that although the majority of grave goods found there are Cypriot, no Aegean imports occur in the graves that date to 1050–850 BCE (Coldstream 1990; Maier 1999). In contrast, imports from Phoenicia were conspicuous from the earliest part of this period (Maier 1999). Consequently, this city that had looked west as well as east during the LBA seems to have acquired only Phoenician ceramic imports during this period. More excavation may change this perspective, but until it does I believe this is a valid working hypothesis.

In the rest of the island, evidence for trade with Phoenicia is scarce from this early period. There is no archaeological evidence that the Larnaca area (which includes Kition) was important to the Phoenicians in IA I (Bikai 1987). At Kition, which became a Phoenician colony in the 9th century BCE, Bikai (1981, 29) remarks that the first thing that can be said about imported pottery in Kition Area II is that there is 'surprisingly' little of it. She goes on to say that very few classes of Levantine pottery are found there and, what there is, is much later, corresponding to Tyre Stratum X – c. 850 BCE (Nunez 2004, 286). The evidence, therefore, suggests contact between Phoenicia and the western part of Cyprus did not stop at the close of the LBA. Palaepaphos had looked west, as well as east, during the LBA; but in IA I it seems to only have Phoenician ceramic imports.

Important recent work in Northern Israel has been carried out by Ayelet Gilboa and Ilan Sharon (2003) using recently excavated data from Tel Dor (which came under Phoenician influence during the early Iron Age). This site has produced one of the most plentiful sequences of Cypro-Geometric pottery outside Cyprus (Gilboa 1999), with the possible exception of Bikai's limited sounding at Tyre (Bikai 1978). Gilboa's 2005 paper also examines the close contact between Phoenicia (including sites along the Carmel Coast) and Cyprus and contrasts this with the apparent lack of contact between Cyprus and Philistia (Gilboa 2005). Suffice it to say that this evidence also supports continuity of maritime trade contacts between Cyprus and Phoenicia in the early part of the Iron Age.

If Phoenicia and Western Cyprus continued to trade in the earliest years of the Iron Age, what did they trade? Giorgos Papasavvas (Papasavvas 2003) has recently argued that Cyprus continued to be an active copper producer and exporter after the end of LC IIC. Michal Artzy (2006, 25) has remarked that it is often difficult to distinguish between LBA manufactured bronze objects and those found in the graves at Palaepaphos-Skales, which date to well after 1200 BCE, attesting continuity in the LBA manufacturing traditions. Given the limited amount of provenience work that has been done on bronze artefacts in Iron Age contexts in the Levant, particularly on the coast, it is not currently possible to prove that Cypriot copper continued to be imported. Scientific studies on bronze objects from Pella (Philip *et al.* 2003), inland in my Zone L3, suggests that copper was obtained from more local sources, accessible overland, during the Iron Age, in contrast to the LBA. If Cypriot copper did find its way to the undamaged Phoenician ports what did Tyre and Sarepta's merchants have to trade in return? Albert Leonard

(1995) has suggested that, although dry goods, spices, beer and olive oil have been put forward as possible contents of Canaanite jars, based on widespread availability of grapes in the Near East since before 3000 BCE, they were principally used in the wine trade. Lebanon remains famous, to this day, for its wines.

At the close of the LBA, a much larger container appears in the southern Levant, namely the collared-rim pithos, or jar. Whereas a typical Canaanite jar would be c. 50 cm in height (Leonard 1995) collared-rim pithoi are usually 1.0–1.2 m in height (Wengrow 1996). These vessels were extremely heavy when full. Wengrow cites the weight of one particular empty jar as 32 kg (close to that of an oxhide ingot of copper) and would have been too heavy for a donkey when full. Artzy (1994) connected the advent of collared-rim pithoi in the archaeological record with the domestication of the dromedary and trade in aromatics from Arabia to the Levant and beyond. The discovery of many collared-rim pithoi in 13th century BCE contexts at the coastal emporium of Tel Nami (on the Carmel Coast of Israel) led her to suggest that one of the reasons behind the wealth of this site was its involvement in the supply of incense. She postulated that these pithoi could have been used as containers to bring incense overland to Tel Nami, from which they were shipped to other coastal destinations in the Eastern Mediterranean. She also pointed out the similarities between the Tel Nami pithoi and ones found at Maa-Palaeokastro (*e.g.* Karageorghis and Demas 1988, II, pl. lxxxii, 563). One such pithos (no. 563) was found on Floor II, dating to the LC IIC period.

In terms of locally available goods, the Phoenician ports also had access to timber and manufactured purple dye and olive oil. The merchants at the undamaged ports of Phoenicia were, therefore, able to continue trading amid the destruction that surrounded them. I have already cited Monroe's work on the merchants of Ugarit which suggests that, despite being under Hittite imperial authority, Ugarit's merchants were engaged in entrepreneurial trade on their own account at the close of the LBA. Andrew and Susan Sherratt (2001) referred to this transfer of control of long distance trade from the palace to the merchants as privatisation.

It is difficult to assess how much control the Egyptians had over the Phoenician ports in the closing decades of the LBA. Susan Sherratt (2003) has suggested that the Phoenician coast may well have been independent by the time of Ramesses II's death. Indeed, there is no evidence of an Egyptian military presence in Lebanon after year 10 of Ramesses II's reign, the date on the badly preserved inscription at the Dog River (Nahr el-Kelb) close to the coast north of Beirut (Higginbotham 2000, 34). A lower degree of Egyptian control would have provided the climate of innovation for private enterprise in the Phoenician coastal city states that already had a long tradition of maritime trade. In Cyprus, the case for a decentralised political structure to the island during the LBA is also strong. Susan Sherratt (1998, 301) has described the 'coastal moguls' of 13th–12th century BCE Cyprus being engaged in decentralised trading activities. Cypriot merchants and their Phoenician counterparts were, therefore, well positioned to capitalise on the opportunities that arose from the catastrophic events at the end of the Bronze Age (Sherratt 1998; 2003).

Phoenicia and the western part of Cyprus were able to seize the day when crisis struck the region. Unencumbered by imperial agendas, and already familiar with operating within a decentralised trading environment, traders and merchants from these two regions used private initiative and resources to continue trading, particularly with each other, in the dark days of the earliest Iron Age. Both Cyprus and Phoenicia had locally produced goods to trade and, unlike the greatest LBA Levantine port, Ugarit, they were not as reliant on goods arriving from long, and now insecure, overland trade routes from Central Asia. We must hope that further excavation, both in Western Cyprus and in the Phoenician homeland, will begin to fill the major lacunae in our data in the next few years to test this proposition.

Acknowledgements

Andrew Sherratt examined my PhD, on which much of this paper is based, in May 2005. I was privileged to benefit from his constructive critique and the enormous depth and breadth of his knowledge. I also thank Sue Sherratt for allowing me to consult her often as my doctoral research progressed. While many others were less than positive about the possibilities of looking at the end of the Bronze Age from an economic point of view, Sue was cautiously optimistic that the issues could be tackled in a systematic way. I owe a huge debt of gratitude to them both and any errors and shortcomings remain my own.

CULTURAL IDENTITY AND SOCIAL INTERACTION IN CRETE AT THE END OF THE BRONZE AGE (LM IIIC)

Katia Perna

According to the traditional interpretation, the beginning of the Aegean Dark Age, which coincides with the transition from the Bronze Age to the Iron Age (hereafter LH/LM IIIC, about 1190–1050 BCE; Warren and Hankey 1989), was a period of harsh instability. In this period, the Aegean political and economic system fell and the regions in this area underwent a profound transformation: a territorial, economic and political reorganization that took place to different degrees in different states, and was influenced by migration of cohesive groups of people from the mainland to the Aegean islands, with the consequent creation of a new cultural *koiné* (Desborough 1972).

The identification of elements typical of distinct cultures, particularly Minoan and Mycenaean aspects, has been the usual framework for interpreting the changes in the cultural reality of Crete at the end of LM IIIB and during the course of the LM IIIC. In fact, the archaeological evidence of LM IIIC Crete makes it clear that a number of cultural regions formed, with different settlement types, burial customs and religious expressions, most notably between upland and lowland settlements, and between the centres of eastern Crete and those on the rest of the island. However, the distinction of phenomena such as cultural interaction, and acculturation or the individuation of different ethnic groups through archaeological data is not without difficulty (Jones 1997, 106–10, 119–27). As post-processualist archaeologists affirm (Hodder 1991), in contrast with normative or deterministic readings of archaeological data, the actions of people and their material productions could have been influenced by many factors, and could have been an answer to needs of affirmation and ideological representation by some groups, or be the product of the manipulation of symbols and ideas.

In light of these possibilities, the aim of this paper is to examine the changes which occurred in LM IIIC/sub-Minoan Crete in each discernable cultural ambit, paying particular attention to the role played by the 'peaceful' interaction between different groups, although these were in some cases based on competitive relationships, and to the reception and revision of old and new symbols, and of foreign cultural influences.

Settlement patterns

At the end of LM IIIB and the beginning of LM IIIC a number of important coastal centers were abandoned in Crete, probably in relation to a decline in the sea-trade or to the abandonment of some trade routes. Nevertheless, the sea-trade did not entirely disappear, as the survival of some coastal centres (Amnisos and Chania) and the installation of the new ones (Elias to Nisi and Palaikastro Kastri) shows. This is also confirmed by the arrival of products of north-European and Italic type on the island (see Bouzek 1985, 143–5, 159–60). Simultaneously, many new settlements arose, particularly on the numerous mountains of the island, which had been usually considered refuge sites (Nowicki 2000). But in many cases the reason for their foundation was probably due to the desire to control land routes, and to exploit the pasture and agricultural potential of the land (Haggis 1993). Indeed, in this period primary production activities became the mainstay for the economy of the inland settlements, and there was an increase in animal husbandry (Borgna 2003, 154–5; Wallace 2003). Because of their economic activities these internal upland settlements probably provided the lowland centres with agricultural products, livestock and textiles in exchange for finished goods. Harbours and lowland centres, on the other hand, would have been the entry points for exotic goods, which could warrant maintaining overseas relations and the survival of a wider exchange system (Borgna 2003, 160–1, 163).

This model is particularly suitable for eastern Crete, where the settlement system seems to have been based on the foundation of small centres around the more productive areas. Some centres arose in a position that allowed the control of the surrounding land, and showed a defined spatial organization, such as those at Kavousi Kastro and Vronda (Coulson 1997; Preston Day 1997), Karphi (Pendlebury *et al.* 1937–38), Chalasmenos (Coulson and Tsipopoulou 1994) and Vasiliki Kephala (Eliopoulos 1998). Gradually the new upland centres grew and consolidated their position on the territory. The presence of 'foreign' products in settlements and tombs (Bouzek 1985; Tsipopoulou *et al.* 2003, 112–18) particularly in the second half of the period, hint to an increased potential to maintain external relationships.

The spatial organization of these centres shows some novelties: they had free standing shrines (Temple G at Kavousi Vronda, Temple 1 at Karphi, Temple E at Vasiliki and the shrine at Chalasmenos), for example, and prominent buildings (Building A–B at Kavousi Vronda, the Great House at Karphi, the Building A at Vasiliki Kephala, the Megara at Chalasmenos) probably designated to the political authority (Mazarakis Ainian 1997, 208–10, 218–20). Some of these building have been related to foreign architectural models. In particular, the megara at Chalasmenos and at Karphi and the room with central heart in the sanctuary at Vasiliki Kephala, as well as other elements such as the presence of many Mycenaean pottery shapes, new cooking habits, new religious iconographies, and so forth, directly referred to Mycenaean people in the opinion of many scholars (Mazarakis Ainian 1997, 219; D'Agata 2001, 350; Tsipopoulou 2005, 322–4), potentially as rulers. Nevertheless, particularly at Karphi and Chalasmenos, other buildings show many traditional architectural features such as the bench rooms in the shrines, or the oblunge rectangular rooms in some houses (Building A–B at Kavousi Vronda), and it is therefore probable that the megaron itself was present in Crete during the palatial period. The mixed character of the architecture does not need to be explained by presence of a mixed population, as it could have resulted through the acquisition of Mycenaean models during a long interaction between them and the Cretan people.

Central Crete shows different situation. The centres of Knossos and Festos, continuously inhabited from the previous period, seem to have been the main centres of large areas of surrounding land. Recently Elisabetta Borgna (2004), starting from the analysis of the pottery of the Acropoli Mediana, has proposed a reconstruction of the LM IIIC Festos as a lead centre in which many groups, some of which extra-island foreigners, formed the social body. The interaction and competition between these groups could be controlled by a central power, and managed by an elite group. In early the LM IIIC at Knossos, a new settlement was established at the current site of the Stratigraphical Museum which was inhabited until the sub-Minoan–early Protogeometric periods. In the preliminary report Peter Warren (Warren 1982–83, 74) noted that some elements hint to direct contacts with overseas people: an imported Italian knife, an apsidal building, and a sub-floor infant burial which recall Mycenaean models and usage. But during its lifetime some old *necropolies* were employed, such as that at Upper Gypsadhes, while old tombs were reused at Kephala and at Aghios Ioannis. During the sub-Minoan, moreover, a new necropolis was established at the North Cemetery. Therefore, it seems that in the LM IIIC Knossos was open to extra-island contacts and received new cultural inputs, but there was a sudden break with the oldest burial traditions and there was a reorganisation of the settlement, in the ambit of a substantial continuity in the occupation of the land.

The new upland settlements at Erganos (Halbherr 1901) and Prinias (Rizza 1996; Perna 2006) show some features similar to the upland eastern settlements, particularly in religious or burial customs (see below), which implies that the settlers perceived some cultural traditions as very important elements. Western Crete was less populated in LM IIIC than in the LM IIIA–B. In the first half of LM IIIC some old centres as Chania remained active (Hallager and Pålsson Hallager 2000) and new ones were founded, such as Chamalevri (Andreadaki Vlasaki and Papadopoulou 2005) near the northern coast, and Sybrita (Prokopiou 1997) in the Amari valley. In these centres a particular ritual practice is attested, in which pits were filled with pottery sherds, pebbles and bronze objects. They have been interpreted as the final act of common meals, during which new settlers, often coming from different areas of the island and involved in the management of the resources of the land, interacted. In the middle of the period either Chania or Chamalevri were deserted, whereas Sybrita grew and developed, transforming its social and political structures (D'Agata 1997–2000, 58–9). Therefore, although Sybrita was an upland centre its rise and development seem to be very different from those of the eastern uplands, less linked to old traditions and tending to the experimentation of new social strategies.

Religion

One of the most distinctive traits of this period was the cult of the goddess with upraised arms (Alexiou 1958; Gesell 1985, 41–6; Prent 2005, 174–84, 616–20). This was a Minoan divinity, who was worshipped during the LM IIIA–B above all in the central-eastern part of the island, at Gazi, Gournià, Haghia Triada and Kannià. In LM IIIB, the shrine of the goddess was an independent building which was often articulated into several rooms and linked to a more-or-less ample open court (Perna in press). According to a specific religious protocol she was furnished with a specialized set of ritual objects (snake tubes, *kalathoi*, *pinakes* and fenestrate stands). In some centres the organization of her cult achieved a noteworthy complexity. The shrine at Kavousi Vronda, for instance contained a conspicuous number of goddess' statues. Given the character of this centre, the main one of a cluster site, as Anna Lucia D'Agata (D'Agata 2001, 349) has observed, it is possible that many groups participated to the festival in honour of the goddess. These meetings could be a useful moment to strengthen alliances and to come to common agreements in order to better exploit the lands' resources.

At Karphi the presence of a number of shrines dedicated to the goddess with upraised arms has been explained as the result of the absence of a central authority (D'Agata 2001, 348–9), or as the sign of the existence of a great sacred area which represented a reference point for the surrounding land (Perna 2004). Karphi was certainly open to overseas trade, as the presence of some European and Cypriot objects shows, and although it is possible that these relations were mediated by other Cretan centres the possibility that this centre received direct external inputs cannot be excluded. Nevertheless, the traditional matrix of the cult is evident. At Vasiliki Kephala, on the other hand, the shrine of the goddess was embedded in a more complex, multi-room sacred building in which diverse ritual activities had to have taken place (Eliopoulos 1998, 310). Here, some architectural features, such as the presence of a room with two columns which flanked a hearth, and the attestation of an enthroned goddess, recall religious practices from the mainland (D'Agata 2001, 350). The Isthmus of Ierapetra was certainly in contact with the rest of the Aegean, as the presence of mainland pottery in the area of Vasiliki shows. The sanctuary at Vasiliki Kephala, perhaps, was also a point of reference in the region and the reception of some mainland characteristics could be due to the presence of a mixed population or to a deep relationship with mainland people.

The religious choice of the upland eastern centres seems to remain in line with local tradition. The cult of the goddess represented a link with the past for the new settlers. Under her protection they could recognize in themselves a common background and became part of a new community. Local differences in the cult of the goddess were probably due to the different composition of the social body, and to the more or less strong reception of new contributors.

In central Crete new forms of religious expressions appeared during the course of the LM IIIC, supplanting the previously widespread worship of the goddess with the upraised arms. However, this cult survived at Prinias (Palermo 1999) and at Knossos, where during the sub-Minoan period the goddess was honoured in the Spring Chamber (Evans 1921–35, II, 129–30), though in a different way. Among the new religious expressions, a cult consisting in the deposition of animal and fantastic-being figurines in open air sanctuaries is attested at Tylissos (Kanta in press)

and at Haghia Triada (D'Agata 1999). In the latter site the open sanctuary was established after the settlement was abandoned, and figurines of bulls, sacred horns and fantastic subjects were placed within it. As well as traditional Minoan figurines, foreign technical and iconographic components (such as the sphinx) have been identified in some of the votive depositions (D'Agata 1999, 233–9). Similar features are shown by the more important cult-place in the western area, the sacred cave of Pathos (Korou and Karetsou 1994), in which animal and human figurines were placed. These cult habits, which were very different from those in eastern Crete, make it clear that in central-western Crete the religious culture incorporated new influences, probably due to a more dialectic relationships with foreign people.

Burials

The burial culture of eastern Crete was very characteristic. Tholoi tombs were widespread in the necropolis, whereas chamber tombs, which were very common in LM IIIA2–B (Perna 2001) became very rare and are attested only in sites continuously occupied from LM IIIA–C, such as Myrsini Aspropilia (Daux 1960, 819–21), Kritsa Kato Lakkoi and Katharos (Platon 1951, 444–5; Tsipopoulou and Little 2001) and Praisos Kapsalos (Kanta 1980, 179–81). In the latter two, however, they coexisted with tholoi tombs. These tholoi presented new features and their aspect was less monumental than Minoan ones. Nevertheless, their link to some oldest Cretan tholoi has been underlined (Kanta 1997), and it is evident in the case of the above-ground ones at Karphi (Pendlebury *et al.* 1937–38, 100–9) and Siderokephala (Taramelli 1899, 402–6). Some Minoan tholoi were reused by the LM III people, such as at Haghia Triada and Archanes in LM IIIA1–2 (Cucuzza 2002), at Knossos Kephala in LM IIIC (Cadogan 1967), and at Valis in the Messara plain during the sub-Minoan (Davaras 1973, 164). Minoan and LM III tholoi were often used as landmarks (Belli 1997, 252–3), or as ideological means to affirm an identity (Cucuzza 2002). The construction of LM IIIC ones required care and tholoi have to have had a visual impact in the territories in which lain, and it is likely that people who chose them shared a common cultural background and recalled it in order to legitimize their presence in a territory just occupied. The contributions of other people who modified the type cannot be ruled out (Belli 2006), but I think that tholos was perceived as a traditional type of tomb and consciously adopted as a symbol of cultural identity by internal settlers.

Continuity with a local tradition is also evident in the use, in the eastern part of the island, of caves and rock-shelters as tombs, such as had been used since the Early Minoan period, and in the custom to place the burial container (usually a pithos) in upside-down position, as attested at

Piskokephalo Berati (Platon 1952, 639–41) and Vrokastro Chavga (Hall 1914, 173) where it had been practised since the Early Minoan at Voros, for example, and in the Middle Minoan at such sites as a Porti, Pachyammos, Sphoungaras and Mochlos. It was still in use during LM IIIA at Palaikastro and Mallia (Perna 2003, 22).

Buried individuals were accompanied by a broad selection of furniture, prevalently consisting of a pottery set. A small number of tombs, however, contained precious objects and weapons, such as at Myrsini (Platon 1959, 372–3), Mouliana (Xanthoudidis 1904) and Vasiliki H. Teodoros (Seager 1906–7, 129–32). In the richer tombs the pottery set consisted of a few closed vessels, and the placing of these beside one or two male corpses, in spite of the presence of higher-value goods, hints at an accentuation of individuality that contrasts with the deposition of complete pottery sets inside family tombs.

The diffusion of cremation in this period is usually adduced to the arrival of newcomers. Cremation had appeared on the island in LM IIIA2 at Olous (Kanta 2001), but during LM IIIC and sub-Minoan became widespread. Nevertheless, in this period cremated corpses were buried in the same tombs with inhumations and, in some cases, were contained in the same burial vase, such as in the tholos at Kapsalos (Platon 1960, 303–5) in the Praisos area, and perhaps in the chamber tomb at Kritsa (Tsipopoulou and Little 2001, 86), where cremation urns were placed directly inside the larnax where the inhumed corpse was lain. The cremated individuals were contained inside a typical Minoan vessel, a decorated pyxis with straight sides. In a tholos at Erganos, this type of vessel was used to contain the bones of an inhumed individual in a secondary burial, and consequently it doesn't seem that cremated individuals were considered 'others' in respect to the social body. They were buried in typical Minoan tombs and, according to Cretan ritual protocol, their burial furniture was very similar to that was laid near inhumed corpses. If the cremation pertained to foreign people then it is plausible to suppose that they were integrated in the host society. Cremation was not a status symbol, because the richer burials of eastern Crete were inhumation. Nevertheless, the cremated corpses of eastern Crete were males and this could hint a social significance in the adoption of this rite.

Few LM IIIC/sub-Minoan cemeteries are known in central Crete, but the evidence offered by the necropolis of Liliana at Festos and, later, by the North Cemetery at Knossos show that the burial culture in the lowland centres of this part of the island had many similarities to those of the previous period (LM IIIA–B). In the necropolis at Liliana (Savignoni 1904, 628–49), burials continued in chamber tombs but without the inclusion of precious objects with the furniture, as had happened in the older cemetery at Kalyvia (Savignoni 1904, 505–27). The absence of status symbols could perhaps be the sign of a poorer society, but the data coming from the settlements of Phaistos seem to

hint a different situation (see above). The homogeneity of the burials, then, could be due to the need to avoid any ostentation, in spite of the presence in the social body of many heterogeneous groups and in order to favour social interaction (Borgna 2003, 171).

In the upland sites of the central area such as Erganos (Halbherr 1901, 262–81) and, in the late LM IIIC–sub-Minoan, Prinias (Rizza 1996; in press), tholoi tombs were adopted. The tombs at Erganos also lacked precious objects and weapons, and contained only an essential pottery set. The later tombs at Prinias Siderospilia portray a different situation. Between the end of the LM IIIC and the start of the sub-Minoan an evident biritualism is attested in this necropolis and contemporaneously at the Knossos North Cemetery: cremations in pit tombs were present at Prinias (Rizza 1996), where inhumed corpses were buried in tholos tombs, while cremation in pit-caves coexisted with inhumations in chamber tombs at Knossos (Coldstream and Catling 1996). In both centres the cremated individuals were accompanied by weapons and precious objects. This situation is consistent with the cremated burials at Tylissos Atzolou (Marinatos 1931) and Archanes Kato Lakkos (Sapouna-Sakellarakis 1990, 75–6), where pit-tombs which contained individual cremated corpses were also accompanied by weapons. This seems to indicate that cremation was linked to groups who differentiated them from those who chose inhumation, but nevertheless these burials show some link with the island burial background. The cremations at Knossos were placed in a traditional local tomb, the pit-cave: in tomb AI at Prinias (Biondi in press) the cremation was placed in a pithos in upturned position, and their grave goods compare with those of other LM IIIC Cretan inhumed burials, whether placed in tholoi or chamber tombs. In my opinion these elements do not favour ethnic separation. From a social perspective it is interesting to note that with the exception of the tombs 200–202 of the North Cemetery of Knossos, in which a group (probably a family group) with rich furniture was buried, cremation was confined to individual male burials and consequently exalted the individuality of the dead. Burnt individuals were in fact buried alone inside a tomb which could contain only one corpse, and were accompanied by few objects, often of 'foreign' type (Catling 1995), which perhaps were intended as exclusive and exotic goods. This tendency could be the sign of a different social organization, in which some individual were emerging and using an elite ideology, very similar to the older one displayed in Mycenaean shaft-graves, and a new ritual to affirm their social role.

Similar features are attested also in western Crete. In this part of the island individual burials seem to have been preferred to family ones, which were the prevailing type during the LM IIIA–B. At Voliones (Pologhiorghi 1981), in the area of Rethymnon, LM IIIB/C *larnakes* with inhumed corpses were buried in the ground, and in the late LM IIIC cemetery at Atsipadhes cremations in urns, accompanied by a few personal objects and one or two closed vases, were placed on the ground (Agelarakis *et al.* 2001). This latter cemetery is the only one in LM IIIC Crete exclusively formed by cremations, and could be inferred as belonging to a non-Cretan people (Agelarakis *et al.* 2001). The building of an above-ground tholos at Pantanassa (Tegou 2001) in the sub-Minoan is consistent with similar burial buildings of eastern Crete. Therefore, the presence of cremations with rich furniture and weapons inside this tomb recall the sub-Minoan cremations of central and eastern Crete. It is very difficult to try to explain the particular situation in this area, but given the similarities noted between it and the central area it is probable that also here changes in the burial customs reflected transformation in social structures.

Concluding remarks

The observation that different areas of Crete had different social, religious and funerary practices clashes with the idea of a cultural homogeneity, sometimes interrupted by the arrival of extra-island newcomers, and testifies to diversified societies which established reciprocal relationships due to a flow communication between the centres of the island. The introduction of new rituals, iconographies and metal objects (Naue II swords, Peschiera daggers, etc.) show that people, ideas, and goods arrived in Crete and perhaps mixed with local people, traditions and productions, but does not presuppose an invasion of consistent groups of people that imposed their habits. The gradual and non-traumatic penetration of new cultural elements could be a consequence of more subtle factors such as trade, peaceful micro-mobility of Aegean groups, and reciprocal exchange of knowledge and traditions. Also the internal movement of Cretan people from some areas of the island to others, testified by the abandonment of some settlements and the foundation of others, probably favoured the syncretism of different traditions. The needs of settlers who occupied new lands likely determined the spatial organization in the new settlements, whereas religious activities and traditional burial symbols allowed them to not be foreigners in a new land.

6

LATE BRONZE AGE EXCHANGE NETWORKS IN THE WEST MEDITERRANEAN

Andrea Vianello

Introduction

One of the most significant developments to occur during the Late Bronze Age was the formation of Mediterranean long-distance exchange networks that spanned the Mediterranean (Fig. 6.1) and influenced many societies by means of the circulation of both commodities and ideas. Continental exchange networks continued the tradition of regional and inter-regional exchanges (Bouzek 1985; Cunliffe 2001), and they were joined by an extensive maritime network in the Mediterranean. The formation of the exchange network happened very quickly: Late Helladic (LH) I pots are already found from the Levantine to the Tyrrhenian

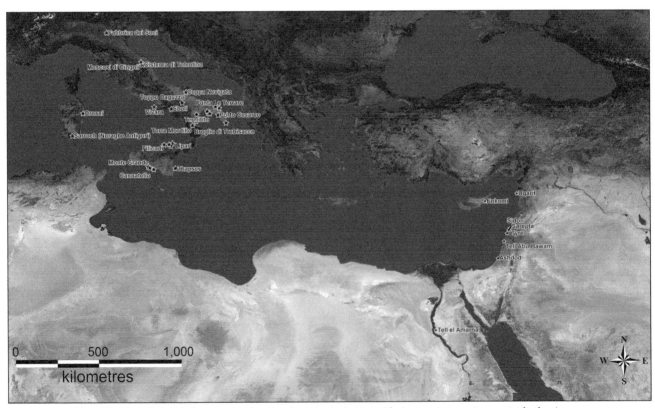

Fig. 6.1: Map of the Mediterranean showing the principal sites with Aegean-type pottery outside the Aegean

coasts. It is noteworthy to mention that Canaanite pottery is also found in the western Mediterranean associated with LH I Mycenaean pottery (Monte Grande and Vivara; Castellana 2000; Cazzella, Marazzi and Tusa 1991), but no Italic products have been recognised in contemporary Aegean contexts. The archaeological evidence consistently points to a Mycenaean origin for the Aegean commodities found in the western Mediterranean and the few Minoan products discovered have also been interpreted as evidence of Mycenaean involvement (Vagnetti 2003). In short, the 'Mycenaean' exchange network formed quite rapidly and introduced the western Mediterranean, excluded in the Minoan exchange network, into the Bronze Age Aegean exchange network.

Sporadic contacts providing at least some awareness of the Mediterranean lands to the west of the Aegean region had probably already taken place (*e.g. ossi a globuli*; Peroni 1994, 205; 2004, 95; Tusa 1999), but regular contacts only occurred from LH I (Vianello 2005; Peroni 2004, 207). There are similarities between the material cultures of eastern Sicily (Castelluccian and Capo Graziano cultures) and the Aegean (Cavalier 1960; Bernabò Brea, Cavalier, and Bernabò Brea 2002), especially the Cycladic cultures. A possible connection with the Cycladic Islands is also strengthened by the presence of an early Cycladic jar at Lipari (Bernabò Brea, Cavalier, Taylour and D'Angelo 1980). However, no Aegean materials in Sicily or elsewhere in the western Mediterranean have been found in depositional contexts that may be earlier than LH I.

Cypriot pottery appear in Italic contexts associated with LH III A2 ceramics (chronology based on the present author's study of ceramic vessels at Thapsos (Vianello 2005); Alberti agrees, pers. comm.), even if Cyprus acted as terminus for Mycenaean products to the Levant from LH I and was probably a port-of-call for the Canaanite pottery that reached the western Mediterranean. LH III A 2 ceramics also mark important changes in the western Mediterranean, such as the end of exchanges of Aegean products at Monte Grande and Vivara as well as the emergence of new sites, such as Thapsos and Cannatello. LH/Late Minoan (LM) III A 2 pottery is also the earliest period for Cretan pottery in the western Mediterranean (Vagnetti 2003: 56, 58). LH III A 2 pottery can be distinguished fairly well from previous ceramics in the existing archaeological record (Vianello 2005), and therefore for all these reasons a chronological division of the exchanges at that point appears both practical and significant.

LH I–III A 1

The eruption of the volcano of Thera probably contributed to the disruption of the Minoan exchange network in many ways. In addition to its immediate destructive effects, it probably caused prolonged devastation at least to some Cycladic Islands, such as nearby Melos. This situation may have forced ships to find new routes, at least temporarily, and perhaps increased exploratory activities, but it also affected the economy, since the Cycladic Islands were an important source of volcanic products such as sulphur. One of the earliest centres to receive Aegean products in the western Mediterranean was Monte Grande, which is located on the southern coast of Sicily (Fig. 6.2). From there sulphur was extracted, worked and traded in a desolate area where no settlement has so far been detected (Castellana, Marazzi, Pitrone and Licata 1998; Castellana 2000; Vianello 2005). As a result we know that the Aegean traders in that case were looking for sulphur, the only product available at Monte Grande. The Aeolian Islands and Vivara, other Italic sites involved in early exchanges of Aegean-type products, are also volcanic areas with deposits of sulphur, but perhaps their involvement in exchanges should be attributed to their geographic position at the crossroads of maritime routes rather than to any local products. We may conclude that Aegean sailors looked, at least, for sulphur during LH I and II (Castellana, Marazzi, Pitrone and Licata 1998; 2000), which they evidently could not source from Melos (as they had done before and were to do so again later). The most plausible reason for sourcing sulphur in Sicily is that the volcanic eruption of Thera interrupted access to Melos during that period.

The route that brought Aegean products to Monte Grande branched on the eastern coast of Sicily, and from there some ships continued northwards to the Aeolian Islands, and then onto Vivara. Monte Grande and Vivara share a number of similarities in the types of Aegean ceramics that they received, considering both their shapes and chronology. The Aeolian Islands appear quite different: the imported ceramics were different from those found at the other two sites; the Capo Graziano culture already had ceramic shapes similar to the Aegean ones in its repertoire; and Aegean ceramics continue to be imported throughout the whole Late Bronze Age. It seems noteworthy that all three areas, Monte Grande, Vivara and the Aeolian Islands are volcanic and remote, in sparsely populated areas. Undecorated pottery was also present in notable quantities at all three sites, suggesting that staple products were exported, or perhaps carried aboard ships and consumed at the place of arrival. The only 'Aegean' architectural monument that cannot be compared locally, and imitates the Aegean architecture sufficiently enough to deserve that name, is the thermal tholos at San Calogero, Lipari, dating to the LH II period according to Bernabò Brea (Bernabò Brea, Cavalier and Belli 1990). Very few Aegean products are found also in the southern Italian peninsula, but they cannot prove more than a simple passage of some ships carrying Aegean products.

The first periods appears relatively homogenous and stable in terms of what might relate to exchanges, but

Fig. 6.2: Map showing the principal sites with Aegean-type pottery dating to the period LH I–IIIA1 and located west of the Aegean

during LH III A 1 the exchanges end at Monte Grande and Vivara, while in the Aeolian Islands the Capo Graziano culture draws to an end. All the Aegean pottery has been found within settlements and, when undecorated wares are also taken into account, storage vessels form the majority of the assemblages. In many cases the Aegean pottery is also found broken and discarded (especially the transport jars) and therefore it seems that the Aegean ceramics were consumed as containers of Mycenaean products being exported. Pottery seems to play a functional role in support of exchanges based primarily on other products (such as sulphur at Monte Grande).

LH III A 2–C

During the subsequent period, LH III A 2–C, the exchanges of Aegean products alter dramatically, involving an area

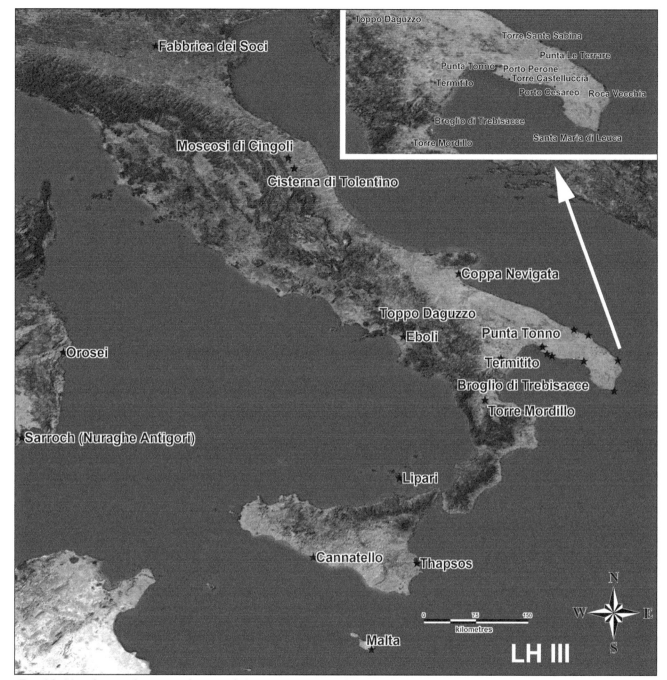

Fig. 6.3: Map showing the principal sites with Aegean-type pottery dating to the period LH IIIA2–IIIC and located west of the Aegean

spanning from Iberia to Apulia (Fig. 6.3). Indirect exchanges can be postulated (this is the case for Iberia even if the ceramics are genuine Mycenaean imports), and Aegean ceramics are also produced within the Italian peninsula (Jones, Levi, and Vagnetti 2002). It seems that the Aegean exchange network reorganised itself during this period with the deliberate intent of maximising its reach; undecorated pottery is absent and there is clear evidence in support of the view that Aegean ceramics were considered a luxury

in many cases at this point (for instance Aegean products in the tombs at Thapsos were part of a 'wealth display' strategy; Vianello 2005). However, this was not the case in the Aeolian Islands, where Aegean ceramics are fairly equally distributed across settlements, and appear to have played no particular role. This view is reinforced by the presence of Aegean pottery in even larger amounts in huts of the southern Italian peninsula, where central or larger buildings (possibly communal, or chiefs' huts) contained the majority of it. Aegean ceramics remain low in absolute quantities (about 5% of all the ceramics at the major sites; Vagnetti 1999), but were prized enough to spur a variety of imitations and Aegean-inspired wares – the 'Aegean-derivative' pottery (Vianello 2005).

During the first part of this period, LH III A 2–III B, Thapsos emerges as an important centre in eastern Sicily. Cannatello (located in the vicinity of Monte Grande) becomes the major centre in southern Sicily and the Milazzese culture marks an increase in Aegean ceramics in the Aeolian Islands; Taranto (Quagliati 1900) and Porto Perone (Lo Porto 1963) are important centres on the Ionian coast of Apulia. Since the lower levels of Taranto (Punta Tonno) were excavated using dynamite, it is possible that exchanges of Aegean products at this site started before LH III A 2, but we have no archaeological evidence for proving this hypothesis. Undecorated Aegean-type wares disappear and decorated Aegean-type ceramics appear at both settlements and funerary contexts. It becomes evident at this time that decorated Aegean-type wares had become in many cases an appreciated commodity. However, each western community seems to have selected certain types of pottery on the basis of local culture and appreciation. This apparent expression of preference on the Italic side suggests a genuine appreciation of the pottery by the Italics. On the basis of similar cultural preference it has also been possible to reconstruct the boundaries of cultural regions, possibly polities (Vianello 2005). Thus, from LH III A 2, Aegean-type pottery appears to have been a very important exchanged product, no longer sidelined by other products. Of course, the contents may have played a role in boosting appreciation. However, the increase of open vessels, especially bowls, the production of Aegean-derivative dolia (recalling Minoan pithoi and associated to new storage techniques), and the production of Aegean-type wares in the Ionian area of the southern Italian peninsula all point to Aegean wares being functional to new needs rather than being a replacement for existing wares. As a result, that area appears to have become a new 'market' for Aegean traders rather than a simple source or destination of specific products.

Both Cannatello and Thapsos received a significant number of Cypriot wares. However, whilst relatively substantial amounts of Aegean pottery have been found at the settlement of Cannatello, very few have been reported from the settlement of Thapsos: most of the Aegean pottery there comes from funerary contexts. There is also no apparent continuity between Monte Grande (last pottery: LH III A 1) and Cannatello (earliest pottery: LH III A 2), but if there was a hiatus in the exchanges, this was so short that the area is unlikely to have been 'forgotten' by Aegean traders. However, the exchanges at Cannatello were not centred on sulphur, as at Monte Grande, and therefore there must have been a change in products needed. From LH III A 2 Crete returns to play an important part in the Aegean exchange network, and with Cyprus formed a key route for the transit of Mycenaean ceramics and other products. Cypriot wares are also found in Sardinia, and Sardinian ceramics appear in Crete from LH/LM III B (Shaw and Shaw 2006, 674–8). Remarkably, the latest study of possible imports of ceramics found at Kommos has ruled out the presence of any other Italic ware, and even restricted the provenance of vessels to southern Sardinia. A direct route from Sardinia to Cyprus is clearly established by the end of LH/LM III B, and this involved the exchange of ceramics in both directions and the importing of copper oxhide ingots to Sardinia (Vianello 2005; Lo Schiavo, MacNamara and Vagnetti 1985; Lo Schiavo 2005).

Of genuine difficulty is the interpretation of the so-called 'Barbarian' ware reported at a number of Aegean sites (Jung 2006; Peroni 2004, 286). Some scholars (Bettelli 2002; Jung 2006) are convinced of its Italic (Apennine) origin, perhaps unintentionally reversing Hencken's (1968) interpretation of the Thracian 'Villanovan' ceramics as the source of influence for the eponymous Italic culture. The present author remains unconvinced that such simple and undecorated ceramics should be interpreted as the product of Italic groups possibly brought to the Aegean by Mycenaean traders, as Peroni (2004, 286) suggests, because they are only finds similar to Italic ones. Furthermore, the production of decorated and undecorated versions of grey ware – and many other Aegean derived wares (Bettelli 2002) – in the southern Italian peninsula demonstrates that the Italics were subjected to cultural influences (in terms of ceramics) from the Aegean during the Late Bronze Age, and therefore Aegean derived ceramics should have been an option for Italic potters. The stylistic and archaeometric analyses carried out at Kommos (and excluding the presence of any other Italic ware) convinces that what Hencken (1968) and Jung (2006) notice is the inheritance of the 'Urnfield' (*Urnenfeldern*) culture (Peroni 1994, 208–9; Bartoloni 2000, 54; Torelli 2005, 33), which influenced the Italian peninsula during the Ancient and Middle Bronze Age (Eder and Jung 2005, 489, for metals; Cocchi Genick 1995, for ceramics), and possibly the earlier 'Bell Beaker' culture, which had a significant impact on the formation of the Apennine style in pottery (Cocchi Genick 1998, esp. 384–95). Lucia Vagnetti (1996, 170–1) suggests that small numbers of Italics who moved to the Aegean may have been responsible for the 'Barbarian' ware. This hypothesis remains possible because it only recognises an Italic influence on 'Barbarian' ware, maintaining that such a style is characteristic of the Aegean.

The second part of this period, LH III B–C, is characterised by a progressive reduction of imported wares. In Sicily there are sweeping changes: Thapsos declines and the site that replaces it, at least for vicinity and importance, Pantalica, a cemetery with about 5,000 tombs, has yielded only one Aegean-type pot and also very few Aegean-derivative products. The arrival of the Ausonian people in the Aeolian

Islands marks a decline in the area: only Lipari remains inhabited and the exchanges of Aegean products wither. The apparent hostility of Tyrrhenian people, such as the Ausonians, towards Aegean products may explain the earlier demise of Vivara and the unusual abandonment of that area in a context of dynamic expansion. In spite of this, Italic productions boom and massive amounts of Aegean-type and Aegean-derivative pottery are consumed in the southern Italian peninsula. When imports, imitations and inspired wares are combined, the overall amount of 'Aegean' wares can be much higher than the estimated 5%. This seems the case at Broglio di Trebisacce (Peroni, Vanzetti and Bagella 1998) and possibly Termitito (De Siena 1986) and Roca Vecchia (Guglielmino 2005; Pagliara 2005). The latter site appears to have been an important harbour during the LH III C period and was also a religious centre influenced by Minoan and Mycenaean symbols. It is evident that people of Mycenaean and Aegean origin reached the Adriatic shores of the Italian peninsula as late as LH III C. Many were probably migrant artisans, such as the potters that started the production of 'Mycenaean' pottery in the Sybaris Plain.

Reasons for the exchange and appreciation of Aegean wares

The exchange and consumption of Aegean wares varies by chronological period and area (Wijngaarden 2002; Vianello 2005; Bell 2006). The different regional patterns of appreciation of ceramic vessels in the western Mediterranean (Vianello 2005, esp. chapter 4) mean that Aegean traders were not trying to exchange any particular commodities (different vessels would normally serve a different purpose), and it is illogical to think that they were trying to exchange small sets of ceramic vessels: ceramics were produced in the western regions and do not seem to have had any exceptional value or role within those societies. The Italics selected the Aegean shapes that were consuming and imitating, and this appears to have been done on the basis of function: not all the Aegean shapes are represented in the western archaeological record and characteristic shapes that may be associated with distinctive uses, like rhyta, are almost absent.

Renato Peroni (2004, 280–5) suggests the term 'diffused exchange' (*scambio diffuso*) to define the Aegean exchanges, and proposes that the Aegeans were trying to source all products available (Torelli 2005, 31, agrees and mentions metals, pottery, slaves, cereals and dyes for textiles as possible products). Peroni considers the exclusion of the mining area of Etruria from direct contacts as proof that the Aegeans were not searching for metals and proposes that the exchanges took place within a framework of inequality in which the Aegeans acted as 'colonisers' sourcing any products they needed from the Italics and helped in forming 'stable political powers' that could act as legitimate

counterparts in the exchanges and be subservient to the Aegean traders that had sustained their establishment. The idea that metals were the main reason for the exchanges is based on Iron Age evidence (*e.g.* Iberia as source of metals would be the reason for the earliest Phoenician colonies in the western Mediterranean, Aubet 1999; Markoe 1992; for the Italian peninsula: Ridgway 2000, 186–7; Giardino 1995), but is often transposed to the Bronze Age (*e.g.* the need for the supply of tin after the fall of Ugarit would have motivated the LH III C Aegean presence in Sardinia; Vagnetti 1996, 170). Peroni accepts the Aegeo-centric perspective and concludes that commercial exchanges could not take place because of the inequality of the exchanges, their similarity in quantity with early colonial trade in the 8th century BC, and the lack of standardisation in the traded ceramics, a recurring feature of Greek trade since the 7th century BC. Of course, Peroni's analysis takes as model the Greeks (and especially the Greek perspective of the events) and only denies a similarity between Bronze Age Aegeans and Greeks in trade. Both ideas, that metals were the main reason for the exchanges and that large elite-controlled 'markets' were needed by Aegean traders (Peroni 2004, 281), seem unfounded.

One reason for its appreciation that emerges from a detailed study of the western evidence (Vianello 2005) is the lack of any ethnic meaning associated to the Aegean pottery. With its abrupt inception in LH I, Mycenaean pottery appears the pottery of a people without history, and whilst the Mycenaeans may have had a local history, for many on the receiving side the Mycenaean pottery was perhaps the first contact, direct or indirect, with that culture. Once the Mycenaean style spread across the Mediterranean, and Italic, Cypriot and other non-Aegean productions had begun, that style must have been perceived as separate from the Mycenaeans themselves. Indeed, the production of Mycenaean pottery lasted longer than the Mycenaean palaces! The lack of ethnic identity appears also evident in the transparent adoption of Mycenaean religious figurines as replacements of Italic figurines (Vianello 2005: 32, 69, 81; Wijngaarden 2002: 221).

Since the period LH III B–C in the western Mediterranean cannot be understood without considering the arrival of foreigners and the perception of a 'foreign' ware as 'own', it is important to briefly discuss the issue. In his pioneering study on the attitudes towards foreigners, Mu-chou Poo (2005) recognises that foreigners often entered a society as equals without any demonstrable biological bias. Opposition and criticism normally address external societies to express a negative example or define the identity of one society, denying that its culture is shared by any of the neighbouring ones. For instance in Egypt foreigners are always depicted as a negative entity, often subdued by the pharaoh, but foreign individuals such as artisans or even soldiers are known to have been present and were not 'hidden' or subjected to any detectable bias (Poo 2005, 110). Looking specifically to the Italic world, the case of Etruria should be noted, where archaeologists have detected Sardinian, Phoenician and Greek individuals integrated within the Etruscan society since the 9th century BC (Torelli 2005, 132–7), suggesting that some western lands were ready to welcome foreign traders perhaps more than long established eastern societies.

The arrival of mobile artisans has been detected first among potters, but the availability of skilled labour may have benefited more professions. For instance, Di Fraia (in Cocchi Genick 2004: 564) emphasises the scarce mobility of Aegean-derivative dolia (local versions of Aegean pithoi) and therefore suggests that they were probably used for local storage at Broglio, noting also that the local architecture develops storage rooms (two small ones unable to contain all dolia; Peroni, Vanzetti and Bagella 1998) during LH III C, after the introduction of dolia during LH III B. Thus, from the new shapes of pottery we can infer new functions, and therefore new practices and skills in agriculture in addition to pottery production. The ceramic evidence – particularly the presence of large Aegean-type stirrup jars – suggests a connection between the exchanges and the exploitation of vines and olive trees at Cannatello (Sicily) and Punta Tonno (southern Italian peninsula). Olive stones have been found in Bronze Age contexts at Taranto (San Domenico; Fiorentino 2002) and Monopoli (Piazza Palmieri; Fiorentino 1995), olive oil production has been proposed at Broglio (Vallino and Ventura 1984: 274) and Roca Vecchia (Fiorentino 2002,

149) and recent studies suggest the presence of olive trees at Archi (Di Fraia 2000). Although this evidence is not conclusive, it supports the possibility of the exploitation of at least olive trees in the western Mediterranean and possibly the introduction of arboriculture during the Bronze Age from the Aegean region, something previously denied by specialists (*e.g.* Hadjisavvas 2003: 56, 'there is no evidence of any kind of exploitation').

During the Late Bronze Age, the western Mediterranean changed profoundly with new routes, people, skills, technologies, and almost certainly ideas reshaping the cultural and social arenas as well as the economy. Most importantly the western Mediterranean joined the Aegean and eastern worlds, both culturally and economically, and as a result the present and future of all the populations involved in the same exchanges became intertwined to some degree. It is not possible at this time to determine if the western Mediterranean played any role in the crisis that affected the Aegean and Levant at the end of the Bronze Age. Nevertheless, we know that the two areas were connected and that the contacts triggered changes: the Mycenaean economy of exchange differed from the pre-existing Minoan one because of the larger geographic area involved and several Italic coastal communities changed substantially their social and economic life because of the exchanges and the arrival of some migrants from the Aegean. The meeting of different people should not be underestimated as a 'force of transformation'.

SICILY AT THE END OF THE BRONZE AGE: 'CATCHING THE ECHO'

Davide Tanasi

This paper aims to analyze transformations in relations between Sicily and the eastern Mediterranean at the end of the Bronze Age, focusing in particular on relations with the Aegean world after the collapse of palatial society. In order to do so, it is necessary to begin with a brief sketch of the earlier history of Sicilian cultural connections so as to set the discussion in as full a context as possible.

The earliest attested Aegean interest in Sicily dates to the Early Bronze Age (EBA; Fig. 7.1), and was probably

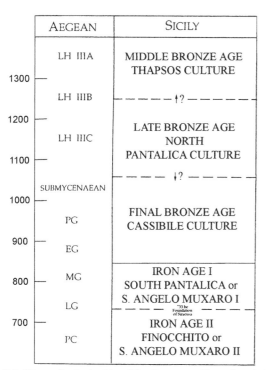

AEGEAN	SICILY
LH IIIA	MIDDLE BRONZE AGE THAPSOS CULTURE
LH IIIB	─ ─ ─ ─ ┆? ─ ─ ─ ─ ─
LH IIIC	LATE BRONZE AGE NORTH PANTALICA CULTURE
	─ ─ ─ ┆? ─ ─ ─ ─
SUBMYCENAEAN	
PG	FINAL BRONZE AGE CASSIBILE CULTURE
EG	
MG	IRON AGE I SOUTH PANTALICA or S. ANGELO MUXARO I
LG	
	⁻⁷³³ ᵇᶜ Foundation of Siracusa
PC	IRON AGE II FINOCCHITO or S. ANGELO MUXARO II

(Left axis dates: 1300, 1200, 1100, 1000, 900, 800, 700)

Fig. 7.1: Chronological table of the Bronze and Iron Ages in Sicily and in Aegean

commercially based and related to the manufacture of sulphur, as the Mesohelladic and Late Helladic I–II Aegean pottery found nearby the manufacturing areas testify (Castellana 1998; La Rosa 2005, 574–5). In the Middle Bronze Age (MBA) an occasional frequentation by Aegean groups (perhaps travelling toward more distant ports) had become a real commercial enterprise involving both freelance merchants and more organised fleets related to the palaces (Militello 2005, 594–5). These ships sailed from Cyprus and the Greek mainland to Sicily, which had now become a terminus of their trade. A more structured relationship required the permanent presence of Mycenaean people in at least the two principal indigenous ports: Thapsos in the east (Orsi 1895, 89–150; Voza 1972, 175–203; 1973, 133–57; 1976–77, 562–8; 1980–81, 674–83; 1984–85, 657–77), and Cannatello in the south-west (de Miro 1996, 995–1,011; Deorsola 1996, 1,029–38; de Miro 1999, 439–49). In all of the sites of the Siracusan hinterland, but mostly in Thapsos, the evidence for a strong process of acculturation, which has been defined as Mycenaeanisation (Tanasi 2003, 600–3), is present in every feature of the indigenous material culture. In terms of domestic and funerary architecture, an urban plan with roads and blocks, and houses with quadrangular rooms articulated around central courts that recall Cypriot examples, appear for the first time at Thapsos (Militello 2004, 314–22; Tomasello 2004, 195–205). An extraordinary diffusion of rock-cut chamber tombs, with a tholoid profile that recalls west-Peloponnesian models, also began simultaneously in both the east and south-west of Sicily (Tomasello 2004, 187–95). It is important, with regard the Thapsian artefacts, to emphasise that every object has been identified exclusively in funerary contexts. The richest Thapsos tombs were furnished with fine Mycenaean pottery of Late Helladic (LH) IIIA–B, and Cypriot vessels of different classes (Fig. 7.2;

Fig. 7.2: Mycenaean and Cypriot vessels from the Thapsos necropolis (Tusa 1997)

van Wijngaarden 2002, 229–36), as well as jewellery and luxury goods in amber, glass, faience and gold, given as gifts to high-ranking chiefs (Militello 2004, 309–12).

A new phenomenon also occurred in indigenous pottery production. The systematic imitations of Mycenaean and Cypriot pottery shapes (Alberti 2005, 344–6), along with imitations of zoomorphic figurative motifs that have precise parallels in Aegean examples of LH IIIB1, sum up the fundamental characteristics of the so-called Sicano-Mycenaean production (Alberti 2004, 122–5; Tanasi 2005, 563–5). Contacts with more specialised metallurgical artisans also led to the diffusion of a new type of indigenous sword which was a hybrid of the Mycenaean types A and B Sandars (D'Agata 1986, 105–110; Tanasi 2004b, 403–6). A small group of clay models of furniture found in Thapsos tombs recalls similar Mycenaean funerary and religious customs (Tanasi 2004c, 21–7). The complex outline of deep acculturation shown by Thapsos does not have a precise parallel in the evidence from Cannatello: if analysis of Thapsos gives the impression of a small Aegean group living within an indigenous village, the small fortified settlement of Cannatello, with circular and rectangular huts that contained rich assemblages of Mycenaean and local pottery, appears to be a Cypro-Mycenaean outpost in indigenous territory. The presence of Aegean storage jars, together with fine ware imports and examples of Cypro-Minoan hieroglyphics, as well as the absence of luxury goods and the lack of Sicano-Mycenaean pottery, all demonstrate the different nature of the frequentation of this site (de Miro 1999, 71–81; Castellana 2000, 237; Vagnetti 2001, 85). Besides Cannatello, other sites in the hinterland of Agrigento have provided examples of pottery or metal artefacts of Cypriot imitation and Mycenaean vessels (Lo Schiavo *et al.* 1985, 30–2; La Rosa 2000, 133–8), usually from rock-cut chamber tombs with a tholoid profile (La Rosa 2000, 125–6). The examples of Thapsos and Cannatello show how the indigenous groups of Sicily were, during three centuries of exclusive contacts, so completely and deeply

acculturated as to assume elements of the Aegean cultures into their common traditions.

Imports of Maltese pottery of the Borg in Nadur type did, however, appear during this time (Trump 2003, 3), and were found in the most important necropoleis of the period, such as Thapsos, Cozzo del Pantano, Plemmiro, Matrensa and Florida. The Borg in Nadur imports are in association with local, Cypriote and Mycenaean pottery, thus indicating a complex relationship between different groups that were probably active in commercial business in the central Mediterranean (Giannitrapani 1997, 438–9; Militello 2005, 592–3).

At about the end of the thirteenth century, the beginning of the collapse of palatial society produced a shock-wave that struck many communities in the Mediterranean, modifying political balances and mechanisms of cultural diffusion. What occurred in Sicily, from this moment on, was clearly a result of that event, and is the echo of that political disaster. Many coastal sites, such as Thapsos and Cannatello, were abandoned, demonstrating how the Mycenaean presence and seafaring were vital to their existence. As a result of a sense of danger emanating from the sea, the indigenous peoples moved back to the mountains, close to river sources in order to maintain control of the territory and the routes to the sea (Bernabò Brea 1990, 43). The most important settlements of the Late Bronze Age are the Pantalica necropolis in eastern Sicily (Orsi 1899, 33–146; 1912, 301–46), and the Mokarta village in the west (Mannino and Spatafora 1995; Tusa and Nicoletti 2000, 963–77; Tusa 2004, 330–3; Bruno *et al.* in press). The first practical effect of the changed situation is the total absence of Aegean imports in the archaeological record, a possible sign that the Mycenaean people who had been involved in commerce with Sicily had been related, in some way, to the palaces – or at the very least a shift had occurred in the maritime exchange routes (Tanasi 2004a, 358; Militello 2005, 594).

However, recent analyses of the material culture present at Pantalica have offered some significant new data. The introduction of the potter's wheel (Cultraro 1998) and its use for the production of Red Lustrous Ware, which together constitute the guide-type of the North Pantalica culture, are considered to be of Mycenaean derivation. Furthermore, the Sicano-Mycenaean pottery was enriched by six new shapes, and reached a high degree of specialization, with imitation of painted decoration such as that testified by the jug from tomb 133 North (Fig. 7.3; Vagnetti 1968, 132–5; Tanasi 2005, 565). Alongside the bronze swords of Thapsian tradition there appear some new shapes of daggers and swords that clearly recall Mycenaean models, such as the examples with duck-head hilts (Tanasi 2004a, 342). Moreover, luxury goods that have close comparisons with the LH IIIB–C culture, such as bronze fibulae, bronze mirrors and massive gold rings, are present in the richest Pantalica tombs (Tanasi 2004a, 344). Architecturally the

Fig. 7.3: Jug from tomb 133 N and bronze mirror, fibulae, short swords and a golden ring from the Pantalica necropolis (Tusa 1997)

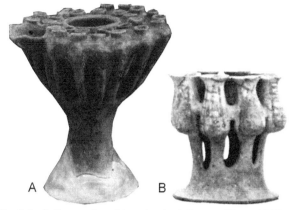

Fig. 7.4: A) Kernos from Metapiccola di Lentini (Rizza 1962); B) Kernos from tomb 122 of Perati (Iakovides 1969–70)

most important structure is the Pantalica *anaktoron* (Bernabò Brea 1990), a palatial building with quadrangular rooms that was planned and completed according to Aegean standards (Tanasi 2004a, 345–7; Tomasello 2004, 208–12). These previously unattested Mycenaean influences of LH IIIB–C culture can only be explained by suggesting that groups of freelance merchants reached eastern Sicily, at the periphery of the Mycenaean world, after the fall of the Palaces, and engaged in a rapport with the indigenous peoples of Pantalica (Tanasi 2003, 335–6).

The outline that emerges from western Sicily, and from Mokarta in particular (Mannino and Spatafora 1995), highlights the beginning of a diversification in the cultural features of the two parts of Sicily. In the material culture there are very few examples of Aegean influences in the west. Pottery and bronze production follows local tradition and a single bone item, perhaps part of a sword hilt, could be interpreted as being of Mycenaean imitation. Some Aegean influences can also be detected in domestic architecture (Bruno *et al.* in press). Other isolated cases of Mycenaean features can also be found in the Agrigentine hinterland, such as the golden rings of Anguilla di Ribera (Panvini 1986, 114). The cultural void left by the lack of contact with the Mycenaean peoples was now filled in terms of pottery production by new influences from the El Argar culture of the Iberian Peninsula (Cultraro 2005, 101–2). It is very significant that these new arrivals appear at the time when relations with the Mycenaean groups had been severed.

In the period of transition from Late Bronze Age to Early Iron Age, the clear situation of cultural diversification between the two parts of the island becomes more complex. In the east a new guide-type is represented by the so-called Plumed Ware, a development of the Red Lustrous Ware (Albanese Procelli 2000, 171–4; 2003, 84–5). This was a

time when small groups of Italic peoples arrived, moved to the central-eastern area and founded settlements such as Morgantina and Molino della Badia, taking with them their material culture and their cremation burial custom (Leighton 1996, 101–15; Albanese Procelli 2003, 66–76). The Italic settlers merged with the local population, as witnessed by the resulting production of artefacts. This peaceful migration and colonisation was most profound and evident in the eastern part, and more superficial and difficult to identify in the western. This act of migration and acculturation had been possible during previous periods, but improbable during the period of Mycenaean frequentation.

New 'western' influences arrived at the same time as these Italic elements, as testified by Iberian metal objects found in several Sicilian sites (Panvini 1997, 497; Cultraro 2005, 103–4) and Nuragic pottery imports found at Cannatello (Levi 2004, 234; Jones *et al.* in press) and Monte Maio (Panvini 1997, 501). A small group of Maltese vessels appears once again in the final phase of the Thapsos settlement, associated with local Plumed Ware (Voza 1973), and in the last level of occupation of Cannatello (Levi 2004, 237; Jones *et al.* in press).

With the collapse of the Mycenaean palatial system new Aegean cultural elements, related to the LH IIIC/ Protogeometric period, emerged in the twelfth- to tenth centuries in eastern Sicily. The development of Sicano-Mycenaean Ware, with new shapes, imitations and painted vessels at Pantalica (Orsi 1899, 50–1), the diffusion of built rather than rock-cut tholos tombs in the Aetnean area (La Rosa 2007, 315–24), the presence of a *kernos* of LH IIIC type at Metapiccola (Fig. 7.4; Rizza 1962, 13–15; Iakovides 1969–70, 424), and a clay model of a pair of horns of Aetnean provenience (Fig. 7.5; La Rosa *et al.* 2002, 247–53), as well as a Protogeometric painted conical lid from the anaktoron area (Bernabò Brea 1990, 97; Coldstream and Catling 1996, 18, no. 57), and the belly handled amphorae imitating LH IIIC/sub-Mycenaean prototypes, from the of tombs Lo Curzio and 8 north-west of Pantalica (Fig. 7.6; Orsi 1889, 174; 1899, 50–1), all testify to new contacts between eastern Sicily and the Aegean world. Until now a corresponding synthesis has not been offered for western Sicily, and so the cultural uniqueness of this region has yet to be formulated.

Current excavations on the Polizzello acropolis, directed by D. Palermo *equipe*, are providing an opportunity to partially fill this void (Palermo 1981, 103–48; de Miro 1988, 25–41; Palermo 1997, 35–45; 2003, 95–9; Palermo and Tanasi 2006, 89–102; Tanasi 2007, 157–70; in press-a; in press-b). The site, in the centre of western Sicily, is located on a 900m high mountain, close to the Gallo d'Oro river, and presents evidence for a nearly continuous frequentation from the tenth to the first half of the fourth centuries BCE. Infrequent and sporadic explorations of the necropolis area have revealed LBA ceramic evidence over the last few decades, but the absence of a precise context for these objects, and their rarity, did not, until recently, lead to further work aimed at comprehending the site as a whole. The recent excavation of an important Sicanian sanctuary of the seventh- to sixth centuries, with its large circular open shrines encircled by a *temenos*, have given my *equipe* the chance to determine the earliest date of frequentation

of the area, its nature and function, and the related cultural assemblage.

The earliest occupation of the area dates to the end of the tenth to the middle of the ninth centuries BCE (Fig. 7.7), and is testified, on the western part of the acropolis, by a large building known as the North Building (Tanasi 2007, 157–70; in press-a; in press-b). This was the site of ritual activities of animal sacrifice and feasting, and is related to an open yard with pebbled floor and two small circular huts on the eastern slope. In addition, small pits with offering goods are cut into the rock in many points of the acropolis. Evidence of animal sacrifice and feasting and drinking activities were found in every context of this period.

The ceramic repertoire was initially composed of hemispherical pedestal cups with incised rims, carinated pedestal cups with multiple grooves, flat-based and pedestal basins, pedestal *pyxides*, *askoi*, strainer-spouted jugs, cooking pots, cup stands and cylindrical tubes. Chalices and pointed-base trefoil mouthed jugs (Fig. 7.8) appeared slightly later. The vases are either decorated with simple incised geometric motifs, or more often with the traditional lustrous red slip. The discovery of a cylindrical amber bead is also highly significant. The cylindrical tube and the pointed-base trefoil mouthed jug with its conical stand are absolutely foreign to the indigenous tradition, and warrant further discussion.

The presence of the clay tube, which was used in ceremonies for the dead, could be related to the contemporary Greek Protogeometric objects that were used for chthonic rituals of libation (Fig. 7.9; Beschi 2005, 33–41). The pointed-base trefoil mouthed jug recalls the white shaved juglets attested in Cyprus (Karageorghis 1974, 78; Dothan and Ben-Tor 1983, 41–3, 67–9; Karageorghis and Demas 1985, 25–6) and the Levant until the end of the thirteenth century and, with some morphological modifications, later (Dothan 1979, 13–17, 38–9; Maeir 2004, 22–3). Likewise, the conical stand, which was previously absent in the indigenous repertoire even though it was widely diffused in eastern Mediterranean communities,

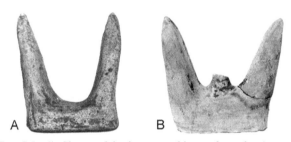

Fig. 7.5: A) Clay model of a pair of horns from the Aetnenan area (La Rosa et al. 2002); B) Clay model of a pair of horns from Phaistos (D'Agata 1992)

Fig. 7.6: A) Clay lid from Pantalica (Bernabò Brea 1990); B) Clay lid from tomb G of the Knossos North Cemetery (Coldstream, Catling 1996); C) Belly-handled amphora with painted decoration from Pantalica (Orsi 1889); D) Sub-Mycenaean belly-handled amphora from the Kerameikos of Athens (Mountjoy 1999)

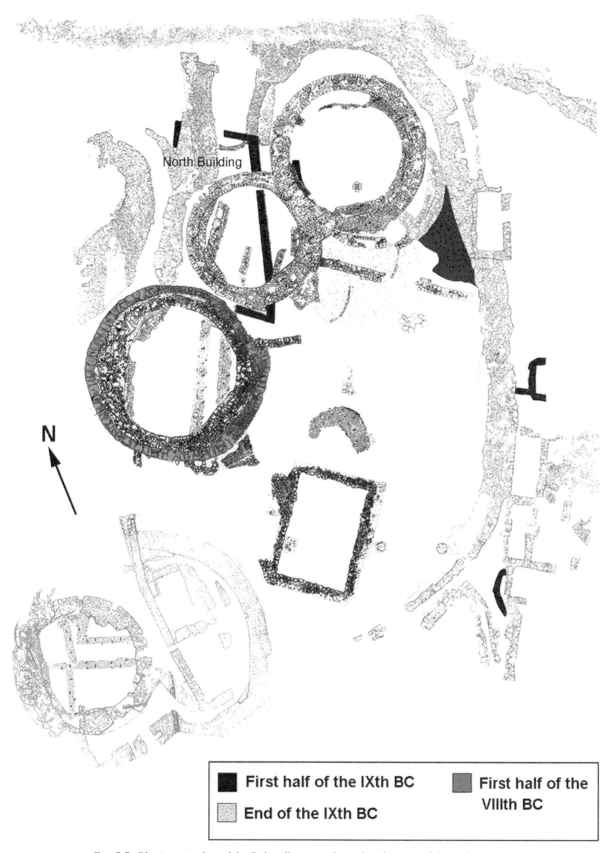

North Building

N

First half of the IXth BC

End of the IXth BC

First half of the VIIIth BC

Fig. 7.7: Planimetric plan of the Polizzello acropolis with indication of the earliest structures

Fig. 7.8: Pointed-base trefoil-mouthed jugs from an offering pit on the Polizzello acropolis

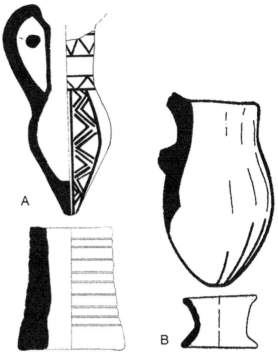

Fig. 7.10: A) Pointed-base trefoil-mouthed jug with the related conical stand from the Polizzello acropolis; B) White shaved jug with stand from Byblos (Dunand 1954)

Fig. 7.9: A) Clay tube from a sacred area of the Polizzello necropolis (Panvini 1993–94); B) Protogeometric libation tube from Kamyros (Beschi 2005)

and the Polizzello examples might therefore have been inspired by contemporary Levantine models (Fig. 7.10). The discovery of the tenth- to ninth century bronze figurine of a smiting god in the sea off Sciacca (Falsone 1993, 55) is another example of an earlier Phoenician interest in western Sicily that seems to support this hypothesis. These new, non-traditional and occasionally exotic features could only be received through new contacts which have not yet been studied in any detail.

Analysis of the indigenous cultural production of the other central-western sites occupied form the beginning of the ninth century enables the identification of other similar features. In this period a local imitation of late Mycenaean ring vases has been found in the S. Angelo Muxaro area (Palermo 1996, 150), as well as a *kernos* imitating LH IIIC models at Mokarta (Buccellato and Tusa in press). Slightly later than those at Polizzello is the pointed-base trefoil mouthed jug of the tomb A9 of Cozzo S. Giuseppe di Realmese (Bernabò Brea and Albanese Procelli 1982, 440–2) and the two examples, now lost, from S. Angelo Muxaro (Bernabò Brea and Albanese Procelli 1982, 599, n. 310). An area with traces of structures was found at Monte Finestrelle di Gibellina, within which a group of indigenous materials of the late ninth century BCE was discovered together with an Egyptian steatite scarab of *men-kheper-ra* type, several amber beads and one glass paste bead (De Cesare and Gargini 1997, 371–4). A few sherds of Phoenician red slip pottery were also found at the site of Monte Polizzo di Salemi (Dixon 2004, 66).

The outline that emerges when all of the data relating to the external influences on Sicily is brought together is that of the presence of several elements of different type and origin, attested in a few cases in both coastal and mountain sites. These isolated testimonies do not support the hypothesis of regular commercial activities or a systematic

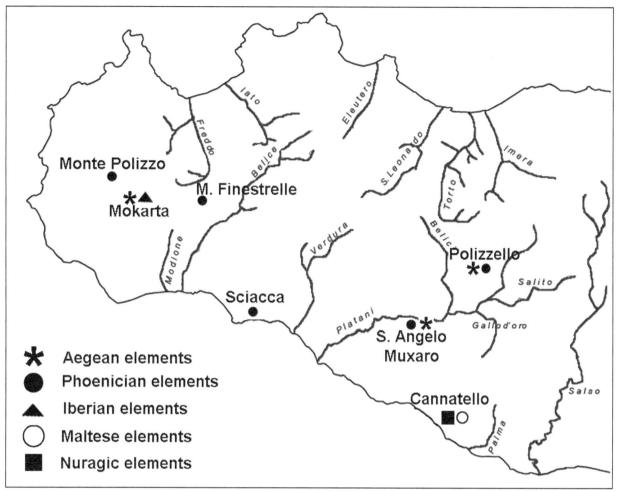

Fig. 7.11: Map of central-western Sicily with indication of the external influences

exchange of goods, but a study of the circulation of the Nuragic pottery outside Sicily can throw some light on these new dynamics. In Crete, after Knossos (Vagnetti 1989, 335–60), the site that recorded the largest amount of Nuragic pottery is Kommos (Watrous *et al.* 1998, 333–45). The coastal site of Kommos is principally characterised by a Phoenician frequentation from the ninth- to the eighth centuries BCE (Stampolidis and Kotsonas 2006, 341–3). It has been plausibly hypothesised that these Sardinian objects were introduced to Crete together with Levantine goods by means of the Phoenicians, who had taken the place of the Cypro-Mycenaean entrepreneurs in the commerce between the eastern and western Mediterranean by the beginning of the ninth century BCE (Bondì 1988, 245; Pulak 2005, 295–310; Bachhuber 2006, 345–63). The motivations behind the Phoenician commercial activities, which involved a large number of the indigenous communities in the western Mediterranean, could largely be explained by means of three non-exclusive theories. The first suggests the sourcing of metals and other resources in large quantities

at cheap expense, particularly in the west, (Bisi 1988, 205–26). Another motivation could have been the search for foodstuffs in addition to the raw materials, which would ultimately include operations to transport cargoes composed of various goods on behalf of others, as intermediaries (Bondì 1988, 243–55). Finally, an interesting suggestion is that the Phoenicians, besides slave commerce, traded in manufactured goods or in other common goods that could be considered exotic in different geographical contexts (Frankenstein 1979, 273).

Returning to the outline of the situation in central-western Sicily, it is possible to make some observations. In all of the sites where objects of Iberian and Aegean derivation were found, either elements of Phoenician type were also found, or these sites were close to others that contained Phoenician elements (Fig. 7.11). The site of Cannatello, which is considered as having been an important port of call on the sailing route from Crete to Sardinia (Day and Joyner 2005, 313), contained several Maltese and Nuragic elements in levels II/III and III, and also exhibited very significant traces of Cypriot frequentation in the preceding levels I and II (de Miro 1999, 71–81). Considering that the foundation level of the Phoenician settlements in sites like Tharros in Sardinia were laid directly over the last levels that contained Mycenaean pottery, it seems likely that the Phoenicians completely stepped into the place of the Cypro-Mycenaean peoples in the western Mediterranean routes at a very early stage (Stager 2003, 233–47).

In central-western Sicily, the majority of the excavated sites have revealed Phoenician and other foreign material culture. The most plausible explanation is that these other elements were introduced through the mediation of the Phoenicians, during the first stages of their interest in the island, preceding their colonising process.

The problem of the location of landing places, which could be solved by an increase in archaeological exploration of the coastal areas, is an important one. It is, however, possible to suggest that at least some small terminals might have existed, perhaps on the ruins of the Cannatello emporium, or that simple forms of exchange were conducted on beaches without proper port structures (Bisi 1988, 217).

The same phenomenon occurred again in eastern Sicily during the eighth century, when the Phoenician merchants exchanged goods with the indigenous peoples of the Marcellino river valley (Villasmundo), and introduced exotic Levantine objects such as scarabs and paste glass, amber and faience items, and the earliest imports of Middle Geometric II Greek pottery (Voza 1978, 104–10; Albanese Procelli 1997, 511–20).

In conclusion, the collapse of Mycenaean Palatial society caused a cascade of events that had severe repercussions on the Sicilian communities, including a decrease in Aegean imports and the abandonment of the two principal emporia and cultural guide sites for the Sicilian Middle Bronze Age. As a consequence of the period of reassessment which followed this event, the settlements relocated into the mountains for defensive reasons in the Late Bronze Age, and an important group of new Aegean features was introduced into the site of Pantalica, perhaps by freelance merchants.

In the tenth- to ninth centuries, after the end of the Mycenaean civilization in the Greek Mainland and the diffusion of the Levantine presence in the Mediterranean, there are a few isolated arrivals of LH IIIC/Protogeometric elements in eastern Sicily, which may have been brought by refugees or people in search of their fortune. At the same time in central-western Sicily, the earliest Phoenician merchants operating on the Sardinia-Sicily-Malta-Northern Africa network and eastern–western Mediterranean route introduced Iberian, Nuragic, Maltese and Aegean elements, together with other objects of a Levantine derivation. While there is an isolated but persistent presence of LH IIIC/Protogeometric features in eastern Sicily until the coming of the first Greek prospectors, the indigenous groups in western Sicily began to have relations with the Phoenician merchants that led to new and different direct and mediated influences. This situation, together with the 'peninsular acculturation' of the two parts of the island, served to increase the deep cultural dichotomy between the two areas that would later, in Greek historiography, lead to a Sicily divided into Sikelia and Sikania.

Acknowledgements

I am grateful to Michael Metcalfe for his advice and assistance with the revision of the text, and to Eleonora Pappalardo for discussing all things Phoenician with me.

PART 3

ICONOGRAPHY AND PERCEPTION

IDENTITY, CHOICE, AND THE YEAR 8 RELIEFS OF RAMESSES III AT MEDINET HABU

R. Gareth Roberts

The year 8 reliefs and inscriptions of Ramesses III at Medinet Habu, which depict what has become known as the Sea Peoples invasion (see principally The Epigraphic Survey 1930 [hereafter *MH*] I, pls. 32–4; 36–44; 45–6), have been studied for over 150 years, but aspects of the compositions remain puzzling. My intention in this paper is to examine two of these problems, namely why the foreigners with horned helmets look slightly different in the two battles of the year 8 campaign and fight on different sides, and why those combatants in 'plumed' or 'feathered' headgear seem to have a number of different names.

The principle

Central to my approach is the view that the main purpose of these reliefs and inscriptions was not to record an attempted invasion by hostile northerners, but rather to record the actions of Ramesses III (Van Essche 1989, 13–14). This definition of perspective is important because it means the depictions of foreigners were an Egyptian choice, and regardless of any historical 'reality' the antagonists would have been presented in a way that accorded with the Egyptian view of the world generally and the dictates of Ramesses specifically. The central character of the reliefs' narrative was the king, the embodiment of Egypt, and not his enemies. Medinet Habu was Ramesses' mortuary temple and the centre of his personal cult, and as such was to serve as a testament to posterity, to the gods, to Egypt's elite and to Egyptian the people, that he had been a king who had ably performed his historic duties.

One of these duties, especially in the New Kingdom, was to defend the borders of Egypt and, as Donald Redford (1984, 16; 1992, 148) has long pointed out, there

are numerous texts from the New Kingdom that refer to kings defeating foreigners who sought to invade Egypt and establish control. Whether any foreigners were actually planning to do this in the reign of Ramesses III is debatable and, for his purposes at Medinet Habu, somewhat irrelevant: it was more important for him to demonstrate that he was a strong king who was able to act decisively and turn back an enemy at Egypt's borders. This is reflected in a number of texts at Medinet Habu, which include statements to this effect in relation to alleged incursions of Libyans in years 5 and 11 (*MH* I, pl. 27.32–35; *MH* II, pl. 79.16–20) and to the Sea Peoples in year 8 (*MH* I, pl. 46.22–6). His strength is also exhibited in the reliefs, for on the walls of Medinet Habu it is the imposing figure of the king that immediately draws the eye and dominates the scene, not the scattered masses of his enemies. It is Ramesses' deeds and qualities that make up the great bulk of the compositions, not the briefly described and ultimately inconsequential actions of his adversaries, whose main role in the narrative is to suffer at his whim. The attackers are minor characters whose motivations are only briefly described in the texts and are shown only as the subjects of Egyptian domination in the reliefs. This perspective has implications for the identity of the antagonists, because if the primary focus of the scenes were the deeds of Ramesses, then the year 8 reliefs only needed to show adversaries who were contextually relevant – in this scenario dangerous seaborne foes from the lands to the north.

The horned helmets

There are many depictions of figures with horned helmets at Medinet Habu, and apart from the sea battle (*MH* I, pl. 39)

Fig. 8.1: Two Sherden, one from the land battle (left; MH I, pl. 34) with the helmet protrusion, the other from the sea battle (right; MH I, pl. 39) without it

Fig. 8.2: A Sea Peoples' chariot, crewed by warriors with circular-patterned headbands, being attacked by a Sherden in Egyptian service (MH I, pl. 34)

they are always shown among the Egyptian military. These helmeted figures certainly represent Sherden (Shardana), as is demonstrated by the fact that the word *šrdn* 'Sherden' is determined in the Qadesh inscriptions of Ramesses II by a seated male figure wearing a horned helmet (*e.g.* Kuentz 1928, 220; pl. I, 2; 6.3; Kitchen 1975–83 [hereafter K*RI*], II, 11 §26), and by the caption *šrdn n pȝ ym* 'Sherden of the Sea' accompanying a bearded figure wearing such a helmet in a prisoner relief at Medinet Habu (*MH* VIII, pl. 600b). However, Harold H. Nelson observed a subtle difference in the depictions of the various Sherden at Medinet Habu. 'It is noticeable,' he wrote, 'that while everywhere else at Medinet Habu the horned helmet always has a ball or disk between the horns, in the naval battle alone the ball is everywhere absent. Is it possible that we have here some other tribe than the Sherden, who are uniformly shown with helmets bearing both horns and ball?' (*MH* I, 6, n. 29).

Nelson was correct in noting that the lack of a central protrusion is the main observable difference between the horn-helmeted figures in those two scenes (Fig. 8.1), because other Sherden characteristics such as clothing and weapons are generally consistent. Exceptions exist but they are few, most notably a figure with a horned helmet attacking a chariot in the land battle who wears an Egyptian kilt and carries an Egyptian shield (see Fig. 8.2; *MH* I, pl. 34), and a group of Sherden in an apocryphal campaign to Amurru where only some have the central protrusion (*MH* II, pl. 94; Noort 1994, 79). This can seem contradictory, particularly because Sherden are not listed among the invaders in the year 8 text at Medinet Habu (*MH* I, pl. 46.18, reproduced below), but they do appear as enemies in the corresponding passage of Papyrus Harris I (76.7), replacing the Shekelesh, and so might be regarded as potential assailants. This puzzled Nancy Sandars (1985, 106) who, like Wolfgang Helck (1977, 9), regarded the identification of Sherden as one of the few 'sartorial certainties' of ancient Egypt; yet in her discussion of the sea battle at Medinet Habu she

observed that she could not be certain that the horned-helmeted figures in the scene were indeed Sherden (Sandars 1985, 127).

I cannot agree with Sandars' conclusion that the figures in the sea battle might not have been intended to represent Sherden because they lack a helmet decoration. Egyptian artists differentiated non-Egyptian groups in ways that were typically consistent and generically representative (*e.g.* Leahy 1995, 155; Redford 2000, 10–11; O'Connor 2003), so that anyone who possessed the requisite knowledge of artistic conventions would have been able to tell which foreign group was being shown when viewing a wall scene. But the principle of generic representation does not mean that the artists were required to depict all foreigners of a certain type identically, and foreigners regularly show slight differences. The overall form of the Sherden helmet, to take a pertinent example, varies widely. In the Qadesh reliefs of Ramesses II, such as those at Abu Simbel (see *e.g.* Wreszinski 1923–35, II, 176), the helmet usually has a level base, while at Medinet Habu the helmet usually extends to cover the ears. However, both level- and uneven-based helmets are present in the land- and sea battle reliefs. Helmet shapes represent variations on a theme, but the figures are still recognisably Sherden.

Furthermore, Sherden had been known in Egypt for many years by the reign of Ramesses III, and the artists responsible for Medinet Habu would have had precedents for how to portray them at a royal mortuary temple. The earliest Egyptian references, as has long been noted (*e.g.* Gauthier 1925–31; Gardiner 1947, I, 194*), are from the el-Amarna archive, where Sherden were mentioned in three letters sent to the Egyptian king by the prolific Rib-Addi of Byblos (*EA* 81, 122, 123; see Knudtzon 1915, 393–7; 526–33; Moran 1992, 150–1; 201–2). Some eighty or ninety years later Ramesses II claimed, in a stela found at Aswan, to have 'destroyed' (*fḫ*) seaborne raiders along the coast (K*RI* II, 344–5, §121), while in what is probably a related stela from Tanis (K*RI* II, 11, §§25–7) he claimed to have faced Sherden who came in ships and, if Jean Yoyotte's reconstruction (1949, esp. fig. 2, pl. VI; repeated K*RI* II, 289–90, §73) is tenable, to have captured them. Ramesses later had Sherden, complete with horns and central protrusion, shown among his bodyguard at Abydos, Karnak, Luxor, Abu Simbel (*e.g.* Wreszinski 1923–35, I, pl. 19; II, pls. 68, 70, 81–2; III, pl. 176), and probably Derr, where Jean-François Champollion (1844–89, I, 90–1) saw Qadesh reliefs that have since been lost. In the accompanying Qadesh 'Poem' he claimed that they were *šrdn n ḥȝkt ḥm=f in.n=f m nḫtw ḫpš=f sdbḥ m ḥʿw=sn nbw dd n=sn tp-rd n mšʿ* 'Sherden of his person's capturing whom he had carried off through the victories of his strong arm, and who had been supplied with all their weapons and there had been given to them instructions for battle' (K*RI* II, 11, §26–7). Sherden were well known and well represented in Egypt before the days of Ramesses III.

The 'different tribe' hypothesis appears implausible, but an obvious alternative, namely that the Sherden in Egyptian service somehow defected part-way through the year 8 campaigns, is less so even if some readings of the reliefs might suggest it. The reliefs of Ramesses III's campaigns at Medinet Habu contain a geographical aspect, with opponents from the south, west and north (Van Essche 1989; 1994), but also a temporal one from west to east, beginning with a Nubian campaign of doubtful historicity on the exterior west wall, continuing on the exterior north wall with the Libyan campaign of year 5, and then further east to the Sea Peoples campaign of year 8. In this sequence the two northern battles are placed between a scene to the west that shows Ramesses issuing equipment for a military expedition in the land of Djahi (*MH* I, pl. 29), and one to the east in which he is presenting the spoils of his campaigns to the Theban triad (*MH* I, pl. 43). These two scenes mark the start of his year 8 campaigns and the end of his military exploits respectively, and because the land battle is furthest west it implies that this encounter took place first. This placing is consistent with the year 8 inscription, which mentions a terrestrial conflict that took place in Djahi (*MH* I, pl. 46.19) before noting a marine one at the *rȝw-ḥȝwt* 'river mouths' (*MH* I, pl. 46.20).

Given this aspect, the presence of 'Egyptian' Sherden in the land battle and 'foreign' Sherden in the sea battle might suggest that the Sherden left Egyptian service at some point between these two episodes, though why they should desert a victorious Egypt for a defeated enemy is not clear. This hypothesis is ultimately premised on the modern perception

that Sherden were 'mercenaries' who fought mainly for loot, as forcefully asserted by Harry Hall (1901–2, 176), and that their normal recruitment mechanism was capture. Ramesses II's statement, above, that the Sherden accompanying him to Qadesh were 'of his person's capturing whom he had carried off through the victories of his strong arm' (K*RI* II, 11, §26) certainly encourages this position, as does Samuel Birch's (1858, 31) influential early rendering of *fḫ* as 'captured' rather than 'destroyed' in his translation of the stela from Aswan, also mentioned above. If Sherden who were taken by Ramesses II, or their descendants, later saw an opportunity to escape and find wealth elsewhere they might have left Egypt for Libya toward the end of his reign, returned with the Libu as adversaries seeking booty, only to be captured again by Merneptah, who claimed to have faced a Libyan incursion that included a Sherden element (see Manassa 2003, pl. 2.1; 4.13–15). The Sherden might then have remained in Egypt until the opportunity came for them to defect once more – this time in the year 8 campaign by Ramesses III, who captured them yet again when he defeated the Sea Peoples.

Implicit in such a reconstruction is the culture-historical assumption that Sherden formed a distinct group and acted accordingly, but this cannot have been the case. It is clear that Sherden were settled in Egypt for most of the Ramessid period and beyond. As noted above, Ramesses II claimed to have incorporated Sherden into the Egyptian military, and there is record of *pr rʿ-ms-sw mry-imn ʿnḫ wdȝ snb (wȝḥ) m nȝ rmtw n nȝ šrdn* 'the estate of Ramesses II, l.p.h., (established) for the people of the Sherden' (Papyrus Amiens, *recto*, 4.10; Gardiner 1941, 40; 1948, 6–7), as Ramesses III did for *nȝ šrdn n nȝ sḥw-nsw mšʿ* 'the Sherden and for the royal scribes of the army' in the same papyrus (*recto*, 5.4). Although this document was probably written after the reign of Ramesses V in the 20th Dynasty (Gardiner 1941, 43) it still suggests that Ramesses II, like Ramesses III, sought to accommodate Sherden during his reign. The best evidence for actual settlement is Papyrus Wilbour, an administrative document that dates to less than ten years after the death of Ramesses III and which names 109 Sherden. Most seem to be living among the Egyptian population, and in several entries (Text A, 27.19; 59.9; 59.25) are noted as having land worked by their children; two of the entries specifically record the death of the landholder, suggesting that Sherden could pass land to their descendants. Family relationships are also recorded in Papyrus Harris I (78.12), where Sherden are noted as having *nȝy=w ḥmwt r-ḥnʿ=w ḥrdw=w r-gs=w* 'their wives with them and their children beside them'. The ethnicity of their wives is not noted but one Sherden couple served as witnesses to a legal transaction on the accession day of Ramesses XI (Gardiner 1940, 24). None of this evidence can prove Sherden settlement in Egypt beyond a second generation, but in aggregate it is strongly suggestive, as is the fact that the latest known piece of evidence for

Sherden in Egypt, a (probable) 22nd Dynasty donation stela of *šrdn p3dsf* 'Sherden Padjesef' (Petrie 1905, 22), shows the deceased as an Egyptian presenting offerings to Khnum and Hathor, and not represented with a distinctive helmet. Sherden could settle and integrate.

Leaving aside the probably unsolvable question of where they 'came from', I suspect that Sherden were also settled as a minority population in other places in the eastern Mediterranean, though the evidence is not as conclusive. There are four surviving tablets from Ugarit, for example, in which Sherden (Akkadian *šerdanu* or *šertannu*) were involved in legal transactions. One of these, *PRU* III 16.251 (Nougayrol 1955, 108–9; pl. lxxv) records that a Sherden named Allan had two plots of land appropriated from him: one described as being in Ilu'ištam'i, which was presumably a settlement, and the other described by a word that probably translates as 'of (his) inheritance' (Heltzer 1979, 10), which if correct is strong evidence for second-generation Sherden settlement at Ugarit. This land was appropriated by king Niqmepa but *PRU* III 15.167+163, 12–17 (Nougayrol 1955, 124; pl. xxxiv), which dates to the reign of his successor Ammistamru II, details what seems to be a civil land transaction between someone described as 'son of the Sherden', whose name is mostly lost in a lacuna, and a Ugaritic purchaser named Kurwanu. In *PRU* III 16.251 the main beneficiary was the king, who received '100 gold' (probably in shekels) in return for handing Allan's land to his vizier (Heltzer 1978, 77), but *PRU* III 15.167+163 simply states that Kurwanu 'bought' the land. This is reminiscent of a record in Papyrus Wilbour (Text A, 32.47) where a cultivator named Khaemope *in n=f* 'purchased for himself' land once held by the Sherden Setemhab, as well as some from an Egyptian travertine worker (Text A, 24.12). These references both suggest that Sherden might have settled and acquired land in a way that implies some freedom of choice (Menu 1970, 127), and which was not held on condition of service to the king but in a way that resembled private ownership (Gardiner 1941–52, II, 55, 75). It is also notable that the reign of Ammistamru probably coincided with that of Ramesses II, and that Sherden were therefore dwelling in both Ugarit and Egypt concurrently.

If Sherden were dwelling as a minority population in several places in the eastern Mediterranean (and had local names – Semitic names are preserved in Ugarit, Egyptian ones in Egypt) then, given the relative frequency of seaborne travel in the Late Bronze Age (see Cline 1994), it is probable that the designers of the reliefs at Medinet Habu would have known it. If Sherden dwelt beyond Egypt and occasionally took part in raiding activity, then it is foreseeable they might have participated in the kind of assault portrayed by Ramesses III at Medinet Habu independently of any Sherden dwelling in Egypt. But regardless of whether any such assault took place Sherden were known in Egypt as seaborne raiders and would therefore have been ideal

subjects for the position they fulfil in the narrative at Medinet Habu, and Ramesses' status as Egypt's defender would have been enhanced because he was able to defeat such powerful warriors. But Sherden were also sought-after as elite guards at Byblos (*EA* 122, 123) and Ugarit (Heltzer 1971; 1979, 11) as well as in Egypt, and it also served Ramesses' status to be able to command such fighting-men. Sherden were ideal for his purposes on both sides of the conflict.

From the discussion above I suggest that the Medinet Habu artists intended for Sherden to participate in the sea battle as well as the land battle, and therefore that they were intended to be seen on both sides of the year 8 conflict. But having identifiable Sherden on both sides of a single campaign might also, as Alan Gardiner (1947, 196*) noted, have seemed ambiguous to an onlooker, and I suggest that the designers therefore incorporated a subtle differentiation into their work to lessen this: they chose to omit the central protrusion from the headgear of the enemy Sherden. The protrusion, or lack thereof, was an identifier; a device employed by the artists at Medinet Habu to identify the 'other' – to distinguish 'our' Sherden from 'their' Sherden in a way that did not detract from the essential character of the figures.

The plumed headgear

Apart from the horn-helmeted Sherden there are other Sea Peoples groups at Medinet Habu, whose names were recorded in the well-known year 8 inscription:

ḫ3swt iry=w šdt m n3y=sn iww tfi ḫnr m ski t3w m sp w⁽ bw ⁽ḥ⁽. n t3 nb r-ḥ3t ⁽wy=sn š3⁽ m ḫt3 ḳd krḳmš irtw irs … t3y=w in-mkt m prst ṯkr škrš dnn wšš t3w dmḏ

The foreign lands made a conspiracy in their islands. Dislodged and scattered by war were all the lands together. No land could stand before their arms, from Hatti, Kode, Carchemish, Arzawa and Alasiya … Their confederation consisting of the Peleset, Tjeker, Shekelesh, Denyen, and Weshesh, lands united (*MH* I, 46.16–18)

The Peleset, Tjeker, and Weshesh were, so far as the available evidence allows, new to the Egyptians during the reign of Ramesses III. A land called *da-nu-na* had been mentioned in Amarna letter *EA* 151.49–55 (Knudtzon 1915, 622–7; Moran 1992, 238–9) and, although some commentators, such as Gardiner (1947, I, 125*), have disagreed it was probably related to the group recorded as *dnn* (Denyen) in the Medinet Habu inscriptions. Gardiner's argument derived from his belief that Denyen could be identified with the Danaans (Δαναοι) of the Argolid, as first suggested by François Chabas (1873, 48–9), but this was based wholly on phonological similarity and, despite repetition in the literature (*e.g.* Luckenbill 1914, 93; O'Callaghan 1949, 195; Barnett 1975, 365), the argument has never been

Fig. 8.3: Tjeker captives (MH I, pl. 43). The caption reads ḏd in nꜣ ḥrw ꜥꜣw n ṯkkr nty m ḥfꜥ ḥm=fꜥ m swꜣš nṯr nfr -pn nb tꜣwy wsr-mꜣꜥt-rꜥ mry-imn wr pḥty tw=k nsw nḫt rꜥ ꜥꜣ n kmt ꜥꜣ ḥpš=k r ḏw n biꜣ šfyt=k mi bꜥr imi n=n pꜣ ṯꜣw ssny=n -sw pꜣ ꜥnḫ pꜣ nty m ḥfꜥ=k rḏt 'Said by the great enemy of the Tjekker (sic), who are in the grasp of his person, extolling this perfect god, the lord of the two lands, Usermaatra Meryamun (Ramesses III), great of strength; "You are the victorious king, great Ra of Egypt, your sword is greater than a mountain of ore, and your majesty is like Baʾal. Give to us air that we may breathe it, the life that is in your grasp for ever!"' '

Fig. 8.4: Peleset captives (MH I, pl. 44). The caption reads ḏ(d) in nꜣ ḥrw n prst imi n=n pꜣ ṯꜣw r fnd=n pꜣ nsw sꜣ imn 'Said by the enemies of the Peleset; "Give us breath for our noses, oh king, son of Amun!"' '

Fig. 8.5: Denyen captives (MH I, pl. 44). The caption reads ḏ(d) in nꜣ ḥrw n dnn ṯꜣw sp-sn pꜣ ḥḳꜣ nfr ꜥꜣ pḥty mi mnṯw ḥry-ib wꜣst 'Said by the enemies of the Denyen; "Breath, breath, oh perfect ruler, great of strength like Montu dwelling in the midst of Thebes!"' '

convincingly developed. Perhaps a better alternative, though also based primarily on philology, is the town of Adana, which is located west of the Amanus mountains in south-eastern Anatolia and was populated in the Early Iron Age by people known as 'Danuniyim'. The town had been part of the Hittite sphere since at least the time of Telepinu (*c.* 1525–1500 BCE; see Hawkins and Çambel 1999–2000, I.1, 38–9), though Denyen were mentioned so infrequently in Egyptian texts that they may have been largely unknown in Egypt in Ramesses' day. Shekelesh were recorded on one occasion before the year 8 campaign, accompanying a Libyan invasion in the fifth year of Merneptah (Manassa 2003, pls. 2, 4, 12–13), but again seem to have been a largely unknown entity to the Egyptians.

It is clear that the Egyptian scribes differentiated between them, and probably knew of at least some, yet three of the names, Tjeker, Peleset, and Denyen, are associated at Medinet

Habu with prisoners who look almost identical, and wear plumed headgear (Figs. 8.3–5; *MH* I, pls. 43–4). There are numerous surviving illustrations from the Mediterranean showing ships crewed by warriors wearing a similar head-dress (see *e.g.* Wachsmann 2000; Mountjoy 2005), so it is not without precedent that warriors so attired, or at least perceived that way, might have been active near Egypt at the end of the Late Bronze Age. Whether Peleset, Tjeker, or any of the other named groups actually wore plumed headgear is debatable, but the Egyptian artists not only chose to depict them that way, they also, despite numerous assertions to the contrary (*e.g.* Nelson 1943, 44; Gardiner

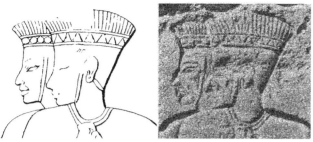

Fig. 8.6: The two predominant headband styles, circular and triangular (MH I, pls. 42 and 52c)

Fig. 8.7: Two Sea Peoples' chariots crewed by warriors with circular-patterned headbands, some of whom are making what is presumably a submissive gesture to Ramesses III (MH I, pl. 34)

1947, I, 200*; Sandars 1978, 134; Drews 1993, 52), sought to differentiate between the groups. As Trude Dothan (1992, 93–4) has observed, there are at least two, and probably more, headband styles represented on the plumed headgear: one that shows a circular pattern, and a second that shows a triangular one (Fig. 8.6). In the land battle the foes with triangular patterned headgear are concentrated in the lower left of the scene, and there are significantly fewer of them than their circular patterned contemporaries. They sometimes occur together in mixed groups, all of whom are fleeing the battle in a rout, but all of the enemies who are unequivocally associated with either chariots or ox-carts in this scene have the circular motif on their headbands, where such a detail is visible (e.g. Figs. 8.2, 8.7 and 8.8). The preservation of the reliefs is good enough that most headband details from the figures in chariots or ox-carts has survived, and while it is possible that an example that would disprove this observation has been lost, the consistency with which only circular patterned headbands are preserved in this way is remarkable. It strongly suggests that the artists intended a distinction. There were at least two groups represented among the mass of plumed adversaries in the land battle: those with circular patterned headgear rode chariots and had dependants, while those with triangular patterned headgear did not.

This differentiation is repeated in the sea battle, where the plumed figures associated with any given ship almost always have the same style of headband: two ships are crewed by warriors bearing circular patterns, and one ship by those with the triangular style (Figs. 8.9–11). There are, it should be noted, two exceptions to this general rule. The first is that the upper middle ship (N1; see Nelson 1943, fig. 4; Wachsmann 2000, 107, fig. 6.2) has one figure with what might to be a cross-hatched headband standing in it (though the cross-hatching might also represent the plumes) with three similarly styled casualties in the water nearby. This style also appears at least once in the land battle (Fig. 8.12; MH I, pl. 34), and probably represents a third group identity. The figures with cross-hatched headbands are far fewer in number even than those with triangular motifs, and their inclusion might be representative in a composition where only three enemy ships were available, two of which

Fig. 8.8: A Sea Peoples' cart, crewed by a warrior with a circular-patterned headband and dependants, being attacked by a Sherden in Egyptian service (MH I, pl. 34)

were crewed primarily by the far more numerous circular patterned warriors. The second exception is that of the capsized ship (Fig. 8.10). All of its crew wear triangular-patterned headbands, apart from one figure with a circular-patterned headband lying across its gunwale with his head mostly obscured by the sail. This inconsistency is not easily explained. It is unlikely that he represents an officer, for example, if in the land battle such figures are shown in greater numbers than those with triangular headbands, and are also seen among the dependants. Nonetheless, the fact that the ships are otherwise so consistently distinguished

Fig. 8.9: Sea Peoples' ship N1, crewed predominantly by warriors with circular-patterned headbands (MH 1, pl. 39)

Fig. 8.10: The capsized Sea Peoples' ship N3, crewed predominantly by warriors with triangular-patterned headbands (MH I, pl. 39)

must be significant, and I suggest that it is a reflection of the perceived identity of the assailants.

It is tempting to associate these styles with the names in the year 8 inscription. The prisoners in the presentation scene captioned *ṯkkr* 'Tjekker' (see Fig. 8.3; *MH* I, pl. 43),

for example, all wear the triangular-style headband, and it could thus be argued that those wearing this style of headband were understood to be Tjeker. Because warriors with circular patterned headbands are much more numerous in the reliefs it could be argued that they were meant to

Fig. 8.11: Sea Peoples' ship N5, crewed by warriors with circular-patterned headbands (MH I, pl. 39)

Fig. 8.13: Libyan dependants under attack, and Sherden in Egyptian service (MH I, pl. 18)

Fig. 8.12: The third, cross-hatched, headband style (MH I, pl. 33)

represent Peleset, who had the greatest effect on the southern Levant in succeeding years and might therefore have been the most numerous migrants in the LBA. But warriors in the ancient Mediterranean need not have worn a uniform, and any headband styles that might have existed could have been adopted freely among them: there is, for example, one well-known anthropoid coffin from Beth Shan that shows

both circular and triangular patterns (from Tomb 90; see *e.g.* Oren 1973, 248, fig. 52.3, pl. 78; Sandars 1978, 173; Dothan and Dothan 1992, 94). Instead, because the choice to depict adversaries with varying headband styles was an Egyptian one, and because the actions of the king were the primary focus, I suggest that establishing an absolute identity for the plumed attackers in the scenes was not the main intention. As such, ascribing identities to the figures has little, if any, interpretive value.

Those who designed the battle reliefs at Medinet Habu,

like all other artists, would have drawn inspiration for their work from the world as they perceived it and from the influences, artistic or otherwise, that they had encountered during their lives. Inscriptions and scenes at Medinet Habu are similar to, influenced by, and sometimes copied from other contexts, as Nelson (*MH* I, 6; 1943, 48–9) himself observed. The compositional forms used in the year 8 text and reliefs were even repeated elsewhere at Medinet Habu. A year 5 Libyan scene, for example, contains the phrase *ii ṯḥnw iry.w šdt* 'Coming by the Tjehenu, having made a conspiracy' (*MH* I, pl. 16.1–4), echoing the year 8 text above, goes on to record that the Tjehenu were a confederation by saying *iw=sn twt dmḏ nn r-ꜥ=sn m rbw spd mšwš* 'They assembled, united without end to them, consisting of Libu, Seped and Meshwesh', and even calls them *tꜣw dmḏw*, 'lands united' (*MH* I, pl. 16. 6–7). One year 5 scene (Fig. 8.13; *MH* I, pl. 18) also includes a Libyan woman and child under attack, indicating that having dependants in battle scenes was not confined to the year 8 Sea Peoples land battle relief.

It is well accepted that there was a tradition or style that was followed for reliefs and inscriptions on royal mortuary temples, and the assailants at Medinet Habu should be seen in such a context. The artists who designed the year 8 narrative scenes would have incorporated into their art the styles and requirements of the commission. Sherden were rendered as Sherden, and not rendered as the plumed attackers, because Sherden were well known in Egypt. They were also contextually relevant to both battle scenes. In one context they were part of the Egyptian world, and in the other they were a part of the outside world, the 'other', and a subtle distinction was used to differentiate between each. Whether a band actually accompanied an invasion of Egypt is almost immaterial because iconographically they provided a suitably powerful opponent for Ramesses to defeat. The Peleset, Tjeker, and so on were less well-known, less immediate to the world of artists in royal employ, but whether or not there was an invasion these groups must have at least been topical, and were used in the composition. The commission called for a collective group of northerners, united in their desire to impose foreign rule over Egypt, against whom Ramesses could triumph. They were therefore shown to be broadly similar, but with subtle variations drawn between them to show their plurality. By depicting Ramesses' enemies as a barely distinguishable mass the artists in effect created the visual equivalent of the 'Nine Bows'; a way of showing that Egypt had many enemies who were acting as one against it.

Acknowledgements

I wish to thank the Arts and Humanities Research Council (AHRC) for their support. All images used in this paper are courtesy of the Oriental Institute of the University of Chicago.

WARRIORS, HUNTERS AND SHIPS IN THE LATE HELLADIC IIIC AEGEAN: CHANGES IN THE ICONOGRAPHY OF WARFARE?

Angelos Papadopoulos

The aim of this paper is to compare the iconography of warfare, and violence in general, before and after the collapse of the palaces in the Aegean region in order to attempt to identify major artistic and social changes. The themes and motifs of palatial military art in the Late Bronze IIIA–B will be compared with post-palatial images (LB IIIC). For the purposes of this paper the chronological terms Late Minoan (LM) and Late Helladic (LH) apply to Crete and the mainland respectively. When the term Late Bronze (LB) is used, it refers to the entire Aegean region. It is not yet possible to give absolute dates, but a useful chronological table is given by Katie Demakopoulou (1988, 27). The media on which these representations from both periods were depicted will be discussed as well. The major objective is to establish if the same motifs were used in the two periods, portrayed on the same materials, and if the same symbolism was applied.

The imagery of martial subjects, if studied properly, provides important information on the social structure of Bronze Age societies, because art in many cases had a symbolic function and was manipulated by local elites for their own purposes and advantages. It can be suggested that scenes of combat were used as elite insignia in LB I societies, as these depictions may hint at the aristocratic past of the ruler(s), and thus underline their legitimate authority.

Late Bronze IIIA–B

LB IIIA–B military iconography includes scenes of combat and battle, hunting, and fights between humans and animals. Nevertheless, some other motifs, such as the figure-of-eight shield, the boar's tusk helmet, the horseman and boxer were also part of the palatial artistic repertoire.

Battles and combats

The fragmentary condition of the wall paintings does not allow a very detailed reconstruction and only the frieze from Hall 64 at Pylos provides evidence for battles between different groups (Fig. 9.1; Lang 1969, 72–4, 22 H 64, 23 H 64, 24 H 64, 25 H 64, 26 H 64, 28 H 64, and 29 H 64). There are, with the possible exception of a seal from 'Athens', upon which two males are engaged in a fight with swords (*Corpus der minoischen und mykenischen Siegel* [hereafter *CMS*] XI, no. 34; Pini 1989, 209, no. 17), no images of battles or duels portrayed on the other media. The duel on a Tanagra *larnax* is a strong candidate for a sword-fighting scene, but like the figures on the seal, the duelists do not wear any kind of military equipment (Demakopoulou and Konsola 1981, 82–3, pl. 42; Demakopoulou in Tzahou-Aexandri 1989, 13–14, no. 13). In addition, the nature of the medium (a larnax) and the overall iconography seems to refer to a religious context, rather than a depiction of a battle.

There is otherwise no clear battle scene at this date, although a number of strong candidates could represent violent moments, particularly two fragments of a stone vessel from Epidauros (Sakellariou 1971, 3–14; Lamprinoudakis 1975, 172–3, pl. 149a). The material is steatite, which was possibly covered with metal. The upper part depicts a group of figures marching along what seems to be a rocky coast. If the rectangular objects are considered as tower shields, they should be warriors similar to the North Wall paintings in the West House at Akrotiri (for the Miniature Frieze, see Morgan 1988, esp. 309–38; Televantou 1990, 309–26; 1994, esp. 309–38). Alternatively they could simply wear short chitons. Three figures are standing to the left and one of them holds a peculiar object, like a stick. On the right is what has been interpreted as an *ikrio* of a ship and a dolphin. The lower fragment shows water, a man, possibly

Fig. 9.1: The Pylos battle wall painting (Lang 1969, 22 H 64, pl. A)

the victim of a battle, and what could be the stern projection of a ship. Whether this is a unique example, copied from or inspired by an older tradition of depicting a town under attack, or there is a continuation of this motif, the important point is that it is most likely part of a violent scene. There are also two helmeted individuals portrayed on two faience fragments from Mycenae (Foster 1979, 126–30, pls. 37–8; Tournavitou 1995, 239–44, pl. 35a–b) and they too could be part of a battle or hunt scene.

Chariots and horsemen

Fragments of wall paintings found at Mycenae outside the West Portal (Pithos Area) were attributed to the 'vestibule' or 'Little Megaron' (Lamb 1921–3, 164; Immerwahr 1990, 124, 192). Large numbers of other wall painting fragments with various themes were found as well, amongst them parts of chariots, horses, and men both armed and not, suggesting

a harnessing scene (Rodenwaldt 1911, 239–40, 245–6; Lamb 1921–3, 162, 164–5; Immerwahr 1990, 123–4). They could have been 'preparations for battle'.

Fragments of a clay figurine of a rider and his horse were discovered in the prehistoric cemetery at Mycenae in a LH IIIB1 context (Fig. 9.2; Crouwel 1981, 161, T18, also pl. 42a–b). According to Sinclair Hood (1953, 84) 'the animal and the rider were moulded separately and were put together while the clay was still soft before firing'. The rider is armed, as he seems to hold a kind of weapon. The figure wears a conical headdress that has been interpreted, probably correctly, as a helmet. This is a unique representation of a rider equipped with both protective and offensive gear (if one accepts the identification of the item he holds as a weapon – Elizabeth French (1971, 176) clearly states that this rider 'appears to be armed'.

A small group of terracotta horsemen were discovered at Methana and their date should be 'within the limits of

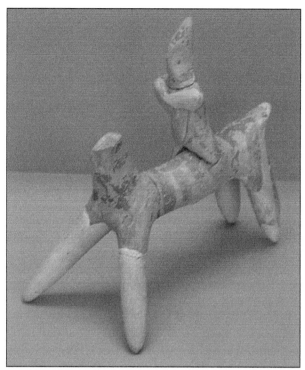

Fig. 9.2: A clay horseman from Mycenae (author)

Fig. 9.3: Larnax from Armenoi cemetery, Rethymno, Crete (author)

the LH IIIB period' (Konsolaki-Yannopoulou 1999). They appear to be unarmed, but all wear conical caps and Eleni Konsolaki-Yannopoulou considers them to be metallic rather than made from boar's tusks, on the grounds of their shape and decoration. According to her interpretation (1999, 432), they are better understood as noblemen exhibiting their riding skills in civil ceremonies and their helmets should be viewed as symbols of high social or religious status and their male character.

Fragments of a krater have been found at Tiryns upon which for the first time warriors armed with round shields and spears are represented, together with a chariot (Sakellarakis 1992, 26–8, no.12). It is possible they also carry swords (Furumark 1941, 240). Unfortunately it cannot be determined whether any passenger(s) were armed, as they do not survive. A dog is painted under the horse.

Hunters

The main focus of LH IIIA–B wall compositions was the boar chase (Rodenwaldt 1912, 96–154, nos. 113–93; Immerwahr 1990, 129–30, 202–3, Ti no. 6). Hunting is a popular theme in LB IIIA–B Aegean portable imagery. A larnax from Armenoi is one of a number of examples from Crete (Fig. 9.3; Vlasaki in Demakopoulou 1988, 84–5, no. 6; Merousis 2000, 112–13, no. 20, pl. 7). In glyptic art, the image of the single hero in close combat with a fierce creature (wild boar or lion) although limited, is present (*e.g.*

CMS I, nos. 165 and 331). The Lasithi dagger shows a heroic moment when a hunter armed with a spear attacks a wild boar (Long 1978, 35–46, esp. 44–6). Ivory plaques from Thebes, so similar to the Tiryns and possibly Orchomenos wall paintings, show that the specific scene was portrayed on both small and larger scale art (Aravantinos 2000, 55–9, 98–9, figs. 20–1). Hunting scenes were depicted in various media during earlier times and the fact that they are now pictured on precious and exotic materials (such as ivory) and weapons hints that they were considered important activities in life, worth commemorating.

Boxers

A fragment of an LH IIIB2 vessel of uncertain shape – perhaps a krater – from Mycenae depicts what may be interpreted as a pair of boxers confronting one another (Vermeule and Karageorghis 1982, 93, 212, IX.17). Only the left-hand figure survives from head to waist, while only the edges of the fingers are shown of his opponent. Additionally, a seal from Pylos possibly portrays two or more men engaged in boxing (*CMS* I, no. 306).

A pottery sherd from Room 4 of the Citadel House at Mycenae shows a male boxer with a helmet or cap and perhaps a uniform (Vermeule and Karageorghis 1982, 93, 212, IX.18). He is looking to the left and the lines on his neck could represent a protective device (Fig. 9.4). The muscles are clearly painted on his thin arm and he seems to be on guard. His helmet is divided by vertical stripes. On the left part of the sherd an opponent can be seen, his nose and equally muscled arm are clear.

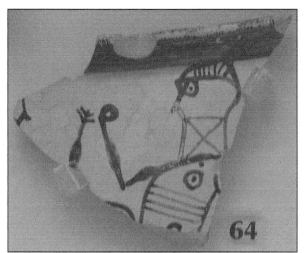

Fig. 9.4: Pottery fragment from Mycenae showing a boxer (author)

Boar's tusk helmets

Boar's tusk helmets appear in most types of media. Most of the warriors from Pylos and Mycenae wear this helmet, and fragments from Orchomenos also show men with this kind of headgear. It appears on a pottery fragment from Tiryns (Crouwel and Morris 1996, 208–9, 217, no. A1, fig. 1; Güntner 2000, 28–9, 199, 207–8, Motiv Mensch 1, Liste Mensch 6, pl. 11.1) and possibly on the boxer sherd from Mycenae noted above. All the other representations of helmets come in the form of the ivory helmeted figures from Crete, the mainland and Delos (see Gallet de Shaunter and Tréheux 1947–8, 156–162, pl. XXV; Krzyszkowska 1991, 107–20; Sakellarakis and Sapouna-Sakellaraki 1997, 721–9, figs. 836–47). These inlays in the shape of helmeted individuals were found in Crete, the Greek mainland and as far as Cyprus, most likely decoration pieces of furniture or boxes. It should be noted that it is not possible to determine whether the ivory figures were considered hunters or warriors.

The boar's tusk helmet represented the hunting abilities and skills of an individual, since killing a wild boar was a very dangerous enterprise (Morris 1990, 149–56). It is clear that it functioned as a symbol of power and martial prowess.

Figure-of-eight shields

The earliest example of a figure-of-eight shield in Aegean iconography appeared in Crete, dates to EM II–MM IA (*CMS* VS. 1A, no. 219; Pini in Marangou 1992, 210, no. 259), and was seen quite often in various media (Daniilidou 1998). In LH IIIA–B times it was part of a common mural decorative repertoire of the mainland centres (firstly at Thebes, then at Tiryns and later at Mycenae), but the earliest example

was painted at Knossos in LM II. Especially at Mycenae, the sacred symbolism of the shields is clear because of the religious environment in which they are represented (*i.e.* other religious wall paintings and the building itself; Immerwahr 1990, 138–40). In the case of Knossos and Tiryns, according to Despina Daniilidou (1998), they could function as the symbol of the palace and the power of the wanax, although there is no proof of the religious character of the architectural context. At the same time, they are important protective weapons as they can be seen in various combat and hunting scenes in earlier Aegean art (combats: *CMS* I, no. 11; no. 12; no. 228; lion hunt dagger: Xénaki-Sakellariou and Chatziliou 1989, no. 1, pls. I–II) and it is not inconceivable that the Mycenaean ruling elite should want their symbolic protection to be transferred to their palaces or important religious centres.

It is clear that shields belong to the repertoire of Minoan religious symbols that have successfully been assimilated to Mycenaean cult. Whether the items decorated with a figure-of-eight shield had religious or other symbolic meaning is difficult to say, as examples do not survive. The footstool from Archanes decorated with the ivory shields and helmeted heads provides strong evidence that it was used by an important person, but not much more can be said. Thus the shields may have had a simple decorative as well as protective function and do not necessarily hint at a martial or purely religious nature.

During Palatial times a plethora of materials were used to portray various scenes of violence, such as battles, duels/combats, hunting and occasionally boxing. The walls of buildings within major centres, such as Mycenae and Tiryns, were decorated with paintings, and also sites such as Orchomenos, Gla and Thebes. Images on pottery were very popular. In addition, objects made of ivory were discovered across the Aegean region, and stone and faience were used as well. In Crete the major medium for depicting mainly hunting scenes were clay coffins, the larnakes. Clay figurines of armed horse riders were discovered in the mainland. Although the motif of the combat between male warriors in glyptic art was never as popular as during LB I, violent engagements between men and beasts were portrayed frequently.

Most of the motifs and complex scenes come from the mainland. These are likely to have functioned as symbols of political authority and the military power of the local elite(s). On Crete, martial images focused on hunting activities and may have had a funerary symbolism, given their context (*i.e.* the larnakes). There are a number of objects, such as the Archanes composition that do not have a clear hunting character, but these are exceptions to the rule. The islands have produced no comparative imagery apart from a seal with a hunter from Rhodes (*CMS* V, no. 656), a spearman from Aplomata, Naxos (*CMS* V, no. 608) and the ivory plaque from Delos.

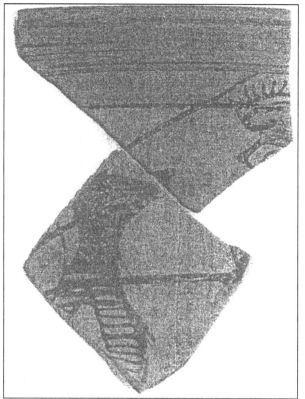

Fig. 9.5: Two probable cup fragments from Palatia, Naxos (Vlachopoulos 2003, 511, fig. 21)

Fig. 9.6: Pottery sherd from Mycenae portraying a man and a horse (author)

Late Bronze IIIC

Battles and combats

Despite their fragmentary condition two combat scenes can be identified on sherds from the islands of Naxos and Kos. A duel between two spearmen is depicted on a cup from Palatia, Naxos, but only two fragments have been recovered (Fig. 9.5; Vlachopoulos 2003b, 498, 511, fig. 21). It must be mentioned though that according to Vlachopoulos the two fragments may not join exactly, but it is rather unlikely that any other scene than a combat could have been portrayed. The torso and parts of the legs of the left figure and the helmeted head of the right individual survive. The helmet is likely to belong to the 'hedgehog' style. Both men carry a spear and a javelin. Judging from the armour of the individuals and their body position it is possible that, even if these sherds do not join, a combat scene was portrayed anyway. A duel between two individuals, at the moment when the left figure is overwhelming his opponent, survives on a sherd from Seraglio, Kos (Karatzali 2003, 513–34, esp. 521, fig. 8.1, 21). It seems that the right-hand warrior has a sword with a round pommel in the scabbard tied at his waist and he uses a second sword against his enemy. The right combatant is falling backwards; his weapons are not pictured, but the line next to his body should be the blade of his sword. No other features are shown and the bodies do not survive above the torsos. No large scale battles (such as the one represented at Hall 64 from Pylos) seem to appear in post-Palatial art. However, 'preparations for battle' in the style of the Pithos area fresco may have existed. Two fragments (see Figs. 9.7–9.8) could be interpreted as showing grooms and their horses, a theme commonly met on wall paintings.

Chariots and horsemen

On a krater fragment from Mycenae, dating to LH IIIC Middle, a warrior and a horse moving to the left are depicted, while the individual is shown overlapping the horse (Fig. 9.6; Sakellarakis 1992, 38, fig. 33). This is the only scene of its kind painted on pottery and it could be understood as preparations for battle or a march. The polychrome nature of the sherd is notable and Jeremy Rutter (1992, 65) highlights the close parallels with painted plaster. He also comments on the overlapping of the figures (the man and the horse) suggesting that together with their polychrome that they 'are as atypical of earlier vase painting as they are characteristic of fresco art'. Equally important and perhaps belonging to a similar scene, is another fragment, also from Mycenae, on which the upper part of a warrior is painted, leading a horse to the right (Fig. 9.7; Sakellarakis 1992, 34, fig. 30). He is holding a staff or a spear and wears a helmet with a long plume.

Amongst the various scenes of armed warriors riding chariots probably the most characteristic is the scene depicted on a krater from Tiryns, on which a chariot with two passengers can be seen (Güntner 2000, wagen 14A,

Fig. 9.7: Another pottery sherd from Mycenae portraying a man
and a horse (author)

Fig. 9.8: A horseman painted on a krater from Mouliana
(author)

pl. 7.1a–d). The first figure holds the reins and the second
behind him holds two spears. As both individuals wear the
same protective gear and armour, perhaps the second male
is holding the spear of his comrade.

Hunters

Various dates have been suggested for a krater from a small
tholos tomb at Mouliana, Crete, but it seems that most
scholars agree that it is LM IIIC (Fig. 9.8; Xanthudides
1904, 32–5, pl. 3; see Greenhalgh 1973, 176, n. 21 for a
presentation of the suggested dates; Crouwel 1981, 165,
V57 'probably LM IIIC'). On one side, a male figure
is engaged in hunting, shown carrying a long spear and
possibly wearing a helmet. Two *agrimia* are shown running
in different directions obviously trying to escape.

The Acropolis of Mycenae has produced evidence of
hunting activities, which, despite the lack of hunters, show
great similarities to the hunting imagery of earlier periods
as hounds are portrayed attacking animals. The surviving
examples decorate a krater (LH IIIC Early) and a kylix (LH
IIIC Middle; Sakellarakis 1992, 46–7, figs. 56–8).

A fragmentary hunting scene from Tiryns has been
characterised by Emily Vermeule and Vassos Karageorghis
(1982, 140, 224, XI.78) as a 'masterpiece'. It deals with
the very popular wall painting motif of the hound in flying
gallop, but this time attacking a deer and biting its leg. The
bodies of the animals are tense and captured in action. It
is believed to be influenced by the Tiryns and Orchomenos
boar hunt paintings.

Although fragmentary, a scene on a krater from Chamber
Tomb K-2 at Englianos clearly depicts another hunting
activity. A possibly bearded male figure wearing what
seems to be a horned helmet is accompanied by two dogs
attacking an animal that has been interpreted either as a lion
or as a jackal (Blegen and Rawson 1973, 229, pls. 289a–e;
Mountjoy 1999a, 355, fig. 122, no. 128). It is possible that

Fig. 9.9: A hunting scene on the same krater from Mouliana
(author)

the hunter carries a spear; although this part does not survive,
the reconstruction seems convincing. On the other side of
the vessel a stag is pursued by one or two dogs.

Horsemen

One example of a horseman can be seen on the Mouliana
krater, on which a rider is shown on his horse armed with
a long spear, a shield and a kind of helmet (Fig. 9.9). A
fragmentary krater depicting a horse, on which a figure is
holding the reins, was found at Grotta, north of the potter's
workshop inside the Mycenaean city wall (Vlachopoulos
1995, 135; 1999b, 74). The schematic human figure seems
to be unarmed and pictured standing on the horse, which has
many stylistic similarities with the horse on the Mouliana

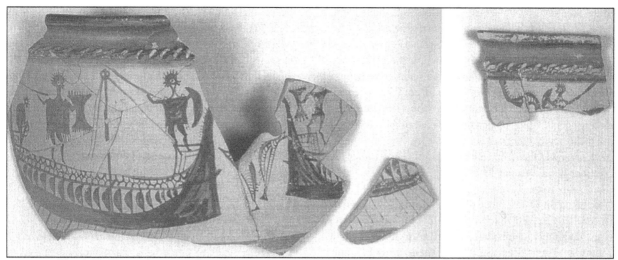

Fig. 9.10: Krater fragments from Kynos, Livanates, depicting a naval battle (Dakoronia 2002, 99, photo 4)

krater. Andreas Vlachopoulos parallels the horseman with the riders on the LH IIIB1 krater from Minet el Beida (in Syria), although he highlights that that one of these figures is armed with a short sword (Vlachopoulos 1999b, 87, fig. 4; see also Crouwel 1981, 45, 170, pl. 80; Vermeule and Karageorghis 1982, 42, 202, V.26). Various interpretations are possible, such as identifying the figure as a 'riding Mycenaean deity', as 'horse races in honour of a warrior or leader', or as the 'prize for the winner of dangerous acrobatics' (Vlachopoulos 1999b, 89–90). Vlachopoulos continues that the lack of arms does not suggest any martial context and perhaps the rider belongs to a class of Naxian pictorial compositions that deals with scenes of everyday life, such as fishing and dancing. At the same time, this horseman ought to belong to an elite group of wealthy people who own and use horses. The large size of the krater (larger than the Warrior Vase from Mycenae) suggests that it was an item of prestige and this is highlighted by its decoration.

Naval battles

For the first time in Aegean iconography clear naval battles are depicted in LH IIIC. Numerous publications have dealt with the material from Kynos Livanates (Fig. 9.10; Dakoronia 1990, 117–22; 1996, 159–71; 1999a, 119–28; 2002, 283–90; Dakoronia *et al.* 2002). Warriors are shown on board ships facing each other and ready to throw their spears at the enemy vessel. Archers and seemingly dead, perhaps drowned, human figures can also be seen. It is clear that the engagements take place in the open sea. A very similar scene is also portrayed on a large krater from Bademgediği Tepe in western Turkey (Mountjoy 2005, 423–6, pls. XCVI and XCVIIa–c). It is not clear whether the krater was locally made, like most of the Mycenaean pottery from the site. Although there are images of violent actions taking place at sea depicted on earlier

representations, such as the EC II–III stone carving from Korfi t'Aroniou (Doumas 1965, plaque V, 52–3, fig. 7, pl. 37α) and the West House miniature paintings (Televantou 1994, 309–38), no ships are shown in such a martial environment that could be described as a naval battle; especially on the plaque, where all fighting is taking place on board and no other ships are shown. Now a new type of warfare has evolved and warriors on board throw spears and fire arrows against their enemies on other ships. Although there is no fighting on the decks of the ships and it is rather a distant exchange of missiles, the full armour of the warriors certainly suggests a full scale combat.

The lack of naval battle scenes on the palatial wall paintings supports the hypothesis that this is a post-palatial activity, or at least it was not a popular subject until LB IIIC. Although there are depictions of ships with armed passengers already from MH III (Siedentopf 1991, 25, no. 162, pl. 38; Wedde 2000, 316, no. 511), it is debatable whether they represent warships at all. At the same time, the shipwreck scene on the north wall of the West House paintings does not show a naval battle, but rather a ship that was damaged while it was docked during a raid (Papadopoulos 2006, 131–7). The fragments from Pylos that may have been part of a ship scene cannot provide any further information (Lang 1969, 186, pl. C, 113, 19 M ne; see also Shaw 2001, 37–43).

It could be argued that the naval battles are in fact images of contemporary events, a period in the Aegean and Eastern Mediterranean that is understood as violent and unsafe, and sea raids and attacks must have been a reality at the time. Although it is not yet agreed who was responsible for them, contemporary artists decided to represent them on pottery.

It is clear from the Bademgediği Tepe and Kynos kraters that rowers were clearly portrayed under the deck on which the warriors are standing. At the same time, a number of sites, such as Seraglio (Kos), Tiryns and Lefkandi, have yelded krater fragments showing rowers (Morricone 1972–3, 360, fig. 358; Güntner 2000, 33, Motiv Mensch 17, Liste Mensch pl. 12.6; Whitley 2004–5, 51). It is plausible that the now-lost scenes originally painted on these vessels may have been sea battles as well. Therefore, the theme of conflict at sea may have covered a large area stretching from Thessaly to the Dodecanese and from Achaea to the coast of Asia Minor. As all of these areas are coastal, it would not be strange that these scenes were seen in real life, if not regularly, at least not on rare occasions.

There are some notable differences with the previous period, as some of the most popular motifs of the palatial artistic repertoire did not survive into LB IIIC. The most obvious disappearance is that of the figure-of-eight shields and boar's tusk helmets. Both of them already appear in Aegean art from the early Late Bronze Age (or even earlier) and became popular in palatial art. It seems that although they could have easily been depicted on pottery, contemporary artists chose not to. The same applies to images of athletes engaged in boxing.

During LB IIIC, pottery seems to be the main medium on which images of martial character were depicted. With a few notable exceptions, there are no artifacts made of stone, ivory reliefs or faience appliqués, no buildings decorated with wall paintings and certainly no glyptic art. These exceptions include a bronze statuette of a spearman from Syme (Lembessi 2002, 16–17, 54–6, 209–14, 335–6, pl. 9. no. 9), a reused painted stele from Mycenae (Tsountas 1896, 1–22, pls. 1, 2.2), a 'menhir' from Soufli Magoula (Karapanou in Demakopoulou *et al.* 1999, 225, no. 60), and a clay figurine of an armed individual from Phylakopi, Melos (French in Renfrew 1985, 223, 225, 226, 230, fig. 6.12, pls. 36a, 37c).

On the mainland, images of warriors and chariots on pottery are quite common. In Crete only a few limited hunting scenes survive and these are painted with a noted aristocratic flavour, recalling old iconographic traditions. Island pictorial art products are now decorated with duels, warriors, horsemen and ships, and three-dimensional figurines were made as well. At the same time, there are signs of prosperity and population increase in the Dodecanese and of wealth in the Cyclades. Perhaps the economic and probably military power gained by the islands is reflected in their art, utilising the insignia of earlier times.

Whether the LB IIIA–B images of fighting warriors and hunting activities functioned as propaganda of the ruling class or as emblems of the elite, it is clear that they did not have the same use in post-palatial times. Generally, scenes of violence in the mainland and Crete may represent moments of everyday life, such as naval battles and transport of troops to the battle. At the same time, some individuals may have attempted to use old symbols of power in order to highlight their own prowess. This could be the case with the Mouliana krater: the uniqueness of the find, in combination with the apparent disappearance from the local iconography of the warrior/hunter ethos and symbolism during this period suggests that this object could indeed have been the property of an individual of some authority, who decided to refer to the old traditions in order to show his prowess. In addition, the motif of the combat that, up to this date, can only be traced on island sites may have survived the abandonment of the palatial symbolism and functioned as an *insignium* of an elite that was either developed on the islands or moved there in LB IIIC.

Conclusions

The collapse of the palatial system marks the end of the elite patron/artist relationship, but not the end of artistic activities. The post-palatial Aegean was certainly not in a state of cultural decline, at least from an iconographic point of view. There was a clear lack of expensive and exotic raw materials, such as ivory, and there were no palatial centres with decoration on their walls, but most of the motifs were transferred to pottery.

The iconographic themes remained more or less the same: warriors, hunters, horsemen and chariots continue to be part of the artistic repertoire. The difference is that in the post-palatial era they do not reflect the kind of propaganda or elite insignia used by the palatial elites or a central authority symbolism. It is possible that a certain individual of power would use these depictions as symbols of authority, perhaps an old aristocrat or a member of a new elite. It must be mentioned though that it is difficult to comment on the character of the LB IIIC elite and to establish whether has been a major elite replacement or not. Bearing in mind that these were probably violent times, the large numbers of images of warriors, together with the representations of sea battles, seem to stand for moments of everyday life. The only exception to this daily activities thematic agenda seems to be the duel/combat (as seen on Naxos and Kos), which functioned as an aristocratic symbol already from LH/LM I and continued perhaps to have a similar meaning in the new urban centres of the Cyclades and Dodecanese. Their very rare occurrence in post-palatial art in comparison with the plentiful warrior depictions underlines the special importance of the duel/combat motif.

It has been suggested that some basic elements of the Mycenaean culture did not change dramatically after the collapse of the palatial system (Rutter 1992, 70). Indeed, it is clear that the survival and continuation of motifs suggests that the iconography remained basically the same, at least concerning martial subjects. Additionally, from the representations provided by this iconography the use of similar weaponry is evident (round shields, spears, greaves and the use of chariot as means of transportation).

Generally, with the exception of the already ancient motifs of the figure-of-eight shield and boar's tusk helmet, most of the LB IIIA–B artistic repertoire continued to exist. The new theme was that of sea battles between warriors on board ships. In the mainland, most of the iconographic agenda remained the same. In Crete, hunting seems to have been the only favourite martial theme during both periods, most likely connected with religion. It seems that military symbolism was deliberately avoided on Crete and political and military status was publicised differently and not via art. The Cyclades and the Dodecanese appear to have taken over from the mainland centres, possibly due to their strategic location. These were violent times with sea battles and a need for skills in weaponry, but these conditions are well known in the Aegean region. To judge from the military iconography of the Aegean and its distribution in various LB IIIC sites, the collapse of the palatial system did not mean population dispersal or a general cultural decline.

Acknowledgements

I would like to express my gratitude to my supervisor, Prof. Christopher B. Mee (University of Liverpool), and Prof. Fritz Blakolmer (University of Vienna) for their comments on an earlier draft of this paper. I was able to participate in the conference thanks to the Thomas Wiedemann Memorial Fund (University of Nottingham). I should acknowledge the patience and help of the editors and conference organisers Christoph Bachhuber and Gareth Roberts. I am also indebted to the Princeton University Press, Dr. Andreas Vlachopoulos, the National Archaeological Museum at Athens, the archaeological museums of Mycenae, Herakleion and Rethymnon and the IΔ' E.P.K.A. (Lamia) for their kind permission to use the various illustrations. In addition, many thanks to Christoforos Agorastoudis for helping me with the images and other technical issues during the preparation for the conference and Ioannis Galanakis for his valuable comments.

PART 4

BUILT ENVIRONMENT
– CEMETERIES, CITADELS AND LANDSCAPES

FORCES OF TRANSFORMATION IN DEATH: THE CEMETERY AT TELL ES-SA'IDIYEH, JORDAN

John D. M. Green

Studies to date focussing on the end of the Late Bronze Age in the Mediterranean and Near East have highlighted major disruptions and migrations, cataclysmic destructions, and other events leading to social and political upheavals – with a less overt emphasis on continuity and revival in the subsequent Iron Age (*e.g.* Ward and Joukowsky 1992; Gitin *et al.* 1998). Recent studies of post-collapse regeneration emphasise the cyclical rise and fall of social complexity, in contrast to the traditional unilineal progression of social evolutionary studies (Schwartz and Nichols 2006). Within such frameworks, one can incorporate human responses to crisis, examining the ways in which societies and individuals reconstitute group and personal identities in such periods of social flux. In this paper, I apply these principles of social transformation to the contextually rich cemetery at Tell es-Sa'idiyeh (Jordan), comparing features of continuity and change from the thirteenth to tenth centuries BCE. This spans a period of prosperity within the Late Bronze Age (henceforth LBA), followed by a period of fragmentation in the twelfth century, and a subsequent period of recovery in the subsequent Early Iron Ages (henceforth EIA).

Far from reflecting conservative attitudes and beliefs, a ritual approach to death and burial provides an opportunity for examining some of the small scale human actions not only reflecting social concerns, but also contributing to the formation and transformation of social identity and social structure (Morris 1992; Voutsaki 1997; 1998). In this paper, I present my analysis of the Sa'idiyeh cemetery, alongside socio-political models for the period and region, with a focus on the Central Jordan Valley. The findings from Sa'idiyeh provide important insights into aspects of ethnicity and cultural identity, changes in the expression of vertical status in death, shifting attitudes to the body, and aspects of gendered identity. It is argued that funerary rituals formed important social arenas in which 'forces of transformation'

were being actively played out; not only reflecting social changes, but also contributing to future outcomes.

Tell es-Sa'idiyeh: background and chronology

Tell es-Sa'idiyeh is located 1.8 kilometres east of the River Jordan, roughly equidistant between the Sea of Galilee and the Dead Sea (Fig. 10.1). The Jordan and the Jezreel Valleys were both important in terms of trade and communication in these periods, not only between coast and hinterland, but also within neighbouring highland regions. The central positioning of Sa'idiyeh in the Central Jordan Valley close to a crossing point of the River Jordan suggests its position was strategically important in terms of east-west trading contacts (Tubb 1995, 142). Sa'idiyeh is also located within prime agricultural land consisting of fertile alluvial soils and several perennial springs and wadis (Dorrell 1988) of integral importance to the local population.

Approximately eleven hectares in area, Sa'idiyeh consists of an Upper Tell with settlement remains dating from the Late Bronze to Roman periods, and a slightly smaller and less pronounced Lower Tell at its western side (Fig. 10.2). The Lower Tell was initially the location of an Early Bronze Age settlement, with burials of the Late Bronze, Iron Age, Persian, and Islamic periods cutting into these ruins and the silted-up spaces between collapsed walls. Tomb-types are highly varied within the cemetery (Fig. 10.3). Most are simple pit-graves for individual or multiple interment, with smaller proportions of mudbrick or stone-lined cists, single jar burials (predominantly for infants), and double-pithos burials. This latter burial type consists of two large store-jars pushed together with an extended primary burial interred inside.

The cemetery has been the focus of major excavation campaigns, firstly by James Pritchard of the University

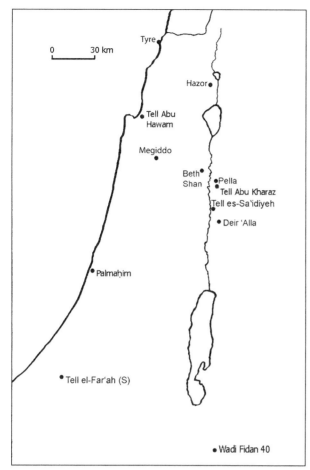

Fig. 10.1: The Southern Levant with sites mentioned in the text

Fig. 10.2: Tell es-Sa'idiyeh viewed from the north, with the cemetery on the lower mound (right). Reproduced with the permission of Jonathan Tubb

of Pennsylvania in the 1960's (see Pritchard 1980), and secondly by the British Museum under the direction of Jonathan Tubb from 1985 to 1996, the results of which are published in preliminary form (Tubb 1988a; 1990; Tubb and Dorrell 1991; 1993; 1994; Tubb *et al.* 1996; 1997). My recently completed PhD thesis (Green 2006) focuses on the LBA and EIA cemetery, combining both Pritchard's published data and the unpublished records from the British Museum excavations. The Persian and Islamic burials are beyond the scope of this paper, and will be presented alongside the LBA and EIA burials in a final report on the British Museum excavations (currently in preparation).

The Lower Tell of Tell es-Sa'idiyeh is an extramural cemetery, a common feature of LBA lowland regions, especially during the thirteenth and twelfth centuries BCE in the Central Valleys (Gonen 1992, 20–21, 32–35). The spatial relationship between settlement and extramural cemetery indicates the deliberate separation of the living

and the dead, with the Upper and Lower Tells demarcated by a major difference in elevation. A detailed discussion of the settlement is beyond the scope of this paper, and its relationship with the cemetery is yet to be refined through post-excavation study. The Sa'idiyeh settlement is one of the few sites in this region where it will become possible to compare settlement and burial data, as strata XV–XII (and related strata 15–13) on the Upper Tell exhibit a close chronological relationship with LBA and EIA cemetery phases. For example, the substantial mudbrick storage and residential buildings of Stratum XII have been extensively excavated and are closely related to the EIA period of cemetery use.

There are several phases and areas of cemetery use on the Lower Tell, providing a diachronic and spatial dimension to the study of death and burial in the LBA and Iron Ages. Pritchard published 44 individually numbered tombs from his excavations in the north area of the Lower Tell. The more recent British Museum excavations have exposed around 450 tombs from the central BB100–600 area, and other areas to the south and southwest (BB700–1400 and DD). Approximately two-thirds (311 individually numbered tombs) are assigned to LBA and EIA periods. The remaining one-third are of later or indeterminate date.

There are three LBA and EIA phases based on stratigraphic relationships between intercutting and superimposed graves, combined with the distribution of diagnostic ceramic types, scarabs, and seals within a relative sequence. In my analysis, these three phases (1–3) are grouped into two main period samples, forming the basis for a discussion of changes and developments over time (Table 10.1). *Period 1* dates to the thirteenth to twelfth centuries BCE (LB IIB–Iron IA) and incorporates Pritchard's 'earliest' and 'intermediate' period burials, and British Museum cemetery Phase 1. A clear horizon is observed at the start of Phase 2, with the construction of numerous mudbrick cists directly over earlier pit graves. *Period 2* dates broadly to the eleventh to ninth centuries (Iron IB–Iron IIA), incorporating Pritchard's 'late'

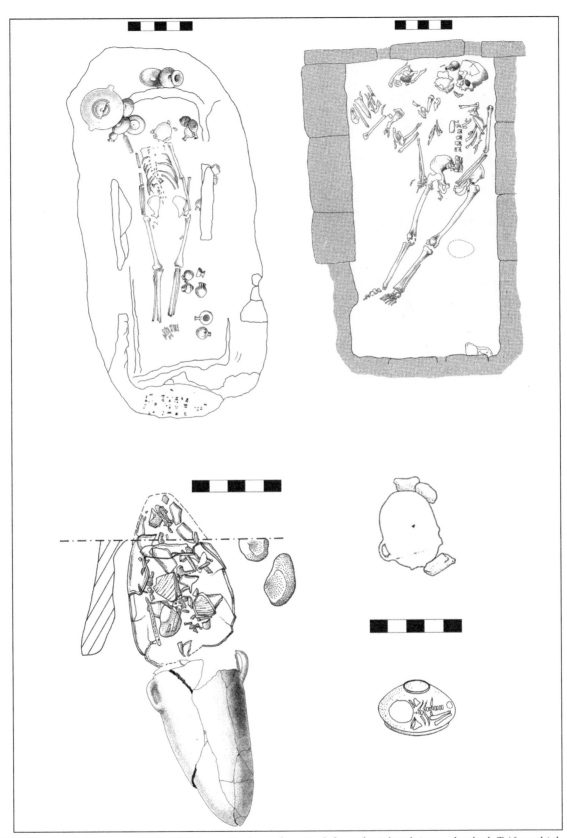

Fig. 10.3: Selected burial types at Tell es-Saʻidiyeh. Clockwise from top left: pit burial with inner clay kerb T.46; multiple cist burial T.188; jar burial T.471; bowl burial T.52; double-pithos burial T.204. Each scale represents 0.5 metres. Reproduced with the permission of Jonathan Tubb

Cemetery periods in this study	Pritchard's periodisation	British Museum cemetery phases	Chronological Period	Approximate dates (BCE)
Period 1	"Earliest" and "intermediate"	Phase 1	LBIIB–Iron IA	Late 13th–12th Centuries
Period 2	"Late"	Phases 2-3	Iron IB–Iron IIA	11th to 9th Centuries

Table 10.1: Periodisation of the Late Bronze and Early Iron Age cemetery at Sa'idiyeh

period burials and British Museum cemetery Phases 2–3. Period 2 could potentially start as early as the late twelfth century, although there is a gap of indeterminate length after the end of Period 1. Phases 2–3 are not subdivided, as the cemetery exhibits continuity in use over time, with close similarities in ceramic types found in both phases.

Ethnicity and elite-emulation

The ethnicities of the Sa'idiyeh cemetery population were given a high priority in previous publications, with the presence of Sea Peoples, central Anatolians (Hittites), and Egyptians implicated in interpretations of grave-objects, body treatments, and burial types (Pritchard 1968; Negbi 1991; Tubb 1995; Negbi 1998). These varied ethnic interpretations were layered onto the Canaanite cultural background of the LBA southern Levant (Tubb 1998), with the Central Valleys (including the Jordan Valley) viewed as a region of Canaanite settlement in LB and Iron I periods (Singer 1994, 310–1). Hittites and Sea Peoples have often been implicated within the upheavals and migrations of populations in the eastern Mediterranean and Near East at the close of the LBA and start of the Iron Age, and their identification has heavily tempered the study of burials from Sa'idiyeh and other South Levantine sites (*e.g.* Dothan 1982; Braunstein 1998; Bloch-Smith 1992; Gonen 1992; Gilmour 1995; 2002).

Ethnic interpretations for Sa'idiyeh primarily focus upon the Period 1 cemetery (LB IIB–Iron IA). Although there is high potential for diversity within populations, and changes in population over time, it is difficult to pinpoint specific cultural or ethnic identities of the Sa'idiyeh cemetery users. The LBA was a cosmopolitan period, with the transmission, transformation, and modification of ideas and material culture over large distances, making the identification of specific ethnic groups difficult and obscure. Fredrick Barth (1969) and Siân Jones (1997) highlight problems in directly linking specific traits (including material culture) with ethnic identity, highlighting the complexity and multi-levelled nature of ethnicity. This can also be applied to burial evidence: there can be no direct one-to-one correlation between ethnic groups and specific burial types, grave-objects or ritual actions.

The role of Egyptian material culture in the South Levant highlights a general problem with interpreting ethnicity and cultural influences using burial data. As Susan Braunstein (1998, 311–15) found in her study of the Tell el-Far'ah South cemetery, it can be difficult to distinguish materially between burials of 'Canaanized Egyptians' or 'Egyptianized Canaanites'. Nevertheless, aspects of the Sa'idiyeh cemetery shed light upon the relationships between local and Egyptian traditions. Locally produced Egyptian-style pottery found in the cemetery includes handleless jars, 'beer bottles' and shallow bowls, occasionally found in large quantities (*e.g.* T.102). According to Mario Martin (2004), this combination is a feature of sites associated with Egyptian control and administration in Canaan. Other aspects of Egyptian-style material culture can be viewed as prestige-related objects, including bronze vessels, ornaments, ivory objects and stone vessels. These are objects potentially linked to status-enhancing emulative strategies, and not necessarily to a direct Egyptian presence (Higginbotham 2000).

Body treatments at Sa'idiyeh suggest intriguing Egyptian influences in death. The so-called 'bitumen tombs' at Sa'idiyeh (T.102 and T.117) show that elaborate rituals took place involving the pouring of heated bitumen over human remains wrapped within textiles perhaps representing 'attempted mummification' (Pritchard 1968, 108; 1980, 15, 20–1; Gonen 1992, 89). It is impossible to say whether those involved in the preparation of the dead intended to replicate Egyptian mummification techniques, or the degree to which they were following Egyptian cosmological concepts. A possible explanation is that Egyptian body preparation rites were actively manipulated and transformed, perhaps an idiosyncratic and emulative adaptation of Egyptian death rituals within a local setting. Other burials exhibit common features such as tight binding of the body and containment of objects within linen shrouds (preserved through mineralised textiles on bronzes), which can also be viewed as a 'partial transfer' or a local modification of Egyptian death rituals (Gonen 1992, 30–1; Tubb 1995, 141).

Other foreign populations implicated in publications to date include Aegean or 'Sea Peoples' groups. Pritchard initially proposed that Sea Peoples were present at Sa'idiyeh (Pritchard 1968) using as an example the T.101 assemblage, which included multiple bronze vessels and a tripod stand

(Pritchard 1980, 10–14, figs. 3–4). Pritchard's interpretation was based partly upon the bronze vessels, paralleled with Hector Catling's (1964) study of Aegean and Cypriote bronzes. These vessels are characterised as 'Levanto-Cypriote' by Ora Negbi (1998, 194). Further material parallels were sought with the nearby Beth Shan cemetery that contained 'grotesque' anthropoid coffins. This appeared to strengthen the argument that these coffins represent the burials of Sea Peoples mercenaries (Oren 1973; Dothan 1982; McGovern 1994), amongst other groups. A link between Sea Peoples and the Jordan Valley was further reinforced by the Biblical reference (I Kings 7:46) to already-established bronze working traditions within the region (Pritchard 1968; Tubb 1988b; 1995). This interpretation may partly depend on the premise that the Philistines and other Sea Peoples groups had a monopoly on metal-working in Iron I (Muhly 1982).

However, Aegean and Cypriote material culture influences at Sa'idiyeh provide insubstantial support for the notion of Sea Peoples settlement as far inland as the Jordan Valley, as subtle material culture features may relate to interaction and trade between coastal Levantine centres and the Northern central valleys during LB IIB–Iron I. For example, the popularity of imitation sack-shaped pyxides at Sa'idiyeh derives from Aegean prototypes; local imitations are already present from the late thirteenth century (Amiran 1969, 186), prior to the posited twelfth century migrations to Southern Levantine coastal regions by Sea Peoples (Dothan and Dothan 1992; Stager 1995).

The double-pithos burial at Sa'idiyeh has been incorporated into many migration and ethnicity-based theories. Interpretations include Sea Peoples from the Aegean sphere (Tubb 1988b; 1995), Anatolians or Hittites (Kempinski 1979; Negbi 1991; Gonen 1992, 30; Negbi 1998; Holladay 2001; Gilmour 2002, 117–18), transhumant migrants from the Transjordan plateau (van der Steen 1996, 68), and Egyptian emissaries (Wengrow 1996, 319). These conflicting interpretations are problematic, and are unresolved. Grave-objects associated with double-pithos burials at Sa'idiyeh include a mixture of local ceramic forms and Egyptian-style prestige goods including ivory objects and metal tools. The objects do not provide a clear indication of ethnic identity, but rather demonstrate the relative status of the double-pithos users within the cemetery, and a potential for Egyptian emulation.

The relatively sudden appearance of the double-pithos burial in northern Israel, Palestine and Transjordan in Iron I (Wolff 2005), and apparently not during the preceding LB IIB period, still requires explanation. Migration theories cannot be ruled out. None of the above authors have cited the Middle Assyrian cemetery at Mari (Tell Hariri) on the River Euphrates, dated to *c.* 1350–1200 BCE, and initially uncovered by André Parrot in the 1930's (Jean-Marie 1999, 42–61). Double-pithos burials are more common at Mari than any other Near Eastern site for this period,

some containing rich finds from north Syrian and Egyptian spheres. This reflects the cosmopolitan nature of Mari on a major crossroads of trade and communication, but it remains difficult to pinpoint an origin for this burial type, or a specific ethnicity for its users. The Mari evidence shows that the double pithos burial is found in regions other than central Anatolia in the LBA, and that migration theories will need to be revised to incorporate Syro-Mesopotamian regions. Possibly some groups settled in northern Palestine and Transjordan in Iron I after the fragmentation of regional exchange networks in northern Mesopotamia, Syria and Anatolia.

The double-pithos burial may be a special case, although as illustrated by the elite-emulation model the expression of social identity at the ethnic level need not be expressed (or detected) materially. Varied 'death-styles' and forms of ritual elaboration may actually mask the expression of ethnic identity. A disproportionate focus on ethnicity therefore needs to be balanced with an overview of other dimensions of social status – including age, gender and vertical status. By examining changes over time in the cemetery we may get closer to identifying patterns independent of ambiguous culture-historical determinations.

Late Bronze Age prosperity and status expression

The relative prosperity of the Period 1 (LB IIB–Iron IA) cemetery is clear from the diversity of types and materials deposited in the burials (*c.* 74 individually numbered tombs). For example, several of the burials excavated by Pritchard (1980 *e.g.* T.102, T.117, T.136B) exhibit a high degree of wealth and diversity, indicated by quantities of bronze vessels, imported or imitation Aegean pottery, ivory items, faience and stone vessels and precious metals. A number of British Museum tombs also contain highly valued items, including from T.232, a bronze bowl and ivory fish box (Tubb 1988a, fig. 47), and from T.46, large quantities of ceramics, bronze items, and an elaborate bead necklace (Tubb 1988a, fig. 46A–B). This sample demonstrates access to a diverse range of types and materials by the Sa'idiyeh inhabitants and their ability and desire to display and dispose of them with the deceased during funerary rituals.

In terms of burial types and spatial organisation, the Period 1 cemetery is characterised by rows and clusters of simple pit graves, with a smaller number of double-pithos burials, stone-lined cists and infant jar burials. Most tombs contain individual, primary interments; a common LBA lowland tradition (Gonen 1992). The practice of individual inhumation partly explains the spacious and regular cemetery layout in this period, noted in BB100–600. Almost all individuals in the BB100–600 area are fully extended and orientated with their heads to the west, often aligned side-by-side in distinct northwest–southeast rows, attesting to a degree of planning

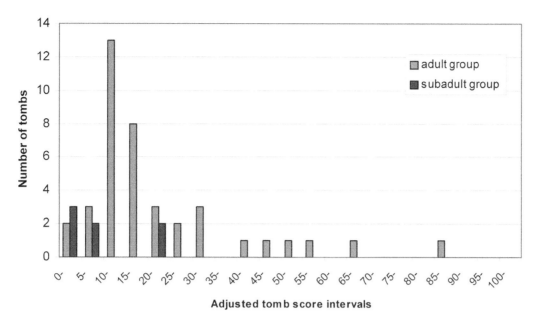

Fig. 10.4: Grave-score distribution for Period 1 tombs

in the selection, maintenance, and control of burial space over time. The presence of small segmented clusters within the rows could indicate a smaller dimension of cemetery organisation, perhaps interrelated kin-groups.

There are also potential chronological differences between the North and Central areas. Pritchard's 'earliest' burials from the North area are assigned to the late thirteenth–early twelfth centuries (Pritchard 1980, 28–29; *e.g.* T.117, fig. 21), containing imported Aegean and Cypriote pottery. The central BB100–600 area overlaps chronologically with Pritchard's (1980, 289) 'intermediate' period tombs, due to the apparent substitution of imported stirrup jars for 'local' LH IIIB imitations in the early twelfth century (Tubb 1988a, T.46, fig. 48A.14). This could indicate a change in cemetery use with the most elaborate and prestigious tombs marking the cemetery 'foundation' in the North area, followed by a gradual shift southwards over time.

A detailed analysis of the better preserved tomb assemblages (Period 1, N=64) utilises a relative scoring system derived from a co-occurrence analysis of object types and materials, in turn producing scores for individual tombs (*e.g.* Jørgensen 1987; Baboula 2000). The sample was further sub-divided into individual adult and sub-adult samples, reducing the respective sample sizes slightly (Fig. 10.4). This method allows particular objects and materials and other features to be singled out as 'rank markers' (*i.e.* highly-valued, or prestige objects) if correlated with high-scoring tombs.

This scoring method, developed from processual approaches to mortuary archaeology, does not attempt to directly link the relative wealth of the deceased with those of living individuals or living society. Status may be masked, inverted, or over-exaggerated in death (Shanks and Tilley 1987; Morris 1992; Rega 1996; Härke 1997). A more explicit intention is to explore differentiations in tomb scores as a representation of relative material investment in the burial ceremony. Distinctions in material investment are considered to represent the wealth and status of the funeral organizers (Härke 1997; cited in Parker Pearson 1999, 84), who inadvertently contribute to the formation of an 'ideal' social structure through death and burial ceremonies (Morris 1992).

The Period 1 grave-scores are hierarchical in structure, with a small number of high scoring tombs (Fig. 4: 40+ points, 8% of Period 1 sample), and a majority belonging to low to medium scoring tombs. High scoring tombs share common attributes. They are furnished with large quantities of Egyptian-style material culture of both a prestige and utilitarian nature, including shallow ceramic bowls and multiple bronze vessels (*i.e.* wine-sets), which are either symbols or actual manifestations of food and drink provision at the funeral. Other rare items include precious metal jewellery, Egyptian-style lotus-seed vessel pendants, and scarab rings.

Imported wares or local imitations are also present, including stirrup jars, pyxides and juglets (often in multiples), and Egyptian-style stone vessels. Such items are generally thought to have contained precious oils or unguents. The most common interpretation of their contents is that they were used to perfume or clean the body (Cook 1981; Shelmerdine 1985, 141–3; Clamer 1986; Sparks 2001, 259). Although it is commonly thought that stirrup jars contained perfumed oils for use in association with the body or clothing, some may have contained wine or flavoured oils for use in cooking or dining (Leonard *et al.* 1993, 105). Cypriote Base Ring juglets may have contained opiate-based products (Merrillees 1962). Until chemical analysis can be carried out on specific vessels, a wide range of contents should therefore be considered.

Another feature of this group is unusual body treatment; including the use of bitumen, or face-down body placement (Fig. 3: T.46). There is also a correlation between tomb elaboration and high scoring tomb assemblages, with the use of larger pits, and stone or mudbrick linings. A greater provision of space around the body within the tombs is evidence of intentionality and the structured orchestration of ritual ceremonies at the place of burial. Deliberate above-ground marking is unclear due to erosion and subsequent tomb-intercutting.

These high-scoring tombs are the closest we can get to a picture of elite burial rituals at Sa'idiyeh, showing that status expression in death was highly individualized, focused on the body, and communicated through repetitive acts involving the deposition of precious oils and symbolic food and drink offerings. A combination of elaborate exotica, repeated deposition of similar items (perhaps indicating multiple ritual participants), multiple serving vessels for food and drink, and elaborate body ornamentation and treatment, contributes to an overall impression of wealth, access to highly valued objects, and innovative rituals. In the context of death and burial, such ritualised provisions and actions might in turn enable the living to acquire a certain level of prestige, contingent upon the interpretation that funerals can be used as arenas for the creation of status, power and legitimacy by the survivors (Voutsaki 1997, 37). Furthermore, the presence of Egyptianizing material and body preparations, suggests a close relationship between elites and the Egyptian administration, reflecting the combined role of direct contacts and emulative strategies within lowland Canaan (Higginbotham 2000).

Mid-scoring tombs (10–40 points, *c.* 50% of the sample) are fairly well represented. Many tombs contain between two and three items that are considered 'highly-valued', such as a single bronze vessel, weapon or tool, an ivory object, a stone vessel, in addition to a small number of vessels representing a typical 'universal' ceramic assemblage (*e.g.* storage jar, lamp, bowl, jug or juglet). A large proportion of cemetery users had access to a few highly-valued items, especially metals, precious oil containers, and other items of specialised craft production. Low ranking groups with just a few ceramic items are under-represented in the sample. This does not appear to fit with hierarchical models, where we might expect a greater proportion of 'have-nots' compared to 'haves' in the cemetery.

At first glance, this could suggest that the cemetery population represents an incomplete social spectrum – *i.e.* those buried by poorer sectors of the population were not given as much access to the cemetery. Just as the cemetery is unlikely to represent a complete demographic population (Leach and Rega 1996, 134), neither should it be expected to represent all social groups or classes. Alternatively, the analysis could suggest that not only elites had access to luxury goods. Perhaps an emergent and fairly affluent middle-status group actively emulated the ritual practices of higher elites through smaller-scale acts of consumption and deposition, participating within elite value systems through the deposition of such items. Such a 'trickle down' effect may on the one hand stabilize and support an inner-elite structure (perhaps through largesse). Conversely such an effect may subvert and transform relationships between lesser and higher elites (Barth 1969, 33; Peregrine 1999).

Twelfth century decline and collapse

The Period 1 cemetery provides an apparent picture of prosperity and wealth in the central Jordan Valley at the close of LB IIB and the start of Iron I. This partly fits Piotr Bienkowski's (1989) interpretation that wealth was concentrated at lowland urban centres and trade routes associated with Egyptian administration and control. This LB IIB–Iron IA regional prosperity model may also fit the posited role of Sa'idiyeh as a frontier garrison or trading outpost associated with Egyptian economic and military control (Tubb 1995, 142). However, there should not necessarily be an equation between wealth, prosperity and socio-political stability. Such concentrations of wealth can be contrasted with an impoverished picture of surrounding highland regions. Resistance to the Egyptian system from non-cooperative city states and semi-nomadic tribal entities living on the margins demonstrates the instability and asymmetry of the wider socio-political situation (Redford 1992; Bunimovitz 1995; Higginbotham 2000): not only were there disparities in wealth between lowland centres and the more isolated highland regions (Bienkowski 1989). The more nuanced picture from the Sa'idiyeh cemetery adds to existing interpretations by suggesting that social tensions between elites and non-elites were felt within lowland centres. Furthermore, it has been argued by Bruce Routledge (2004) that high-status elaborations in the use of material culture in ritual settings, in addition to more permanent symbols of power such as temples, palaces, and residencies, helped to maintain a fragile system of rule that was in 'perpetual crisis'. At the same time this reinforced socio-economic distinctions between town rulers *(hazannu)* and the peasantry *(hupšu;* Routledge 2004, 67–71, 76–77).

During the first quarter of the twelfth century, maritime trade routes between the Levant, Cyprus and the Aegean were already in decline and becoming disrupted by migrations, conflict, and destructions of key centres on the Levantine coast and Cyprus (Karageorghis 1992; Redford 1992, 241–56; Yon 1992). Despite these disruptions, the twelfth century in the South Levant had a different trajectory due to a period of military resurgence by Egypt in the 20th Dynasty on its northern frontiers, extending the relative political, cultural and economic stability of the region well into the twelfth century (Weinstein 1981, 22–3; 1992; Bietak 1993, 301; Finkelstein 1998, 141). The finding of a small number of imported Aegean and Cypriote vessels alongside locally made Aegean-style vessels in the Period 1 cemetery at Sa'idiyeh could suggest a continued demand for such locally made versions. Although emulative strategies played a role in the appearance of locally made Aegean-style vessels, a shift towards local production may have intensified as such imported products became increasingly scarce following a decline in Late Bronze Age maritime trade.

Eveline van der Steen (1999) suggests that the mid-twelfth century Egyptian withdrawal had a devastating impact on the local economy of the Jordan Valley, previously geared towards servicing the Egyptian-led system. The withdrawal particularly affected markets in the Deir 'Alla area (close to Sa'idiyeh), and over-dependent Transjordan centres. Stephen Bourke (2006) suggests that parts of Transjordan, including the Pella region, had already entered into a steady but gradual economic decline from the thirteenth century due to the cumulative impact of Egyptian military campaigns. Despite this decline, as Bourke argues, there is settlement continuity in the Pella region throughout Iron I, arguing against an entirely cataclysmic interpretation for the Jordan Valley.

Partly due to a lack of textual sources for the thirteenth to twelfth centuries (such as equivalents to the El-Amarna letters), a question remains as to whether there was direct Egyptian involvement in the central Jordan Valley, or semi-autonomous political control (Savage and Falconer 2003, fig. 4, clusters 6 and 13). Regardless of whether an Egyptian withdrawal hastened a gradual decline, or caused a sudden collapse, combined disruptions and limited military support would have resulted in greater insecurity along trade routes. Prior to their decline, the inland trade routes were an important conduit through which local elites obtained luxuries and exotica through direct or indirect contacts with the Egyptian sphere, perhaps enhancing status and political power through elite emulation. If conduits of trade and their administration were disrupted, this may have led to a legitimization crisis (Peregrine 1999) and a breakdown of an already fragile social order. As Egyptian power waned from the mid-12th century BCE, semi-nomadic groups previously on the margins and listed as enemies of Egypt, including the Hapiru, Shasu, and Israel (Redford 1992), and non-cooperative Canaanite states, were able to take fuller advantage of a fragmented political landscape. Within such a scenario, a frontier trading outpost such as Sa'idiyeh would have become highly vulnerable and potentially unserviceable, prompting an end to this period of relative prosperity.

Communality and egalitarianism in the Early Iron Age

A specific end date for the Period 1/Phase 1 cemetery remains unclear. At some point in late Iron I, numerous mudbrick lined cist tombs were constructed, marking the start of cemetery Phase 2. The stratigraphic sequence is clearest in squares BB100–200, where cists were found immediately overlaying Phase 1 pit graves (*e.g.* T.232 under T.41; Tubb 1988a, 64; 1990, 106–7). A series of cists (T.32, T.24, and T.42) were laid out on a west-east 'head-to-toe' alignment differing from the side-by-side pit graves in Phase 1. The Phase 2 tomb builders apparently took care not to disturb the underlying burial deposits, perhaps indicating population continuity over time, or at least a degree of respect and awareness for the earlier burials.

In material culture terms, there are several important developments. Phase 2 mudbrick-lined tombs contain new ceramic types, including the 'ridge-necked' jar with Iron IB–IIA parallels at Deir 'Alla and Beth Shan (James 1966, fig. 64.10; Franken 1969, fig. 62.30), and red slipped and hand-burnished sack-shaped pyxides and long-necked juglets (*e.g.* James 1966, fig. 61.5; Franken 1969, fig. 70:50, 51). Egyptian-style stamp-seal amulets (*e.g.* T.118, T.33, T.65) include those assigned to the 21st–22nd Dynasties (Münger 2003, 75; Eggler and Keel 2006, 372–375, nos.13–18). 'Hippo-jars' are often used as infant burial containers, differing slightly from the less baggy 'ridge-necked' jar (Alexandre 1995). A small number of black-burnished juglets and pyxides are clearly assigned to Iron II traditions (Amiran 1969, 256–7, pl. 86.12–13, pl.96).

A key finding is a decline in the quantity of grave-objects, from between five to six objects per individual in Period 1, to an average of one or two objects in Period 2. Another feature is the relative decline in the diversity of types and materials within tomb assemblages, often limited to a single juglet or pyxis, or a few bronze or iron body ornaments and beads. Bronze vessels, and metal tools and weapons have a more restricted distribution, and ivory and gold are absent. Imported precious-liquid containers such as stirrup-jars and Egyptian-style stone cosmetic containers are substituted by ceramic juglets, pyxides and local style stone-vessels. This reduction in high-value materials and imports could be partly attributed to a decline in long-distance trade networks and also a change in the local specialised craft production in late Iron I. If considering burial contents to be a general indication of the relative affluence of living society, the pattern indicates general poverty at least in material terms. This mirrors the view from nearby Tell Abu Kharaz, where a general concern with basic survival is interpreted from the EIA settlement remains (Fischer 2001, 307).

In total, 135 tombs are assigned to Period 2, of which 76 are of adequate preservation for analysis. Tomb-score distributions are lower on average (compared to Period 1)

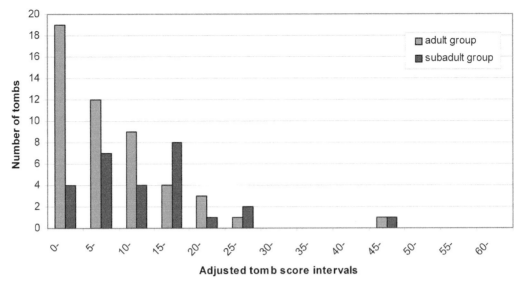

Fig. 10.5: Grave-score distribution for Period 2 tombs

and more evenly distributed across the sample (Fig. 10.5). The highest scoring tomb (T.282: 45+ points) contains up to eleven individuals, equivalent to less than one object per individual, and demonstrating the accumulation of objects after successive reuse. More limited tomb score differentiations could indicate a more egalitarian social structure with fewer vertical social distinctions being expressed in death.

Single inhumations continue, although multiple-interment becomes a common feature. Cists such as T.282 (Fig. 10.6) contain multiple interments of males, females, adults and sub-adults suggesting that 'family' tombs were now being maintained and re-used in Phase 2. This marks a change from the Phase 1 pattern of single interments within clusters or rows. Secondary treatment becomes common, with body parts such as the skull and long-bones being re-interred alongside primary burials, or within separate installations (Tubb 1988a, 61–63, fig. 44). This suggests that attitudes to death and the body were changing, with a greater emphasis on kinship relations, and a focus on elaborate death rituals involving commemorative and communal activities – including the manipulation of decayed remains after death.

An intriguing feature of Period 2 is a drastic reduction in ceramic bowls and lamps, which were common in Period 1 (in approximately 50% of tombs). Why should such a significant component of the burial assemblage no longer be emphasized? A possible explanation is an ideological change affecting the range of funerary rituals enacted. John Ribar (1973, 80–2) posits that social prohibitions in the provision of symbolic food offerings for the dead, due to the apparent reduction in ceramic bowls within mortuary contexts, may have been due to a rejection of Canaanite ideology, and 'feeding the dead'. Alternatively, there may

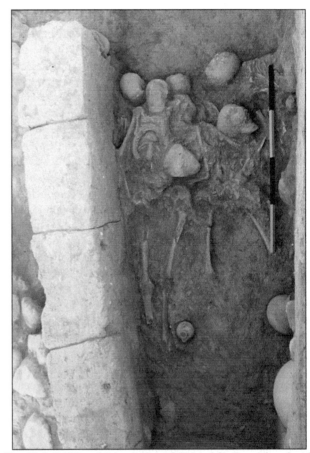

Fig. 10.6: T.282 multiple cist burial (Period 2). Reproduced with the permission of Jonathan Tubb

have been a shift in ritual arenas where food and drink is presented and consumed, *i.e.* away from the place of burial. However, it is noted that both animal offerings and bronze bowls continue in Period 2 tombs, arguing against this food prohibition theory. More convincing explanations are sought from excavations at Wadi Fidan 40 in Southern Jordan, where EIA burials contain wooden bowls and pomegranates (Levy *et al.* 1999, 299–302). Organic remains are preserved at Fidan 40 due to the arid conditions of the Faynan district (only carbonized or mineralized organics would survive at Sa'idiyeh). Thomas Levy *et al.* (2004, 86–7) argue that ceramic bowls and lamps are less likely to be carried over long distances by nomadic groups, and therefore 'unbreakable' metal and wooden vessels are more commonly used. An absence of ceramic serving vessels at Sa'idiyeh could be partly explained by a shift towards wood or reed vessels.

The absence of ceramic bowls and lamps from tombs could indirectly suggest that some of the cemetery users were expressing a semi-nomadic lifestyle in death. This might fit with interpretations of changing settlement patterns and the re-sedentarization of semi-nomadic groups in the Jordan Valley during Iron I (van der Steen 1999). For example, the ephemeral pits, postholes, and furnaces at Iron IA Deir 'Alla are seen as evidence for seasonal activities of nomadic groups after the destruction of the LBA settlement (van der Kooij and Ibrahim 1989, 80–1). Mixed groups including displaced farmers, traders, craftsmen, and semi-nomadic groups (including 'early Israelites') may have coalesced within new settlements in the Jordan Valley during Iron I (van der Steen 1999). There does appear to be some continuity of burial populations at Sa'idiyeh, due to the implied awareness of the Period 1 cemetery users. However, a shift towards communality, reduced status expressions in death, and an ideological shift in social practices and attitudes to death could suggest a partial change in population as well as social structure during Iron I.

Early Iron Age status and gender distinctions

The apparent decline in material expressions of status in Period 2, may indicate a generally poorer society, although the potential for maintaining wealth through valued items above-ground should not be overlooked. There are some (albeit limited) manifestations of high-status in Period 2. These may include the widespread use of mudbrick lined tombs for single and multiple burials, and bronze bowls and wine-sets. For example, the T.32 wine-set includes a bronze dish with an incised cable-band and rosette net medallion (Tubb 1988a, figs. 49–50), resembling Cypro-Phoenician bowls from Iron Age Cyprus and Italy (Markoe 1985, 232 [type Ca1], 242–3 [Type Cy1]). This could suggest that the bowl was an import from the Phoenician coastal sphere (although survival from LBA traditions cannot be ruled out).

Iron knives also appear occasionally in Period 2. The adoption of iron as a prestige material (especially iron knives) increases during the twelfth–eleventh centuries in Cyprus and the Levant, prior to its more common and widespread usage in Iron II (Waldbaum 1978; Sherratt 1994a). Another indication that iron was regarded as having a greater prestige-value at Sa'idiyeh is supported by a significant increase in the wearing of ornamental iron by sub-adults (especially bracelets). An amuletic or apotropaic role of iron ornaments is also possible given their strong association with sub-adults.

A concurrent feature of the Period 2 shift to less diverse tomb assemblages is the decline of individualized elite burial traditions of Period 1. The disappearance of the traditional elite is one of the expectations noted in a cross-cultural study of collapse in early state societies by Colin Renfrew (1979, 482 ff.; cited by van der Steen 1999, 185), which could be potentially applied to this period in the Jordan Valley. Period 1 elites may have been absorbed into the local population after the Egyptian withdrawal and Iron IA decline, and were no longer able to, or compelled to, express high status death-styles in such diverse and innovative ways. Another possibility is that elites no longer chose to use the cemetery as a focus for their elaborate rituals, perhaps using alternative burial locations, or utilising burial methods that are no longer preserved or detected archaeologically.

Alternatively, destabilised elites may have physically abandoned the site (and the Jordan Valley), at the time of Egyptian withdrawal. Which social groups might be continuing to use the cemetery after this time? A number of ritual features common to the Period 1 low- and mid-scoring groups include the bending or breaking of weapons and tools, and occasional depositions of bronze bowls, are also found in Period 2, suggesting local continuity in ritual practices. This could indicate that some Period 1 non-elites continued to use the cemetery in Period 2, filling a power vacuum left by the departed traditional LBA elites. This resulted in the transformation and modification of somewhat muted and associative high-status practices within a new socio-political setting.

Changes in the nature of animal offerings are also implicated in this new setting. Priscilla Lange's (in preparation) analysis of faunal remains demonstrates the deliberate selection of specific species and age-sets. In Period 1, most depositions consist of discrete butchered animal parts such as the forelimb of a young sheep or goat (lamb or kid; (*e.g.* T.204), fish (T.232), and a collared dove (T.204), usually found in the grave-fill immediately overlaying the upper body. This is tentatively identified as a 'closure ceremony', a ritual stage occurring after the deposition of the body and associated objects (see Aubet 2003, 61–3 for examples at Tyre al-Bass). This practice is also apparent at LBA coastal cemeteries at Palmaḥim and Tell Abu Hawam (Gonen 1992, 86, 92). In Period 2, continuity in forelimb depositions is accompanied by a marked change within some of the mudbrick cists, where the whole carcasses of sheep, goat, and young cattle are deposited (*e.g.* T.32, T.34, and T.41). These are frequently larger than lambs or kids, some nearing adult maturity. This is a notable change from Period 1 'closure ceremonies', with these substantial meat offerings in close bodily association. This suggests that the deposition of meat and related feasting rituals became more important at EIA funerals. The removal of specific meat cuts at Sa'idiyeh also indicates a range of 'above-ground' ritual activities, perhaps involving communal feasting by mourners during the funeral.

Gender distinctions are marked in Period 2, and may also be divided along status lines. In the Period 1 cemetery, prestige-objects are found with both males and females, with some of the highest scoring assemblages belonging to female interments (*e.g.* T.46). The gender dichotomy in Period 2 is indicated by the finding of several females (but no males) with bronze body ornaments and beads (*e.g.* T.92, T.123A, and T.218A). A greater degree of ornamentation of both women and children could also be significant in terms of 'wearing wealth' in both life and death (Green 2007). Also in Period 2, animal offerings, iron knives and/or bronze vessels are found within a small group of tombs containing adult male interments (*e.g.* T.32, T.34, and T.41/97), suggesting that feasting and elaborate food and drink depositions were restricted to relatively high-status males. This may fit with Avraham Faust's (2002) interpretation that gender divisions became heightened in the period leading up to Iron IIA, as public feasting ceremonies were confined to males, with women's roles becoming more narrowly focused within domestic settings. If, as Justin Lev-Tov and Edward Maher (2001, 106) suggest, animal offerings in tombs served as 'an economic rite of inheritance', such rituals may have reinforced patrimonial lineages.

Summary

The Sa'idiyeh cemetery provides an opportunity to examine subtle and marked changes in the negotiation of status, cultural identity, and gender in death across the Late Bronze-Iron Age transition. At the close of the LBA, the Sa'idiyeh population was closely integrated with the Egyptian economic, cultural and political sphere. This was a fairly prosperous and cosmopolitan society with access to a range of high value material objects including imports and valuable metal items. Their death-styles were innovative and individualistic, indicative of a syncretised Egyptian and Canaanite cultural *koiné*. This system was dependent upon links with the Egyptian sphere, and unstable partnerships between local elites and Egyptian emissaries and governors. It was a system inherently prone to collapse in the period leading up to, and as a consequence of, the

twelfth century Egyptian withdrawal. With the destruction of major coastal and inland urban centres and trade-routes disrupted, Sa'idiyeh's role changed irreversibly as the region became more isolated in terms of long-distance contacts. Future reassessment may shed further light on the Upper Tell sequence and its relation to the cemetery during this transitional period.

In late Iron I a different community was settled at Sa'idiyeh, perhaps including descendants of the local population, increasingly sedentary semi-nomadic groups and migrants from neighbouring regions. The emergent economic and political structure was now the coastal region of Northern Palestine and the Central Valley urban centres, including revived Canaanite polities such as Megiddo (Harrison 2004). This phenomenon is labelled by Israel Finkelstein (2002) 'New Canaan' due to the increase in the numbers and sizes of settlements re-emerging after the LBA collapse. Other socio-political entities were forming: Israel in the Samarian Highlands, Philistia in the southwest coastal plain, and Phoenicia in the Northern coastal plain. Zvi Gal (1995) posits that as Israelites expanded and occupied both sides of the Jordan Valley, Phoenicia became the dominant political and economic entity influencing lowland regions, including the North Jordan Valley. This may be reflected in features at Sa'idiyeh including 'hippo' jars, spheroid flasks, and the T.32 bronze platter. Sa'idiyeh was slowly re-integrated within trade networks, testifying to the ability of lowland settlements to return after collapse.

EIA death-styles reinforced kinship relations, with multiple family interments and rituals aimed at commemoration through secondary burial treatments and increased handling of the dead. Communal burial reinforced an ideology of kinship in death. In the absence of traditional LBA elites, modified forms of status expression developed, some looking back to the LBA (wine-sets and mudbrick cists) and others focusing on new forms of prestige and personal display (iron knives and an increased focus on animal offerings). A reduced emphasis on displays of quantity and luxury goods suggests an idealised representation of an egalitarian society in death (Faust 2004), despite the emergence of new status and gender inequalities.

In summary, there is continuity and change at Sa'idiyeh, both in the period of the LBA decline, and the subsequent EIA revival. Social identities and status distinctions were actively constructed and transformed through death-rituals in both periods. This demonstrates the way in which societies are able to respond to and survive major upheavals – reinventing themselves by blending old traditions with new ones, and dynamically reordering social relations within ritual arenas and communal activities. These developments are not only related to external factors such as migrations and settlement destructions, but also to internal societal transformations and the creation of new identities.

Acknowledgements

Special thanks to Jonathan Tubb (The British Museum) for permission to access the material and records from Saʻidiyeh, and for his continued support in bringing my research to fruition. My PhD research on the Saʻidiyeh cemetery was supported by the Arts and Humanities Research Board (now AHRC). Continued work on the final report for the Saʻidiyeh cemetery at the British Museum (Department of the Middle East) is supported by the White-Levy Program for Archaeological Publication and the Seven Pillars of Wisdom Trust.

THE SOUTH-EASTERN AEGEAN IN THE LH IIIC PERIOD: WHAT DO THE TOMBS TELL US?

Mercourios Georgiadis

The south-eastern Aegean is a region that has been either overlooked or overemphasized by different scholars. On the one hand it is frequently considered, at best, to be a mere Mycenaean province or periphery either to the Argolid (Voutsaki 1993, 166–8; Mee 1998, 143; Karantzali 2001, 79–80; Voutsaki 2001, 210–11; Hope Simpson 2003, 236–7) or to Thebes (Niemeier 2002, 20). On the other it is treated *a priori* as a unified polity, important enough to be the kingdom of Ahhiyawa attested in Hittite records (Page 1959, 15–16; Desborough 1964, 219; Boysal 1967, 55–6; Vermeule 1972, 272; Gates 1995, 296; Benzi 1996, 967; Mountjoy 1998, 50–1; Sherratt 2001, 217–8, n. 9). For the purposes of this paper the south-eastern Aegean is a term used to define a geographic region that contains what today is the Dodecanese, Samos, Ikaria, and the Anatolian coast separated from the interior by high mountains (Georgiadis 2003, 1). The importance of this region is its strategic location: it is at the edge of the greater Aegean, very close to Crete, Anatolia and the Cyclades. It is also the gateway to the Aegean for any movement to, and from, the eastern Mediterranean. Rhodes, for example, is almost equidistant from both mainland Greece and Cyprus.

Among of the main sources of evidence for the mature Mycenaean period in this area are its numerous cemeteries. In this paper I will address some of the mortuary evidence and assess it to investigate socio-political developments in the south-eastern Aegean, up to and including the LH IIIC period. The cemeteries, I suggest, can shed light on the degree of change and continuity in the 12th century BCE, the character of exchanges and contacts, and whether or not any migration theories can be applied to the region. This will in turn lead to a consideration of the hypothesis of Greek colonisation on 12th century Cyprus.

The character of the Mycenaean culture in the south-eastern Aegean from LH IIB to IIIB

The proximity of the south-eastern Aegean to Crete meant that Cretan cultural influence came into the area from the Middle Bronze Age (MBA), and reached its highpoint early in the Late Bronze Age (LBA). Similarities between these areas are clear, both in architecture and in items of everyday use such as pottery. This is particularly evident from an LB I cemetery that was recently discovered at Trianda on Rhodes (for any site that lies in the south-eastern Aegean and is referred to in this paper, see Fig. 11.1; for the wider Aegean, see Fig. 11.2), which is set in an area that lay on the coast at that time (Marketou 1988, 615–25; 1991, 482). Nonetheless, from LH II increasing quantities of Mycenaean pottery reached Trianda, and in LH IIB the old burial location was abandoned and new burial clusters appeared at Makra Vounara and Moschou Vounara, hills in an inland region often referred as Ialysos (Morricone 1972/3, 392–4; Mee 1982, 81–2; Papazoglou-Manioudaki 1982, 184).

The relocation of the cemetery probably reflects an attempt by the inhabitants of Trianda to differentiate their burial practice from that of the past, and to create a new tradition and identity. From the LH IIB onwards there was a gradual but relatively rapid adoption of the new burial tradition; the introduction of the multiple-burials within chamber tombs, along with all the rituals associated with this burial type, occurred across the south-eastern Aegean reached its height in LH IIIA2. In this period there were at least 46 active cemeteries with numerous tombs, containing far more burial offerings that were of a higher quality than previously attested. Already a regional tradition had formed, primarily with the use of chamber tombs of the standard type but of smaller size than those on the mainland. At the same time local variations and preferences appeared in the

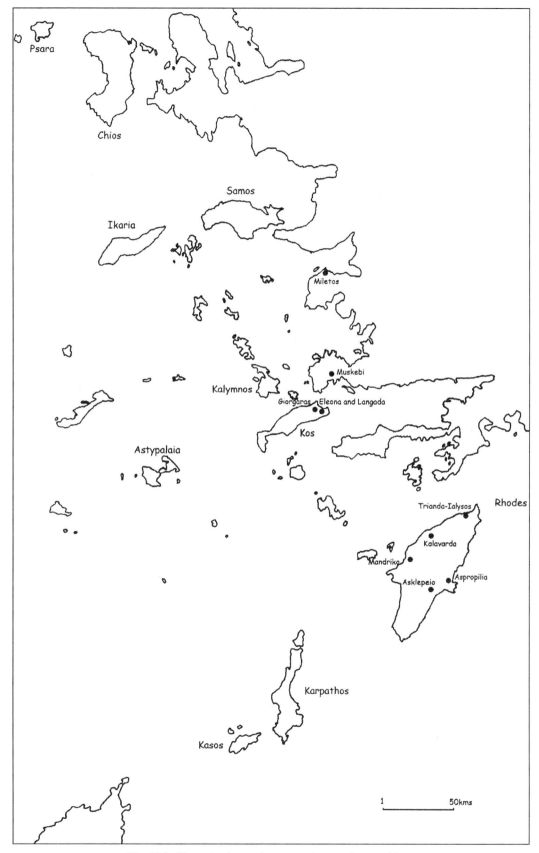

Fig. 11.1: Places in the south-eastern Aegean discussed in text

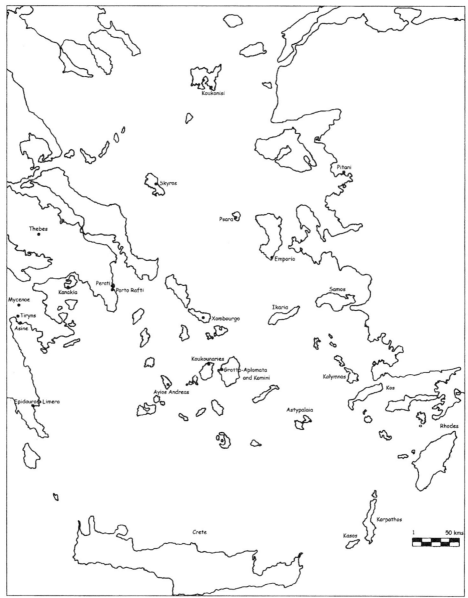

Fig. 11.2: Places in the Aegean discussed in text

south-eastern Aegean. For example the construction of tholos tombs is attested so far only on Kos, close to the main town of the island (Skerlou 1996, 690; 1997, 1,110–1; Georgiadis 2003, 40), whilst the existence of tombs with a side chamber is found only in three cemeteries, close to each other, in southern Rhodes (Passia, Apsaktiras, and Aspropilia; Dietz 1984, 36, 37; Karantzali 2001, 16; Georgiadis 2003, 72–3). The only instances of chamber tombs with an antechamber are at Ialysos, T.19, T.24 and T.43 (Georgiadis 2003, 70). Probably the most notable idiosyncrasy in the south-east is the tendency in each cemetery for all tombs to have more or less the same orientation (Georgiadis 2003, 46–8). This trend is not associated with a common orientation of all tombs to

the east, as seems to be the case in the contemporary Cretan cemeteries (Blomberg and Henriksson 2001, 78, fig. 6.6), but with a symbolic view/use of the landscape oriented towards streams and plains. The relation between the Mycenaean cemeteries and the landscape is believed to be associated with afterlife beliefs and the importance of the ancestors in the Mycenaean belief system (Georgiadis 2003, 108; Gallou 2005, 74–5; Gallou and Georgiadis in press). In other words, the focus of the cemeteries is towards the fertile parts of the landscape and the deceased/ancestors were probably thought of exercising powers of protection and regeneration over the land. The importance of the ancestors in the south-eastern Aegean is emphasised by various other burial practices.

Closely related to this observation is the preference for the practice of the secondary treatment of the deceased across this region. This custom is common in mainland Greece as William Cavanagh (1978, 171–2; Cavanagh and Mee 1998, 76) has suggested, and in the south-eastern Aegean this practice represents more than half of the burials (Georgiadis 2003, 85). Ialysos is the only site where the practice is not as marked as in the other cemeteries. The prevailing practice in this cemetery was to retain the primary burial, with the deceased placed in an extended position with the head close to the *stomion*. It is also interesting to note that the open vessels seem to be especially popular in contrast to the finds from most cemetery sites in mainland Greece. Although this trend underlines either symbolically or physically the role of communal drinking as part of the burial ritual we cannot define in which part of the ritual this was meaningful. Still, it appears to be closely associated with the secondary treatment and possibly with the deceased becoming anonymous, a necessary step to be elevated to the status of ancestor.

In the LH IIIB period there is clear continuity and the funerary practices were not altered in any discernable way. Nevertheless, on Rhodes and Karpathos there was a change in the number of cemeteries and tombs used in comparison to LH IIIA2, as well as in the offerings deposited inside the tombs (Georgiadis 2003, 106). On Rhodes there were 28 active cemeteries in LH IIIA2 with a small decrease to 25 during the LH IIIB period. The decrease between the two phases is more graphically seen in the case of Ialysos, where there is a sharp decrease in the number of tombs used and in the quantity of offerings deposited in them (Georgiadis 2003, 68, fig. 9.2). In the other cemeteries on Rhodes a similar picture can be observed, though there are some notable exceptions. This change may be associated with the decline in contacts with Crete, and/or of trade between mainland Greece and the Near East. Thus, the strategic position of Rhodes and Karpathos on the sea trade routes in the 13th century BCE seems to be not as significant as in the previous era. Nonetheless, imported pottery from the Greek mainland continued to predominate and comprised 90% that found in the Trianda settlement and Ialysos cemetery, as was also the case in LH IIIA2 (Jones and Mee 1978; Jones 1986, 501–8). The recent analyses of pottery from Aspropilia in southern Rhodes confirm this picture, strongly suggesting large numbers of mainland imports for the whole island (Karantzali and Ponting 2000, 235; Ponting and Karantzali 2001, 107). Analysis of sherds from the Serraglio settlement on Kos suggests that the majority were locally made, but some were also imported from the Greek mainland (Jones 1986, 508–9). On Kos, Kalymnos and Astypalaia in the northern part of the south-eastern Aegean, it seems that these islands flourished more than in the previous periods, with more tombs, cemeteries and burial offerings. Thus, it seems that there were different politico-economic developments conditions between these islands and southern part of the

south-eastern Aegean (Rhodes and Karpathos). Already it is clear that there was regional diversity in the south-eastern Aegean during LH IIIB, something that continued in the LH IIIC period.

The LH IIIC period

From the beginning of the 12th century BCE a major change can be seen in the south-eastern Aegean, which seems to differ from the various mainland Mycenaean centres. Overall there is a small decrease of cemeteries, but in most of the active ones both the tombs and the offerings are more numerous than in LH IIIB. This rather distinct increase of tombs and offerings is emphasised in both the largest cemeteries in this region, Ialysos, and Eleona and Langada in Kos town. In particular at Ialysos six times more pots were deposited in the tombs, and more than twice as many at Eleona and Langada. Furthermore, at Ialysos there was a strong tendency to re-use older, LH IIIA, tombs, attested in 16 cases out of the 50 LH IIIC tombs (Cavanagh and Mee 1978, 36–8; Benzi 1982, 325–33; 1992, 225, 227). The same trend can be observed to a lesser extent at Kalavarda (4 tombs) and Passia, and possibly Mandriko and Asklepeio on Rhodes, as well as at Eleona and Langada (in ten tombs out of 50 in LH IIIC), and Giorgaras tholos on Kos (Cavanagh and Mee 1978, 39–40; Benzi 1982, 334–5; 1992, 419; Dietz 1984, 98–9; Georgiadis 2003, 74). There was also a new fashion at Ialysos, where pits inside the chamber tombs appeared in significant numbers. Inside 18 tombs one to three pits were recovered – all, with one exception, in tombs in use or re-used in LH IIIC. A similar practice of cutting pits inside a tomb is also observed at Perati (see Fig. 11.2) in Attica (Iakovidis 1970, 14–5) and Kephallonia (Marinatos 1932, 20–2). Another common element between Ialysos and Perati is the practice of cremation in urns or pits. At Ialysos this is attested in eight or nine tombs, though at Eleona and Langada only one case has been recovered (Iakovidis 1970, 40; Georgiadis 2003, 79, 82). However, it should be noted that sporadic cremations existed in the south-eastern Aegean possibly from as early as the LH IIIA2 period (Georgiadis 2003, 84), a tradition probably coming from the north-western part of Anatolia (Iakovidis 1970, 43–57; Melas 1984, 24–33; 2001, 17). In contrast with the situation at Ialysos, a different impact can be obscured in LH IIIC in the other areas under review. On Karpathos and Samos there was seemingly no cemetery used in this period, and indeed no LH IIIC remains have been recovered anywhere on these two islands, while only a few sherds from this period have been found on Kasos, and only two pots from an unknown site on Ikaria. In the rest of Rhodes there was a small decrease in the number of cemeteries, but in most of them more offerings were deposited. On Kos most of the cemeteries went out of use, but overall more pots were deposited in the tombs of those that were. On Astypalaia and at Müskebi there was a decrease in the number of tombs and offerings, but on Kalymnos and at Miletos more finds from this period have been recovered. The regional diversity in the south-eastern Aegean that was already apparent from the time of the introduction of Mycenaean burial practices is also evident in the LH IIIC.

Despite the fact that most of the changes in this period have been observed at Ialysos, there are also strong elements of purposeful continuity in the local traditions. The orientation of the tombs in the burial clusters remained unaltered in this period, as well the tendency for a greater percentage of primarily burials. Similar signs of continuity can be found in all the cemeteries in the south-eastern Aegean, while the secondary treatment was still dominant.

The cemetery of Aspropilia in southern Rhodes has yielded the only reliable anthropological analyses of the deceased (McGeorge 2001, 82–93). In LH IIIA and B there was a balanced representation of genders in the tombs, something that changed dramatically in LH IIIC when the presence of children was emphasized with seven examples out of the total of ten that were deposited in the cemetery. The focus on child burial could indicate a fear of continuity for the local community (McHugh 1999, 24–6), possibly reflecting a period of wider socio-political unrest in the Aegean and in the eastern Mediterranean.

In order to assess the exchanges and the contacts of this period it is important to understand the pottery tradition of the south-eastern Aegean. In contrast to LH IIIA and B when the majority of the pottery at Ialysos was imported from the mainland or followed mainland prototypes, in LH IIIC *c.* 75% of the pottery was locally produced on Rhodes (Jones and Mee 1978; Jones 1986, 501–8). The rest came from various sources on the mainland Greece, the Cyclades and Crete. Clay analyses conducted on samples from Aspropilia cemetery have confirmed a similar change at this cemetery, where the majority of the LH IIIC vessels were locally produced (Karantzali and Ponting 2000, 235; Ponting and Karantzali 2001, 107). During the LH IIIC period the local pottery style is idiosyncratic, with many local characteristics, some strong stylistic influences from Crete, and fewer from the Greek mainland. Horns, half-moon stemmed spirals, outlined solid lozenges, triangles, semi-circles are some of the main motifs from Rhodes (Mountjoy 1999a, 985–9). On Kos, Kalymnos and Astypalaia the Pictorial style seems to be more common, using motifs such as humans, birds and fish, along with panelled decoration, spirals, framed wavy lines and semi-circles; all comprising the east Aegean *koine* that incorporates these areas and, possibly, Miletos (Mountjoy 1999a, 967–8, 1078–81, 1126–7, 1139). The most distinct LH IIIC shapes on Rhodes were the ovoid piriform jar (FS 37, 38), the belly-handled amphora (FS 58), the two-handled amphoriskos (FS 59), the strainer jug (FS 155), the cup spout (FS 157) and the kalathos (FS 291; see Mountjoy 1999a, 987–8). The ovoid piriform jar (FS 37,

38) and the belly-handled amphora (FS 58) were equally common in the rest of the south-eastern Aegean with the addition of the amphoroid krater (FS 56; see Mountjoy 1999a, 1079–80). Nonetheless, the most characteristic example of the new LH IIIC Rhodian style is the Octopus stirrup jar. Its inspiration originates in LM IIIB examples from Crete and belongs to the LH IIIC middle phase (Kanta 1980, 304–5; Benzi 1992, 9–10; Mountjoy 1999a, 1,044). It was produced mainly at Ialysos, but also at Kos and possibly Kalymnos, while nine out of the 36 examples from Ialysos were imported from Crete. Octopus stirrup jars have also been found at a number of sites across the Aegean, on Crete (Kanta 1980, 255–6), Naxos (Kardara 1977, 9–21; Mountjoy 1999a, 951–7; Vlachopoulos 1999a, 305–6; 2003a, 221–3), Skyros (Parlama 1984, 146–51), Perati (Iakovidis 1970, 181–8), Porto Rafti (Stubbings 1947, 23, pl. 2.3), Epidauros Limera (Demakopoulou 1968, 168, pls. 74 d, e), Pitani (Mee 1978, 143) and as far as Scoglio del Tonno in southern Italy (Vagnetti 2000–1, 111), a range that reveals the extent of contacts and interactions in this period across the Aegean. A most intriguing fact is that stirrup jars are not found in any of the other cemeteries on Rhodes, suggesting a kind of monopoly in their manufacture and traffic centred at Ialysos (Mountjoy 1998, 60). A similar picture is seen with the strainer jugs which were very popular at Ialysos, and only two examples have been found at Aspropilia cemetery in Southern Rhodes, two more come from Eleona and Langada, and one from Ikaria (Morricone 1965/6, 183–7, 235–7; Benzi 1992, 60; Mountjoy 1999a, 1,113, 1,146, fig. 471; Karantzali 2001, 58). Although strainer jugs are sporadically attested in the Argolid and Attica (Iakovidis 1970, 233), the co-occurrence of strainer jug and octopus-style stirrup jars is found only at Perati, Aplomata and Kamini on Naxos, Epidauros Limera, Eleona and Langada and Ialysos, suggesting an interactive network. This indicates a vibrant local pottery production with regional characteristics and contacts with other Aegean areas.

In addition to the pottery there is a more varied picture in the small finds deposited in tombs, with some interesting trends. There were 25 silver, 26 gold and 4 bronze rings recovered in a number of tombs at Ialysos, all dating to the LH IIIC period and suggesting a new fashion (Benzi 1992, 183, 188–9, 191). At Eleona and Langada the same picture appears, but with smaller numbers: 4 gold and 16 bronze rings (Georgiadis 2003, 102). This may mark an attempt to underline social differentiation during LH IIIC, while at the same time it is possible to argue that there was a greater abundance of precious metal, and perhaps local workshops, in this region. The same picture is also attested at Perati (Iakovidis 1970, 291 n. 4, 373–6), and Aplomata and Kamini (Kardara 1977, 4–7; Vlachopoulos 1999a, 308–9), but not at other Mycenaean cemeteries of this period. All these sites had an active, central role in the trade contacts during the 12th century. The connection between Ialysos,

Kos, Naxos and Perati has already been noted in the pottery, and is reinforced by the small finds.

Moreover, there is evidence of contacts with areas beyond the Aegean. At Ialysos six bronze mirrors and two stone mortars have been recovered, all of which seem to come from Cyprus (Benzi 1992, 182, 206). From the same cemetery twelve seal stones have been found, six of which have been identified in LH IIIC tombs; two are of Hittite provenance, and one is northern Syrian (Benzi 1992, 206–7). Scarabs have been recovered at Ialysos, Eleona and Langada inside LH IIIC tombs, and are most probably of Egyptian manufacture (Benzi 1992, 206–7). Additionally, at both cemeteries amber beads have been found in burials of this period, coming from the Baltic region via the central Mediterranean. The amber manufacture centre at Frattesina in the Po valley may have been an important nexus in the circulation of this material during the 12th century, either as a raw material or as finished articles (Bieti Sestieri 1996, 126, 279; Pearce 2000, 109–10). All these finds reveal the active role the south-eastern Aegean played in trade during the 12th century in an exchange network extending from Syria-Palestine and Cyprus to the Aegean and the central Mediterranean. It is important also to note the similarities between the finds from the Gelidonya shipwreck, notably stone mortars, sealstones and scarabs (Taylour 1964, 95; Buchholz 1967, 148–53; Shulman 1967, 143–7), and the imported Near Eastern goods recovered at the cemeteries at Ialysos, Eleona and Langada. This strongly suggests the links that both major centres had maintained with the eastern Mediterranean exchange network of the 12th century.

The migration model and the LH IIIC period in the Aegean

The extraordinary increase in burials and offerings, particularly in the largest two cemeteries of the south-eastern Aegean, led many scholars to propose a migration from the Greek mainland after the collapse of the palatial socio-political structures at the transition of LH IIIB–C (Mee 1988, 57). The decrease of LH IIIC settlements in mainland Greece and the shorter- or longer-lived prosperity of island settlements in the Cyclades and the eastern Aegean islands provided enough evidence to support the migration theory. This movement from the mainland to the Aegean islands and Crete, was seen as a necessary first step before the colonisation and Hellenisation of Cyprus further east (Iakovidis 1995, 216; Kanta 1998, 40). An Aegean origin for the Philistines in Syria-Palestine has been developed by some scholars out of this hypothesis (Iakovidis 1995, 217).

Migration and colonisation are very complicated processes both in antiquity and in modern times. Many types of them exist, but the ethnographic parallels suggest that the commonest form is the movement to familiar areas close to the place of origin where common cultural elements are shared (Anthony 1997, 24). Migration tends to be a series of time-lapse events involving individuals or family groups, rather than waves of people or 'cultures' covering whole landscapes in single events (Anthony 1997, 23). When long distance migration does occur in unfamiliar areas, it tends to be based on kin information and following well-established exchange routes (Schofield 1983, 295): long distance migration involves the movement of individuals or kin groups at the most, and depends on the positive conditions of the destination and the cost of transportation to that area (Anthony 1997, 26–7). In contrast to migration, colonisation needs a strong socio-political background for the people attempting to colonise as well as considerable planning (Rowlands 1998, 327), and it should be noted that Klaus Kilian (1990, 465) tried to trace and define Mycenaean colonisation but concluded that there was no plan or any homogeneous effect in the Mycenaean cultural expansion.

As more evidence becomes available in the Aegean, different patterns emerge. Although in mainland Greece the large palatial centres were destroyed, Mycenae, Tiryns and Asine continued to be occupied (Shelmerdine 1997, 581–2). In some regions LH IIIC settlements were scarce, as in Messenia (Shelmerdine 1997, 581). In other areas there was an increase in settled sites, as in Elis and Achaia in the Pelopennese, and Locris and Phthiotis in Central Greece (Shelmerdine 1997, 581–2; Dakoronia 1999b, 181; Eder 1999, 263). In the areas where more settlements have been found, it could be suggested that a local migration had taken place from neighbouring regions. Nevertheless, a more diachronic analysis of these areas is necessary in order to confirm this hypothesis.

Different conditions are attested on the Aegean islands (Fig. 11.2). For example, early in LH IIIC the settlement at Kanakia on Salamis was destroyed and never reoccupied again (Lolos 2003, 113). At Koukounaries on Paros the fortified stronghold was built in LH IIIC early and sacked at the beginning in the middle LH IIIC, only to be partly re-inhabited in the LH IIIC late phase (Schilardi 1992, 632–5; Vlachopoulos 2003a, 230). Ayios Andreas on Siphnos was most probably abandoned at the end of LH IIIC early and reoccupied late in the LH IIIC (Mountjoy 1999a, 887–8; Vlachopoulos 2003a, 229 *contra* Televantou 2001, 209). Grotta on Naxos (Lambrinoudakis and Philaniotou-Hadjianastasiou 2001, 166; Vlachopoulos 2003a, 229–31), Emporio on Chios (Hood 1981–2, 579–80), Skyros (Parlama 1984, 274–5) and possibly Psara (Achilara 1996) and Koukonissi on Limnos (Guzowska and Yasur-Landau 2003, 475), appear to flourish during the whole 12th century, giving a more diverse picture for the Aegean islands. The case of Xombourgo on Tinos remains an open issue without clear LH IIIC strata (Kourou 2001, 187).

A similar prosperity is observed in the south-eastern

Aegean in the LH IIIC, though the significance of the change in this region with its important increase in the number of tombs and offerings, and with the new local pottery style remains to be assessed. The most fundamental burial practices in the south-eastern Aegean appear to be unaltered in the transition from LH IIIB–C with no change in the orientation of tombs or the symbolic use of the landscape. More importantly there is no change in the burial practices and traditions already formed from the LH IIIA period. The only new characteristics in LH IIIC are the use of pits inside the tombs and the kalathos vessels with mourning figurines on them, both found only at Ialysos, and the introduction of cremation in a small scale, all of which are elements of a wider phenomenon also seen at Kephallenia, Perati and the north-western Anatolia. It is thus possible that the introduction of pits reveals a new fashion of limited distribution and no clearly identifiable origin, and cannot be taken as evidence for the arrival of migrants. Additionally, the introduction of cremation dates back the LH IIIA2 in the south-eastern Aegean and became progressively more popular (Melas 1984, 33; Kontorli-Papadopoulou 1987, 156; Georgiadis 2003, 84). Furthermore, the pottery tradition is for the first time overwhelmingly of local production with new elements deriving mainly from local inspiration and some Cretan influence, rather than from the Greek mainland. Therefore the only point that leads through to an explanation of a change imposed by newcomers is the appearance of greater number of tombs and more finds in the two largest cemeteries of the south-eastern Aegean. At Eleona and Langada this change is more gradual with a linear growth of offerings deposited in tombs over time. In the LH IIIC period it is interesting to note that there is a decrease in the number of cemeteries on Kos and it is possible that nucleation was taking place, centred at one well-defended site with strong overseas contacts. This prosperity is reflected in the tombs where more offerings in precious metals and foreign imports were deposited with the deceased. On Rhodes there is a more complicated picture with many sites continuing to be active across the island. Rhodes can be divided into a northern and a southern part divided by the two large mountains, Attaviros and Profitis Ilias, with their foothills forming a natural barrier. In the southern part if the island the number of cemeteries remains the same from LH IIIB–C with more offerings deposited inside the tombs, but less marked than the increase attested at Ialysos, Eleona and Langada. In northern Rhodes some of the cemeteries went out of use in LH IIIC, revealing an abandonment of the dispersed settlement pattern in favour of nucleation centred at Ialysos and Kalavarda. Thus, a similar pattern to the one seen at Kos emerges here in contrast to the picture of southern Rhodes, arguing against the application of the nucleation hypothesis for Rhodes as a whole (Macdonald 1986, 132; Benzi 1992, 224–5; 1996, 974). Curiously, Ialysos, Kalavarda, Eleona and Langada, share another characteristic, the re-use of

abandoned tombs, strengthening this argument. It seems that any regional migrants that came to these centres used the older abandoned tombs, mainly of LH IIIA2 date, to deposit their own deceased in the 12th century. The nucleation hypothesis proposed here provides an alternative explanation for the growth of Ialysos, Eleona and Langada in the LH IIIC rather than the migration theory. This does not mean that was no long distance population movement in the 12th century. Rather, if there was one it was not as massive as proposed and it did not influence significantly the cultural character of the south-eastern Aegean.

Conclusions

The south-eastern Aegean is a vital stepping stone if one wishes to sustain a hypothesis for a massive movement to the east, but the burial evidence from this region demonstrates a period of continuity of older practices and traditions. The structure of the tombs, their symbolic relation to the landscape and the rituals performed in them emphasize this point. This picture is reinforced by the development of a stronger local pottery production than ever before with affinities to local and Cretan influences. At the same time the local and regional prosperity in the south-eastern Aegean is reflected in the valuable items and the foreign goods from the eastern and central Mediterranean.

The new local social conditions in the LH IIIC period were the result of economic development as a result of the 12th century exchange network and the regional nucleation observed at Kos and north-western Rhodes. Each island has at its centre respectively Ialysos and Eleona and Langada, two ports which played an active role in the exchange network that formed in the Aegean after the collapse of the palatial politico-economic structures. These LH IIIC centres maintained strong ties with other islands as well as with mainland sites. More importantly, they were significant nodes in the newly formed exchange networks of the 12th century that connected the eastern with the central Mediterranean. This development was partly responsible for the process of nucleation around these settlements, possibly along with social insecurities as observed in the burials of children at Aspropilia. A similar trend can be seen in other Aegean islands such as Naxos and possibly in some mainland regions such as the Argolid and Attica. Nonetheless, the data when put together emphasize the regional nature of developments in the south-eastern Aegean, with strong local variations in burial practice and in the socio-economic conditions.

The evidence presented here for the 12th century does not support a migration influx, nor can any new major mainland cultural influence be observed in the south-eastern Aegean. Such a large-scale population movement would have been bound to cross and consequently affect this area in a visible way, either directly with at least some new settlers or indirectly with new cultural elements from the Greek mainland. Overall, this area provides no evidence for mainland migration for the LH IIIC period, and moving a step further it raises questions over the migration hypothesis proposed for Cyprus and beyond. After all, in 12th century Cyprus a process of nucleation or synoecism is also attested with more emphasis on the coastal sites, which prospered thanks to the exchange network of this period (Steel 2004, 188, 190). This picture is not unlike that witnessed in the south-eastern Aegean, and indeed in several areas across the Aegean, and for similar underlying reasons. It should also be noted that the Mycenaean and/or Mycenaeanising pottery, which is considered an important criterion for identifying migrants or colonisers, is not a reliable one. Apart from the obvious methodological problem of equating pots with the ethnic identities of individuals (Niemeier 1998, 26), this local imitation of Mycenaean pottery has a rather wide distribution in the Mediterranean, attested in Sardinia (Ferrarese Ceruti *et al.* 1987, 35; Jones and Day 1987, 263), Sicily (Leighton 1998, 172; D'Agata 2000, 64), southern Italy (Jones and Vagnetti 1991, 131–4; Vagnetti 1999, 138),

Macedonia (Buxeda I Garrigós *et al.* 2003, 264), Troy (Mee 1978, 147), Cilicia (Mee 1978, 150; Sherratt and Crouwel 1987, 340–1), Cyprus (Steel 2004, 165), and Philistia in Syria-Palestine (Yasur-Landau 2003b, 588). Although the bulk of these pots were made in the 12th century with different character and impact in each area, the trend in most cases is older, dating back to the 14th and 13th centuries BCE in more modest numbers at Sardinia (Lo Schiavo 2003, 15), Sicily (Tanasi 2003, 599), South Italy (van Wijngaarden 2002, 241), Macedonia (Buxeda I Garrigós *et al.* 2003, 275), Troy (Mee 1978, 147), and Cyprus (Sherratt 1994b, 42; van Wijngaarden 2002, 271–2). The increased popularity of these pots may be traced to the new politico-economic conditions of the 12th century and the change in the modes of exchange (Artzy 1997; Sherratt 2000, 89; 2001, 238), rather than to a population exodus, linked with the Sea Peoples. Perhaps it is time to look more carefully at the evidence which the Aegean islands offer us to assess the Aegean influence on Cyprus and Syria-Palestine, giving more credit to cultural interaction, rather than migration and large-scale population movements.

THE LAST DAYS OF A CANAANITE KINGDOM: A VIEW FROM HAZOR

Sharon Zuckerman

The 13th century BCE was a period of social and political tensions threatening the cohesion and the mere existence of the palatial societies of the eastern Mediterranean. Interpretations of these 'crisis years' and of the processes leading to the final collapse of the Late Bronze Age system are varied (Ward and Sharp-Joukowsky 1992). Scholars have suggested a myriad of factors, including environmental stresses, changing climatic conditions, adoption of technological innovations and new military techniques, as well as internal social tensions and the appearance of new groups of people, as possible factors (for a recent review see Dickinson 2006, 43–57).

I would like to focus my discussion of this period on one site, Tel Hazor in northern Israel. Hazor was a major kingdom in the complex system of Canaanite petty kingdoms characterizing the southern Levant during the Late Bronze Age. A detailed discussion of the changes visible in the archaeological record of the city towards its final days will help to illuminate the forces operating within it during this crucial period, and will enhance our understanding of the gradual processes leading to its final destruction. The theoretical and conceptual basis and the detailed description of the archaeological features were presented elsewhere (Zuckerman 2007). Here I would like to formulate, in more general terms, an interpretation of the last days of Hazor as can be gleaned from the archaeological remains. I believe that a detailed description of this phase holds the key to our understanding of Hazor's decline and final destruction, and can serve as a case-study for the wider trajectories evident in the Eastern Mediterranean throughout the 13th century.

The final phase of the Late Bronze Age city was uncovered in several areas of Hazor during the 1950s' excavations (Fig. 12.1). The latest Bronze Age stratum (Stratum XIII on the upper Tell and Stratum 1A in the Lower City) was

described by Yigael Yadin (*et al.* 1960, 113; 1972, 108) as a short-lived and degenerated occupation, preceding the final destruction and the wholesale abandonment of the Lower City. This apparent decline is reflected in many aspects of the material remains of the site, including architectural features, technological and typological aspects of the ceramic assemblages and various other finds. In the following, I will highlight some of the phenomena characterizing this phase, in an attempt to identify the possible factors of the violent destruction putting an end to this stratum and the Late Bronze Age settlement of Hazor. No written records documenting this phase have survived, and the only possible textual reference in Ugarit to the troubles encountered by the king of Hazor in the 13th century (Arnaud 1998) was recently refuted and cannot be considered an unequivocal source (Durand 2006). Thus, we are left with the material remains and their interpretation.

'Crisis architecture' and the abandonment of monumental buildings

The social and symbolic function of the built environment is emphasized in recent studies of ancient architecture (Parker-Pearson and Richards 1994). Monumental and public buildings form an important aspect of the process of materialization of social ideology, representing the transformation of ideas and values into concrete physical form (DeMarrais 2004). The endurance of building as a significant social and ideological symbol necessitates its continuous maintenance, so when a building deteriorates due to social and political changes, its social and ideological message is weakened or profoundly transformed (Knapp 1996, 11–12). Such cases have been detected in the

Fig. 12.1: Hazor, the Lower City and the Upper Tel (from the north)

archaeological record and identified as 'crisis architecture', a term coined by Jan Driessen (1995, 65–6) and applied to architectural responses to short-term changes in socio-cultural conditions. These architectural changes usually involve a decrease of energy input in construction and maintenance, a change in original plan, and a change in the original function of the structures (Driessen 1995, 67–76; Driessen and MacDonald 1997, 41–7).

A relevant case for the period under discussion is the latest phase of the Mycenaean palace at Pylos, which shows several architectural changes resulting in a diminishing of the spaciousness and elegance of the main structure (Wright 1984; Shelmerdine 1987). This last phase of crisis architecture marks the culmination of a long and gradual process of decline of the Pylos polity and the Mycenaean palatial system as a whole (Sherratt 2001). I have argued that similar processes can be identified in other contemporary cases'in the 13th century eastern Mediterranean, such as Lachish and Megiddo and, most notably Hazor (Zuckerman 2007).

The apex of Late Bronze Age Hazor can be dated to the 15th and 14th centuries BCE, a period roughly corresponding to the Amarna period in Egypt. Strata XV–XIV on the upper tell and Strata 2–1B in the Lower City of Hazor

show a major rebuilding activity throughout the city (Fig. 12.2). Structures of the Ceremonial Precinct on the acropolis are erected on top of a massive constructive fill covering earlier monumental buildings (Ben-Tor and Rubiato 1999). The royal 'Podium Complex' is built on the northern edge of the Tel facing the Lower City, covering the remains of earlier buildings (Zuckerman 2006). These activities were initiated by an ambitious ruling dynasty at Hazor, vividly reflected in the Amarna archive letters of Abdi-Tirshi ruler of Hazor and his peers (Moran 1992, 235 [*EA* 148], 288–90 [*EA* 227–8], 362 [*EA* 364]). It seems that the acropolis of Hazor was then re-designed as a center of political and religious authority, as part of the reorganization of the city and its re-foundation by an aggrandizing ruler (Margueron 1994).

Hazor of the 13th century, the time of the Egyptian 19th Dynasty, was only a pale shadow of the splendour of its 14th century predecessor. The Lower City was unfortified during its final phase (Ben-Tor 1989, 286–93, and esp. 297; Mazar 1997a, 382), and traces of deterioration and partial abandonment are visible in most public buildings and communal areas. The Orthostats Temple of Area H undergoes changes in both plan and construction, showing several features of crisis architecture (Zuckerman 2007, fig. 7). Noteworthy are the blocking of the rear niche, the

Fig. 12.2: Late Bronze Age Ceremonial Precinct on the Acropolis (from the east)

diminishing size of the various spaces, and the haphazard nature of the construction during this phase (Yadin 1972, fig. 20; Ben-Tor 1989, 258, plans XL–XLI).

On the upper Tell, the final phase of the Podium Complex in area M is characterized by changes and alterations to the overall plan of the building, and it seems that the structure was cleaned out and abandoned prior to its destruction (Fig. 12.3). The royal ceremonial precinct on the Acropolis (Area A) underwent similar alterations during its last phase. These included the intentional removal of orthostats and architectural features, which were then thrown into pits dug in the pavements of the courtyard (Fig. 12.4). Some of these were re-used as building materials for the meager installations built haphazardly along the walls of the monumental Ceremonial Palace/Royal Sanctuary. Flimsy walls attributed to this phase were also built in the paved courtyard to the north of the building and all around the once impressive Ceremonial Precinct.

Stratum 1A marks a profound change in the urban landscape of Hazor, as a series of architectural changes and alterations affected the most important spaces of the public buildings. There is significant decrease of energy input into the maintenance of the buildings, and an on-going neglect of the architectural expressions of political and religious authority. These deteriorating architectural and material features of the public buildings at Hazor reflect signs of crisis and disintegration of the royal strategy which was carefully

planned and executed during the 14th century. The partial abandonment of certain royal buildings and the disuse of the city's gates and fortification walls might indicate the inability of the elite to maintain its control over the city, and it seems that members of the ruling class had already left Hazor by this time, leaving behind other less fortunate residents of the city. These changes are closely related to phenomena such as the deliberate mutilation and burial of the material indices of these ritual activities.

Mutilation and burial of statues and architectural features

Cases of intentional mutilation and burial of royal and cultic statues at Bronze Age Hazor were already discerned and described by Yadin, and recently discussed in detail by Amnon Ben-Tor (2006). These activities point to significant changes in the attitude of Hazor's inhabitants towards the once important material symbols of royal and divine power and authority. The intentional mutilation of eleven objects, including Egyptian royal statues and Canaanite statues of deities and kings, was interpreted by Ben-Tor as cases of 'political iconoclasm' motivated by political reasons. Most of these were found in the destruction layer of the Late Bronze Age and are attributed to those who brought about the final destruction of the city (Ben-Tor 2006, 14). In light of the

Fig. 12.3: Area M, 'Podium Complex', final phase

Fig. 12.4: Area A, Ceremonial Precinct, final phase in the Northern Courtyard

above discussion of the gradual violation of ritual spaces, it seems that these acts had also strong religious motifs, an observation suggested also by Ben-Tor (2006, 12–13).

The burial of statues, identified in five cases, is understood by Ben-Tor in a somewhat different way. The interment of the seated figure in area H, the lion orthostats in Areas H and A and the bronze statues in the Area A Ceremonial Palace/Royal Sanctuary, is interpreted as an act of veneration or protection of these value-laden objects from an impending disaster (Ben-Tor 2006, 12). This is also the explanation preferred by Yadin (1972, 91) for the burial of the lion orthostat in the wall of the porch of the Area H temple. In this latter case, I believe another explanation might fit better the archaeological evidence. The lion orthostat was found buried in a pit and covered by a heap of stones that included a bull-shaped base of a god's statue whose torso was found close-by in the courtyard (Yadin *et al.* 1961, pls. CXV, CXVIII–CXX; Beck 1989, 335–7; Ben-Tor 1989, 248, plan XXXIX). The pit was dug into the south-western corner of the front wall of the porch, deliberately destroying the possible entrance into the Stratum 1A temple. I suggest that this act should be understood as a 'termination ritual' ending the ritual and sacred function of the temple (Mock 1998).

Another example of a termination ritual was noted in the 'Podium Complex'. In the final phase, the passage from the entrance of the complex through the podium area and into the courtyard is blocked by a row of broken orthostats and stones, sealing the semi-circular libation installation in front of the podium (Fig. 12.3). It is obvious that these stones were laid by people who knew the original function of the building, recognized the importance of its plan and associated features and intended to obliterate its ritual and symbolic functions.

'Ritual closure' or 'sealing off' of ritual, ceremonial and domestic structures, usually through burning or ceremonial burial, was identified in diverse archaeological contexts (see Zuckerman 2007 for a detailed discussion and references). Such 'ritual closures' are interpreted as the theologically appropriate way to end the existence of a structure (Bjork-man 1999, 115) or, alternatively, as 'an act of rejection or 'ideological closure' of the ideas and practices that defined and integrated a community' (Nelson 2000, 56). This could have been done either during the phase of alterations made inside the monumental buildings or simultaneously with their final destruction.

While it is difficult to pinpoint the exact chain of events that lead to the final destruction of Hazor, it seems that some intensification of cultic and ritual activities accompanied the deterioration of public and monumental buildings and their subsequent abandonment in the last phase of the city. One possible hint to this process is the unusual nature of the faunal remains attributed to the final phase of some of the public structures, probably representing events of communal and sacrificial meals held at the eve of Hazor's destruction.

'Calamity feasts' at Hazor?

Feasts, defined as events of ritual activity that involve communal food and drink consumption and display in contexts that are different from mundane consumption (Dietler 1996, 89), were no doubt a common feature in Canaan of the Late Bronze Age. The elites ruling the Canaanite city-states of the second millennium BCE, a closely-knit system of centralized and hierarchical polities involved in never-ending conflicts for control over limited land and human resources, probably held 'Diacritical' feasts (Dietler 1996, 98–9; 2001, 85–8) as a vehicle of social cohesion and elite legitimation as part of their daily routine (Bunimovitz 1995).

Large-scale feasting activities were identified in the last phase of Canaanite Hazor on the basis of material indices of feasting preserved in the archaeological record (Hayden 2001, table 2.1). These include the faunal remains, usually animal bones and ashes, and the ceramic assemblages which are usually characterized by large quantities of serving vessels, oversized storage and cooking vessels and special function vessels. Another group of prestige objects such as incised bone and ivory inlays provides iconographic clues to the existence of elite sponsored feasts at Hazor and other contemporary Canaanite sites (Liebowitz 1980, 165; Ziffer 2005, 150–4).

The Royal precinct in Area A, and especially the Ceremonial Palace/Royal Sanctuary and its courtyard (Ben-Tor and Rubiato 1999), was probably a major locus of feasting events. The faunal assemblage of the courtyard at Hazor was recently published by Justin Lev-Tov and Kevin McGeough (2006), and was shown to fill most of the requirements of a feast-related corpus: it is unusually abundant, shows clear preference for certain species, and the intentional selection of specific body parts of animals of certain age/gender. The bones were found accumulated on the floors of the courtyard, with a clear concentration around the central podium (Lev-Tov and McGeough 2006, fig. 5.4). The thickest accumulation of bones was found on the latest floor contemporary with the latest phase of the podium, and was sealed by the ashy destruction layer marking the violent end of the whole complex. It is plausible that this large assemblage contains bones and other food residues accumulated during a longer period, and thus might represent several feasting cycles rather than a single final event. It should however be stressed that several restorable bowls were found close to the Ceremonial Palace/Royal Sanctuary entrance, and these might represent remnants of such final feasting event, just prior to the violent destruction and desertion of the Royal precinct and of the whole city (Lev-Tov and McGeough 2006, 89–90).

Ancient Near Eastern feasting events have been shown to serve a myriad of social and political functions (Schmandt-Besserat 2001). In the context of Late Bronze Age Hazor, feasts were probably used as a socio-political vehicle of maintenance and manipulation of power relations within the Canaanite city and between it and its neighbours. Legitimization of elite authority and the formation and reification of identity were also an important function of state-sponsored religious feasts (Lev-Tov and McGeough 2006). Against the specific background of 13th century Canaan, when the increasing Egyptian control became a burden on the socially and economically impoverished country, feasts such as those reflected in the Hazor material record of the last LBA phase might be explained also as 'calamity feasts', or large-scale communal meals initiated by rulers in situations of environmental or social crisis and impending catastrophe (Hayden 2001, 37). According to Brian Hayden, in times of emergency people are willing to surrender surpluses and labor for the promise of relief and compensation of infuriated deities through their mortal agents. In the case of Hazor, these events might be seen as a last measure taken in the face of the impending political, social and economic crises. The evidence of conspicuous consumption in LBA cities was already interpreted as a sign of unstable political situation and culminating social stress and conflicts within the Canaanite city-state system (Bunimovitz 1995, 157–9; Herzog 1997, 272–5), and such large-scale events might be interpreted as signs of weakness rather than of strength. The fact that remains of feasts characterize the last phase of the royal precinct of Hazor, just prior to its abandonment and the final destruction of the site, lends support to this interpretation of Canaanite feasting at Hazor. Though this interpretation remains speculative in the lack of contemporary written sources, it does enrich our understanding of the complex function of feasts and suggest future directions for the study of this social practice.

The final destruction of Hazor

Remains of a 'general conflagration' ending the Bronze Age city were already identified by John Garstang in his limited soundings of the Lower City (Yadin 1972, 18, 28). The excavations by Yadin in the Lower City and on the upper tell revealed more evidence of this destruction level, although a clear destruction level was identified in the Lower City only in the Orthostats Temple in area H (Yadin 1972, 108; Ben-Tor 1989, 257–64). It seems that none of the smaller-scale domestic and cultic buildings in the Lower City were similarly burnt or violently destroyed.

Yadin's excavations on the upper tell were inconclusive concerning the existence of a clear destruction level at the end of Stratum XIII (Yadin 1972, 126). The renewed excavations on the acropolis revealed two LBA monumental complexes which were both destroyed in a fierce conflagration (Ben-Tor and Rubiato 1999; Zuckerman 2006). The results of the renewed excavations thus corroborate the existence of a

preferential conflagration of the public buildings that were erected during the phase of the implementation of the royal strategy, and witnessed a phase of crisis architecture and abandonment (Ben-Tor 1998, 465).

The identity of those responsible for the final destruction of Hazor is debated, and they could be either foreigners (for a review see Ben-Tor 1998) or local Canaanites. The inhabitants of Hazor, who suffered the mounting social conflicts and the economic burdens of financing, construction and maintenance of the elite large-scale building projects throughout the LBA, could well have been the agents of the final destruction campaign. Although the suggested internal revolt might have served foreign interests it is predominantly an internal affair. The visible features of stratum 1A described above are the material indices of the social and political processes leading to the violent, and in a sense inevitable, destruction campaign that ended the physical existence of the Canaanite kingdom of Hazor.

'Ruin cults' at Iron Age I Hazor?

Following the violent destruction of its Canaanite monumental buildings, the city of Hazor was abandoned for an unspecified period, throughout which the remnants of the ruined monumental buildings on the acropolis were clearly visible on the surface of the site (Ben-Ami 2001). The area of the ruined Ceremonial Palace/Royal Sanctuary was consciously avoided by later inhabitants of the Tel until well into the 9th century BCE. This avoidance was interpreted as a reflection of a ban placed on these remains, a *taboo* preventing re-use of the destroyed buildings or the rebuilding on top of them (Ben-Tor and Rubiato 1999, 27–8).

Architectural remains of the Iron I period include a large number of rounded pits, meagre walls and foundations of huts or tents. Especially noteworthy are the remains of two cultic installations (*bamot*), consisting of one or several standing stones (*masseboth*) and stone offering-tables. The first one, located in Area B on the western tip of the Tel, is a structure with an attached paved area and installations (Ben-Ami 2006, figs. 7–8). This precinct was termed by Yadin's team a 'high place', based on the apparently cultic finds attributed to it, especially several incense-stands and a clay jar full of bronze objects (Yadin *et al.* 1960, pls. CCIV–CCV; Yadin 1972, 132–4). The bronze objects, a warrior deity figurine and several weapons, are reminiscent of earlier Canaanite types and might have been scavenged from the ruins of the Late Bronze Age royal precinct (Negbi 1989, 362). Other finds include serving bowls and cooking and storage vessels (Yadin *et al.* 1960, pl. CCIII), as well as a rich assemblage of basalt vessels used for food preparation (Yadin *et al.* 1960, pl. CCVI). The second cultic installation (Fig. 12.5) is located very close to the Ceremonial Palace/

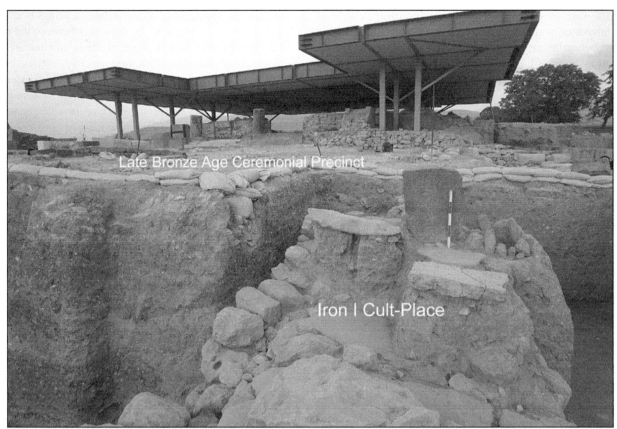

Fig. 12.5: Area A, Iron I 'ruin cult'

Royal Sanctuary, and was dug into the north-eastern corner of the LBA courtyard (Fig. 12.2; Ben-Ami 2006, 123–5). It consists of a large basalt standing stone, reminiscent of LBA orthostats, and a group of smaller standing stones beside it (Fig. 12.5; Ben-Ami 2006, figs. 2–3). Its related assemblage consists of bowls, cooking pots and smaller vessels, as well as a small zoomorphic figurine (Ben-Ami 2006, figs. 5–6).

The occurrence of two apparently contemporary cultic installations, in the context of an otherwise meagre Iron I settlement, is noteworthy. Most telling is the persistence of cultic activities in and around Area A's Ceremonial precinct on the one hand, and the continuation of Canaanite features such as the standing stones, the incense stands and the bronze figurine on the other. I suggest that these two phenomena are closely related and should be interpreted as the remnants of 'ruin cults' performed in connection with the visible ruins of the Late Bronze Age acropolis. This means that the ceremonial and sacred precinct of Canaanite Hazor preserved its meaning and significance for more than a century after its violent destruction, and continued to be venerated by the later inhabitants of the site. Assessing the exact nature of the ritual activities is impossible, but it is clear that Canaanite rituals of burnt offerings (represented

by the incense stands and offering tables) and probably also cultic feasts (prepared and consumed within the 'high place') were conducted in Area B, overlooking the impressive ruin of fallen mud bricks and stones that once was the Canaanite ceremonial precinct (Ben-Ami 2006, fig. 1). The figurine of the seated god resembles the typical bronze figurines of Canaanite deities found in the main temples of the Late Bronze Age city (Negbi 1976, 137–8; 1989, 359–62). It is of course impossible to say if the same deity continued to be venerated by the builders of the Area B 'high-place' or, alternatively, was collected as scrap metal and intended to be re-melted and re-used (Ben-Ami 2006). In any case, its existence points to the fact that the Iron I inhabitants of Hazor knew and frequented the huge accumulation of debris in the central part of the site, but nonetheless chose not to build their walls nor dig their pits into it. In this sense, the attitude of Hazor's Iron Age I inhabitants towards the destroyed remains of their predecessors should be interpreted as one of awe and respect for the age-old Canaanite ruins, generating a cultic emphasis on the association with the past and its veneration. Similar phenomena are known in other contemporary archaeological contexts, such as the Early Iron Age continuity of cult activities at the Minoan palatial ruins during the beginning of the first millennium

BCE (Prent 2003). These activities represent the revival of interest in a glorious past, and are sometimes connected to the rise of heroic literary forms such as the Homeric poems. At Hazor, similar memories of a glorious past find an echo in the much later biblical narrative of the Israelite conquest of Canaanite Hazor 'once the head of all those kingdoms' (Josh. 11.10; see also Ben-Ami 2001, 168–9).

The last days of a Canaanite kingdom

The picture emerging from the above discussion of Hazor's last phases is profoundly different from that drawn by Yadin concerning the destruction of the Late Bronze Age city. Yadin (1972, 108) noticed 'signs of decline' in Stratum 1A of the Late Bronze Age, but he still maintained that the Hazor destroyed by the conquering Israelite tribes was a powerful Canaanite center to be reckoned with (Yadin 1982). But detailed scrutiny of the archaeological remains of Hazor reveals a different situation. In its last phase Canaanite Hazor was a weakened and deteriorated city, only a pale shadow of its past grandeur. The Lower City seems to have been unfortified, leaving the acropolis less protected. The temples and cultic precincts reveal clear signs of 'religious crisis architecture' and termination rituals ending their religious significance (Zuckerman 2007). Some of the elite monumental buildings were probably abandoned during this phase, and were probably no longer used as such at all.

Evidence of squatter activities is present in all public spaces on the acropolis, including the Ceremonial Palace/Royal Sanctuary and its surroundings and the Podium Complex on the northern slope of the Tel. The only sector that seems to have been less affected by these profound changes were the domestic buildings, which continued to function and seem to have been deserted rather than destroyed in the final phase of the city.

The identity of Canaanite Hazor's agents of destruction is still debated, although the culminating social tensions hinted by the archaeological remains point to internal rather than external causes. The seeds of Hazor destruction were already sown in its rise as a megalopolis in the Middle Bronze Age, and clear signs of its decline are visible in its last phase. The Biblical phrase 'Hazor, once the head of all those kingdoms' (Josh. 11.10) could have well been coined already in the 13th century BCE, rather than the 11th or even the 8th centuries, when it was finally embedded in the Joshua conquest story for generations to come.

Acknowledgments

I wish to thank Prof. Amnon Ben-Tor, who encouraged me to pursue and present my interpretation of the last days of Late Bronze Age Hazor, despite our profound disagreement over many of the views expressed here. Photographs are by Manuel Cimadevilla, Hanan Shafir, and SkyBalloon.

THE SIGNIFICANCE OF
CHANGES IN SPATIAL USAGE AT MYCENAE

Elizabeth French

Immediately after the '1200 Destruction', however it may have been caused, the citadel of Mycenae was a mess. As far as we can tell almost all structures were unusable (Fig. 13.1). Both fire and collapse were widespread and we have evidence of a layer of mud wash covering large areas of the west slope which we surmise was the result of heavy rain on the debris.

The extensive building programme of earlier in the century consisted of tallish buildings built on sturdy stone terraces but the upper storey was built of mud brick with wooden cross ties placed both vertical and horizontal along and through the wall. Fire usually causes this part of a structure to collapse totally but leaves standing the heavy foundation basements and terraces. The north-south section across the Citadel House Area on the west of the citadel shows this very clearly (Fig. 13.2). This type of building had been adopted during the second half of the 14th century (recent confirmatory evidence comes from the Petsas House excavations by Dr Kim Shelton) and was used throughout the early 13th century development. After the earthquake at the cusp of LH IIIB1 to B2, the repairs were made in a newly adopted technique of *pisé*, which was quicker and obviously seemed adequate. The relatively unpretentious nature of the repairs is shown clearly in the palace court where the floor is plastered rather than being re-laid in the water-resistant materials of the original structure. It seems likely that the damage caused by the earthquake was underestimated – because, for instance, it may have led to

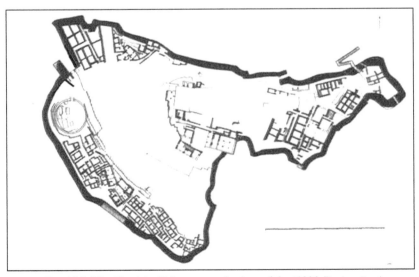

Fig. 13.1: The Citadel of Mycenae at the time of the '1200 Destruction'

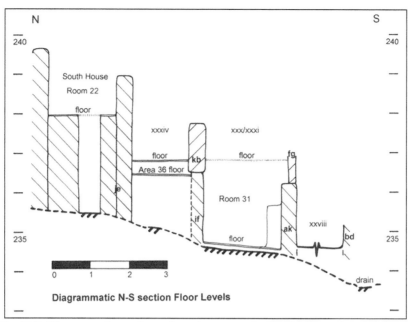

Fig. 13.2: Diagrammatic north–south section across the Citadel House Area at Mycenae

the later collapse of the terrace supporting the megaron of the Palace.

I have suggested elsewhere that there was a strong element of town planning in the early 13th century development (French in press-a). In this planning one area seems to have been deliberately left as a 'public' open space. This was the space between the Lion Gate and the Grave Circle, *i.e.* just inside the entrance to the citadel which allowed a clear view of and easy access to the Grave Circle.

Here in the aftermath of disaster an entirely new building was constructed using an adaptation of the terrace structure but with very firm foundations. This is the building now known as The Granary from the plant material found in the strata of its own final destruction. It was excavated first by Heinrich Schliemann and finally cleared by my father in 1920. The early history of the building is generally ignored because of the striking destruction deposit. It is usually included in general plans of the site in the 13th century – for no other reason than it is very much there today; but it is the period of its construction, particularly the background to it, that requires consideration here. The heavy terrace on which it is built is supported on the north by the western extension of the citadel wall – this use of the wall is the significant innovation of this period of building and is paralleled in another structure which we excavated in the Citadel House Area. The terrace of The Granary is founded on the rock which at this point drops significantly from east to west.

Looking at the east-west section (Fig. 13.3), which is redrawn here to incorporate both The Granary and the area immediately to the west of the Lion Gate into one drawing

and at the same scale, we can see this drop, and the width of the wall in the terracing that was deemed necessary in order to build upon it. Note that the entry level to the Grave Circle is 240.53 m above mean sea level. The excavation of 1920 examined the fill of the terrace, and the publication states that it resembled that from levels I–V of the Lion Gate strata and it is thus directly comparable with the material from the terrace constructed in the Citadel House Area to the south using debris from the '1200 Destruction' (what we now call LH IIIB2 late; French in press-b). The building was later strengthened by the addition of two further buttress-like structures and the so-called 'corridors' at the East were altered. Of course the so-called east corridor is NOT a corridor of the building but a passage leading beside the south boundary wall of the forecourt to the citadel to an entrance at the north end. This passage was NOT floored with cement but consisted of trodden earth and clay. As we can see from the section, the ground level had now risen considerably and both Wall g and the so-called west corridor forming a solid barrier on this side against which the new building could be constructed. Based on these facts, we can see how this area develops before and after the 1200 BCE destruction.

What kind of governance is implied by the well thought-out and extremely sturdy construction of a building like The Granary in a conspicuous position on what it may be suggested was public land (Fig. 13.4)? We could interpret this as continued town planning. Moreover this is not the only sign of organized government. It now seems likely that a new structure was constructed in the Court of the palace which can be compared with that built at this time within

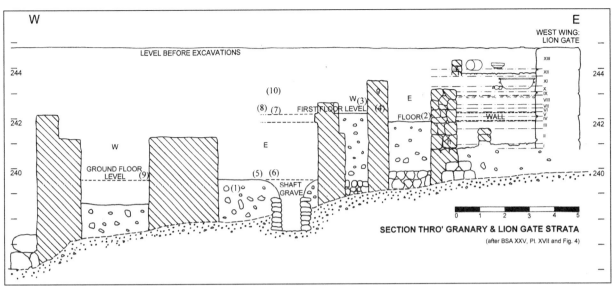

Fig. 13.3: Section from the Lion Gate through the Granary (adapted from The Annual of the British School at Athens 25, fig. 4 and pl. XVII)

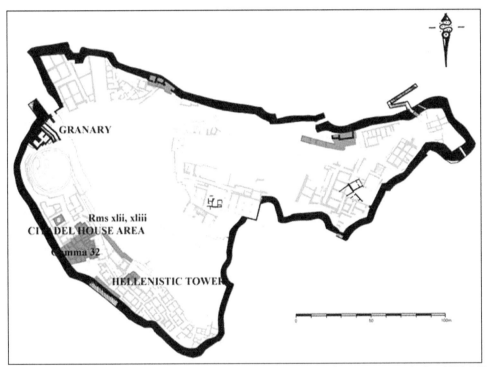

Fig. 13.4: The building within the Citadel of Mycenae known to have been constructed after 1200 BCE

the megaron at Tiryns (Maran 2001a), which could form a central and perhaps religious focus. In pottery studies it has become clear that the period following the Great Destruction is marked by a distinct controlled regulation of production. There is no fall-off of quality but the range of design is severely restricted. To me it bears a striking resemblance to the 'utility' wares of post WWII Britain – strong economic control.

Thus Mycenae does not exhibit the post-catastrophe society put forward many years ago by Colin Renfrew (1981, 30). It is rather the scenario suggested slightly more recently and very cogently by the late Klaus Kilian (1988b, 135). We might even debate whether such a society is really POST palatial – a supposition based on negative evidence that is perhaps disintegrating – or merely the tangible evidence of altered priorities on the part of a continuing bureaucracy.

FROM *DA-MO* TO ΔΗΜΟΣ: SURVIVAL OF A MYCENAEAN LAND ALLOCATION TRADITION IN THE CLASSICAL PERIOD?

Michael Franklin Lane

I argue here that the principles of land division and allocation seen in the Linear B archives of Mycenaean Greece (*c.* 1450–1150 BCE) are fundamentally the same as those applied in Archaic and Classical Period (8th–4th centuries BCE) Greek cities and colonies. I suggest that the common structures may represent a continuing agronomic tradition or political institution superficially transformed.

Describing and measuring land

The following tablet series from Mycenaean palace archives describe the allocation and possession of land: Knossos E, Uf; Pylos E–; Mycenae Eu; Tiryns Ef. The data of the archives of Knossos and Pylos corroborate each other in crucial details, while the other archives share in common terminology and offer nothing to contradict these details. The parcels of land recorded in the Linear B texts very likely represent allotments that were involved in a regular cycle of cultivation, abandonment and redistribution – cultivated especially by persons performing certain political and religious roles and subject to a particular kind of collective tax.

The parcels of concern here are described as *ktoinai* and together make up an area and jurisdiction known as a *dāmos*. *Ktoinai* are qualified in two ways: *ktimenai* (currently) 'cultivated' or *khekhemenai* (already) 'abandoned' (see Deroy and Gérard 1965; Ruijgh 1967, 365–6; Calderone 1968; Duhoux 1976, 9–10; De Fidio 1977; Carpenter 1983). Named persons 'have' whole cultivated or abandoned *ktoinai* or fractional 'profitable' parts (*onāta*) of them. The possessors of whole *ktoinai* are called *ktoinohokhoi*, whereas possessors of fractional *onāta* are called *onātēres*. It is clear that whole *ktoinai* or their remainder, less fractional

onāta, also constitute *onāta* (Bennett 1956, 120). The terms *ktoinohokhoi* and *dāmos* are used interchangeably (PY Eb 297, Ep 704.5), indicating that the *ktoinohokhoi* represent the community of landholders.

Some *ktoinohokhoi* are known as *telestai* (PY En 609.2, Eb 149.1; KN Uf(2) 839, 970, 990), evidently because they 'perform a duty' (*teleiahen*), or 'do work' (*wordzehen*), whereas others 'pertain to the leader of the army' (*lāwāgesioi*). Still others, such as a certain priestess and a 'companion' (*hequetās*) have special allotments called *e-to-ni-ja,* comprising abandoned parcels (PY Eb 297.1 = Ep 704.5, Eb 473.1 = Ep 539.14). Most *onātēres,* when they are not servants of some titled person, are 'royal' craftsmen or 'servants of (the) god'. Finally, a celebrated analysis of the Pylian Er–Es–Un 718 series shows that the *onāta* of a single *ktoinā* parcel, however split into fractions, are directly proportional to the amount of tribute in agricultural products (*dosmos*) paid from it to certain persons and divinities (De Fidio 1977, 7–75).

Areas of land are measured in amounts of seed grain. The usual formula, seen at Pylos and Tiryns, is the word for 'seed' or 'sowing' followed by a symbol known technically as 'GRA', which most likely represents 'wheat' (Halstead 1995a), and a dry-measure value. Two texts from Knossos (E 9295, 9322) include an abbreviation of the same formula, and measures of GRA following personal names at Mycenae (Eu 654, 655) are probably records of individual landholding. Emmet L. Bennett Jr. (1950) reconstructed the Mycenaean system of dry measurement even before the decipherment of Linear B. One major unit – for present purposes, GRA – has three aliquot fractions, conventionally represented by the Latin characters T (1/10 GRA), V (1/60 GRA or 1/6 T) and Z (1/240 GRA or 1/4 V). When the seed grain formula was eventually translated, the question arose of how to convert the sowing density represented into areas of land that could be measured geometrically.

The debate about absolute values of the dry measure units is too involved to discuss in detail here. Suffice it to say that estimation has been based on: internal textual evidence, including 'conversion factors' between one kind of capacity and another, and records of subsistence allocations; external textual evidence, comparing known figures from the Ancient Near East and Egypt, as well as from other places and times where similar agricultural methods were followed; empirical studies of sizes of vessels found at Mycenaean palaces; and detailed consideration of minimum nutrition requirements of adults and children, with reference to ration figures in Linear B texts.

In short, there are two competing series of values, both seriously considered, one of which I call Ventris and Chadwick (VC) values, the other Chadwick and Palmer (CP) values. While the CP values have some basis in empirical studies of vessel size and nutritional requirements (see Lang 1964; Ventris and Chadwick 1973, 393–4; Palmer 1989), the VC values are supported by internal evidence, including the equivalence of dry measure T to liquid measure S, the latter of which is probably empirically observed (Ventris and Chadwick 1973, 55–6; see also proportions in Palmer 1963, 96–9; Chadwick 1966; De Fidio 1977, 102–14; and discussion of sizes in Shelmerdine 1985, 141–8).

VC Values			CP Values		
GRA	≈	120 litres	GRA	≈	96 litres
T	≈	12 litres	T	≈	9.6 litres
V	≈	2 litres	V	≈	1.6 litres
Z	≈	0.5 litres	Z	≈	0.4 litres

Table 14.1: Theoretical absolute values of Mycenaean dry measures

Sowing densities

An intensive agricultural strategy is historically typical of cultivation by hand in the Aegean, and it is defined by relatively high human labour inputs (planting, weeding, harvesting) per unit area of land, with the goal of assuring yields from each of various crops high with respect to dependent population (usually the cultivators themselves); among other benefits, a wealth of different crops buffers the consumer–cultivators against the risk of failure of any crop in a season (Halstead 1987; Forbes 1989; Halstead 1989; 1992b, 65–70). An extensive agricultural strategy is historically typical of cultivation with animals in the region, and it is defined by low human labour inputs per unit area, with a limited number of crops, aiming to attain a modest surplus relative to dependent populations (often more than just the cultivators) over the long term. Land areas exploited in intensive agriculture are perforce smaller than those

exploited in extensive agriculture. A smallholder with a small work gang, perhaps four to five family members or servants, can cultivate and harvest about 2 to 3 hectares maximum of land under crops in a season in the eastern Mediterranean (Halstead 1995b, 14–16). In contrast, employing animals under similar conditions is only sustainable if one has at minimum 3 to 4 hectares of arable land. Furthermore, the larger the animal one keeps, the more land one must have for pasture or fodder (Halstead 1995b, 12–13).

From early days, Linear B scholars doubted the seed grain measures represented the high sowing densities typical of intensive farming (Webster 1954; Ventris and Chadwick 1973, 237). Ventris and Chadwick assumed, in order to test the hypothesis of high sowing densities, that plots could have been sown with between 150 and 200 litres of seed grain per hectare, as recommended by various Roman and Near Eastern sources. Revisiting their study, one observes that a medium-size fractional *onāton* of area T 1 would be between about 0.05 and 0.08 hectares, and *onātēres* could easily plant and harvest it as individuals, perhaps with the help of other *onātēres* or a family and dependants. However, the largest remainder belonging to a *ktoinohokhos,* measuring GRA 3 T 2 (Eo 269.B = En 659.18), would be between about 1.5 and 2.5 hectares. This size is close to the 2 to 3 hectares a smallholder can cultivate with a small work gang by hand (see above), and the *telestās* in question has a single *onātēr* claiming GRA T 2. The *e-to-ni-jo* of the *hequetās,* measuring GRA 4 T 6 (Eb 473.1 = Ep 539.14), would be between about 2.2 and 3.7 hectares. The mean hypothetical area of this plot, 2.95 hectares, presses the limit even harder, if it does not in fact exceed it – even assuming that the *hequetās'* servants are not occupied tending their own plots.

If whole *ktoinai* or partial *onāta* thereof were intensively cultivated by hand, then one would expect a wide variety of crops to be grown in them. However, the evidence of crop yields in pertinent Linear B records indicates a very narrow range of crops: two types of grain, olives, figs and flax. This stands in contrast with the half dozen or more varieties of grain traditionally cultivated in the region. Critically important is that the Linear B texts record no staple pulses, though these have been found in archaeological contexts (Jones 1987; Halstead 1992a, 108–9; 1992b, 65–6; 1995a; Jones 1995). Therefore, it is quite unlikely that any of the plots, including fractional *onāta,* was cultivated intensively.

On the contrary, it is very likely that all the land plots recorded in Linear B texts were cultivated with extensive methods, one of which is remarkably low sowing densities in areas of land large enough to sustain them. Ventris and Chadwick (1973, 237) cited figures of 50 litres per hectare in Neo-Sumerian (*c.* 2200–2000 BCE) and Kassite Period (*c.* 1600–1150 BCE) Mesopotamia and 60 litres per hectare in Mittani Period (*c.* 1500–1350 BCE) Nuzi in northern Mesopotamia. Further study of sowing densities in the Ancient Near East support Ventris and Chadwick's observations. Kazuya Maekawa (1984; 1986) observes sowing of approximately 60 litres per hectare in the Ur III Period (*c.* 2100–2000 BCE) and later in Mesopotamia, while Carlo Zaccagnini (1979; 1990) observes densities ranging from about 38 to about 64 litres per hectare in Nuzi.

Juliet Du Boulay (1974, 27–32) gives wheat yield figures in the modern Greek village of Ambéli, Euboia, before the introduction of artificial fertilizers, that also support the argument for light sowing on relatively large arable areas. There families, usually of 4 to 6 members, cultivated on average about four hectares, usually ploughed with horses and sown by broadcasting. Expected yields were about 300 kilograms, or 260 litres, per hectare (Du Boulay 1974, 29), using a factor of about 0.85 litres of cleaned seed corn per kilogram (Bennett 1987, 91). Assuming a modest ratio of seed sown to yield of 1 to 5, the implicit sowing density is 52 litres per hectare. Even if the ratio was at the low end of the range, 1 to 3, the sowing density would be just 86 litres per hectare (for examples of yield ratios under similar conditions, see Sterling 1966, 44–82).

More significant is the recently discovered evidence of sowing densities of the same low order in *çiftlik* estates in Ottoman Period Pylos. An eighteenth-century fiscal survey of Anavarin, the area around Pylos, clearly describes a *çiftlik* of 500 *dönüms* (46 ha) on which 100 *kiles* (2,800 kg) of wheat were sown (Zarinebaf *et al.* 2005, 68–9, 194). Using the conversion factor of 0.85 litres per kilogram, this too amounts to about 52 litres per hectare.

Table 14.2 distils the metrological discussion above, giving the hypothetical areas of land corresponding to sowing 40 to 60 litres per hectare.

		Sowing density		
System	Unit	40 litres/ha	50 litres/ha	60 litres/ha
VC	Z	0.0125 ha	0.01 ha	.0083 ha
(equivalent	V	0.05 ha	0.04 ha	0.03 ha
areas)	T	**0.30 ha**	**0.24 ha**	**0.20 ha**
	GRA	3.00 ha	2.40 ha	2.00 ha
	GRA 10	30.0 ha	24.0 ha	20.0 ha
		40 litres/ha	50 litres/ha	60 litres/ha
CP	Z	0.01 ha	0.008 ha	0.007 ha
(equivalent	V	0.04 ha	0.032 ha	0.027 ha
areas)	T	**0.24 ha**	**0.192 ha**	**0.16 ha**
	GRA	2.40 ha	1.92 ha	1.60 ha
	GRA 10	24.0 ha	19.2 ha	16.0 ha

Table 14.2: Hypothetical areas of land measured in seed grain, using Ventris and Chadwick's (VC) and Chadwick and Palmer's (CP) values of Mycenaean dry measurement

Broadcasting and ploughing

Broadcast sowing was probably employed throughout the Ancient Near East to achieve some of the low densities recorded (Maekawa 1990, 115), and there is good reason to believe that it was used in Bronze Age Greece as well.

Efficient seeder-ploughs, such as were used in ancient Mesopotamia, are unknown in Mycenaean Greece, and the Iron Age poet Hesiod probably alludes to broadcasting when he recommends hiring an experienced farmhand who 'avoids over-sowing' (Hes.*Op.*446). Effective, non-wasteful broadcasting requires several, usually interdependent conditions: abundance of land with respect to dependent human population; low ratio of human labour input to land available; tracts of fertile land large enough for regular fallowing of considerable parts of them, on which animals contribute to fertility and control weeds by grazing; and use of some of the same animals, which do not compete directly with humans for crops, to plough these tracts.

Hence it should be clear that ploughing, especially with powerful animals like oxen, and broadcast sowing are very compatible methods. Citizens of Athens and other Classical Greek polities who were wealthy enough to own a pair of oxen with which to plough required 50 to 60 *plethra*, about five hectares, of land or more according to law and custom (Burford 1993, 67). In Mycenaean terms, this area is about GRA 2 (see Table 14.2). In fact, the mean size of a *ktimenā* parcel in the Pylian Eo–En texts, including all fractional *onāta*, is GRA 2 T 5. The largest estates in ancient Attica seem to have been no larger than about 300 *plethra*, or 27 hectares – on the order of Mycenaean GRA 10 (Burford 1993, 68; Table 14.2). Single farms within these Attic estates were on the order of 60 *plethra* – again about GRA 2 or a little more.

The Mycenaean palaces lie near areas of well drained, fertile land suitable for extensive application of low human and seed inputs along with animal labour: the Mesara Valley of south-central Crete (Watrous 1993); the coastal and upland plains of Messenia (McDonald and Rapp 1972; Zangger *et al.* 1997; Cosmopoulos 2006); the Argive Plain (Jameson *et al.* 1994); and the Boiotian plain (Bintliff and Snodgrass 1985; Knauss 1996). Furthermore, the Linear B records indicate a great number of oxen and ox-drivers in some of these very areas (see Bennet 1985; Palaima 1989), as well as very large harvests of GRA, probably a single variety of wheat (Godart 1968; Killen 1994–1995; see also Halstead 1999, 320–1). In this context, several aspects of the use of the *çiftlik* described in the Ottoman fiscal survey discussed earlier in 'Sowing densities' are significant. Its area is large compared with most others catalogued therein, and so it can be cultivated extensively. In fact, it was cultivated entirely with grain or row crops (including 'fodder'). Ten pairs of oxen were used on its 46 hectares. Each pair ploughed land for 10 *kile* of seed (*i.e.* 4.6 ha), and each of these allotments was presumably an individual constituent *çift;* none of the people recorded as tilling these *çifts* appears to have had a plot smaller than 10 *kile*, such as are found in other, generally smaller *çiftliks* in the region (Davies 2004, 111; Zarinebaf *et al.* 2005, 68–9). These *çifts*, then, are on the order of Mycenaean GRA 2.

Ploughing and organisation of plots

Although the modern Greek *stremma* is officially 0.10 hectares, it is traditionally the ground a pair of draught animals can plough in one day. According to one authority, it has ranged between 0.09 and 0.16 hectares, corresponding to square fields 30 by 30 metres and 40 by 40 metres, respectively (Psychoghios 1995, 24–5, citing various sources). Ethnographic data show that a day's ploughing in moderately well drained, alluvial soils of Messenia and the Argolid ranges in fact between 0.1 and 0.3 hectares per day, the upper end of the range associated with oxen ploughing, particularly teams of them in rotation (Aschenbrenner 1972, 57; Du Boulay 1974, 242–4; Jameson *et al.* 1994, 388). Paul Halstead has noted that consecutively ploughed and sown strips of land are commonly about 10 metres wide. Thus a plot of 0.09 hectares can be thought of as a field consisting of three strips 30 meters long, a plot of 0.16 hectares as a field consisting of four such strips and a plot of the median size observed above (0.2 ha) can be thought of as a field consisting of four strips 50 metres long (Halstead, pers. comm. 2006). Halstead has also noted that in deep, well drained soils of the flatlands of northern Greece, oxen can plough a furrow of 50 to 100 metres or more before they have to rest. The cultivator usually ploughs a strip of length appropriate to the animal employed, sows it and ploughs the seed in before birds eat the seed or weather drives the cultivator off the land. This procedure is repeated as necessary (Halstead, pers. comm. 2006).

Standard classical measures of area that correspond in principle to the *stremma* vary in size. The Attic *plethron* was 100 by 100 feet (*c.* 30 × 30 m = 0.09 ha), and the Roman *actus* was 120 by 120 Roman feet (*c.* 35 × 35 m = 0.12 ha), while the Roman *iugerum* was twice the size of an *actus* – 120 by 240 feet (*c.* 35 × 70 m = 0.25 ha; see Burford 1993, 113; Columella *Rust.*5.1.6). It is important to observe that historically where a central authority assesses large extents of land, this authority usually tries to create standard areas and dimensions. This practice is particularly well documented in the Venetian administration of the Peloponnese (Davies 2004).

As a rule, the space between furrows is equal to the length of the yoke or some multiple thereof, the former reflecting turning the draught animals so that one animal walks back down the tracks of the other, and the latter reflecting turning the animals to give the last tilled furrow or concomitant ridge a wide berth. Assuming paired draught animals, as is evidently the rule in the Linear B texts from Knossos and probably Pylos (Killen 1992–1993; Halstead 1999), yoke-length is between about 1.7 and 2.5 metres (Kumwenda 1999, my own observations). Yokes longer than about 1.8 metres are usually reserved for mouldboard ploughs that create large ridges for drainage in wet climates (Kumwenda 1999, 141). The ploughs used in Late Bronze Age Greece were almost certainly simple ards, perhaps with a metal ploughshare.

As the calculation of *dosmos* implies (see above), as perhaps does a Pylian text describing an official visually inspecting 'ploughlands' (*arourai*, Eq 213), the minimal units of land ploughed and sown at any time in a *ktoinā* parcel should be easily observable on the ground. No texts describe an *onāton* claim smaller than V 1 (= Z 4), and it is therefore reasonable to assume that V represents the equivalent of the minimal ploughed and sown 'strip' described above. Fraction Z could nevertheless correspond to a ploughing dimension. One may hypothesise that Z is a furrow roughly of length 65 metres – the mean of 30 and 100 (see above) – of which four make up a V-size strip (the result of setting out and returning with the plough twice). If V is about 10 metres wide, as observed in modern Greece, then furrows would be spaced about 2.5 metres apart, at the outside limit of a yoke-length and a strange distance, even if furrow spacing is measured in multiples of yoke-length. However, if V is about seven metres wide, then four Z furrows would be about 1.75 metres apart. This is a more likely yoke-length for an ard, as well as a fairly round number with which to elaborate hypotheses.

Seven metres is still a plausible strip width, even for broadcasting; broadcast-sown English furlongs, making up a traditional acre, are 5 metres wide (one 'rod'; Hall 1982, 22). Given 1.75-metre furrow spacing, the next largest fraction of land, T (= V 6), would consist of six successive strips – that is, an area of about 42 by 65 metres, or 2,730 m² (0.273 ha). Area T would thus be a reasonable day's ploughing on flat land with tractable soils. If one assumes the furrow spacing was 1.5 metres, then area T would be about 36 by 65 metres, or 2,340 m² (0.243 ha), whereas if the furrow spacing was 2.0 metres, then T would be about 48 by 65 metres or 3,120 m² (0.312 ha). These figures are respectively close to the lower and upper end of the observed range of a day's ploughing with oxen.

Using the dry-measure figures in Tables 14.1 and 14.2, one can now calculate the seeding density from the hypothetical ploughing rate. Fraction Z of seed can be thought of as 0.4 to 0.5 litres per area between furrows of 0.011375 hectare within a 42-by-65-metre plot; the sowing density would thus be between 35 and 45 litres per hectare. This range is rather lower than that of area figures in Table 14.2. However, one should bear in mind that the figures are hypothetical: those of seed could be a little larger, and those of land a little smaller. For example, an area of T amount of seed equal to 0.24 hectares, highlighted in the 40 litre and 50 litre columns of Table 14.2, can be thought of as a rectangle of dimensions 40 by 60 metres (yoke-length 1.67 m). To achieve an area of about 0.273 hectares, hypothesised in the last paragraph, the furrow length would have to be closer to 45 metres – which would be tantamount to the 42-by-

Area	'Rectangular' dimensions		Square dimensions	
	Sown (40–50 l/ha)	Ploughed	Sown (40–50 l/ha)	Ploughed
T	40.00 × 60.00 m	42.00 × 65.00 m	49.00 × 49.00 m	52.25 × 52.25 m
GRA	200.00 × 120.00 m	210.00 × 130.00 m	196.00 × 98.00 m	209.00 × 104.50 m
GRA 10	400.00 × 600.00 m	420.00 × 650.00 m	490.00 × 490.00 m	522.25 × 522.25 m

Table 14.3: Dimensions of hypothetical plots based on sowing density and ploughing rate

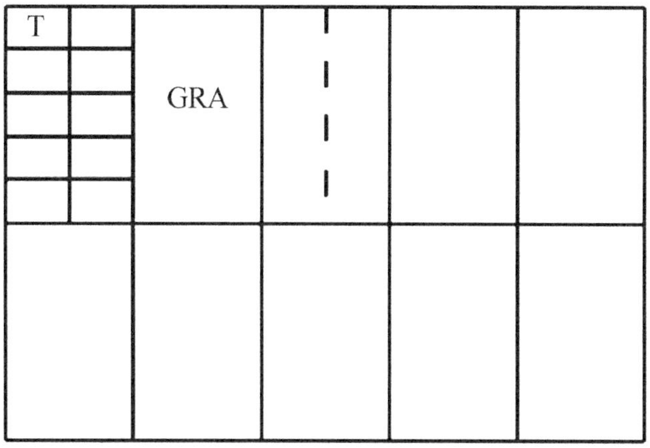

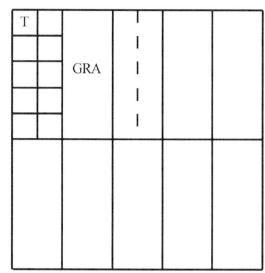

Fig. 14.1: Hypothetical layout of Mycenaean land plots using 'rectangular' dimensions

Fig.14.2: Hypothetical layout of Mycenaean land plots using square dimensions

65-metre plot already described. A square field of the same area would be 52.25 metres on a side and would require furrow spacing of about 2.18 metres. This furrow spacing is awkward but not implausible, and a V-size 'strip' would be about 8.72 metres wide. A field of 0.24 ha size, such as is presented in Table 14.2, could be realized as a square 49 metres on a side (furrow spacing 2.04 m).

The Linear B scribes were interested not only in allotments of fractional size V and T but also of whole unit size GRA and, especially, multiple GRA 10, the latter evident in several summary texts from Pylos (Ed 236, Eq 213, Er 312). One may assume that plots of size GRA and multiples thereof were laid out optimise (1) traverse along any dimension, because cultivators, harvesters, claimants and perhaps fiscal agents would have to move efficiently across any parcel, and (2) 'packing' of plots of regular dimensions within an extent of easily arable land, so as to make the most complete use of the few large areas of suitable soil in the region. Given these parameters, area GRA consisting of average-size 'rectangular' T plots (42 × 65 m) would be 130 by 210 metres (2.73 ha, *c.* 3:5 dimensions), and area GRA 10 consisting of such GRA plots would be 420 by 650 metres (27.3 ha, *c.* 2:3 dimensions). Assuming a square T plot, GRA would be 104.5 by 209 metres (1:2 dimensions), and GRA 10 would be a square 522.5 metres on a side. All the hypothetical dimensions discussed above are presented in Table 14.3, and the hypothetical layout of plots is given in Figs. 14.1 and 14.2.

One can see in Figs. 14.1 and 14.2 that GRA 10 is readily divided into viable *ktoinai* of GRA 2 and GRA 2 T 5. These would be between 5.4 and 6.9 hectares, given the ploughing data above, though perhaps as small as 4.8 to 6.0 hectares, if sown with 40 to 50 litres per hectare.

Comparison with later Greek *khōrai*

The concept developed above is consistent with Classical Greek tradition: a large expanse of habitable land, almost invariably called the *khōrā* 'space', comprising perhaps several *dāmoi* and other groups with special interests (*e.g.* temple officials looking after precincts or estates), was divided into plots of standard size, *khōria,* from which allotments of whole units or aliquot fractions were made (Lewis 1973; Burford 1993, 112–4). The extant evidence of the far-flung Greek colonies makes this arrangement even clearer. The best preserved is in the colony of the Crimean Khersonesos, which Megarians established in the fifth century BCE. There the major plots of land – also the major allotments, or *klēroi* – are nearly all 420 by 630 metres (varying by only a few metres in any dimension), plots of 420 by 420 metres and 420 by 735 metres being the main exceptions (Dufkova and Pečirka 1970; Saprykin

1994; Figs. 14.3 and 14.4). Each of these constituted a single estate, usually with a single farmhouse. Inscriptions from the colony indicate that the *klēros*-holders rented fractional parcels of their estates (Saprykin 1994, 87–94, 150–1), sometimes to tenant farmers who probably did not continuously inhabit the land (see Burford 1993, 54, 172–7).

The smallest recognisable fraction of an allotment of 420 by 630 metres was a plot 52.5 metres on a side, of which 96 made up a typical *klēros* (8 × 12). These smallest plots, or *plethra,* were usually demarcated with walls, ditches or access roads, and each appears to have been dedicated to a single crop (Dufkova and Pečirka 1970). Although clearly square, they are very nearly equal in area to my hypothetical Mycenaean *plethron / stremma* (area T) – 52.5 by 52.5 metres making 2,756.2 square metres, or 0.276 hectares (*cf.* 42 × 65 m / 52.25 × 52.25 m = 2,730 m²; Table 14.3). The usual size of a tenant farm in the Khersonesos was one sixth of a *klēros,* that is, a square parcel of 16 local *plethra* (4 × 4), 210 metres on a side, being 4.41 hectares in area – though they are known to be as small as half of a sixth-parcel, that is, a rectangle 105 by 210 metres (2.2 ha), consisting of eight local *plethra* (Saprykin 1994, 83). The former size is safely above the lower limit of what can economically be cultivated with oxen. Allotments of the latter size were usually turned over to intensively cultivated vineyard or orchard (Saprykin 1994, 83).

It is hard to dismiss as mere coincidence the 2-to-3 proportions the Crimean *klēroi* share with one of the hypothetical reconstructions of Mycenaean plots of size GRA 10. For fear of seeming to overstate the similarity of the later Greek evidence, I feel I should emphasise the

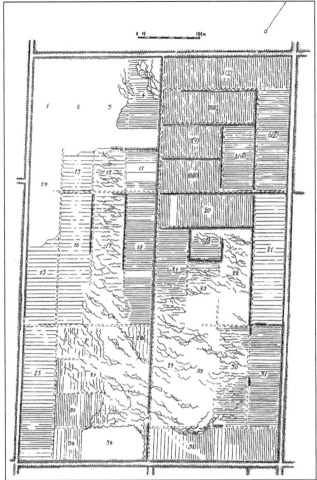

Fig. 14.3: Plan drawing of land-plot 137 in Crimean Khersonesos (Saprykin 1994, 130)

Fig. 14.4: Aerial photograph of land-plots 9, 10, and 11 in Crimean Khersonesos (Saprykin 1994, pl. 25)

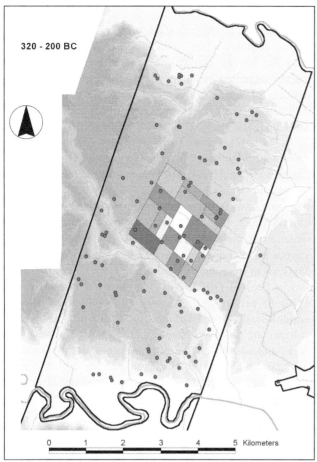

Fig. 14.5: Reconstructed land plots in the Metapontion during the Hellenistic Period (Carter 2006, 120)

differences. For example, the Khersonesian *klēroi* estates appear to represent a compromise between the alternative 1-to-1 and 2-to-3 proportions of Mycenaean agricultural plots hypothesised in above (see Table 14.3, Figs. 14.1 and 14.2). Here the *plethra* and most common farm subdivisions are square (52.5 × 52.5 m and 210 × 210 m), while the *klēros* is rectangular (420 × 630 m). In contrast, the 2-to-3 proportion of the Mycenaean *ktoinā* system would be established at the level of the *plethron / stremma* (area T) and repeated at the level of GRA 10 (assuming conventional optimisation of space). One upshot of this difference is that the Khersonesian *klēros* is readily divided into halves, thirds, quarters, sixths and twelfths – there normally being 6 to 12 tenant farms and 96 *plethra*. The Mycenaean plot of GRA 10, again in contrast, is readily divisible into halves, fifths and tenths (there being T 100), as well as into quarters, if one allows a hypothetical plot of T 10 to be split in half (see Figs. 14.1 and 14.2).

In spite of this apparent difference, Pia De Fidio's (1977) analysis of the Pylian Er–Es–Un 718 series, cited earlier in 'Describing and measuring land', may also be relevant to understanding the Khersonesian system of land division. Three sectors of landholders described therein, each representing an area that is a multiple of GRA 10, collectively pay one sixth of their agricultural product to certain entities. The tax assessment is facilitated by the *onāta* of each of the landholders being measured in amounts of GRA T, the major fraction of which is V (= 1/6 T), if the method of assessment is not actually designed around the fractions. However, the Khersonesian *dāmos* consisted of only one jurisdiction of *klēros*-holders. It was divided into 'hundreds', probably four, consisting of 100 *klēroi* (Saprykin 1994, 87–94, 150–1). Thus collectively each 'hundred' could be assessed for one sixth of the product of the constituent *klēroi*, measured either in proportion to *plethra* or, in most cases, tenant farm subdivisions consisting of whole *plethra*. Put another way, the relationship of Mycenaean V to T (1:6) is written at a larger scale in the Khersonesian system of *klēroi*: to wit, Mycenaean V : T : GRA 10 :: 16 Khersonesian *plethra* (1/6) : 1 *klēros* : 1 'hundred'. Epigraphy especially makes clear that tribute in multiples of sixths and tenths was common in Archaic and Classical Period Greece – for example, the Athenian *dōdekatē* 'twelfth' tax, or the 1/60 assessment Athens imposed on the Khersonesos and other states in the later fifth century (Meiggs and Lewis 1988, 83–9).

What is more, evidence from Archaic Greek colonies in lower Italy and the French and Spanish Riviera seems to support the theory that the parallel between the Mycenaean *ktoinā* system and Khersonesian *klēros* system is not simply coincidental, reducible to agricultural conditions or technologies, but rather reflects an already ancient tradition or institution of land allocation. Greeks from Akhaia were systematically colonising the Metapontion in Italy by the eighth century BCE (Graham 1971; Boardman and Hammond 1982, 174–5; Graham 1989; Carter 2006). Running across the plain from the coast to the foothills, between the rivers, are parallel ditches spaced approximately 210 metres apart, with very little variation (Adamesteanu 1973; Carter 2006, 103). Perpendicular to these, also at intervals of 210 metres or multiples thereof, are other ditches, which may also have assisted with drainage, as well as walls and roads, which together break the landscape up into parcels that consist of square units as small as 210 metres on a side. In at least one well excavated place, the distance between a perpendicular 'division line road' and the next perpendicular division (a ditch), both lying across a 210-metre interval, is about 630 metres, which strongly suggests a standard way of dividing land, seen also in the Khersonesos (Carter 2006, 97; see Fig. 14.5).

Likewise, in the Phokaian colony of Emporion in present-day Catalonia, founded in the early sixth century BCE, the major land division appears to be 210 metres, with multiples of 630 metres frequently occurring. Rosa Plana-Mallart (1999, 1) has pointed out that if one assumes that the Emporiote foot was 0.35 metres long, the same as the so called 'Samian' foot, then 210 metres make up a classic stade of 600 feet (see *Hdt.* 2.149). Just across the modern border in Hérault, France, is the colony of Agathe Tykhe, which Phokaians from Massalia founded, perhaps as early as the seventh century. Its remains reveal the major land division interval to be about 180 metres, in contrast with the figures I just discussed, squares of this dimension on the sides comprising 3.2 hectares. However, Monique Clavel-Lévêque (1999, 189–91) points out that if one assumes the so called 'Attic' foot of 0.293 to 0.297 metres for the layout of this colony, then 180 metres is approximately one stade of 600 feet (see 'Measures', *Oxford Classical Dictionary*; recent discussion in Stieglitz 2006).

I can now work with hypothetical foot measurements to reconstruct the area of Mycenaean GRA 10. If a foot was 0.35 metres, then furrowing spacing of 1.75 metres would have been 5 feet, or the classical 'double-pace' (*diploun bēma*; see Davies 2004, 114). T could then have been 120 by 180 feet, and GRA 10 could have been 1,200 by 1,800 feet – or 2 by 3 stades. Conversely, if furrow spacing was 1.67 metres (as though for GRA 10 = 400 × 600 m), then a foot would have been 0.33 feet, slightly more than the classic 'Doric' foot. Assuming for purposes of hypothesis that a Mycenaean foot was equal to J. Walter Graham's (1987, 222–9, 250–2, 254–5) 'Minoan' foot of 0.304 metres, the furrowing spacing for area Z would have been 1.52 metres – rather small. However, GRA 10 could have been 364.8 metres by 547.2 metres, or 19.96 hectares. This area is about that sown with 60 litres per hectare using VC measures, or a little less than 50 litres per hectare with CP measures (see Table 14.2). Of course, there are other permutations, especially for square dimensions (see above).

Conclusions

Important cultural historical questions remain. For example, all the colonies whose land division systems I compare with the Mycenaean *ktoinā* system were founded and mainly inhabited by Greeks who wrote or spoke Dorian dialects of Greek, in contrast with the generally 'Old Akhaian' or 'East Greek' character of Mycenaean (Ventris and Chadwick 1973, 73–5, 396–7; Dunkel 1981; Bartoněk 2003, 446–97). Recent valid critiques of this and other traditional linguistically based distinctions between Greek communities aside (*e.g.* Hall 1997), one possible explanation of the similarities may involve geographical, rather than linguistic, association: cities in mainland Greece, as opposed to Asia Minor, founded these colonies. Mainland Greece is where most major Mycenaean sites are found and where various populations may have adopted and transformed the Mycenaean tradition of landholding.

Lin Foxhall (1995, 249) has asserted that no reason exists to believe that 'socially and politically coherent, agriculturally based communities' did not survive the collapse of the Mycenaean palace system around 1150 BCE, and she has challenged archaeologists to illuminate the 'darkness' between this date and the eighth century BCE, when 'coherent, well-organized political entities' appear again on the archaeological horizon. Contemporary archaeological remote-sensing technologies afford the opportunity to test both my model of Mycenaean land allocation and Foxhall's historical conjecture.

LANDSCAPES OF POWER AND PROTO-URBAN DEVELOPMENTS TOWARD URBANIZATION IN BRONZE AGE AND EARLY IRON AGE *LATIUM VETUS*

Francesca Fulminante

The old debate over urbanisation in central Italy (Ampolo 1980) has recently been revitalised by new excavations conducted in the central area of Rome (see Sommella Mura *et al.* 2001 for the Capitoline hill; and Carandini 2007 with previous references for the Palatine hill) and by recent research conducted by Italian (Peroni 1996; di Gennaro and Guidi 2000; Pacciarelli 2001; Peroni 2000; Guidi in press) and international scholars (Damgaard Andersen *et al.* 1997; Attema 2004; Osborne and Cunliffe 2005). In simple terms the main questions of this debate have always been whether the city began in the 8th–7th or the 6th century BCE, what political structure preceded the city, and to what extent were changes generated by external factors. With reference to this third issue, some scholars, mainly historians, Classicists and Etruscologists, have placed a great emphasis on external stimuli, such as Greek colonisation, and on the priority of the process in Etruria as opposed to other Italian regions. Other scholars, principally pre-historians, have placed more emphasis on early and fairly rapid internal transformations, and see a weak asymmetry between Etruria and some other regions (for a summary and further references see Vanzetti 2002; and Fulminante 2003, 244–9). This papers aims to contribute to this debate by reconsidering these new excavations, combined with a re-evaluation of old settlement data, in the light of fresh ideas.

The new excavations which have uncovered an earth wall around the Palatine central cult place and a regal residence in the area of the Vesta Sanctuary (see Carandini 2007 for a synthesis of his excavations on the north slope of the Palatine and interpretations on the foundation of Rome), together with a re-examination of materials and contexts from old excavations (Carafa 1997; 2004; 2005; Filippi 2005; Gusberti 2005), seem to date the very beginning of Rome as a city to as early as the middle of the 8th century

BCE. In addition, a reorganisation of the north slope of the *Capitolium*, excavated in the area of the Giardino Romano and dated to the Recent Bronze Age, confirms the presence of a permanent settlement on this hill and which probably dates as far back as the Middle Bronze Age (Cazzella 2001).

The very beginning of Rome and its first development is a controversial subject, with opinions ranging from the generous size estimations by Andrea Carandini (1997) to the minimal calculations of Alberto Cazzella (2001), and cannot be debated exhaustively within the limits of this paper. However it is generally agreed that a major stage of this development is represented by the shift of formal cemeteries from the area of the *Antonino* and *Faustina* Temple, at the foot of the Palatine hill, to the Quirinal and Esquiline hill, which implies a significant enlargement of the settlement (Guidi 1982; Cazzella 2001). Estimates of the size of this growth, dated to the Latial IIB period (9th century) or, according to Marco Bettelli (1997), possibly to Latial IIA (the end of 10th and the beginning of 9th centuries), have varied. Alessandro Guidi (1982, 282) has calculated that the area comprising the Palatine, *Forum* and *Capitolium*, and possibly Velia, covered an extension of 95 ha in the Latial IIA period, while Alberto Cazzella (2001) gives a similar estimation (about 100ha) but only from the Latial IIB onward. My own calculation gives a figure of about 54 ha for the area around the Quirinal (*Colles*) and from 37 to 60 ha for the system around the Palatine, Velia, *Cermalus* (*Montes*), totalling about 90–114 ha. Paolo Carafa (1996, 799) gives a figure of about 150 ha for the Latial IIA period, including both the *Colles* and the *Montes*. According to Carandini's (1997) reconstruction, the unification of the *Colles* and the *Montes* into one unified settlement, by the Latial IIB2/IIIA period (the end of the 9th to the beginning of the 8th centuries), saw Rome reaching

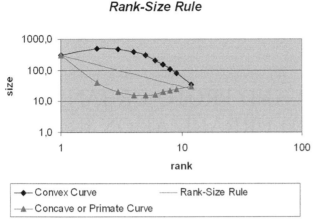

Rank-Size Rule

Fig. 15.1: *Types of deviations from Rank-Size log-normality: concave (or primate) and convex curves*

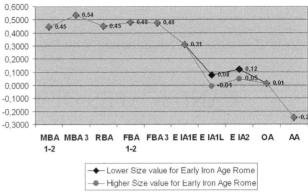

Fig. 15.2: *Latium vetus: Rank-Size index graph*

the remarkable extension of about 250 ha, which made the city approximately as large as the main contemporary Etruscan settlements, such as the plateaux of Veio, which Guidi (1982, 283) has estimated at around 242 ha.

From the above figures, even adopting the lowest prudent calculations by Cazzella, it is clear that the transformations that occurred in Rome during the 8th–7th centuries represented more a qualitative revolution than a physical modification of the city itself (already suggested by Guidi 1982, 279). The appearance of monuments such as the wall around the Palatine, the Vesta Sanctuary and the Capitoline hill votive deposit, or the Forum and the *Comitium* for civic assemblies, indicate the birth in Rome at that time of a unified community of citizens and a new political entity, even though the complete urban realization of the city (with stone buildings, monuments and temples) would only have been completed by the Archaic period.

By combining this new evidence from the central area of Rome with location analyses conducted at the regional level (Rank-Size rule, the Spatial Efficiency model, and Voronoi diagrams applied to *Latium vetus*' Bronze and Early Iron Age settlements), this paper aims to demonstrate that urban formation in central Italy was not simply a secondary phenomenon imported from Greece, but a primary process whose origin dates back well into the Bronze Age, and whose development was influenced, but not triggered, by external stimuli.

The Rank-Size model

It is a commonly held belief that by the end of the Final Bronze Age or the beginning of the Early Iron Age a process of settlement nucleation and centralization led to the formation of large proto-urban centres on the *tufa* plateaux, later occupied by the cities of the Archaic Period (Peroni

2000). This process, revolutionary in Etruria and more gradual in *Latium vetus*, is also confirmed by the application of the Rank-Size model (compare Guidi 1985 for Etruria and *Latium vetus*; and Cardosa 1993 for Etruria).

The Rank-Size rule, developed from theories advanced by George Kingsley Zipf in the late 1940s (1949), notes the relationship between the rank of cities and their population. The formula is $P_n = P1/n$, where P_n is the population of towns ranked n, P1 is the population of the largest town, and n is the rank of the town. The formula states that the population of a town ranked n is equal to the population of the largest town divided by n. Thus, if the largest town has a certain population, the second largest town will have a population of one-half that number, the third largest will have a population of one-third, and so on.

If the common logarithms of rank and size (generally used in archaeological applications) are plotted against one another, the result is a straight line with a slope of -1. This classic, 'ideal' distribution is called log-normal and is typical of a state-system with a high level of integration between settlements. Two deviations from the log-normal are possible: concave or primate distributions, where the largest settlement is unexpectedly 'large' (typical of imperial or colonial systems), and convex distributions, where the largest settlement is unexpectedly 'small' (typical of systems with a low level of integration; see Fig. 15.1).

Gregory Johnson (1977; 1980; 1981) applied the Rank-Size rule to the Susiana plain (Iran) in the fourth millennium BCE and demonstrated that an increasing system integration (with the development of a state-level society) was shown by the development of a log-normal rank-size distribution from a convex distribution. After this pioneering study the Rank-Size model has been applied by a number of scholars in as many geographical and historical contexts (see for example Falconer and Savage 1995; Liu 1996; Mudar 1999), but there are still unresolved issues attached to the application of this model.

First, Zipf's law is empirical and even though several

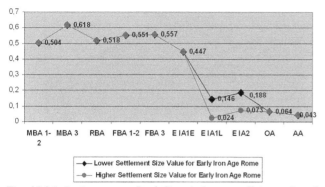

Fig. 15.3A: Latium vetus: Rank-Size A-shape coefficient: plotted values

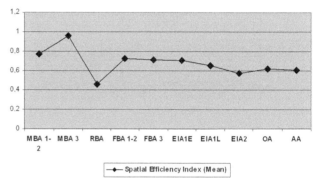

Fig. 15.3B: Latium vetus: Rank-Size A-shape coefficient: statistical confidence zone for plotted values

attempts to demonstrate its mathematical validity have been undertaken there is still no theoretical basis for its application (Hodder 1979; Laxton and Cavanagh 1995). On the contrary, as demonstrated by Ian Hodder (1979, 143), *'the structure in each rank-size curve is the composite result of a complex balance between original forces and survival and recovery processes'* and it is very difficult to establish whether a deviation from the normal distribution reflects the real interplay of forces or just biases in the actual data.

Second, Johnson noted that the interpretation of the rank-size graphs could be related to scale and boundary problems (1980, 241; 1981, 167) or that a log-normal distribution, which misses middle range settlements, could become a primate distribution (1981, 173). In order to minimize these problems, Rank-Size Index (hereafter RSI; Johnson 1980) and A-shape coefficient (Drennan and Peterson 2004) can be calculated from the curves of the rank-size graphs in order to mathematically estimate the degree of convexity of the curves and to plot their trends through time.

RSI and A-shape coefficient values of 1 indicate the highest degree of convexity of the rank-size curve, values around 0 indicate a log-normal distribution, and values between 0 and -1 indicate a primate distribution. The calculation of A-shape coefficients can establish the statistical confidence of the rank-size curve, and demonstrates if a certain curve and the corresponding sample are really representative of settlement pattern and market forces, or if the result is due to vagaries in the sampling or errors in the definition of the regional limits.

Finally, as suggested by Johnston (1981, 171), the rank-size analyses in this work have not been conducted in 'isolation', but have been combined with the results of independent analyses (other locational models such as the Spatial Efficiency model, and Voronoi diagrams) and compared with different types of evidence (funerary evidence and urban excavations), to help to verify the internal consistency of the general historical interpretation.

The rank-size graphs for Bronze Age settlements in

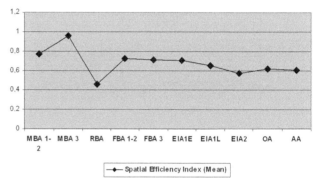

Fig. 15.4: Latium vetus: spatial efficiency index

Latium vetus show convex curves for the whole duration of this period, as confirmed by RSI values of around 0.4–0.5. This suggests that at this time the region was still characterised by a low level of integration between different settlements. Such a model is consistent with the settlement pattern proposed by Marco Pacciarelli (2001, 87–8) for this period: a continuous and capillary occupation of the territory with small open sites, generally less than 1 hectare in extent. However, it is possible that a certain level of hierarchy was already present at this time.

Francesco di Gennaro distinguishes between 'monocentric' communities, those concentrated in one settlement only, with polycentric communities that have several settlements within their territory – one central and others dependant – and has identified polycentric communities in late Middle Bronze Age Etruria (see Peroni 1996, 196 ff.). It is possible that this kind of organisation is also present in *Latium vetus*, as is demonstrated by the higher value of the RSI for the Middle Bronze Age 3 (see Fig. 15.2).

During the Early Iron Age the rank-size graph shows a straightening of the convex distribution, still present for an early phase of the Early Iron Age 1 (the Latial IIA period, with a RSI of 0.33), towards the log-normal distributions

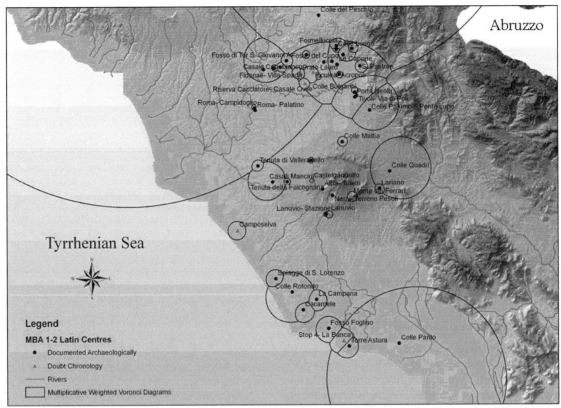

Fig. 15.5A: Latium vetus: multiplicatively weighted Voronoi diagrams: Middle Bronze Age 1–2

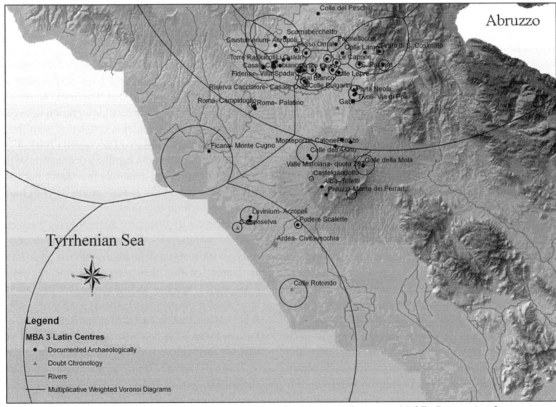

Fig. 15.5B: Latium vetus: multiplicatively weighted Voronoi diagrams: Middle Bronze Age 3

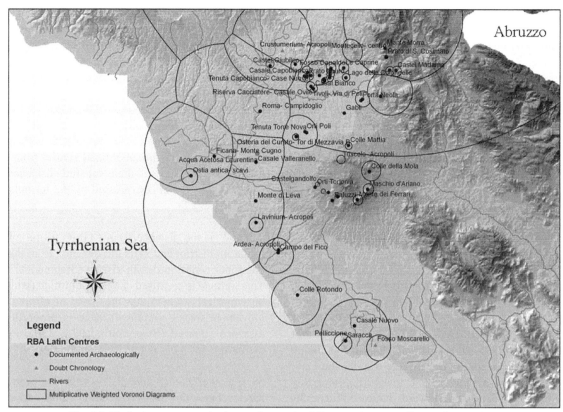

Fig. 15.6A: Latium vetus: multiplicatively weighted Voronoi diagrams: Recent Bronze Age

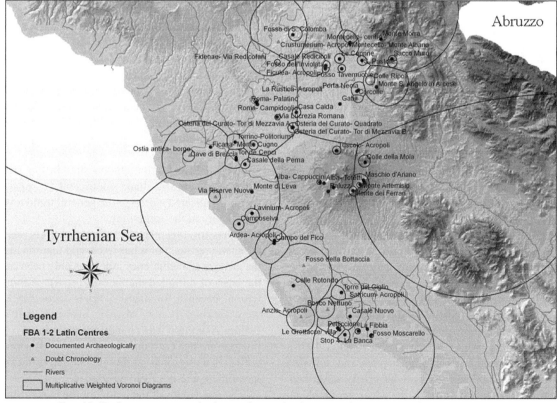

Fig. 15.6B: Latium vetus: multiplicatively weighted Voronoi diagrams: Final Bronze Age 1–2

that appears during the second phase of the Early Iron Age 1 (Latial IIB) and persists during the Early Iron Age 2, before ending in almost imperceptible convex distribution for the Orientalising and Archaic Periods (values of the RSI around 0.00, and slightly below for the Archaic Period). A tendency toward a log-normal distribution during the second phase of the Early Iron Age 1 (Latial IIB) has been noted by Guidi (1985, 224), who nevertheless underestimated and disregarded the development of *Latium vetus* toward an increased complex and hierarchical settlement organisation as compared to Etruria (on this point see also Vanzetti 2004).

The trend of the rank-size curves indicated by the RSI is also confirmed by the A-Shape coefficient. The calculation of this index for the Bronze Age confirms a convex distribution, with value around 0.5–0.6. The value of the A-shape coefficient then decreases slightly during the first part of the Early Iron Age 1 (Latial IIA) with a value of 0.44, and then more dramatically from the second part of the Early Iron Age 1 onward (from Latial IIB) with values around 0.00 (Fig. 15.3A). The graph of the error ranges for the A-shape coefficient shows that its values have a higher statistical confidence for the Bronze Age than for the Early Iron Age. However a general trend toward log-normality can still be detected, pointing towards increased hierarchy and settlement integration (Fig. 15.3B).

The Spatial Efficiency model

In the late 1970s, Vincas Steponaitis (1978) questioned whether the Central Place Model could be applied to the study of pre-capitalistic societies, and developed a new locational model to analyse settlement hierarchies in pre-state societies and complex chiefdoms. Steponaitis' model is based on assumptions regarding the locational constraints of chiefly centres. Any community is a closed environment with a certain finite amount of energy. The costs of maintaining the central institutions of complex chiefdoms (nobility, craftsmen and other non-productive classes, public and religious architecture, sumptuary goods, etc.) are supported by the surplus production and *corvée* labour of the commoners. The 'effort' invested by commoners in surplus production and *corvée* labour could only be maximised by minimising the 'effort' spent in movement of goods and people to and from chiefly centres. As a consequence, it can be demonstrated that minimising this cost can best be achieved by an efficient location of the chiefly centres.

A mathematical explanation of the model does not form part of the present work (instead *cf.* Steponaitis 1978), but its principles and the basic procedures and software applications used in this work will be briefly described. According to Steponaitis' model, the ideal geographical position of a chiefly centre is calculated in relation both to local and second-order settlement location and take into account the chiefly centre's population size. But, as he stressed, with a high degree of political centralization the position of the lower-order centres is more important than the distribution of local settlements, and the capital would ideally be located 'at the centre of gravity of the minor centres' (CGMC; Steponaitis 1978, 435).

According to Steponaitis then, the spatial efficiency of a chiefly centre location can be calculated as the sum of the squared distances of the subordinate centres from the capital, divided by the sum of their squared distances from the CGMC. This model is expressed by the formula: $\dfrac{\sum_{i=1}^{I} R_i^2}{\sum_{i=1}^{I} D_i^2}$

where R_i is the distance from CGMC to the minor centre in the ith district and D_i is the distance from the capital to the minor centre in the ith district (Steponaitis 1978, 436). This formula is premised on the assumption (which is based on empirical studies) that the 'cost' of effort involved in movement over a certain distance is proportional to the distance squared (Steponaitis 1978, 430). Because by definition: $\sum_{i=1}^{I} D_i^2$ = is less than or equal to $\sum_{i=1}^{I} R_i^2$ =

the spatial efficiency index is 1.0 when the centre is ideally located, but as the observed position of the 'capital' diverges from the ideal location the value of the index decreases (Steponaitis 1978, 436). In order to identify which centres pertain to each district, planar and multiplicatively weighted Voronoi diagrams have been used (and will be presented in the following section). Arc View 3.2 and Arc GIS 9 have been used to perform the analysis and, in particular, the Weighted Mean of Points (v. 1.2c) extension for Arc View has been adopted to calculate the CGMC (Jenness 2004).

Quite unexpectedly the spatial efficiency index (Fig. 15.4, below) showed a very high value for the Middle Bronze Age 3, and then a generally decreasing trend with Early Iron Age values lower than Bronze Age values. The spatial efficiency value for the Middle Bronze Age 3 indicates a particularly good spatial integration among sites in this period, while the RSI and the A-shape coefficient (compare previous section) indicated a drop in the general trend toward higher complexity in the same time.

Thus, for this period the two models seem to give antithetic results, but it has to be said that the high value of the mean spatial efficiency index has only been calculated on the basis of a limited number of districts within the whole region, because for many districts secondary settlements were lacking. It may also be probable that during the Bronze Age there was already a certain level of settlement integration, but only on a local scale and in certain areas, while at a regional global level the process was still incomplete and not fully developed.

The low values of the index for the Early Iron Age could indicate that the Spatial Efficiency model is suitable for the Bronze Age period, but does not fit later phases. This model, in fact, was specifically elaborated by Steponaitis for chiefdom-level societies, where full market forces were not yet in practice. Therefore for the Early Iron Age, other models, such as the Central Place Theory (Christaller 1933), may be more appropriate, or other constraints, such as political choices, may have influenced site location.

Multiplicatively weighted Voronoi diagrams

In order to define the development of *Latium vetus* territorial patterns from the Middle Bronze Age to the end of the Iron Age, multiplicatively weighted Voronoi diagrams have been applied by using the programme *MWVD_Shape 1.0* (Lan 2004; for a similar application, the *Gambini* program, see Rajala 2005). This analysis will define areas of territorial dominance and detect dynamic changes through time. Multiplicatively weighted Voronoi diagrams are an evolution of Planar multiplicatively weighted Voronoi diagrams (or Thiessen Polygons), which take into account not only distance but also settlement sizes. In this procedure each site is given a weight, which is proportional to the distance from the site, so that, after the distance to the site is measured, it is multiplied by its weight. This model is quite similar to the X-Tent model (proposed by Renfrew and Level 1979; applied by Stoddart 1990; and recently by Stoddart and Redhouse 2005, and Ducke 2006 within a GIS environment), but simpler. This means that it is less flexible but also that there is less scope for errors and uncertainty.

In my recent paper (Fulminante 2007) the analysis was conducted with a less refined distinction between phases (the Middle Bronze Age and the Final Bronze Age were considered without internal distinction) and with a smaller sample of sites. The new analysis has confirmed the general patterns of this paper but has also identified some new features. The previous analysis showed that in the Middle Bronze Age there were approximately eight larger but similarly sized districts in the region, all vying for influence with some smaller, but still medium-sized, districts in the Alban Hills and in the northern part of the region.

However, the new analysis, which distinguishes between Middle Bronze Age 1–2 and Middle Bronze Age 3, shows that there were only a few settlements (Rome, Gabi, the area of the Alban Hills, and the costal zone) which seem to have had some sort of influence on very large territories. It is possible that at this time settlement activity had influence over a wider area, and that there were some sort of inter-site alliances and treaties on matters of general interest such as war, exploitation of resources of general interest, trade, and so on, but that each settlement only maintained a strict control over a more limited area.

In particular two areas, the valley of the Aniene and the coastal area between the modern cities of Ardea and

Anzio, seem to have had a markedly higher concentration of settlements: the first area both in the older and more recent phases of the Middle Bronze Age (MBA 1–2 and 3) and the second one only in the MBA 3. The high concentration of settlements in those two areas could be connected with economic activities practised during this time, such as fishing or hunting in the costal area (most of them were on the borders of ancient, and now dried-up, lagoons; Alessandri 2007) and transhumance for the high valley of the Aniene, which lies at the foot of the Tiburtine mountains and is a crucial area of confluence of the main transhumance routes from the Latin plain to the mountains. Quite a few settlements were also located in the Alban Hills, again on the mountains and near a lake (Fig. 15.5A–B).

In the Recent Bronze Age both the previous and the new analyses seem to show the same pattern: the coastal territory is divided equally between different settlements from the mouth of the Tiber to the southern part of the region, while the rest of the territory is dominated by three major poles (Rome, Gabii, and the Alban Hills; Fig. 15.6A). During the first part of the Final Bronze Age (FBA 1–2) the same pattern as in the Recent Bronze Age seems to be present, but with an increased number of medium and small-sized subordinate centres (Fig. 15.6B). By the later phase of the Final Bronze Age (FBA 3) the centre of *Lavinium* also seems to emerge as a major pole (Fig. 15.7A).

In this work I have accepted Guidi's hypothesis that at least part of the large plateaux, later occupied by the city of *Lavinium* in the Archaic period, was already partially inhabited from this time (di Gennaro and Guidi 2000). This interpretation is based on the fact that by the Latial I period burials had already moved from within the plateaux to external areas in the surroundings. This indicates that a formal distinction between the inhabited sites and areas reserved for burials, that is between the 'city of the living' and the 'city of the dead', had already been established (Fulminante 2003, 233).

In the first part of the Early Iron Age 1, the territories of large proto-urban centres start to delineate: on the coast there are *Lavinium* with the smaller Anzio to the south, and possibly *Satricum* and Cisterna di Latina further inland (an extensive occupation of Ardea in this phase has not yet been documented for this phase, but can be postulated hypothetically); the central area of the Alban Hills has Alba and Velletri, and possibly *Corioli* (only documented by literary sources) as major centres; Praenestae dominates on the west, at the foot of the Prenestine Mountains (Appenine), while in the north three major centres are dominant (Rome, *Gabii* and *Crustumerium*); other first rank centres of less importance (*Fidenae*, *Ficulea*, Montecelio and *Tibur*) control smaller territories (Fig. 15.7B).

It is remarkable that Rome's influence had already extended to all the territory on the south bank of the Tiber, including Ficana and probably Castel di Decima (Fig.

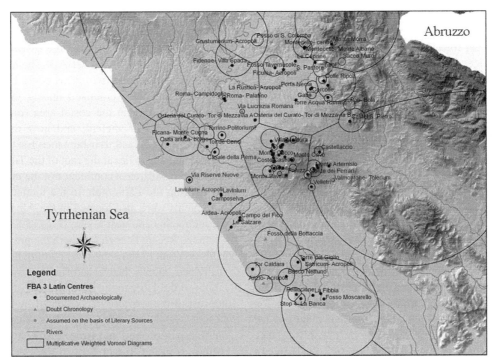

Fig. 15.7A: Latium vetus: multiplicatively weighted Voronoi diagrams: Final Bronze Age 3

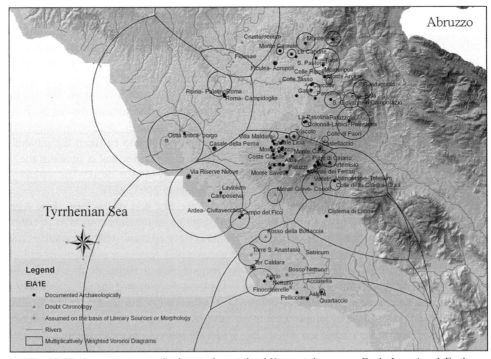

Fig. 15.7B: Latium vetus: multiplicatively weighted Voronoi diagrams: Early Iron Age 1 Early

15.7B). In a later phase of Early Iron Age 1 and in Early Iron Age 2 the centre situated at Rome consolidated and extended its power in the region; it is absolutely dominant over all other centres of *Latium vetus* (Fig. 15.8A–B). The

Orientalising and the Archaic Age confirms the pattern already established during the later phase of the Early Iron Age (Fig. 15.9A–B).

The application of multiplicatively weighted Voronoi

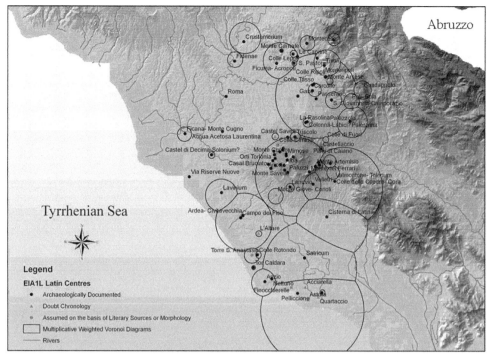

Fig. 15.8A: Latium vetus: multiplicatively weighted Voronoi diagrams: Early Iron Age 1 Late

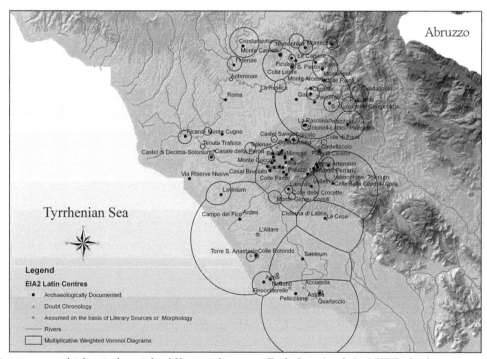

Fig. 15.8B: Latium vetus: multiplicatively weighted Voronoi diagrams: Early Iron Age 2 (in MWVD the dominant centre is left without a 'polygon')

diagrams shows that three major areas of influence existed around Rome, *Gabii* and the Alban Hills from at least the Recent Bronze Age, if not earlier. In the Final Bronze Age and the beginning of the Early Iron Age large proto-urban centres started to develop on the plateaux, later occupied by archaic cities, within defined territories. At this time the area of the Alban Hills was dominated by the presence of Alba, and this settlement, together with *Gabii*, seem to be

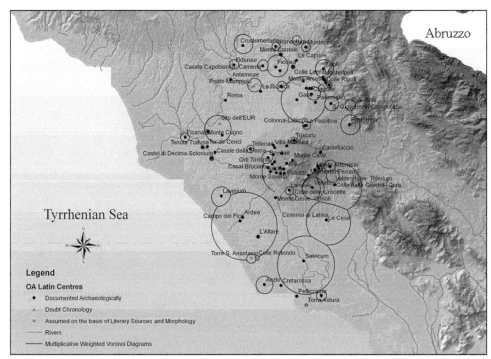

Fig. 15.9A: Latium vetus: multiplicative weighted Voronoi diagrams: Orientalising period

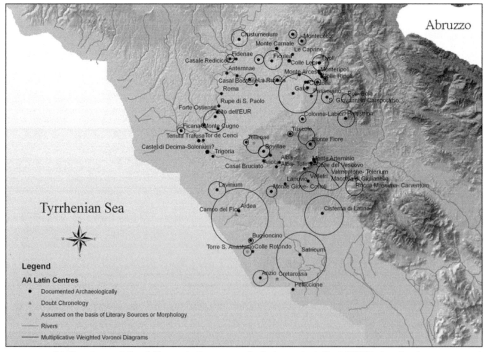

Fig. 15.9B: Latium vetus: multiplicative weighted Voronoi diagrams: Archaic period (in MWVD the dominant centre is left without a 'polygon')

more influential than Rome (if the latter is considered as constituted by two separated settlements). Only from the later stage of the Early Iron Age does Rome, which is now unified into one large proto-urban settlement, become the dominant centre at the regional level.

Conclusions

In an earlier work (Fulminante 2003), I analysed Early Iron Age burials of *Latium vetus* and demonstrated the early presence and development of social stratification in that region. This paper, building on the previous funerary approach, presented some traditional locational analyses (the Rank-Size rule, Spatial Efficiency model and Voronoi diagrams) not yet fully applied to *Latium vetus* (though for an early application of the Rank-Size rule see Guidi 1985) and has provided a complementary picture of the social and political landscape of early Rome and *Latium vetus*.

The application of locational models at the regional level has confirmed that the Latin cities of the Archaic Period are the product of a long process of Bronze and Iron Age pre- and proto-urban formation originated locally rather than under the influence of external stimuli. In fact, both the RSI and the A-shape coefficient show a regular and constant increasing trend toward higher hierarchy and settlement integration with a particular rise at the beginning of the Early Iron Age 1, well before the foundation of Greek colonies in southern Italy. In addition, the application of multiplicatively weighted Voronoi diagrams showed that these large centralised proto-urban centres dominated large districts that were regularly and evenly spaced.

This general picture of the development of regional dynamics defines the context for the urbanisation of Rome (and other Latin cities), which had already started during the 8th century, as proposed by Hermann Müller-Karpe (1962) and confirmed and better defined by recent excavations (Carandini and Carafa 1995; Cazzella 2001 with a different interpretation; Carandini 2004; 2007) and recent studies (Peroni 1989; Bettelli 1997; Pacciarelli 2001). Monuments such as the fortification wall around the Palatine, a regal residency (House of the Kings), cult places (Vesta Sanctuary, Capitoline votive deposit, Volcanal) and spaces for assemblies (the *Forum* with the *Comitium*) point to the existence of a centralized power, governing a unified body of citizens.

The power, that was previously shared and contended among aristocrats, was finally unified under the control of one single *rex*, a position that included both the religious and political power. However, the general picture delineated from burial and settlement evidence of the regional socio-political dynamics, showed that development toward higher complexity and hierarchy (social stratification, settlement centralization and hierarchy) were already ongoing processes from at least the Bronze Age, certainly accelerated but not fully initiated by external influences at the end of the Early Iron Age.

Intensified contacts with Greeks and the Near East are evident from the presence of proto-Corinthian and Corinthian pottery and exotic objects, in urban contexts (for example the S. Omobono area) or rich burials of the late 8th century and early 7th century (La Rocca 1976). But it is also probable that communications and connections between the western and the eastern Mediterranean, established in the Mycenaean Period, were never completely severed. This may be suggested by the presence of an inscription in Greek letters found in the necropolis of Osteria dell'Osa in a tomb dated to the end of the 9th or beginning of the 8th centuries (Ampolo 1997).

In this perspective, the traditional 'orientalist', diffusionist model, according to which the concept of the city (and specifically of the 'polis') migrated from the eastern Mediterranean to the west through the mediation of Greek and Phoenician colonists, has to be revised. Similarly, the more recent 'occidentalist' model, which claims for a priority of the city-state model to the west (namely with the foundation of Rome, according to Carandini 2007), has also to be rejected.

New research perspectives suggest that the city-state model developed in parallel at a number of sites around the Mediterranean during the first half of the first millennium BCE (central and southern Italy, Greece, Spain, Cyprus, Sardinia, Israel, etc.). The process differed in the various regions and did not always occur at the same pace, but was synchronic and almost certainly developed as a 'network' (Malkin 2003), where the advance and progress of each single node was favoured by reciprocal cultural, commercial and social contacts (see also the 'hybridization' concept adopted by van Dommelen 2006).

Acknowledgements

This paper presents some of the results of my PhD dissertation written under the supervision of Dr. Simon Stoddart at Cambridge University. This research was made possible by the generosity of several institutions, which provided funding (University of Rome 'La Sapienza', AHRC, IFUW and Dan David Prize) and digital data (*Provincia di Roma* and *Regione Lazio*), and scholars who have granted permission to use unpublished data in this paper (in particular Dr. Clarissa Belardelli from the *Regione Lazio*).

Phase	Latium	Veio	Tarquinia	Abs Chronology
Middle Bronze Age 1–2	Grotta Nuova-Protoapenine	Grotta Nuova	Grotta Nuova	1700/1650–1400
Middle Bronze Age 3	Apennine	Apennine	Apennine	1400-1325/1300
Recent Bronze Age	Subapennine	Subapennine	Subapennine	1325/1300–1175/1150
Final Bronze Age 1–2	Protovillanovan	Protovillanovan	Protovillanovan	1175/1150–1025/1000
Final Bronze Age 3	I	Protovillanovan	Protovillanovan	1025/1000–950/925
Early Iron Age 1 Early	IIA	IA	IA	950/925–900/875
Early Iron Age 1 Late	IIB	IB–IC	IB	900/875–850/825
Early Iron Age 2 Early / Late	IIIA	IIA–IIB	II	850/825–775
Early Iron Age 2 Final	IIIB	IIC	II	775–730/725
Early Orientalizing Age	IVA1	IIIA	IIIA	730/725–670/660
Middle Orientalizing Age	IVA2	IIIB	IIIB	670/660–640/630
Late Orientalizing Age	IVB	IV	IV	640/630–580
Archaic Period	AP	AP	AP	580–509

Fig. 15.10: Bronze Age and Early Iron Age: absolute chronology in central Italy (based on Pacciarelli 2000 and Nijboer 2005). All dates are BCE

Appendix: Bronze Age and Early Iron Age
Latium vetus – absolute and relative chronology

There has been much debate recently on the absolute chronology of Bronze Age and Iron Age central Italy. Scholars seem to agree that the Early Iron Age ends by the middle or end of the 8th century, but there is still no consensus on the absolute chronology and the duration of the Bronze Age and the Early Iron Age (for the current state of this topic see Bartoloni and Delpino 2005). The table presented as Fig. 15.10 is based on recent proposals by Marco Pacciarelli (2001) and Albert Nijboer (2005), and is intended to help orientate readers unfamiliar with local material culture and chronology.

16

THE IRON AGE
TRANSITION AT TROY

Maureen Basedow

The 1998 and 1999 excavations in the Trojan Agora Area D9 uncovered well-sealed deposits providing an uninterrupted stratigraphic sequence of successive Troy VII, Protogeometric, Geometric and Archaic phases (Aslan 2002; this volume). The knowledge that what had been described as Troy VII type wares continued as part of Early Iron Age ceramic assemblages transformed our understanding of the wide range of Iron Age material from the Tübingen excavations in the West Sanctuary (Hnila 2006, 69–70). What we had in the Sanctuary was seemingly an earlier Sanctuary from at least the late 9th/early 8th century BCE onward, with a significant Early/Middle Protogeometric activity phase as its predecessor (Figs. 16.1 and 16.2; Aslan, this volume; Aslan and Basedow in final preparation; Basedow 2007; in press).

In this paper the identification of distinctive Geometric

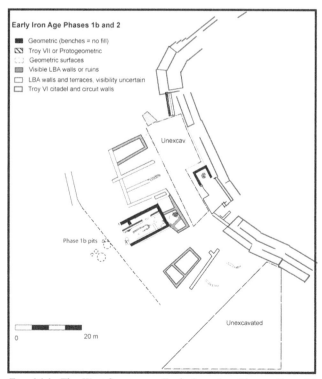

Fig. 16.1: The West Sanctuary, Early Iron Age Phases 1b and 2 (author)

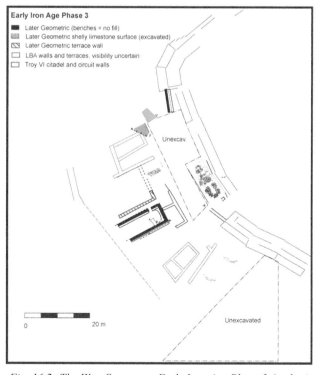

Fig. 16.2: The West Sanctuary, Early Iron Age Phase 3 (author)

and Early Archaic architecture and related ritual features serves as the starting point for a re-evaluation of the post-Bronze Age archaeology of the Pillar House/South Gate areas excavated by Carl Blegen. This reassessment began as part of a continuing investigation of the role of Late Bronze Age ruins in the topography of Early Iron Age at Troy (Basedow in press; Morris 2007) and elsewhere in the eastern Mediterranean (Felsch 1980, 66; 1987, 3–5; Kienast 1992, 173; Shaw and Shaw 2000, 9, 25–7). It ended with questions about the methodology behind Blegen's assignation of ceramic phases to architecture in general, but especially for the period of the Bronze Age–Iron Age transition.

Identifying the Bronze Age–Iron Age transition at Troy, historical problems and solutions

A lack of information regarding the form and function of Iron Age ceramic and architectural contexts contributed to Blegen's conclusion that there was an Early Iron Age hiatus instead of what we now understand to be an active period of ritual culture at Troy. Until recently, the evidence for Early Iron Age activity at Troy was considered meagre. Wilhelm Dörpfeld recognized *frühgriechesch* pottery, but given the limited state of investigation at the time in the Aegean he reserved judgment on its interpretation and stratigraphic associations (Dörpfeld 1902, 200; Schmidt 1902, 298–9). In the view of Carl Blegen, his successor, settlement at Troy came to a calamitous end with a newly identified Late Bronze Age phase he called Troy VIIa. The subsequent phases VIIb1 and VIIb2 were understood as distinct, still 'Aegean Late Bronze Age' assemblages influenced by developments outside the region, including the introduction of 'Barbarian Ware' (VIIb1) and 'Knobbed Ware' (VIIb2), as well as new architectural styles, most famously the 'orthostat' walls (VIIb2). What followed was a 400-year hiatus lasting into the 7th century BCE (Blegen *et al.* 1953, 250). Although, like Dörpfeld, Blegen had uncovered a representative sampling of Early Iron Age decorated pottery dating from the Protogeometric through to the Geometric (Hertel 1991, 137–38, figs. 1–3; Aslan, this volume), limited understanding of the associated assemblage context, together with the continued poor state of investigation for the period elsewhere in the Aegean, left his conclusions essentially unchallenged.

Prior to the 1998–2001 re-investigation of Area D9, the Early Iron Age deposits from the West Sanctuary at Troy were similarly under-interpreted. Although it was no longer possible to speak of an Iron Age hiatus in the presence of a wide range of Protogeometric through Geometric decorated wares and distinctive small finds, no conclusion could be reached regarding the circumstances of their deposition (Rose 1995, 89–93; Lenz *et al.* 1998, 194–7). The Tübingen

excavations had introduced a Troy VIIb3 phase as a means of categorically separating Troy VII deposits that included Early Iron Age pottery. Unfortunately, in the absence of an intact transitional sequence, the VIIb3 phase could not be employed consistently, severely limiting its utility (Korfmann 1995, 22; Koppenhöfer 1997, 341–7; Korfmann 1997, 27–8; 1998, 33, fig. 27b). Once the excavation of intact transitional stratigraphy in Area D9 permitted a more precise division into chronologically and functionally diverse deposits and architectural phases, the known sequences of imported Aegean ceramic styles could be easily related to the Trojan Iron Age deposits. In the interest of clarity, the Aegean categories and terminology form the basis of the Early Iron Age phases used here.

Identifying Early Iron Age features in the Pillar House/South Gate area

Pillar House and the South Gate area generally (Fig. 16.3) had long been recognized as parts of Late Bronze Age Troy that had remained visible into post-Bronze Age periods. One of the pillars, P2, had been repaired with a butterfly clamp (Blegen *et al.* 1953, 222) and more recent excavation had confirmed that the South Gate Tower and its row of stele were visible into the Hellenistic period (Korfmann 2003, 17).

Covered by an enormous Schliemann spoil heap at the time of the Dörpfeld excavations, Pillar House itself was relatively untouched when Blegen dug there. Both field notebooks and final report agree that the excavation of the post-Sixth Settlement Pillar House area did not produce the expected stratigraphic sequence known from the smaller-scale Troy VII excavations nearby. Near the pillars P2 and P1, 'Troy VIII' material, the phase the Blegen excavation used collectively to describe layers with G2 or -3 Ware and/or Archaic and/or Classical pottery, was found to within ten centimetres of the presumed Troy VI floor (Blegen *et al.* 1953, 225). The Troy VIIb1 phase was difficult to identify (Blegen *et al.* 1958, 203, 209–10) while the associated ceramics of what were assumed on the basis of the presence of Knobbed Ware to be Troy VIIb2 features had less of the type ware than expected, and much more Troy VIII pottery than could be easily explained (Blegen *et al.* 1958, 212, 217–18). While later Roman and Byzantine intrusions no doubt contributed to the lack of a consistent stratigraphic horizon, the excavators recognized that this did not provide all the answers (Blegen *et al.* 1953, 228–9; Blegen *et al.* 1958, 85). That the area was frequently cleared and levelled, leading to what the Blegen reports repeatedly refer to as 'telescoping' (Blegen *et al.* 1958, 215, 243–4), was surely also a factor. The research presented here offers another explanation: that features assigned by Blegen to the various Troy VII phases actually belong to the Early Iron Age.

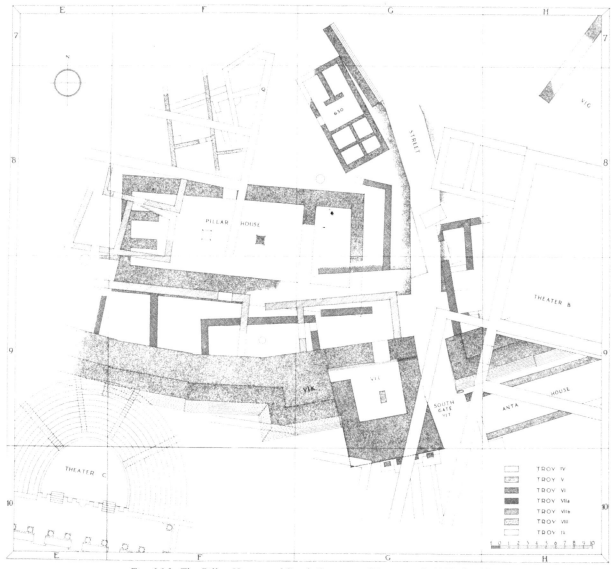

Fig. 16.3: The Pillar House and South Gate area (Blegen et al. *1958, fig. 324)*

Throughout the work presented here, Blegen's tendency toward minimalist interpretation, if not outright dismissal, of clearly Early Iron Age material is very much in evidence. While his somewhat mysterious categorical rejection of an Iron Age at Troy and other sites has been discussed in detail elsewhere (Popham 1991; Basedow 2007), a few specifics relating to the areas under discussion are worth mentioning. While Blegen did not recognize Early Iron Age stratigraphic continuity or topographical relationships with the Late Bronze Age site (Blegen *et al.* 1958, 247–8), these relationships were recorded explicitly in the field notebooks and plans (Cox [1932], 32, 80; Caskey [1933], 151; [1936], 53). Although Blegen reports that the Pillar House and South Gate areas had more Troy VIII material than any other part of Troy except the Sanctuary, the Troy

VIII from Pillar House is consistently misrepresented in the final publication. The most egregious example is the one published Troy VIII phase plan from this part of the mound (Fig. 16.4). For reasons that are not clear, the individual features are joined to one another into a single, strange building, despite the text making clear that these walls were not contemporary (Blegen *et al.* 1958, 288, fig. 336). The revised plan presented here (Fig. 16.5) is based on a thorough reading of the field notebooks and comparison of the Pillar House excavation with features exposed by the Tubingen excavation of the Early Iron Age West Sanctuary.

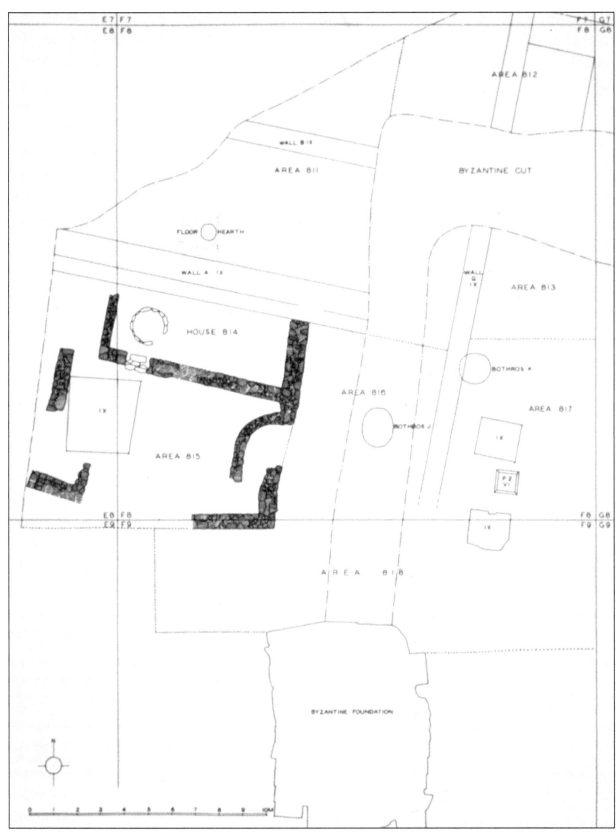

Fig. 16.4: The Blegen excavation plan of Troy VIII in the Pillar House area (Blegen et al. 1958, fig. 336)

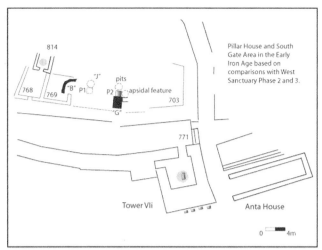

Fig. 16.5: Plan of Early Iron Age features in the Pillar House/South Gate area (author)

Fig. 16.6: House 850 in the West Sanctuary (University of Cincinnati Troy Excavations Archive, photo no. not recorded)

The Early Iron Age in the West Sanctuary

In the interest of brevity, I will describe the features from just two West Sanctuary Early Iron Age phases and the relationship they bear to material from Pillar House and adjacent South Gate area. The ceramic analysis and dates for the West Sanctuary Early Iron Age Phases 2 (825/800–725 BCE) and 3 (750–650) are the work of Carolyn Aslan (this volume). The majority of the Iron Age architectural and contextual parallels in the Pillar House/South Gate areas fall within this range. There are, however, certainly deposits in the general area of Pillar House and the South Gate that contain material comparable to the West Sanctuary Phases 1 (1075–950 BCE) and 1b (975/950–875 BCE), which are respectively Protogeometric and Early Geometric in date. The nearby D9 stratigraphy includes these phases, and it is likely, based on the amount of Protogeometric pottery found there, that parts of Area E8/9 excavated by Tübingen to the west of Pillar House belong to these phases as well. Likewise, there are also West Sanctuary Phase 4 (650–550 BCE) features in the Pillar House area, some of which will be briefly mentioned in the discussion below.

West Sanctuary Phase 2 (Fig. 16.1)

The West Sanctuary is located on a terraced slope in front of Section 5 of the Sixth Settlement citadel wall. Phase 2 is the first clear Early Iron Age architectural phase that can be defined within an area that, based on the excavation of votive pits belonging to the previous Phase 1b, had already been the site of ritual activity. During Phase 2 specialized activity is focused in two areas. The first is a walled, hypaethral space in front of a Late Bronze Age terrace between two pre-existing parallel northeast–southwest walls belonging either to Troy VIIb2 or the Protogeometric

period we call Early Iron Age Phase 1. Also in Phase 2, the space, which has both long (north) side and short (west) side entrances, underwent a number of modifications. An apsidal structure with irregular, sharply angled orthostats at one end dominated the western half. It was filled with ash and burnt bone fragments. Another early feature is the spur wall that defined the eastern end of the complex. The spur wall bonded with a bench built up against the inside face of the south wall of the structure. The south wall also had a bench built against its exterior face. Somewhat later in Phase 2, a non-weight-bearing parastade wall was erected along the north side to make the central space longer and narrower. A bench built along the inside face of that wall incorporated an unusual, secondary, partial burial of a female adolescent. Toward the end of the period, the eastern section of the building was further distinguished by a series of three postholes arranged in oblique triangle plan. Comparable to similar arrangements known from a range of Early Iron Age ritual sites (Morgan 1999, 320, n. 85), in this context they probably supported a table.

The second focus area of Phase 2 is a terraced platform constructed up against the Troy VI citadel wall, more or less on the same northeast–southwest axis as the hypaethral area below to the west. The earliest structure here is the building Blegen called 'House 850'. Shown here in an unpublished excavation photo (Fig. 16.6), this was not, as Blegen (*et al.* 1958, 273–9) described it, a simple dwelling. Viewed with its interior stone platform intact, there can be little doubt that we have a structure comparable to the Kultmahl at Miletus and similar structures elsewhere (Held 1993, 11–12, 33–45). By the end of Phase 2, the first of many stone circles that would dominate this space in Early Iron Age Phase 3 were already in place on the southern, lower-lying part of the terrace.

Fig. 16.7: House 814 in the Pillar House area (Blegen et al. *1958, fig. 66)*

Phase 2 Parallels in the Pillar House area

Blegen's 'House 814' is set atop a terrace crossing the northwest corner of the ruins of Pillar House. Both House 850 (Fig. 16.6) and House 814 (Fig. 16.7) in the West Sanctuary are small, nearly square buildings with orthostat walls and central stone platforms. The original plan in the Blegen report extends the foundations of House 814 to connect it, over a gap, with walls further east, reconstructing it as a long, rectangular plan building (Fig. 16.4). There is, in fact, no physical connection between these two structures and, indeed a difference in elevation of nearly one metre that does not suggest that these walls are part of the same phase, let alone the same structure (Blegen *et al.* 1958, 292).

House 814 sits on a terrace formed by the walls Blegen called 'House 768' and 'House 769', each of which were assigned a phase VIIb1 and VIIb2 occupation (Figs. 16.3 and 16.5). House 768 has no VIIb1 floor deposit and no line of division between it and the VIIb2 version of House 768 lying above (Blegen *et al.* 1958, 203). The VIIb1 phase is given no ceramic support by the published catalogue, where the expected VIIb1 type ware proportions were not observed. Pottery 'resembling the fabric of Troy VIII' is mentioned instead (Blegen *et al.* 1958, 203–4). Blegen concluded the existence of a VIIb1 phase based on the higher-than-expected elevation of a south wall doorway in the south wall with respect to the level of an adjacent street ('Street 751W'). Since this area was terraced going back to the Late Bronze Age, as elsewhere at Troy, it would seem a more acceptable explanation to suggest that there were a few steps or low ramp in place to access a building situated at a higher level instead, especially given the lack of ceramic support for any intervening VIIb1 occupation level.

The Phase VIIb2 House 768 has a floor that slopes to the south from the north, where its elevation is equivalent to the threshold of House 814 (Blegen *et al.* 1958, 204, 292).

Houses 814 and 768 share a wall, the lower course of which has orthostats. Although Blegen notes the difficulty of sorting out all these 'differences and irregularities', his elaborate explanation (Blegen *et al.* 1958, 204) is less convincing than simply seeing House 768 as part of a terrace constructed or reconstructed to serve as a forecourt to House 814. This is something that Blegen's phase criteria could not admit as a possibility. With Knobbed Ware present in House 768, and present but, according to Blegen (*et al.* 1958, 292) 'surely out of context' in House 814, the two structures, with their shared walls and comparable elevations, would have to have been separated by at least 400 years. While stratigraphic telescoping to this extent is not unknown at Troy – the Late Archaic and Early Hellenistic phases in the Northern section of the West Sanctuary share virtually the same ground level – there is typically considerable architectural distinction between the much earlier and much later buildings when this is the case. We now know that Knobbed Ware is integral not only to Troy VIIb2 ceramic assemblages, but also to the Protogeometric and Early Geometric as well (Aslan, this volume). With this knowledge in hand, seeing House 768 and 814 as potentially part of the same complex is a reasonable proposition.

With House 814 paralleled in the West Sanctuary at Troy, House 768's high proportions of fine wares compared to coarse wares, finds of gold leaf and ivory, along with its doorway's elaborate jambs and pivot stones do not suggest that this was the 'so simple an establishment' concluded by Blegen (*et al.* 1958, 204–5). New insights on House 768 and 814 may be forthcoming from the re-evaluation of the material excavated by Tübingen further west in Area E8/9. Excavated before the discovery of the continuous stratigraphy in nearby D9, Area E8/9 produced considerable Early Iron Age material from comparable levels.

House 769 (Figs. 16.3 and 16.5) is a continuation of this same terrace to the east. According to Blegen (*et al.* 1958, 209–10), it too had an ephemeral VIIb1 phase dated primarily based on its proximity to a Troy VIIa version of the same terrace wall ('House 725') directly below and walls with orthostats directly above. Knobbed Ware, for Blegen an unequivocal indicator of the VIIb2 successor phase, occurs in unexpected quantities in association with House 725's southern walls (Blegen *et al.* 1958, 210). The argument for a VIIb1 stratigraphic phase again, seems weak at best.

As with House 768, the northern wall of Blegen's VIIb2 phase of House 769 is distinguished by a row of orthostats. Whatever lay further north has not survived (Blegen *et al.* 1958, 211). There is a pithos taking up most of the floor of the first VIIb2 level covered by stones, burnt debris and whole pots, which Blegen interpreted as destruction. Above, the second phase of VIIb2 is nondescript and may have been open air. No floor was observed. The pottery is characterized by 'Troy VIII' in 'increasing quantities' (Blegen *et al.* 1958, 212), a description that fits Early Iron Age deposits in the

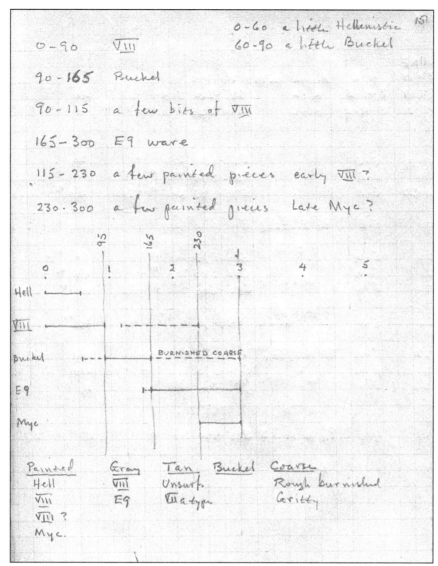

Fig. 16.8: Chart prepared by Caskey ([1933], 151) documenting the assemblage overlap of Knobbed Ware and Troy VIII pottery in the same deposits

West Sanctuary and Area D9 very well. Although a field notebook chart shows that the excavators were aware that Troy VIII pottery and Knobbed Ware regularly occurred together in the same deposits (Fig. 16.8), in the final report on this area Blegen nevertheless restated his conviction that 'the Knobbed Ware cannot be doubted' as an indicator of the VIIb2 phase only. He explained the suspect Knobbed Ware proportions as a matter 'differing tastes' from house to house and the unexpected amount of Troy VIII pottery as the result of later 'levelling and grading' (Blegen *et al.* 1958, 212). On the evidence presented here it seems a more likely, and considerably more straightforward, explanation that the terrace is actually Early Iron Age.

The terrace almost certainly continued even further east although it cannot be directly followed due to the interference of a Byzantine robbing trench. 'House 703' (Figs. 16.3 and 16.5), near the South Gate Street and really just a series of walls of irregular plan with no associated floor level (Blegen *et al.* 1958, 69–70), represents its likely conclusion. According to Blegen, House 703 was a Troy VIIa building later used as a terrace during Troy VIIb, when its westernmost extent, 'Wall L', served as the border to the street entering the South Gate. It seems to have been assigned to Troy VIIa primarily on the base elevations of the walls and indirect associations with an area of burning further west. The pottery is described as coming from 'in and about' the walls, making the stratigraphic integrity of the mostly non-diagnostic fragments questionable at best (Blegen *et al.* 1958, 69–71). At the same time, the shape of the space defined by House 703 clearly recalls that of

Fig. 16.9: Upper part of pit against the east side of P2 in Pillar House (University of Cincinnati Troy Excavations Archive no. 36.cb.15)

Fig. 16.10: Lower part of pit against the east side of P2 in Pillar House (University of Cincinnati Troy Excavations Archive no. 36.cb.26)

the Phase 4 enclosures of the Upper Sanctuary in the West Sanctuary area. What began as a terrace may have become, with a later addition ('Wall M'), a means of defining an Early Iron Age sacred space. Lying at a lower elevation than the House 814 end of the terrace system, the space that the House 703 walls enclosed would have been dominated by the eponymous pillars of Pillar House.

There is considerable support for Early Iron Age interest in the pillars. Both P2 and whatever stood on the foundations of P1 had large deposits of fine ware ceramics, probably originally in pits, on their northern and, for P2, eastern sides. These pits had 'Troy VIII' pottery in them that continued down to within ten centimetres of the Troy VI floor level.

Fig. 16.11: Apsidal structure and Structure G near P2 in Pillar House (Blegen et al. 1958, fig. 48)

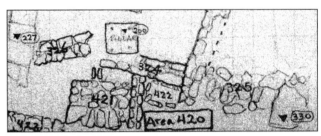

Fig. 16.12: John L. Caskey's ([1936], 53) sketch plan of Area 770 showing features clustered around P2, including the apsidal structure (422 on sketch), Structure G enclosure and the platform on top of it (421)

While Blegen dated Pit J (Figs. 16.4 and 16.5), near P1, to Troy VIII, the deposits east and north of P2 were called Troy VIIa, presumably because they were very strongly burnt as well (Caskey [1933], 42; [1936], 82–83; Blegen *et al.* 1958, 86). Unpublished photographs from different stages of excavation show that these P2 pits or deposits began well above Late Bronze Age levels (Figs. 16.9 and 16.10). Taking into account their burnt content, that the pillar pits were ritual in function seems likely.

There are additional features associated with the pillars that permit us to date the ritual use of the area to the Early Iron Age. Most of these features are comparable to West Sanctuary Phase 2. While all later activity around P1 was cut away by the Byzantine robbing trench, there an apsidal structure (Figs. 16.5, 16.11, 16.12, and 16.13) comparable in size and construction to the ash-retaining apsidal structure in the West Sanctuary (Figs. 16.1 and 16.13) just the south of the top of the easternmost P2 burnt deposit described above. As in the West Sanctuary, the apex of the P2 apsidal feature is distinguished by sharp-edged, angular, thin slab orthostats. Blegen dated it and other bits and pieces of wall around P2 ('Area 770') to Troy VIIb1 or VIIb2 based on the presence

Fig. 16.13: Apsidal structure in the Early Iron Age Phase 2 West Sanctuary (Troia Projekt, Tübingen University)

or lack of orthostats, noting however that 'surprisingly little Gray Minyan Ware of the type characteristic in the earlier phase and little of the Knobbed Ware normally associated with the later is found anywhere in Area 770' (Blegen *et al.* 1958, 217–18). A later structure or series of structures ('Structure G'), comparable to Phase 3 or 4 rectilinear orthostat enclosures and pavements in the West Sanctuary, succeeds the small apsidal feature at a higher level (Figs. 16.5, 16.11, and 16.12).

West Sanctuary Phase 3 (Fig. 16.2)

During West Sanctuary Phase 3, the hypaethral area was rebuilt into a longer, narrower, roofed building with an apsidal eastern end. It retained the long and short side entries of the earlier structure, though this time the one long side doorway has a pivot stone preserved. Phase 3 involved a complete renovation of the southern wall, with its upper courses seemingly completely re-laid at this time. A number of small finds familiar from votive pit contexts were found built into the new courses of the wall at regular intervals. The southern wall interior benches were not retained, but the exterior bench was expanded into a double-stepped structure. During Phase 3, the eastern end of the building became more clearly the focus of the cult. The spur wall was rebuilt, fitted out this time with a course of rectilinear orthostats along its eastern face. Early in the phase, a mortised stone statue base was centred against the rear, eastern wall. A final adaptation late in Phase 3 seems to represent an effort to make the eastern end of the building apsidal. The stone base is covered over with an apsidal platform and the single stone post support, found *in situ*, would have been sufficient to support the sloping roof of an apsidal-ended structure. A large deposit of bronzes, including fibula and a projectile point, were found buried near this base. With a date range from the beginning of Phase 3 to its end, the fibula could have been buried either as a group to mark the building the going out of use, or individually over time to mark the conclusion of a ritual that may have involved dressing or draping a cult image.

During Phase 3, the platform against the citadel wall becomes crowded with stone circles (Fig. 16.2). These too are functionally ritual based on finds (Rawson [1936–1937], 59; [1937–1938], 156; Aslan and Basedow in final preparation) and structure. The abundance of fine ware drinking and pouring vessels, the regular association with burnt deposits, as well as the many *comparanda* from other ritual sites (Farnell 1921, 5, 413; Hägg 1983; Deoudi 1999, 2–3) do not support Blegen's interpretation of the circles as places to dry figs or thresh grain (Blegen *et al.* 1958, 275).

Phase 3 parallels in the Pillar House area

Three courses of a partial, well-built, apsidal wall were excavated atop the north wall of the terrace formed by the House 769 terrace (Figs. 16.5 and 16.14). Called 'Wall B' or 'House B' in the field notebooks (Cox [1932]), and 'another wall' in the final report (Blegen *et al.* 1958, 294), and dated to Troy VIII based on content, this curious wall, which is stratigraphically later than House 814, enclosed burnt debris and bones of the kind also reported by Blegen from the nearby Anta House. Blegen noted that its three courses enclosed a deposit that could actually be followed very nearly 'down into the underlying debris of the preceding phase, which in this case happened to be of the same consistency and color' (Blegen *et al.* 1958, 294). Because no floor could be discerned, the excavator described it as a pit (Cox [1932], 38, 80). What it most resembles is the apsidal end of a building, much like the Phase 3 structure in the central part of the West Sanctuary.

Other interpretations are possible. Though no apsidal or oval retaining structures of comparable size are known from Troy there is large one known from the pre-Archaic levels of the Artemis Temple at Ephesos (Weissl 2002, fig.

Fig. 16.14: Wall B in the Pillar House area (University of Cincinnati Troy Excavations Archive no. 32.cc.13)

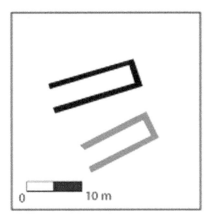

Fig. 16.15: Anta House (black outline) compared to the West Sanctuary Early Iron Age 3 building (grey outline) (author)

5). While apsidal, circular, oval, or rectangular ash and burnt bone depositories of all sizes are common in Early Iron Age sanctuaries (Goldman 1940, 398, fig. 24 and plan 1; Felsch 1980, 50, 63–4; Tuchelt 1984, 199–201; Deoudi 1999, 11; Ekroth 2002, 25–60), they are seldom as sturdily built as our Wall B.

With Phase 3, it is possible identify features comparable to the West Sanctuary Early Iron Age not only in the Pillar House area, but in the South Gate area directly east as well. Just outside South Gate lies Anta House. Its long, narrow proportions baffled Blegen (*et al.* 1953, 249–50). Given the evidence from the Phase 3 West Sanctuary, there is no longer any reason to view Anta House as some kind of a Bronze Age architectural anomaly. It is very clearly comparable to the long, narrow Geometric Building in the Phase 3 West Sanctuary (Fig. 16.15). Although Blegen dated Anta House to the Late Bronze Age Sixth Settlement, he admitted that this was not based on content but on the (freely acknowledged) slim evidence from exterior deposits (Blegen *et al.* 1953, 249–53). Filled with burnt debris, including animal bone, Anta House also had at least one stone circle

inside (Blegen *et al.* 1953, fig. 164). The stone circles are, as mentioned, a feature of the West Sanctuary from Late Phase 2 through 3, and deposits of burnt debris and bones from the feasting associated with sacrifice are common during the Geometric period (Morgan 1999, 316–17). The West Sanctuary stone circles, for example, are associated with burnt debris that was pushed back against the citadel wall (Rawson [1936–1937], vol. 5, 55, 58–59, 90; vol. 6, 47, 59; and photos 37.A.6 and 37.7.3–4). The function of Anta House is indeed, as Blegen (*et al.* 1953, 252–53) noted, likely to have been sacred, but Early Iron Age rather than Late Bronze in date.

That the South Gate area should be the focus of Early Iron Age attention is not surprising. We know from the West Sanctuary that the Troy VI wall was a significant element in the Early Iron Age ritual landscape (Basedow in press; Morris 2007). The South Gate, with its tower fronted by a row of stele, was visible into the Hellenistic period. In addition to Anta House, other potential Early Iron Age elements are associated with the gate area. A non-bonding stepped platform was built up against the street-facing short side of 'House 771'; a building dated to Troy VIIb by Blegen and located directly to the left as one enters through the gate (Figs. 16.3 and 16.5). It recalls the stepped platform on the exterior face of the north wall of the Phase 3 building in the West Sanctuary. Then there is the matter of the stone circle inside the Tower itself (Fig. 16.16), which served as the basis for a monolithic block, atop which stood, perhaps, an object with a double cylinder base (Fig. 16.16; Blegen *et al.* 1953, 99). A circle with such a monolithic block is known from the Phase 3 West Sanctuary (Fig. 16.2; Blegen *et al.* 1958, figs. 163, 369 [circle #25]) where, as may be the case with the South Gate tower, the circles go through multiple phases (Blegen *et al.* 1958, 275). Recent excavation noted six predecessors to the South Gate Tower circle (Korfmann 1998, 30–1), which may however represent deep foundations for a platform meant

Fig. 16.16: Stone circle in the South Gate Tower VIi (Troia Projekt, Tübingen University)

Fig. 16.19: Tapering, pillar-like structure in the Early Archaic Phase 4 West Sanctuary (Troia Projekt, Tübingen University)

Fig. 16.18: West Sanctuary Archaic Phases 4 and 5 monolithic blocks in Area Z6 (Troia Projekt, Tübingen University)

Fig. 16.17: Pavement in the Early Iron Age West Sanctuary (Troia Projekt, Tübingen University)

to support considerable weight rather than renewal phases. The distinctive bread-loaf cobble paving style of the South Gate paved circle can also be found in Early Iron Age levels in the West Sanctuary (Fig. 16.17).

Finally, there is the question of the stele, or 'baetyl' stones, as Blegen sometimes called them. These are found in front of the South Tower, but also in abundance throughout the Pillar House and Iron Age West Sanctuary areas, where they can be either freestanding or built into walls as distinctive corner and end elements (Fig. 16.18). The north wall of Anta House terminates with one of these blocks – the 'anta' from which the building received its name. Almost certainly dating to a variety of phases, there is no evidence for the unequivocal interpretation of the baetyls as Bronze Age gate or doorway stele (Blegen *et al.* 1953, 104–105, figs. 72–76; Korfmann 1998, 471–88). In the South Gate area, the similarity of the Anta House baetyl stone to the P2 pillar reinforced Blegen's conviction that this must be a Bronze Age building (Blegen *et al.* 1953, 249). Yet the find of a similar, though much more weathered, tapering pillar in the Lower Sanctuary area dating to the Early Archaic Phase 4 raises questions even about P2 (Fig. 16.19). In the West Sanctuary, some of Blegen's baetyl stones are perhaps best understood as boundary stones, so-called *horoi*, that at Iron Age and later ritual sites demarcate sacred space. The questions of who placed the row of stele in front of the South Gate Tower, and to what end, need also be reconsidered in this context. The reuse of Sixth Settlement blocks is documented for nearly every later period at Troy (Blegen *et al.* 1958, 215, 243–4, 286). The use of monolithic blocks salvaged from the Sixth Settlement citadel wall in clear post-Bronze Age ritual settings like the West Sanctuary shows that this well-documented reuse could be sacred as well as profane.

Conclusions

The plan of the identified Early Iron Age features offered here (Fig. 16.5) is necessarily sparse and incomplete. That a terrace stood here in the Early Iron Age at least as early as our West Sanctuary Geometric Phase 2 seems secure. Houses 814, 768, 769, and 703 make up parts of that structure. The pits on the south sides of P1 and P2 may also be part of that general plan. The curved wall and built structures at the base of P2 are somewhat later, and not necessarily contemporary with each other. Lacking a complete stratigraphic record, including precise descriptions of associated ceramics, little more can be said. That P2 excited Early Iron Age interest is clear. Certain unusual features associated with Blegen's plan of the Troy VI Pillar house, such as the stairs near P2 that descend nearly half a meter from a level that was not preserved (Fig. 16.20; Blegen *et al.* 1953, 228), should represent post-Bronze Age interest in keeping P2 accessible.

The nearby South Gate features, Anta House, the South Tower circle and the stepped bench outside House 771 fit models familiar to us from the West Sanctuary phase 3. The many monolithic blocks set throughout the area, including the ones lined up in front of the South Gate Tower, were without a doubt the focus of Early Iron Age attention. Whether these were actually erected in the Early Iron Age or Late Bronze Age needs to be carefully considered.

Detailed consideration of the focus of the Early Iron Age cult identified in the Pillar House area is outside the scope of this paper. The hundreds of spindle whorls, needles and loom weights found associated with Pillar House deposits, numbers so exceptional as to be remarked upon by every excavator working within the area defined by its walls (Cox [1932]; Caskey [1934]; Blegen *et al.* 1958, 233–7), may point to a connection with the cult of Athena Ergane, evidence for which has been found in the form of large numbers of votive loom weights from a secondary dump in Area D9 (Wallrodt 2002, 179–96).

Also to be mentioned only briefly here is the likelihood that other parts of the prehistoric citadel were, like the West Sanctuary and Pillar House/South Gate area, the site of Early Iron Age cult activity. The Northeast Bastion area K4 is a strong candidate. The bastion was visible into the Hellenistic period, when a stairway is built alongside it. There is an unusual apsidal feature, the so-called *Brunnenfassung* around the bastion's interior well, where Dörpfeld found a Geometric and Protogeometric pottery (Hertel 2003a, 187, n.2, with full bibliography). Curved wall structures were

Fig. 16.20: Pillar House during excavation. Two flights of stairs can be seen descending to the level of P2 (Blegen et al. 1953, fig. 4)

excavated on the terraced slope directly outside it (Dörpfeld 1902, pl. 45; Blegen *et al.* 1958, 286).

Finally, this attempt at identifying Early Iron Age elements near Pillar House and the South Gate exposes Blegen's less-than-secure basis for the phasing of many of the architectural features in the area, from entire buildings (Anta House) through terrace elements (Houses 703, 768, and 769) and smaller excavation units (Area 770). Phase VIIb1, already suspect as a ceramic assemblage, has been shown to be fragile as an architectural phase as well. For Troy VIIa, proximity to the Sixth Settlement levels and signs of burning are frequently given precedence by Blegen over more rigorous categories of information. Troy VIIb features in the Pillar House area (Houses 768 and 769) have been shown to uniformly share the same orientation, plan and functional elements (large sunken pithoi) as underlying features (Houses 703 and 725) that Blegen dated to this Troy VIIa phase. The architectural and functional concordance between Blegen's Troy VIIa and VIIb, and lack of the same between Troy VIIa and Troy VI, has never been adequately addressed. That the VIIa ceramic assemblage is to be associated with the final phase of the Sixth Settlement, rather than a later architectural phase has been suggested before (Finley *et al.* 1964, 6; Mellink 1986, 100; Hood 1995; Korfmann 2004, 14–15). That the VIIa architectural phase is an early version of VIIb would logically follow. There is nothing in the Pillar House area, or in what this study says about Blegen's difficulty in reconciling ceramic and architectural phases, to contradict this conclusion. Further review of the Blegen model is recommended on every level.

PART 5

SOCIAL IMPLICATIONS FOR THE PRODUCTION AND CONSUMPTION OF POTTERY

END OR BEGINNING? THE LATE BRONZE AGE TO IRON AGE TRANSFORMATION AT TROIA

Carolyn Chabot Aslan

When excavations began again at Troia in the late 1980's, the end of the Bronze Age was understood according to the model proposed by the previous excavator, Carl Blegen. Evidence from the recent excavations has prompted a re-evaluation of some of his phases, in particular the ceramic sequence. New information has emerged concerning the Protogeometric and Geometric periods, which needs to be considered when rewriting the narrative of events and developments at Troia after the Bronze Age. The transition from the Bronze Age to the Iron Age at Troia can be characterized by the migration of people most likely from the area of Thrace and Bulgaria, creating a mixed population with the remaining local inhabitants and a ceramic tradition with elements of both groups. This ceramic assemblage continues into the Protogeometric and Geometric periods, while contacts with Greek and northern Aegean sites slowly increase and ritual activities begin to concentrate around visible Bronze Age remains at the site.

Carl Blegen's stratigraphic interpretation

Carl Blegen's interpretation of the stratigraphy should be briefly reviewed. According to Blegen, the phase VIIa settlement suffered from a destruction event, which he interpreted as the Trojan War. After this event, a small population of survivors reoccupied the site. In this VIIb1 reoccupation phase, the earlier ceramic tradition continued with some modification, and a new type of handmade pottery was introduced. This handmade Coarse Ware is distinguished by finger impressed rope decoration found around the upper part of large jars, which was the most common shape (Fig. 17.1, shapes C85, C86; Blegen *et al.* 1958, 10–13, 141–7, 158–9; see also Mountjoy 1999b, for a discussion of this phase).

In the following VIIb2 phase, Blegen saw evidence for much more extensive changes in ceramics with a migration of people bringing Knobbed Ware. Knobbed Ware is also a handmade ware, and has distinctive knobs and incised or stamped decoration (Fig. 17.2). After some deliberation, Blegen concluded that Knobbed Ware was not directly related to the previous Coarse Ware and saw the introduction of these two wares as separate episodes (Blegen *et al.* 1958, 154, 158–60).

From the evidence available, Blegen (1958, 146–48) concluded that at the end of the VIIb2 period, occupation ceased and the site remained uninhabited for about 400 years until resettlement in 700 BCE. Archaic Grey Ware ceramics from the seventh century BCE appear very similar to Bronze Age Grey Ware. This situation has been explained by various scholars, usually by proposing that Aeolian colonists learned how to make Grey Ware somewhere else in western Anatolia or Lesbos, and then brought the ceramic type back to Troia in the seventh century (Lamb 1932, 1; Blegen *et al.* 1958, 147; Bayne 2000, 210–11, 266–7).

New evidence and evaluation

When excavation began again at Troia the aforementioned stratigraphic sequence was expected, but soon it was noted that Protogeometric amphora sherds were being found in many areas of the site, often in mixed contexts in areas around the edges of the mound (K/L4, E8/9, West Sanctuary; see Fig. 17.3). Reinvestigation also revealed that previous excavators had found some Protogeometric material (Hertel 1992; Catling 1998; Lenz *et al.* 1998; Hertel 2003b), which at least partially disproved the theory of a long hiatus marking the end of the Bronze Age. However the Protogeometric amphorae were assigned to a new phase

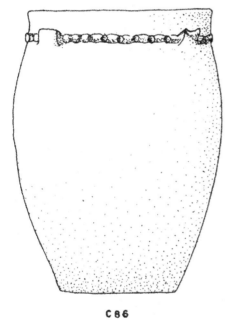

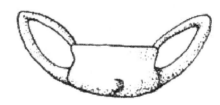

Fig. 17.2: Knobbed Ware cups (reproduced with permission from Blegen et al. *1958, fig. 218)*

Fig. 17.1: Handmade coarse ware jars with finger impressed rope decoration (reproduced with permission from Blegen et al. *1958, fig. 218)*

(VIIb3) without well-stratified contexts from this phase, there was still much that was unknown about the Bronze Age to Iron Age transition.

Knowledge of the Protogeometric and Geometric periods increased through careful excavation in sector D9, which is located on the southern side of the mound (Fig. 17.3). A small room was located under Archaic levels, perhaps part of a house and including an assemblage of ceramics that can be dated to the Geometric period, a previously undocumented phase at the site. Under this room were two Protogeometric levels, which in turn were found directly over a VIIb2 phase (Aslan 2002). One important contribution of the D9 contexts was that once the components of the Protogeometric and

Geometric assemblages were understood, it was much easier to identify other such contexts at Troia. This was especially important for understanding the West Sanctuary, where we now have evidence for multiple phases of activity in the Protogeometric and Geometric periods under the Greek and Roman cult buildings (Fig. 17.4). The D9 sequence allowed us to better study entire assemblages, instead of isolated ceramic types, and this allowed us to begin revising our understanding of the ceramic phases.

Troia VIIb1 and VIIb2

There are several aspects of the original model that are now undergoing renewed investigation. Beginning with the VIIb1 phase, its designation as a separate ceramic phase is now being reconsidered. Although in Blegen's report, it would

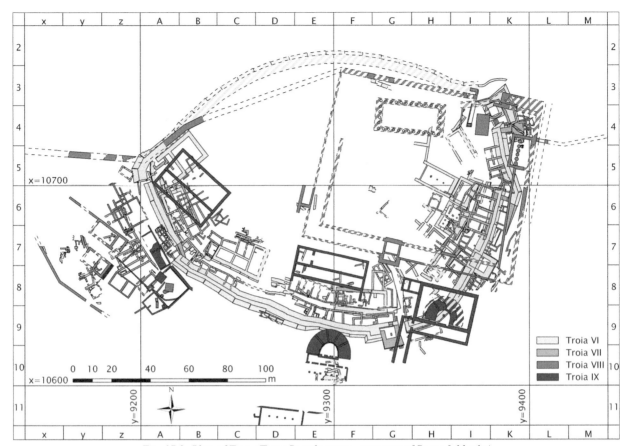

Fig. 17.3: Plan of Troia (Troia Projekt image, courtesy of Peter Jablonka)

seem that evidence for this phase was found in many areas, in the recent excavations it has been very difficult to find any contexts that fit Blegen's description for VIIb1 (Pavol Hnila, pers. comm.). When re-examining Blegen's final publication (1958), in many areas he reports that there was not such a clear division between VIIb1 and VIIb2 and the ceramics are often described as mixed. The difficulty in finding VIIb1 contexts either indicates that the reoccupation was by a small population that was unevenly distributed at the site, or else it may be a symptom of ceramic classification problems.

The main difficulty with identifying VIIb1 contexts is finding assemblages where the Coarse Ware jars with finger impressed rope decoration occur without Knobbed Ware vessels, which is how Blegen had described the VIIb1 assemblage. It was previously thought that vessels with the finger-impressed rope decoration were the type-artefact for the VIIb1 period, but it is now clear that such vessels are one of the most common types in the VIIb2 period, and continue to be found in the Protogeometric period and even occasionally in Geometric levels (Aslan 2002). Analysis of the overall assemblage shows that it is better to consider handmade Coarse Ware as a general group with certain types used for utilitarian purposes, while other types are used as serving or dining vessels. One variant, Coarse Ware jars with

rope decoration, are the utilitarian ware of the assemblage used for food storage, production, and perhaps cooking. They occur together with Knobbed Ware vessels, which are used for eating, drinking, and serving. Knobbed Ware vessels include various cups and mugs, often with large loop handles, characteristic knobs and may be highly decorated with polished surfaces and incised or stamped decoration (Blegen *et al.* 1958, 154, 158–160; Koppenhöfer 1997). Although the fabric of Knobbed Ware can be quite coarse their decoration, highly burnished surfaces, and shapes place them into a category of fine table ware. Some of the differences in manufacture, fabric and decoration within the handmade Coarse Ware tradition can be explained by functional and display needs.

Previously at Troia we had incorrectly seen coarse handmade jars and Knobbed Ware as primarily chronological categories rather than functional categories. Although Blegen saw the two handmade Coarse Ware types as separate ceramic traditions coming to Troia in different time periods, this idea should be reconsidered. Research is underway to examine if there is any chronological pattern to the introduction of different shapes of handmade Coarse Ware, which may be an important factor in tracing the mechanisms for the introduction of handmade ware at

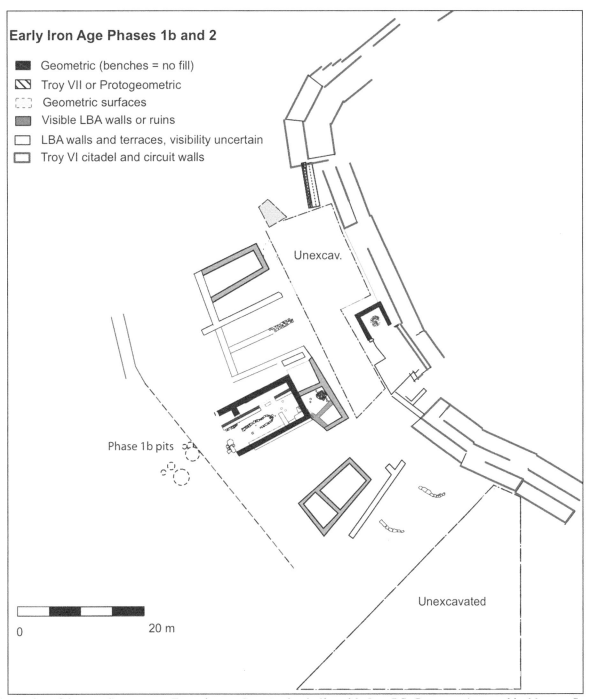

Fig. 17.4: Plan of the West Sanctuary at Troia showing Iron Age levels 1b and 2: Late PG–Geometric (prepared by Maureen Basedow, Troia Projekt)

Troia. The introduction of handmade Coarse Ware both in Anatolia and in Greece has been the subject of much debate (Hood 1967; Rutter 1976; Walberg 1976; Bloedow 1985; Bouzek 1985; Özdogan 1987, 14–15; Rutter 1990; Small 1990; Sams 1994, 20–2; Bankoff *et al.* 1996; Genz 1997; Koppenhöfer 1997; Small 1997). At least in the case of Troia, several factors suggest that the appearance

of this new handmade ceramic assemblage represents a migration of people, perhaps extending over a period of time. Compared to sites in mainland Greece, which received only a small amount of handmade pottery in a limited shape range, at Troia handmade Coarse Ware forms between 50% and 70% of the assemblage in phase VIIb2 and has a large shape range. The evidence for an actual migration of

Fig. 17.5: Protogeometric amphoras (Troia Projekt image)

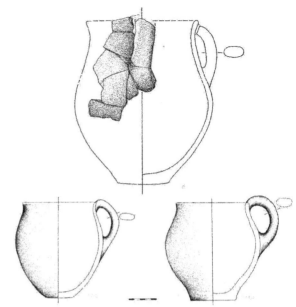

Fig. 17.7: Protogeometric cooking pots (Troia Projekt image)

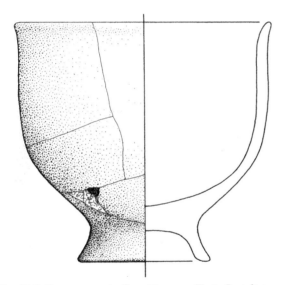

Fig. 17.6: Protogeometric Grey Ware cup (Troia Projekt image)

suggests that some local potters were still producing wheel-made wares. The handmade and wheel-made ceramics are found in the same contexts, but the range of shapes in each tradition is evocative. Most of the shapes and wares retained from the previous tradition consist of fine ware vessels that would have been used in food service, and may have been retained as status markers. Late Bronze Age cooking pots of the late VI and VIIa period do not appear to continue into the VIIb2 period and the handmade Coarse Ware vessels probably replaced them. The large numbers and new shapes of handmade utilitarian ware vessels may be indicative of a wider shift in subsistence and food production and cooking practices. Further research in faunal and botanical remains may provide more information about these changes.

Protogeometric period

As mentioned above, Blegen's interpretation of a hiatus following the VIIb2 period can also now be revised. There is evidence for two Protogeometric phases following the VIIb2 phase. Most of the ceramics from this period have been found in areas on the edge of the mound (West Sanctuary, sectors D9, E8/9, KL4/5; see Lenz et al. 1998; Aslan 2002). Presumably there was more occupation on the mound itself, but these layers were removed by ancient building activity or by earlier excavations. Even so, there are fewer architectural remains that can be associated with the Protogeometric period compared to the number of VIIb2 house remains, and there is an overall sense that the population has decreased somewhat.

The first Protogeometric phase at Troia does not represent

people is also supported by petrographic analysis (Pintér 2005), which indicates that the handmade Coarse Ware at Troia was locally made. This is in contrast to limited NAA results (Guzowska et al. 2002) that indicated that some of the pieces might be imported. The combined results indicate that a new group of people arrived at Troia and began to make their pottery types with local materials, but it would also not be surprising if there were a few pieces from the original homeland. Whether the VIIb1 period indicates the first sporadic movement or initial contact with this culture group, or whether it should be cast off as a separate phase, is now an ongoing research question.

Previous local Bronze Age types of Grey and Tan Ware also continued, although they were much reduced in number. Even so, the continuation of the previous ceramic tradition

Fig. 17.8: Late Protogeometric fenestrated stand (Troia Projekt image, drawing by C. Haussner)

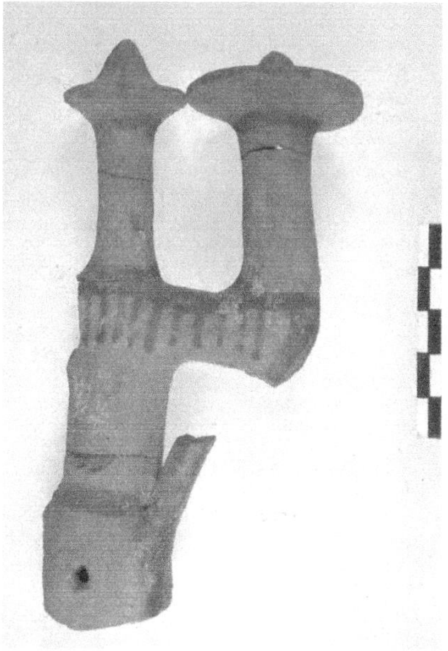

Fig. 17.9: Late Protogeometric ceramic pronged object (Troia Projekt image)

significant change at the site, but instead demonstrates strong continuity with the previous VIIb2 culture. Handmade Coarse Ware is still common, ranging between 30% and 70% of the assemblage depending on the context. The Protogeometric phase is recognized by a few new ceramic types, which were added to the previous VIIb2 assemblage. These ceramic types include Protogeometric amphorae, which stand out from the rest of the assemblage because of their distinctive decoration of concentric circles (Fig. 17.5). The amphorae in this first phase are mostly from Troia Group I, which is a type common at North Aegean sites (Catling 1998), and Grey Ware continues to form a large percentage of the assemblage (20–50%). Many of the shapes were continuations from the previous period, but there are a few Grey Ware cups (Fig. 17.6) that have the same shape as painted cups found at Greek mainland sites such as Athens and Lefkandi (*cf.* Catling and Lemos 1990, no. 103, pl. 8; Lemos 2002, 27–30, nos. 24.10, 24.11).

A new type of plain cooking jug also seems to have been introduced in this phase, or perhaps earlier (Fig. 17.7). The origins of the Protogeometric cooking pots are somewhat problematic. Petrographic analysis has shown that they were locally made and have similar fabric as VIIb2 handmade Coarse Ware vessels (Pintér 2006). Examples of such cooking pots have not yet been clearly found in VIIb2 contexts, although they may have been overlooked and assemblages are currently being re-examined to identify exactly when this shape is introduced at Troia. There are some small flat-based mugs (Blegen shape B44) that have a similar shape and are found in the VIIb2 period, but they are much smaller. Somewhat similar flat-based cooking jugs

also became common at Greek sites in the Protogeometric period (Wells 1983, figs. 50, 207; Reber 1991, figs 2–4; Lemos 2002, 85–7), but the ones at Troia are not quite the same. It is possible that the cooking jugs were developed out of the local handmade Coarse Ware pottery tradition in the region of Troia, but were also influenced by wider trends in cooking techniques. It is likely that different cooking practices were introduced in the Protogeometric period, with the new cooking jugs used for smaller portions of liquid or semi-liquid foods such as stews or soups.

The combined evidence from Grey Ware imitations, the Protogeometric amphorae, and perhaps shared trends in cooking techniques indicate a limited, but growing interaction between Troia and other sites, and the distribution patterns of Group I amphorae (Catling 1998) indicates trade routes up along the rim of the north Aegean linking Troia to Greek sites. However, the contact was still quite limited and the local culture remained dominant.

A pattern of slowly increasing imported material can be seen in the next phase, the late Protogeometric period. The range of imported amphorae and other painted vessels increased somewhat, but they were still a small percentage of the overall assemblage (Aslan 2002, nos. 10–23). Some of these imports were unusual types of vessels probably used in ritual. A pit was found in the West Sanctuary containing a large and fragile fenestrated stand (Fig. 17.8; Rose 1997, 82–3; 1998, 74–7). Two ceramic pronged objects were also found in this pit, one painted and one in Grey Ware. The painted example has three prongs topped with mushroom-shaped caps, although one has broken away. The paint appears to represent some type of fringed garment that was

Fig. 17.10: Late Protogeometric Grey Ware krater (Troia Projekt image)

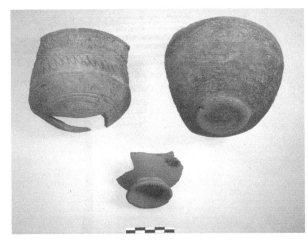

Fig. 17.11: Late Protogeometric cups and bowls (Troia Projekt image)

tied around the figure and two spots of paint may indicate breasts (Fig. 17.9). It is likely that the objects had symbolic meaning and can be considered as some type of figurine or idol. Within this pit were also a large Grey Ware krater (Fig. 17.10) and some bowls and cups, many of which have unusual shapes and fabric for Troia and were probably imported (Fig. 17.11). The krater has a similar shape to painted kraters found at Lefkandi (*cf.* Lemos 2002, 74–5).

Research by Maureen Basedow on the excavation notebooks of Blegen's expeditions, currently held in the archives at the University of Cincinnati, has revealed that his team found a similar Grey Ware krater in association with a Grey Ware cup and a painted jug in an area near House 850 on top of the Troy VI fortification wall. This assemblage probably represents a second pit deposit from the late Protogeometric period, although it was not described this way in the final report (Blegen *et al.* 1958, 273–4, figs. 300, 302, nos. 31.1070, 37.968, 37.971).

The ceramic material from these two deposits has been interpreted as votive or ritual equipment. The combined evidence from the late Protogeometric material from the West Sanctuary indicates ritual activity had begun at least by this period, perhaps involving ritual feasting as indicated by the sets of kraters and cups. Impressive Bronze Age remains, including the Troy VI fortification wall and a large Bronze Age building, were located in the area of the West Sanctuary (Becks *et al.* 2006; Basedow, this volume), and it is likely that the partial ruins of these structures formed the focus for the ritual activity perhaps connected to Bronze Age heroes.

Above late Protogeometric levels in D9 and in the West Sanctuary are Geometric levels, probably dating to the eighth

century BCE, which leaves the ninth century as something of a mystery. It could be that there was a significant decrease in population at Troia in the ninth century, or simply that ceramic classification and stratification is not fine enough to distinguish ninth century from eighth century material. There may have still been some activity at Troia in the ninth century, as indicated by the continuation of religious activity in the West Sanctuary. In the Geometric period a cult structure became more formalized over time, eventually resulting in a closed structure. The evidence that a late Protogeometric votive pit was located opposite the entrance of the new building suggests some continuity at the site and not total abandonment in the ninth century BCE. There is also continuity seen in the pottery, especially in Grey Ware. At no point in the Protogeometric through Geometric periods at Troia is there evidence for a significant influx of Greek-style pottery, only a trickle of imports, which casts some doubt on the historical validity of the Aeolian migration (Rose 2008).

Conclusions

The overall nature of the changes from the Bronze Age to the Iron Age can now be better understood. In the VIIb2 period, both the large numbers of handmade vessels and the range in the types of vessels indicate that a new population group moved to Troia. The similarities between this assemblage and pottery from Thrace and Bulgaria make it very likely that people with this pottery tradition were moving south into the Troad.

In the Protogeometric period, and certainly in the Geometric period, Troia slowly began to be more tied into North Aegean and Greek networks and ceramic styles. The early Geometric period, especially the ninth century BCE, is still not fully understood and there may have been times within this period that the population at the site was either absent or much reduced in number, but there was certainly not a 400 year abandonment period. The fact that Archaic period Grey Ware is very similar to Bronze Age Grey Ware can now be better understood as a factor of the continuation of the ceramic tradition from the Bronze Age through the Iron Age period in the Troad region.

In conclusion, it is apparent that the key transformation at Troia occurred in the VIIb2 period, with the likely arrival of a new population group that mixed with an existing local population. The situation at Troia is just part of the evidence that attests to population movements at the end of the Bronze Age and it marks the beginning of a new Iron Age culture at the site.

Acknowledgements

I thank C. Brian Rose and the late Manfred Korfmann for their support in the study of this material. Much of my research was done in collaberation with Bronze Age and post-Bronze Age researchers at the Troia excavation. I am especially thankful to Pavol Hnila, Maureen Basedow, Peter Jablonka, Diane Thumm, Ralf Becks, Penelope Mountjoy and Wendy Rigter, although some of our interpretations differ. More information about the West Sanctuary Iron Age remains will soon be forthcoming in final reports published by Philip van Zabern. Handmade Coarse Ware at Troia is currently undergoing study in a dissertation project by Pavol Hnila at the University of Tübingen.

HANDMADE AND BURNISHED POTTERY IN THE EASTERN MEDITERRANEAN AT THE END OF THE BRONZE AGE: TOWARDS AN EXPLANATION FOR ITS DIVERSITY AND GEOGRAPHICAL DISTRIBUTION

Bartłomiej Lis

The handmade and usually burnished pottery that appeared around 1200 BCE in the eastern Mediterranean is a phenomenon that was correctly recognized only some 30 years ago. Since then all such pottery has been placed in a single category called Handmade Burnished Ware (hereafter HBW) or, more subjectively, Barbarian Ware, though names such as Dorian- or North-Western Greek Ware have been used sporadically (Kilian 1978b; Avila 1980). A false impression of a more or less homogeneous group of pottery has thus been created, which has led to a failure in locating a single area of origin. Some (Reber 1991, 162) connect HBW with Greek Early Iron Age handmade pottery, which as used here starts with the onset of the Protogeometric period, around 1050–1000 BCE. This discussion will only focus on locally produced dark-surfaced handmade pottery that can be recognised as new or novel within specific sites. Therefore, imported Sardinian or western Anatolian pottery from Kommos (Watrous 1989; Rutter 2006), handmade pottery from Macedonia (*e.g.* Hochstetter 1984) or pale-surfaced pottery from Kalapodi (Jacob-Felsch 1996, 78) will not be treated.

Distribution of handmade pottery

The earliest occurrence of HBW dates to the first half of the 13th century BCE and is associated with the Cretan site of Chania (see Fig. 18.1). During the second half of this century, HBW appears at a few new settlements, including the important centres of Mycenae, Tiryns and Midea. The first decades of the 12th century mark a short-lasting apogee of the HBW phenomenon. On the Greek mainland it is found almost at every LH IIIC Early settlement excavated since 1975 and has also appeared on the Levantine and Anatolian coasts. In the last stage of LH IIIC Early (*i.e.* Tower phase or Rutter's phase 3), HBW is identified for the first time in settlements on Cyprus. This peak is followed by a sharp decline in a total number of sites where HBW is still present (for a useful summary of HBW finds see Pilides 1994; for an up-to-date bibliography see Jung 2006, 255f.). There are, however, many new Greek sites that witness the appearance of handmade pottery towards the end of the Late Bronze Age, and will be referred to in the second part of the paper.

This rather uncomplicated distribution pattern may be refined by incorporation of a few simple variables concerning the HBW pottery and its context. The first of these is the relative quantity of handmade pottery. Although much significance is attached to the finds of such pottery, it usually occurs in quantities not exceeding 1% of the total number of sherds. Only a handful of sites reach or exceed 2.5%, including Troy (Koppenhöfer 1997, 306, tab. 1), Kalapodi (Jacob-Felsch 1996, 90) and Mitrou moreover, the share of handmade pottery exhibits an upward trend over time. The second variable is the general character of the assemblage. Open shapes seem to form the majority of HBW only from Chania and Lefkandi. A relative balance between both open and closed shapes is characteristic for Korakou, Dimini and Troy, but most of the surveyed sites feature an assemblage that is in a greater part composed of closed shapes used for storage and cooking, with a

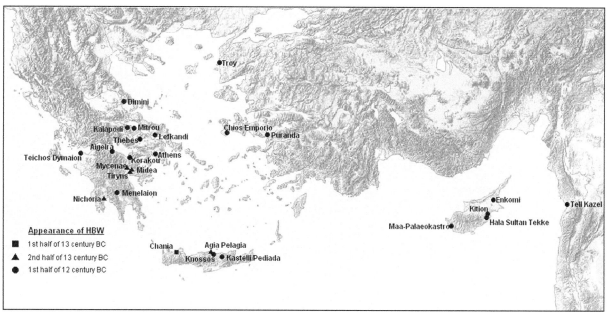

Fig. 18.1: Distribution of dark-surfaced handmade pottery in the Eastern Mediterranean between 1275 and 1150 BCE

substantial addition of open shapes such as carinated cups. However, Kalapodi and, to some extent, Mitrou stand out for their assemblages composed exclusively of closed shapes. The presence of carinated cups showing close morphological similarity to southern Italian examples can be a third variable. This particular shape was used by Reinhard Jung (2006) to establish a comparative chronology between southern Italy and southern Greece. A fourth variable is the co-appearance of HBW with Grey Ware, which shows links with ceramic assemblages of southern Italian peninsula. So far such pottery has been identified at Chania (Hallager and Hallager 2000, 166f.; 2003, 254–6), Tiryns (Kilian 1988a, 146–9), Dimini (Adrimi-Sismani 2006) and Tell Kazel (Jung *et al.* 2005, 31, n. 48). Finally there is the presence of decoration in general, and of the plain plastic band in particular. Closed shapes from Kalapodi and Mitrou do not bear any decoration, while vessels at Troy and in the southern part of the surveyed area feature mainly plastic decoration. The plain plastic band is missing at Troy and it has been shown that this particular decoration cannot be derived from the Balkan region. The only reasonable origin is therefore southern Italy (Jung 2006, 26; pl. 25). Many other variables could be included here, but enough evidence has been gathered to establish three distinct groups of handmade pottery (Fig. 18.2 and Table 18.1)

Group I: Handmade Burnished Ware

The first group, for which I propose the name Handmade Burnished Ware should be reserved, has following char-

acteristics: It occurs in very small relative quantities, not exceeding 1% at its highest frequency; yet the assemblage is both typologically and functionally varied (it includes jars of different types, cooking utensils, other closed shapes as well as bowls and cups); it often includes carinated cups of southern Italian affinities; HBW constitutes a rather ephemeral phenomenon – in single cases when it survives for a longer period (such as Tiryns; *cf.* Pilides 1994, fig. 15), its quantity diminishes rapidly; it is sometimes associated with the Grey Ware of a very probable Italian inspiration or origin; HBW bears mainly plastic decoration, including a plain plastic band on simple jars; and its influence is visible mainly in the fine decorated pottery.

No distinct concentrations of HBW have been convincingly documented as yet. Concentrations of both HBW and Grey Ware, reported from Raum 127 in the Lower Citadel (Belardelli and Bettelli 1999), is probably illusory as it may include pieces from the debris hump below the earliest floor (Tobias Mühlenbruch, pers. comm.). Moreover, with an exception of Athens (Athens; Rutter 1975, fig. 16), HBW has been found only in settlement material. However, both these observations are probably due to the random nature of archaeological discoveries and may be amended by future excavations. The number of the HBW vessels recovered at Tell Kazel (Badre 2003), can be cited, where the number of the HBW vessels recovered suggests that there were some concentrations, but exact statistics for this site are not available. Several features of this group, such as chronological and geographical distribution (first appearance in western Crete, then the Mainland, and finally Levant and Cyprus), co-appearance with Grey Ware, and typological

Fig. 18.2: Distribution of sites with handmade pottery attributable to one of the three groups

Site/Variable	Relative Quantity	Character of assemblage	Carinated cups	Grey Ware with Italian links	Frequent decoration/plain plastic bands	Group
Dimini	n.e.d.	VARIED	YES	YES	n.e.d./YES	1
Kalapodi	HIGH	RESTRICTED	NO	NO	NO/NO	3
Mitrou	HIGH	RESTRICTED	NO	NO	NO/NO	3 (1)
Lefkandi	LOW	n.e.d.	YES	NO	YES/NO	1
Korakou	LOW	VARIED	YES	NO	YES/YES	1
Aigeira	n.e.d.	VARIED	YES-	NO	NO/NO	~1
Tiryns	LOW	VARIED	YES	YES	YES/YES	1
Mycenae	LOW	n.e.d.	NO	NO	n.e.d./YES	1
Menelaion	LOW	VARIED-	NO	NO	YES/YES	1
Chania	LOW	VARIED	YES	YES	NO/YES	1
Troy	HIGH	VARIED	NO	NO	YES/NO	2
Kition	LOW	VARIED	NO	NO	NO/NO	1
Tell Kazel	n.e.d.	VARIED	NO	YES	YES/YES	1

Table. 18.1: Division of handmade pottery from selected sites into three distinguished groups according to five variables (author's own compilation based on published data, except for Mycenae. I would like to thank Elizabeth French for sending me the chapter on LH IIIC Mycenae from Susan Sherratt's unpublished PhD thesis; n.e.d = not enough data; YES – in terms of Aigeira; cf. Jung 2006, 43–6)

similarities to contemporary *impasto* pottery from southern Italy pointed out by Marco Bettelli (2002) and Jung (2005; 2006; in press), indicate an Italian origin for the major part of this pottery. However, as petrographic and chemical analyses have shown at Aegira (Deger-Jalkotzy 2003, 465f.), Chania (Jones 1986, 261; Hallager and Hallager 2003, 253),

Mycenae (Jones 1986, 261; French 1989, 47f.), Menelaion (Whitbread 1992), Tell Kazel (Jung *et al.* 2005), and Thebes (Mommsen *et al.* 2002, 608) the lions' share of HBW was produced locally.

In light of these observations the most reasonable conclusion is that this material attests to the presence of foreign groups. The alternative explanation, that indigenous populations of Crete and Greek mainland locally emulated pottery common in southern Italy, seems to be very unlikely. Naturally, adopting foreign influence (ceramic styles, exotic goods, etiquette) was a common practice in closely connected cultures of the eastern Mediterranean, but for several reasons this does not seem to relate to HBW. First of all, on Crete and the Greek mainland there is no contextual indication of any special value (for instance due to their exotic origin) that would have been ascribed to such vessels. Secondly, in the case of HBW we are dealing not with possible imitation of a few shapes or attractive mode of decoration, but with production of more or less complete assemblages with the use of technology diverging in all possible respects from the one that was locally employed. Moreover, earlier imports of pottery originating from southern Italy are not attested, thus there are no predecessors, whereas the common situation with Mycenaean pottery outside of its core production area is that it was first imported and than locally imitated (Cyprus, Southern Italy). Finally, the HBW assemblage consists mainly of shapes of purely utilitarian function. If it was imitated for prestigious reasons, an abundance of open shapes, tableware, would be expected.

The occupation and role of foreign groups in local societies on the Greek mainland constitutes a challenging point of research, and I would suggest three main categories. The first instances of finds related to Italian metallurgy on the mainland such as the very early Naue II sword and winged-axe mould at Mycenae (*cf.* Eder and Jung 2005, 486), immediately precede the appearance of HBW and suggest that there were foreign craftsmen working under the auspices of palaces. They and their companions might have been responsible for the first occurrences of such pottery, especially given that HBW first appeared mostly in major palatial, or at least administrative, centres. The contexts of HBW from Cyprus also reveal a pattern connecting it with metallurgy (Pilides 1994, 72f.). Contemporary appearance of simple clay spools at Chania (Wiman and Bruun-Lundgren 2003, 266) may indicate that weaving was another craft in which the newcomers were specialized. Similar clay spools are sometimes associated with HBW at other sites (*e.g.* Lefkandi; Popham and Sackett 1968, 13). However, as the research of Lorenz Rahmstorf (2005) has shown, the chronological and ethnic significance of these tools is far from being well understood.

Settlers lured by newly-created opportunities may constitute a second group of newcomers, and highly mobile traders could make up the third category. Both settlers and traders might have immensely profited from the dramatic events around 1200 BCE. The former would gain easier access and more freedom to settle; the latter would be able to take part in re-establishing and reshaping trade connections within these new conditions, and it is therefore possible to attribute the dynamism of the HBW phenomenon to these two groups. The traders were probably quite flexible in their profession, turning into pirates if the cost calculation was favourable. Settlers may have been equally opportunistic. However, at least the history of the Aigeira settlement in Greek Achaea shows that there was a rather peaceful coexistence between the group who produced HBW and the Mycenaean population that adjoined, and did not eliminate, the former (at Aigeira there is a stratum that contains some HBW material but no Mycenaean pottery, which appears only in the next settlement layers; Deger-Jalkotzy 1977; 2003). Nothing conclusive can be said about the connection between HBW and the groups of Sea Peoples. However, the association of HBW with highly mobile individuals capable of travelling great distances by the sea and present in the Aegean, Cyprus and the Levant, implies that these people might have been a part of the phenomenon that was reflected in the historical sources as the Sea Peoples.

Why did HBW (but not necessarily the people behind it) disappear or at least diminish in quantity so quickly? The assimilation of its producers must have been one of the major factors. Many settlements were simply abandoned after the outset of 12th century BCE. The migration to Cyprus, where HBW appeared in the later stage of 12th century together with an increased Aegean influence, might have contributed to this process. Finally, the incorporation of HBW features and forms (plastic bands on kraters, the carinated cup) into the Mycenaean repertoire could have accelerated the fading of the HBW phenomenon, yet this factor played a rather minor role in the whole process.

Two more features of this pottery group deserve a short mention here, namely the intra-site distribution of HBW, characterized by a wide scatter without any distinct concentrations, and very small quantities of such pottery. They are indeed quite striking when compared with Troy, where the presence of a new population is also very probable. In my opinion this would suggest that the newcomers were not fully integrated into local societies, living probably in small concentrations or communes on the edges of settlements, from where single pots and/or their contents were traded and 'leaked' into the settlement proper. Naturally, such reconstruction does not presuppose any hostility between the Mycenaeans and newcomers.

Group II: West Anatolian Handmade Pottery

The second group of handmade pottery shares some characteristics with HBW (composition of assemblage, presence of decoration), yet it differs considerably in the relative frequency. So far only one site, Troy, can be attributed to this group, but safely ongoing and future excavations on the western Anatolian coast, such as at the site of Bademgediği Tepe (Puranda), will undoubtedly add to this list, though not enough material has been published as yet (Meriç 2003, 89). Troy features two types of handmade pottery: Coarse Ware (simple domestic pots) and Knobbed Ware (mainly decorated table ware; for a recent summary with illustrations see Koppenhöfer 1997). Carl Blegen (*et al.* 1958) believed that there was a chronological distinction between the two: Coarse Ware appeared in Troy VIIb1 and was joined by Knobbed Ware in Troy VIIb2. However, some of Blegen's observations and, above all, recent discoveries suggest that these two wares were in fact contemporary (Hawkins and Easton 1996, 115, 118), and constitute a common ceramic tradition. Knobbed Ware was quite rare in the beginning, yet its percentage rose with time. It seems that the development of handmade pottery after the LH VIIb2 phase led, on the one hand, to a simplification of forms and reduction of decoration, but on the other hand to an increase of its share to an astonishing 70% (Aslan 2002, 84).

The major traits of this group of handmade pottery include: it forms a functionally complete assemblage; handmade pottery has a strong appearance from the beginning, and its frequency rises constantly over the time; handmade domestic pottery (Trojan Coarse Ware) replaces completely traditional Coarse Ware (Gritty Ware), while table pottery (Knobbed Ware) coexists with local fine wares (Tan and Grey Minyan Ware); the presence of table ware is weak at the beginning, yet displays a rising tendency; there is a trend towards simplification of forms and decoration.

Group III: Handmade Domestic pottery

The third group of handmade pottery has very little in common with HBW (Group I). Substantial share in the total ceramic assemblage is its common feature with Group II (Western Anatolian) However, unlike the HBW and Western Anatolian groups, this third group forms a functionally impoverished assemblage, limited to closed shapes for cooking and storage. Thus this pottery should be newly categorized to distinguish it from HBW, which it is all too often associated with. My suggestion is to call it Handmade Domestic Pottery (hereafter HDP). The name has already been proposed by Irene Lemos (2002, 97) for the typical Early Iron Age handmade pottery. In the early stage of its use (the 12th century BCE), HDP may be already distinguished at sites of Kalapodi and Mitrou (Fig. 18.3:1–9).

It can be characterized as follows: the assemblage is typologically and functionally limited – only closed shapes of storage/cooking function are represented; it has a substantial share in the total amount of pottery and its frequency tends to rise (Fig. 18.4); the assemblage was much later enriched by new types of vessels for other purposes (for Kalapodi see Nitsche 1987, 36); sites where this group of handmade pottery is represented are located close to regions where handmade pottery had been in wide use for centuries; HDP gradually ousts traditional wheel-made cooking pottery.

At this point it is necessary to present the evidence from Mitrou, a settlement in eastern Lokris (*cf.* Fig. 18.2). Although these are still very preliminary results after two excavation seasons, though it is worth illustrating to show that Kalapodi cannot be treated as an exceptional site in terms of Greek handmade pottery. The site and its 12th century BCE pottery were presented by Jeremy Rutter (in press) during the LH IIIC Middle workshop held in 2004 in Vienna, Austria. I would like to suggest that both HBW and HDP are represented at Mitrou. The lack of substantial pure LH IIIC Early deposits makes it difficult to analyse the interrelations between both groups at the same site and to understand how the HBW assemblage at Mitrou looks like. Yet a dark burnished kylix stem with a part of the bowl (mixed context, object No. LO784-007-013), a simple jar with impressed plastic cordon below the rim (a surface find, LN785-001-011), and a cup with high-swung handle (LN784-028-015) most probably belong to the HBW group (see Fig. 18.3:13–15). Only the cup comes from a plausible LH IIIC Early unit and has a parallel from Tiryns (Kilian 1982, fig. 7:1). In the same unit, a horizontal loop handle from a closed vessel executed in a grey fabric was found (LN784-028-014). It is clearly different from Middle Helladic Grey Minyan, yet its attribution to the Italian Grey Ware is disputable. If proved correct, however, it would constitute another argument for the designation of the cup to the HBW group (see above). Another interesting link with the Italian Grey Ware is provided by the kylix stem. Until recently, there were no published examples of HBW kylikes, but this form is, after the carinated cup, the most common among the Grey Ware vessels found in Chania (Hallager and Hallager 2003, 255). The coexistence of handmade pottery belonging to two different groups at the same site (HBW and HDP in the case of Mitrou) is hardly an exception and poses a serious obstacle in correct identification and interpretation. Such situations point to the necessity of defining clear criteria, given the macroscopic similarity in fabric and surface treatment between HBW and HDP. The presence of these groups is highly probable at sites like Tiryns or Mycenae, where HBW is a long-lasting phenomenon.

Based on a dozen datable pottery units, it is possible to observe the changes in the share of handmade and burnished pottery during the final stages of the Late Bronze Age at Mitrou. It is not possible, however, to assess the duration of the HBW tradition and its prominence. However, it seems that most of the dark-surfaced handmade pottery consists of cooking pots that feature flaring rims and distinguishable necks, which find their best parallels in the material from Kalapodi (*cf.* Fig. 18.3:1–6). Moreover, judging from the evidence from other sites, HBW at Mitrou should also be a short-lived and weak phenomenon. The difference of the situation at Mitrou from that attested at Tiryns can be seen in Fig. 18.4 (see also Pilides 1994, fig. 15 and her note on p. 13 concerning 0.9% share of handmade pottery in the

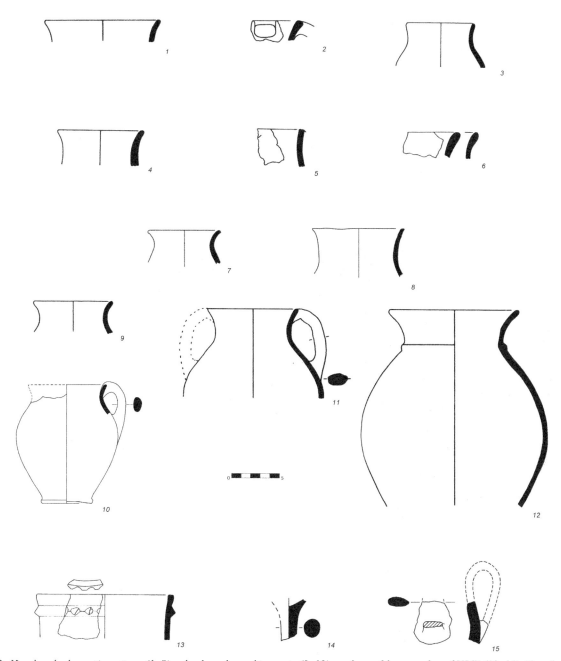

Fig. 18.3: Handmade domestic pottery (1–8), wheel-made cooking pots (9–12), and possible examples of HBW (13–15). Nos. 1–6, 9, and 11–12 are from Kalapodi (after Jacob-Felsch 1996, table 24:35 [1], 27:67 [2], 31:156 [3], 41:332 [4], 40:300 [5], 27:77 [6], 38:259 [9], 44:397 [11], 35:223 [12]). Nos. 7–8, 10, and 13–15 are from Mitrou (LM786-040-014 [7], LN782-018-014 [8], LN784-018-014 [10], LN785-001-011 [13], LO784-007-013 [14], LN784-028-015 [15])

total assemblage at Tiryns), which also clarifies how similar the cases of Mitrou and Kalapodi are – both in terms of chronology and relative frequency. The share of handmade burnished pottery (only the medium-coarse dark class) rises from 2.5% in LH IIIC Early to 12% in Early Protogeometric, whereas its share within the whole medium-coarse dark class soars from 15 to 66% respectively. The major visible

difference is that Kalapodi experienced a rapid increase in the share of handmade cooking pots during the Advanced stage of LH IIIC. This change is even more acute if we assess all groups of the handmade pottery from Kalapodi (including also unburnished cooking pots and handmade Kitchenware) – between the LH IIIC Advanced and Submycenaean period their share sky-rocketed from 10% up to 40%! This data

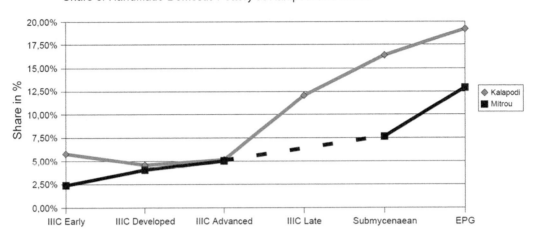

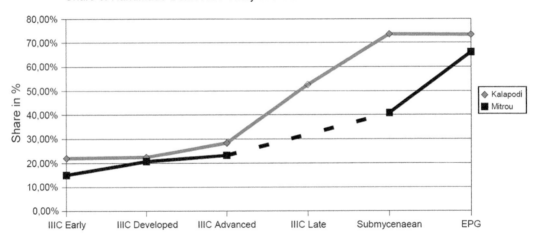

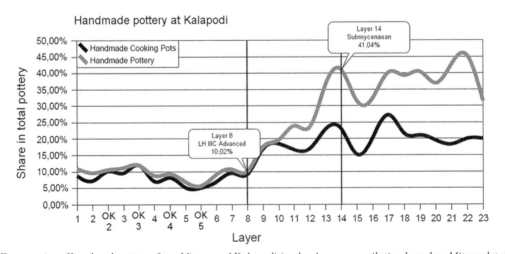

Fig. 18.4: Frequencies of handmade pottery from Mitrou and Kalapodi (author's own compilation based on Mitrou database and statistical data from Jacob-Felsch 1996)

attests to a major shift in pottery production, which may be a reflection of more fundamental changes. The development at Mitrou, as it seems at the moment, followed a much more stable course than at Kalapodi, though both experienced broadly similar development.

Explaining the origin of Handmade Domestic Pottery

Returning to the general discussion of Handmade Domestic Pottery, one has to consider two basic theories explaining its appearance. Both have already been discussed in the literature as possible explanations for the occurrence of the HBW group (*cf.* Rutter 1975; Walberg 1976 for two opposing views).

The theory of an indigenous appearance seems to offer a satisfactory explanation. The general similarity with Mycenaean cooking pottery points to a local development, and the occurrence of handmade domestic pottery may be seen as a reaction, on a household level, to difficult access to workshop products of similar function. The model of household pottery production and its exchange to meet agricultural shortfalls, suggested by David Small (1990), may find a good application in this situation, an idea already suggested by Jeremy Rutter (1990, 32). Burnishing may be explained as the simplest technique for strengthening the fabric, a crucial feature in the case of cooking pots, and is also said to increase the effectiveness of heat transmission (Schiffer 1990). A group of handmade but not burnished cooking pots from Kalapodi may be seen as an evidence for some degree of experimentation in search for optimal solution – it is exactly what one would expect from people not very experienced in making the pottery on their own.

The example of pottery workshops on the island of Aegina shows that shortages in domestic pottery production might have occurred. After LH IIIC Early this pan-Hellenic cooking pottery supplier no longer functioned, or at least ceased to export its products (Lindblom 2001, 38, 41). This may have been the case for other workshops in Mycenaean Greece as well, which nevertheless continued producing fine pottery. The appearance of HDP did not take place where ceramic workshops continued manufacturing, apparently undisturbed, all sorts of pottery. Kynos, a settlement only a dozen kilometres away from both Mitrou and Kalapodi, may serve as the best example. Handmade pottery appeared there for the first time during the transition to the Early Iron Age. It seems that the activity of the local workshop (attested at least for LH IIIC Middle, Dakoronia 2003, 38) and the strength of Mycenaean tradition obstructed the indigenous appearance of handmade pottery for a very long time. A similar situation may be observed at Lefkandi, some 80 km down the cost on the island of Euboea. Only two possible HDP vases (Evely 2006, figs. 101:1 [phase 2b/3] and 101:5

[phase 3]) were found there in the LBA levels. The notion that wheel-made cooking pots are present throughout all phases of the Xeropolis settlement comes therefore as no surprise (Popham and Milburn 1971, 336, 344; Evely 2006). The same 'deterrent' factors were evident in Dimini, a Mycenaean centre in Thessaly, at the beginning of 12th century BCE. Although the handmade pottery tradition was in all probability present in the region surrounding Dimini, and the HBW has been found in the settlement itself, HDP was not found even in domestic contexts (Horejs 2005, 14).

The indigenous explanation, no matter how convincing, should be weighed against a theory of foreign origin – that such pottery was either introduced by newcomers or at least appeared under foreign influence. In the case of Troy, this theory receives much credibility. The shapes and decoration of Coarse Ware (the local HDP) were different from Gritty Ware, its functional predecessor. Moreover, Coarse Ware was accompanied by another handmade and burnished pottery group, Knobbed Ware – the two formed a functionally complete assemblage with a substantial share in the whole ceramic material.

What about the two Greek Mainland sites, where similar developments took place, but only in relation to domestic pottery? The shapes of handmade cooking pots from Kalapodi and Mitrou are similar, but not identical, to their Mycenaean counterparts. An ordinary handmade cooking pot is morphologically different from what seems to be a typical 12th century Mycenaean one- or two handled jar with short everted rim and globular body (compare Fig. 18.3:1–9 with Fig. 18.5), not to mention a complete lack of tripod cooking pots among handmade vases. Moreover, a new variant of wheel-made cooking pot from Kalapodi (appearing at the end of the LH IIIC Advanced period) and Mitrou (LH IIIC Late context) with its taller flaring neck and elongated body, seems to have been borrowed from the handmade repertoire (Fig. 18.3:10–12). The same features can be observed in cooking pots from the later phases of the Xeropolis settlement at Lefkandi (Evely 2006, figs. 45:3 [phase 2a], 61:3 [phase 3]). The lack of any obvious Mycenaean pottery imitations within the HDP group is interesting when compared with the so-called Kitchenware from Kalapodi (*Küchengeschirr*; Jacob-Felsch 1996, 78f.). This is a group of medium-coarse pottery made of light-coloured clay, although initially manufactured also with the use of the wheel, was later predominantly handmade. This group features many exact imitations of Mycenaean pottery (Jacob-Felsch 1996, figs. 29:121 [amphora/hydria/jug]; 31:159 [hydria/jug]; 40:302 [cup]; 40:304 [tray]; 40:305 [kylix]; 40:314 [krater]; 40:371 [deep bowl]). In my opinion, it is *Küchengeschirr* that should be referred to as an example of indigenous ceramic development. A clear indication in favour of this idea is that the clay of *Küchengeschirr* is just a finer and better-fired version of the standard pithos

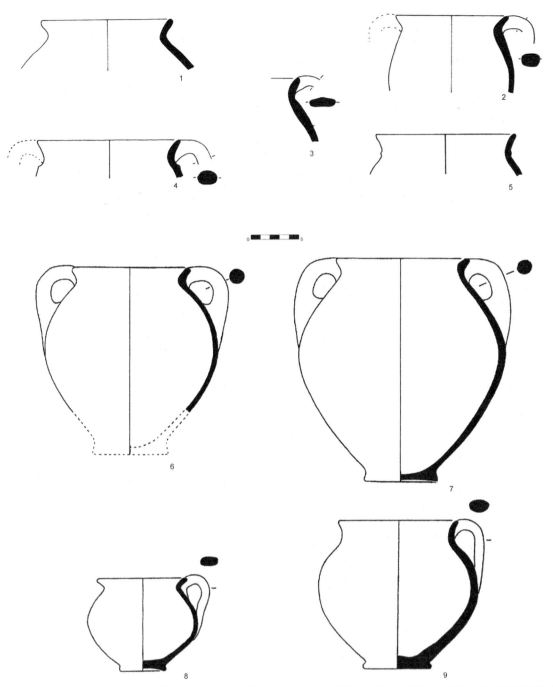

Fig. 18.5: Typical LH IIIC Mycenaean cooking pots. Nos. 1–5 are from Kalapodi (after Jacob-Felsch 1996, table 24:34 [1], 29:123 [2], 29:122 [3] 38:258 [4], 32:174 [5]). Nos 6 and 7 are from Athens (after Rutter 2003, figs. 7.5 [6], 7.6 [7]). Nos. 8 and 9 are from Lefkandi (after Popham and Milburn 1971, fig. 2.5 [8], 2:6 [9])

clay (Jacob-Felsch 1996, 78). *Küchengeschirr* seems to be a different response of the local potters to the same conditions as those the potters producing so-called White Ware were faced with. Interestingly, both White Ware and *Küchengeschirr* covered a very similar array of shapes, mainly used for storage and transport of water (Popham and Milburn 1971, 344; Jacob-Felsch 1996, 79). Not without significance is the fact that only small amounts of White Ware were found in Kalapodi, even though Lefkandi, possibly a major producer of this ceramic class, is located at a close distance.

As it was suggested previously, the use of burnishing may

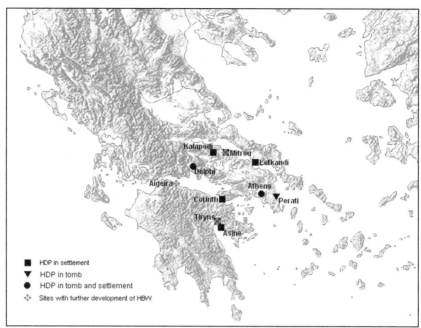

Fig. 18.6: Handmade pottery in Greece at the transition to the Early Iron Age

simply be a reinvention. Yet the borrowing of both shape and technology from adjacent regions also seems to be a reasonable explanation. Not only in the case of Troy does the influence coming from the north have to be taken into consideration. Unfortunately, the lack of any decoration, as well as the fragmentary character of the settlement material, makes it hard to find a possible inspiration or area of origin. Even more frustrating is the fact that there are no published contemporary settlement deposits from Thessaly (the nearest region to the north), apart from the already mentioned Dimini.

The derivation of such pottery from the (semi-) nomadic populations (pastoralists) should also be considered. Such an explanation, especially for the handmade forms closely resembling Mycenaean types, was suggested by Jung (2006, 46f.). However, this theory is more plausible for the appearance of the so-called 'Leather-bag Ware' attested at Kalapodi (Jacob-Felsch 1996, fig. 45:424), Kynos (Dakoronia 2003, figs. 12–13), Elateia (Deger-Jalkotzy 1983, figs. 1–2) and Delphi (Lerat 1937, pl. 5) at the transition to the Early Iron Age. This handmade pottery seems to form yet another group, whose ancestors should be sought among vessels made of organic materials.

None of the two presented origin theories can be currently accepted or fully rejected. As a temporary solution I would suggest a model that is a balanced combination of both. A successful and long-lasting accommodation of foreign influence, including those coming from a neighbouring region, would not be possible without the occurrence of particular socio-economic conditions, mainly difficulties

in accessing wheel-made domestic pottery. The example of HBW illustrates the course of events when foreign influence is confronted with a different economic background: HBW remained a marginal phenomenon that was never truly incorporated into the local ceramic assemblage.

HBW, HDP and the Early Iron Age handmade pottery in Greece

Having discussed the three distinct groups of handmade pottery in the eastern Mediterranean around 1200 BCE, I will now move to the last issue of this paper's concern: the relation of HBW and HDP to handmade pottery in Early Iron Age Greece. In this period, exclusively handmade cooking pots are one of the most characteristic features and represent, as Richard Catling and Irene Lemos (1990, 60) wrote, one of the important breaks with the Mycenaean tradition.

In order to address this issue, the discussion has to move away from the two sites in central-eastern Greece, where developments outlined above continue smoothly into the EIA, and shift our focus southwards (Fig. 18.6). There are a few sites that feature handmade and burnished pottery postdating the Early stage of the LH IIIC period (*i.e.* after 1150 BCE). Two vessels from the settlement of Lefkandi dated to phases 2b and 3 (both falling roughly within LH IIIC Late) have already been mentioned. At Delphi, several fragments of handmade and burnished cooking pots were found in the Late Mycenaean settlement levels (Reber 1991, 45). Unfortunately, an exact date of these pieces is

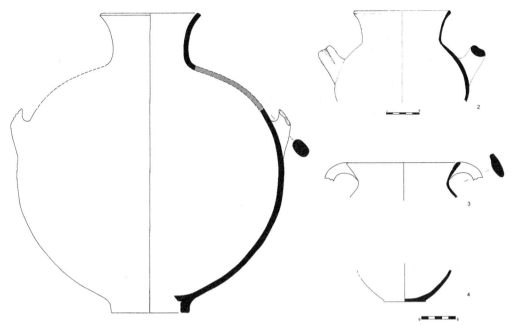

Fig. 18.7: Examples of HBW development. No. 1 is from Tiryns (after Kilian 1982, fig. 7:5). No. 2 is from Aigeira (after Jalkotzy 2003, fig. 8.6). Nos. 3 and 4 are from Mitrou (LM786-023-011 [3], LM786-040-015 [4])

unknown, yet the Mycenaean settlement at Delphi continued until the sub-Mycenaean phase (Mountjoy 1999a, 747). A one-handled handmade jug was found in a chamber tomb with the latest vases dating to the sub-Mycenaean period (Lerat 1937). Aigeira, across the Corinthian Gulf, together with Tiryns form a special group of settlements, where HBW not only survived (in diminished number) for a longer time, but also experienced certain development. It is represented by a fusion of HBW elements (fabric and surface treatment, yet not the decoration) with traits typical of Mycenaean pottery production (shapes and use of wheel). At Aigeira, such vessels occurred in the second phase of the settlement (dated to LH IIIC Advanced, Fig. 18.7:2); at Tiryns, a handmade but thin-walled amphora came from a LH IIIC Late context (Fig. 18.7:1). At Mitrou, similar vase(s) came from a LH IIIC Middle context (Fig. 18.7:3–4): it is a typical wheel-made Mycenaean cooking pot, with extremely thin walls that are, surprisingly, burnished on the exterior. However, discovery of such vessels in a LH III B2 Late dump undermines their interpretation as a later development of HBW, which was either not present in this deposit at all or was represented only in very small quantities.

At the settlement of Corinth, a group of handmade burnished and undecorated domestic pottery (pots with flaring rims, complete profiles are not preserved) appeared in layers dated to LH IIIC Advanced and Late (Rutter 1979, 390f.). In Athens, in the LH IIIC Late settlement deposit, there is some handmade and burnished domestic pottery, accompanied by an overwhelming presence of wheel-made Mycenaean cooking pots (Smithson 1977, 78) – a situation

similar to that of the first layers at Kalapodi, some 75 years before. In the subsequent sub-Mycenaean period, this kind of pottery occurred in the tombs of the Kerameikos cemetery (Kraiker and Kübler 1939, 65f., 75f.). At the chamber tomb cemetery of Perati there is a single handmade pot identified in Tomb 4, dated to the local phase I or II (LH IIIC Middle at the latest; Iakovidis 1969, 157, pl. 45γ, no. 35).

Further to the south, in the Argolid, the first non-HBW handmade pottery is dated to the sub-Mycenaean period. Examples are known from Tiryns (Papadimitriou 1988) and Asine (Frizell 1986). In Asine, this kind of pottery makes up a substantial part of the assemblage. At both Tiryns and Asine the handmade pottery is executed also in pale fabric, a feature characteristic of the Protogeometric assemblages in Argolid and Corinthia.

The amount of handmade material from the period between LH IIIC Middle and the Early Iron Age is very limited. However, it seems that at most of the sites presented here, handmade and burnished pottery forms a functionally limited assemblage, consisting mainly of cooking pots. Such a situation resembles closely, though not chronologically, the evidence from central-eastern Greece. The chronological pattern of the appearance of handmade domestic pottery suggests that the whole process began in that region. Over the last decades of the Greek Bronze Age HDP spread southwards, where it developed further to become a significant part of the Early Iron Age pottery assemblage. Naturally, these might have been unrelated processes at every single site, yet the chronological pattern and similarities are undeniable. Moreover, the beginning of this diffusion-process might have been established in the second half of LH IIIC Middle, which is exactly the time when the handmade pottery in Kalapodi experienced a remarkable growth in use. There are, however, two specific phenomena worth highlighting that do not seem to have their equivalent in central-eastern Greece, namely handmade pottery deposited as grave goods and the appearance of pale fabric for shapes like amphorae, hydriae and large open shapes. This situation may be interpreted as a later, local development that did not reach the area of origin, but another explanation may prove to be more plausible. The custom of depositing domestic handmade pottery as a grave offering might already have been present in central-eastern Greece at the beginning of the LH IIIC period. However, there are no tombs of that period associated with settlements like Kalapodi or Mitrou, and when this tradition was introduced in the south, handmade pottery was already attested in Elateia, a chamber tomb cemetery located close to Kalapodi and Mitrou (Deger-Jalkotzy and Dakoronia 1992, 70). The lack of domestic pottery executed in pale fabric at Kalapodi may be attributed to the development whereby this niche was filled by a different product – the locally developed *Küchengeschirr*, which basically comprises the same shapes as pale-fabric vessels from the Greek Early Iron Age. At Mitrou, on the other hand, the use of pale fabric for handmade vases is attested, but as yet not fixed chronologically.

The derivation of Early Iron Age pottery from HBW is highly improbable. The development of HBW traced in Aigeira and Tiryns is very marginal in terms of quantity and seems to have reached a dead end. Thin-walled Mycenaeanizing and partly wheel-thrown vases are more remote from the typical Early Iron Age handmade pottery than HBW itself. The same applies to the wheel-made and burnished examples from Mitrou. Moreover, at sites where HBW survived until the end of the Late Bronze Age it had a constantly diminishing share in the assemblage – a sharp contrast with the abundance of handmade pottery at the beginning of the Iron Age. The well-stratified settlement of Lefkandi provides more negative evidence: the possible HDP appears there after the disappearance of HBW (Evely 2006).

Summary

The existence of at least three distinct groups within the Late Bronze Age handmade pottery should be stressed. As far as the two groups present in Greece, HBW and HDP are concerned, not only did they have different determinants of appearance, but they followed different development paths. HBW was most probably introduced by foreigners from the Italian peninsula and retained its foreign character where it survived. The appearance of HDP on the other hand is far more related to the local conditions and the pottery itself was integrated within the local assemblage, transforming its appearance considerably. This kind of pottery appeared in southern Greece during the last stages of the Greek Bronze Age, probably due to an unfavourable change in the economic conditions. This process covers the gap, both chronological and geographical, between handmade domestic pottery appearing as early as 1200 BCE in the central-eastern Greece and the handmade pots present at every Early Iron Age site in Greece. Therefore another element of the Iron Age material culture seems to have had its roots in the 'forces of transformation' that began in the preceding Late Bronze Age period.

Acknowledgements

I would like to thank Aleydis Van de Moortel and Eleni Zachou for inviting me to take part in the Mitrou project and giving me the permission to study and present the material from the excavation. I am very grateful to Jeremy Rutter and Reinhard Jung for inspiring discussions and helpful comments. My thanks also go to several members of the Mitrou team, especially to Tina Ross who did the pottery drawings and to Evi Gorogianni who designed a perfect database that made all the calculations possible at this early stage of research. Last but not least, I would like to thank Weronika Ruszecka for her support and constant readiness to correct every new version of the English text.

THE CHANGE OF POTTERY'S SOCIAL MEANING AT THE END OF THE BRONZE AGE: NEW EVIDENCE FROM TIRYNS

Philipp Stockhammer

This article focuses on the change of pottery's social meaning in the transition from the palatial to the post-palatial period in Mycenaean Greece. This analysis will concentrate on the Argolid, and for the post-palatial period especially on Tiryns, where the excavations of Klaus Kilian in the 1970s and 1980s and those under the supervision of Joseph Maran since the late 1990s have provided new important insights into this period.

Production and significance of pottery in the Argolid in palatial times

During the palatial period, the production of ceramics and other goods seems to have been at least under the partial control of the palace. Mycenae's pottery workshop in Berbati is a well-known example of this control. By the Late Helladic (LH) IIIA2 period at the latest, the palatial administration oversaw the production of a specific export-oriented repertoire in some identifiable workshops in the Argolid, which subsequently produced elaborately decorated craters and other tableware, and supplied the palatial oil and perfume industries with high-quality containers (Åkerström 1968, 51; Sherratt 1982, 183; Jones 1986, 599 f.; Åkerström 1987, 119; van Wijngaarden 1999a, 6 f.; 1999b, 26; Voutsaki 1999, 29 f.). The present data from neutron activation analysis on LH IIIB pictorial pottery found in the Eastern Mediterranean suggest that the majority of these vessels were produced in workshops around Mycenae, probably in Berbati itself (Mommsen and Maran 2000/1). Gert van Wijngaarden (1999b, 24 f.) proposes a multifaceted picture of Mycenaean pottery production which, in his view, was only partially controlled by the palace administration. Based on the results of Frederick Matson (1972) for Messenia,

he postulates a household level of production at least for cooking and coarse ware (van Wijngaarden 1999b, 24). However, the cooking ware as well as some of the Coarse Ware from the Argolid shows a degree of standardisation of form and production similar to that of the fine wares. It therefore seems more plausible that the cooking and smaller Coarse Ware vessels were also produced in specialised workshops, while the pithoi may have been made by specialised and probably itinerant potters. In the context of his analysis of the pottery found in Pylos, Todd Whitelaw (2001, 75), doubts that the palace at Pylos was very much interested in pottery production in Messenia (*contra* Palaima 1997, 409–12; Galaty 1999, 49). Concerning the Argolid, however, he does not exclude the possibility of palatial control for part of the pottery production (Whitelaw 2001, 78 f.). The palaces of the Argolid, as the largest single consumers of tableware and storage vessels, might have been of considerable importance to the production of a high-quality, highly standardized pottery in LH IIIA2/B1. Regarding the palace at Pylos, Whitelaw (2001, 61 f.), assumes a demand of *c.* 12,000 vessels per year. The three palatial centres of the Argolid – Mycenae, Tiryns and Midea – taken together will have needed an even higher quantity of pottery. By demanding a large number of high-quality vessels, the palaces set high standards and very probably also influenced the workshops that were producing for the local market. The outstanding quality of LH IIIA2/B1 pottery, its homogeneous appearance in the whole valley of the Argolid, and the simultaneous, far-reaching standardisation with regard to raw materials, form and decoration can only be explained by its production in a distinct number of workshops, possibly organized on a family basis. The picture of scattered, seasonal part-time potters working mainly for their local communities as suggested by Whitelaw (2001,

68 f.) for Messenia does not seem to apply to the Argolid. Indeed the pottery preferences of the average household in the Argolid may not have had any influence on the workshops that were producing for them.

Moreover, it is beyond question that the *wanax* was able to monopolize certain pictorial media (for a definition of 'media' *cf.* Rutter 1992, 71 n. 4) and raw materials and to endow them with a specific meaning. Consider fresco painting or the ivory and faience industries. Pottery as a palatial mass product seems to have had no special function in the context of representation of power. The simplicity of the tableware found in huge numbers in the palace at Pylos (Blegen and Rawson 1966, esp. 350; Whitelaw 2001) and in the so-called House of Kadmos in Thebes (Keramopoullos 1909, 71; Dakouri-Hild 2001, 98) corroborates this hypothesis. On occasions of special importance, one would expect the elite to use metal vessels instead of pottery. At least in the elite's sphere of living in Messenia and Boeotia, Mycenaean fine ware does not seem to have possessed any conspicuously symbolic meaning. Its value was entirely utilitarian. On the basis of the Linear B textual evidence, Whitelaw (2001, 74) reaches the conclusion that pottery of the palatial period was not an object of prestige, but presumably an everyday article. In the Argolid, however, some symbolic function for pottery should not be excluded, considering the dynamic development and elaborate decoration of the palatial pottery produced there (compared with Messenia and Boeotia).

Pottery's social meaning at the beginning of the post-palatial period in the Lower Town of Tiryns

The excavations in the northern Lower Town of Tiryns (*cf.* Maran 2004a, 262, fig. 1; Maran and Papadimitriou 2006, 100, fig. 1) form the basis for my reflections on the social meaning of the post-palatial Mycenaean pottery. In 1976, an initial excavation in this area was conducted to the north-west of the Lower Citadel under the supervision of Klaus Kilian. During this excavation, a small area of the settlement systematically built around the Citadel at the beginning of LH IIIC was revealed (Kilian 1978a, 449–57; Mühlenbruch 2005). A further excavation was undertaken to the north-east of the Lower Citadel under the supervision of Joseph Maran in co-operation with the Fourth Ephorate of the Greek Antiquity Service in 1999 and 2000 (Maran 2000b, 574; Touchais *et al.* 2000, 803 f.; Maran 2001b, 30; 2001c; Touchais *et al.* 2001, 831–33; Maran 2002, 7–11; 2004a, 277–83; Maran and Papadimitriou 2006). The findings from the two excavations north of the Tirynthian Citadel owe their special importance to the fact that this area had been left undeveloped since the beginning of LH IIIB, because it was situated in an area flooded by a river. The re-routing of the river by the building of a huge dam-and-channel system in late LH IIIB made this area potential building land.

However, no building activity can be detected there until the beginning of LH IIIC. Immediately after the extensive destruction of the settlements in the Argolid around 1200 BCE, a high proportion of the surviving population seem to have settled together around the Citadel of Tiryns. There, they founded a large settlement, probably instigated by the post-palatial elite (*cf.* Kilian 1980, 173; 1988b, 135; Maran 2002, 11; 2004a, 283 f.; Maran and Papadimitriou 2006, 130). The part of the Lower Town north of the Citadel was situated on relatively sterile river sediments. Therefore, it can be deduced that the findings of the excavations in the North-eastern and North-western Lower Town were all brought to this area in the post-palatial period, be it intentionally as household equipment or unintentionally in the form of small sherds embedded in the earth used for the mudbricks. In the context of my article, I will focus on some selected and largely preserved vessels, which can be safely assumed to have been brought intentionally into the post-palatial buildings there. Although a continuous settlement activity from the beginning of LH IIIC until the end of this period can be observed in the North-eastern Lower Town, my analysis will concentrate on the findings from the two settlement phases of LH IIIC Early, which were located in the North-eastern and in the North-western Lower Town.

Significant architectural remains of the first settlement phase of LH IIIC Early were only preserved in the North-western Lower Town. Despite lacking architectural evidence and closed floor deposits *in situ*, a number of complete or restorable pots were also found in Phase 1 of the North-eastern Lower Town (Stockhammer 2006, 140–2). In the bulk of LH IIIC Early pottery, three vessels stand out, and whose presence in a LH III C context is surprising (FS and FM refer to Furumark Shape and Furumark Motive as classified by Furumark 1941).

First, in the North-eastern Lower Town, a jug with a cutaway neck (FS 136) was discovered. The shoulder depicts a staggered arrangement of vertical whorl-shells (FM 23:9) with a knob and a small dot rosette (FM 27:23) under the handle base (Fig. 19.1). Second, the presence of a qualitatively outstanding conical-piriform stirrup jar (FS 166), which features a polished surface and glossy orange paint (Fig. 19.2). Third, in the autumn of 2005, the re-study of the findings from the North-western Lower Town revealed many fragments of a large piriform jar (FS 19) bearing a frieze of argonauts (FM 22) on the shoulder zone with their arms stylised as spirals (Fig. 19.3).

The analysis of formal, stylistic and technical features suggests that these three vessels were produced long before LH IIIC Early. This impression was confirmed by Elizabeth French and Kim Shelton, who were able to examine the two pots from the North-eastern Lower Town in August 2005. The jug with cutaway neck was probably produced in LH IIIB1, and possibly earlier in late LH IIIA2. The stirrup jar finds its best parallels in Mycenae in LH IIIA2 (*e.g.* in the

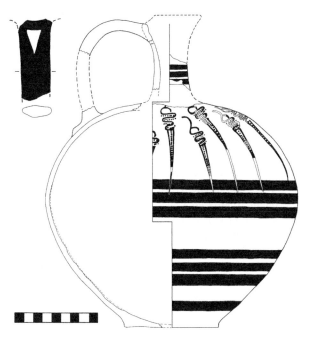

Fig. 19.1: North-eastern Lower Town 2000. Jug with a cutaway neck (FS 136), Phase 1 (beginning of LH IIIC Early); LXVIII 30/55.64.65.66.75 Ost.85 XI

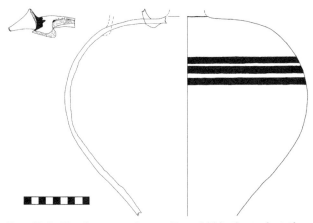

Fig. 19.2: North-eastern Lower Town 2000. Conical-piriform stirrup jar (FS 166), Phase 1 (beginning of LH IIIC Early); LXVIII 30/56.64.65.85 XI and LXVIII 30/64 Oberfläche XII Nr. 188/00

Fig. 19.3: North-western Lower Town 1976. Large piriform jar (FS 19), Horizon 19A (beginning of LH IIIC Early); LIII 30/59 IV, LIII 30/36 V Raum 302, LIII 30/53 V, LIII 30/88 Vb, LIII 30/87 VI grau, LIV 30/43 II, LIV 30/42 IIb, LIV 30/50.60 V, LIV 30/71 VIa, LIV 30/63.73 VIIa and LIV 30/52.53.62 VIIb; probably also from LIII 30/47 Va, LIII 30/45 VIIb Grube 15 and LIV 30/49 IV

stirrup jars from Petsas' House; Papadimitriou and Petsas 1950, esp. 208, fig. 6; French 1965, 171 f.). The piriform jar from the North-western Lower Town should be dated to LH IIIA1 at the latest on the basis of the argonaut motive (*cf.* Niemeier 1985, 24–8; Mountjoy 1986, 52 f., esp. 53, fig. 58).

It is not necessarily surprising that large and elaborately decorated Mycenaean vessels were kept over a long period of time. The foundation deposit of the temple discovered

at Amman Airport in Jordan contained a full spectrum of Mycenaean pottery ranging from LH IIA to LH IIIB, although the temple was in use until the end of the 13th century BCE or the beginning of the 12th century. According to Vronwy Hankey, this pottery was collected for cultic deposition long after its production (Hankey 1974, 142; van Wijngaarden 2002, 107; 2005, 408 f.).

The three vessels from Tiryns discussed above were certainly brought to the Lower Town after the destruction of the palace. Consequently, there is evidence that immediately after 1200 BCE the inhabitants of Tiryns had access to pottery which was over 100 years old. It is hard to imagine that those vessels could have survived within buildings through the earthquake that destroyed Tiryns at the end of the palatial period. Large ceramic vessels were probably not people's first choice of salvage when fleeing, but a search in the ruins of the houses would, in all likelihood, have revealed only sherds. In my view, the only plausible explanation is that at the beginning of the post-palatial period, some families took conspicuous, representative vessels out of the old and often still used chamber tombs in the surroundings and integrated them with their household pottery. Therefore, it is not surprising that the best parallels for two of the three vessels from the Lower Town can be found in the palatial chamber tombs of the Argolid, especially at Asine, where in chamber tomb I, 2 a piriform jar (FS 19) with Argonauts on the shoulder (Frödin and Persson 1938, 379 fig. 248.3, 380) and another piriform jar (FS 34) with vertical whorl-shells, rosettes and knobs on the shoulder (Frödin and Persson 1938, 378–9, fig. 248.2) were found.

I believe that the meaning of these vessels for the inhabitants of Tiryns should be seen in the context of semiotic transformation from the palatial to the post-palatial period. At the end of the palatial period, both the rule of the *wanax* and his power over images and symbols broke down. Some palatial media came to an end with the palatial system, while others like ivory carving and fresco painting continued (*cf.* Maran 2006, 127 f., 134 f. n. 19) but on a much reduced scale. These developments may have been the result of a shortage of raw materials, the absence of potential customers, or due to social restrictions (*cf.* Rutter 1992, 62, 65, 70, 72 n. 10; Maran 2006, 128, 142–4). The liberation of media from the monopolized palatial canon resulted in the symbolic revaluation of the media which were still accessible to the surviving old elites and those trying to join this social group at the beginning of LH IIIC.

The end of the palaces seems to have lead to the replacement of the *wanax* and his administrative system by a group of aristocratic families, whose position within society was based on a network of personal relations and had to be defended and justified competitively on a constant basis (Deger-Jalkotzy 1991b, 57–9; Borgna 1997, 207; Maran 2006, 125, 128, 142–4). In order to improve their position in this contest for power and legitimacy, members of the elite manipulated their material surroundings. With regard to pottery, this took the form of increasing the depiction of topics like competition, hunting and fighting in pictorial pottery (Deger-Jalkotzy 1991a, 147–9; 1991b, 64; Rutter 1992, 63; Deger-Jalkotzy 1995, 376; 1996, 20–2; Güntner 2000, 198; Maran 2006, 143). Considering the important social function of common feasting, it was very possible, and plausibly desirable, to acquire a set of pottery breathing the spirit of the palatial system in its heyday. What could be more obvious than helping oneself in the family's chamber tomb when it was opened for a new burial? Maybe some vessels were also taken from the chamber tombs of those families who did not survive the catastrophic events at the end of the palatial period. An antique set of pottery enabled a family to show off its own traditions before guests and thus also to lay claim to an important position in the post-palatial period. The strategies of the 12th century elite to identify with the past palatial period in order to legitimize their position in society are also discussed by Sigrid Deger-Jalkotzy and Joseph Maran (Deger-Jalkotzy 1991a, 148 f.; 1991b, 64–6; 1995, 375 f.; 1996, 25; Maran 2001a, 119–21; 2006, 142–4).

The phenomenon of manipulating material culture in order to strengthen symbolically one's own social position has been described frequently in ethnology and sociology (*cf.* Bourdieu 1987). At this point, I would only like to refer to the ethnoarchaeological research on the production and meaning of pottery by Daniel Miller (1982; 1985) in the Indian village of Dangwara. Members of this community used pottery in a systematic way to emphasize their own position within the hierarchical caste system (Miller 1982, 91–4; 1985, 154–60). Moreover, Miller was able to demonstrate a dynamic process in this system of symbolic communication: although the membership of a particular caste is fixed by birth, members of the lower castes intentionally use vessels that are associated with the next higher caste. As a consequence, the representatives of the higher caste demand new vessel types from the potters in order to dissociate themselves from the members of the next lower caste. These dynamics result in the creation of ever new forms of status representation (Miller 1982, 89 f., 91–4; 1985, 185–7). It is of particular interest that, in some cases, it was not so much the presence of elite pottery forms in lower castes which bothered the members of the elite, but rather the improper usage of the vessels which induced them to renounce the use of these contaminated forms any longer (Miller 1982; 1985).

This dynamic process may possibly explain why there was no continuous use of antique dishes in Tiryns in later LH IIIC Early. However, a process was triggered, which can be clearly shown in the second settlement phase in the North-eastern Lower Town.

The social meaning of pottery in the second settlement phase of the Lower Town

Of special importance in this context is a building with a large room (Room 8/00) divided by at least two parallel rows of columns on stone bases, which was arranged around a courtyard with other buildings (Maran and Papadimitriou 2006, 105–11). Architecturally, this building belongs to the small number of buildings representing post-palatial architecture, together with the Building T on the Upper Citadel of Tiryns, Megaron W in the Lower Town and the post-palatial megaron at Midea (Walberg 1995, 87–9; Maran 2000a, 12 f.; 2004a, 278). This room with columns was destroyed by fire at the end of LH IIIC Early, thus preserving many complete vessels *in situ* (Stockhammer 2006, 142–5). Three ceramic objects are of special interest to our analysis: a marvellously painted mug (FS 226) of astonishing dimensions (Fig. 19.4), a huge coarse ware transport stirrup jar (FS 164) with the depiction of a stylized octopus (Fig. 19.5; FM 53:14), and a ceramic wall bracket of Cypriot inspiration (found in squares LXVIII 30/44 *Ost* X, LXVIII 30/86.87 X and LXVIII 30/44 *Oberfläche* XI *Nr.* 150/00). While the mug and the wall bracket are local products (for the wall bracket *cf.* Rahmstorf 2001, 135 f.; 2003, 65; Maran 2004b, 12 f.; Maran and Papadimitriou 2006, 108; Maran in press), the coarse ware stirrup jar has

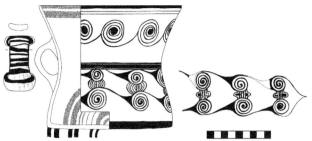

Fig. 19.4: North-eastern Lower Town 2000. Mug (FS 226), Phase 2 (end of LH IIIC Early); LXVIII 30/100 Oberfläche X Nr. 106/00

Fig. 19.5: North-eastern Lower Town 2000. Coarse ware transport stirrup jar (FS 164), Phase 2 (end of LH III C Early); LXVIII 30/80 VIII–IX Profilabbau, LXVIII 30/80 IX, LXVIII 30/80 Oberfläche X Nr. 196/00 and LXVIII 30/80 X–XI Profilabbau

certainly been imported from Crete into the post-palatial Argolid. The special meaning of these three vessels becomes evident if their shapes and find contexts are analysed.

When approaching the representative room with column rows (Room 8/00) during the time of the second settlement phase, the huge Minoan stirrup jar could be seen standing at the threshold right outside the building (Fig. 19.5). Its architectural context was quite impressive for post-palatial times. The room with column rows will have struck the visitors first of all because of its dimensions, which were unusual for post-palatial conditions. The monumental character of the room was reinforced by the use of large single blocks of stone in the foundation courses of the walls (Maran 2001b, 30; Maran 2001c, 640; 2004a, 278; Maran and Papadimitriou 2006, 105). During palatial times, those stirrup jars seem to have been usually stored securely at special places at Mycenae, Thebes and Tiryns (Raison 1968, 15–17; Haskell 1981; Podzuweit 2007, 173; Dakouri-Hild 2001, 86, n. 21; 119–22; Maran 2005, 417). Although it is probable that they were not frequently displayed in public, their meaning as an import from a subjugated Crete – maybe as part of the island's tribute – was generally understood (Maran 2005, 427 f.). Irrespective of the continuation of this tribute situation into LH IIIC, the Minoan stirrup jar in front of the representative building demonstrated that the head of the *oikos* had far-reaching contacts like the *wanax* of palatial times, and was still able to obtain those vessels from Crete. The change of contexts from the palatial period, during which a huge number of these stirrup jars was kept inside storage facilities, to the post-palatial placement of a single imported stirrup jar in front of one's doorway reinforces the change of meaning and the symbolic revaluation of the vessel in LH IIIC.

On entering the conspicuous room, the visitor would have immediately noticed the wall bracket, which was attached to one of the wooden columns directly beside the hearth (Maran 2004b, 13, 15, fig. 2, 16 fig. 4; Maran and Papadimitriou 2006, 108, 109 fig. 11; Maran in press). In the last few years, a connection between such wall brackets and cult as well as metal-working could be demonstrated for the palatial period (Rahmstorf 2001, 116 f., 140; *cf.* Schlipphak

2001, 49; Maran 2004b, 14, 16; in press). The visitor still familiar with the old palatial meaning of this object might have recognised the particularity of the object and remembered the atmosphere of cult and magic connected therewith. The power of the master of the house, who had this object at his disposal, was thus further emphasized.

It is easy to imagine that the marvellously painted, large mug, which was found immediately south of the building, was offered to guests as a drinking vessel during receptions (Fig. 19.4). It was certainly produced by a post-palatial potter, who combined features of LH IIIA2/B1 mugs with decorative elements of LH IIIC. The ridges under the rim and at the waist together with the division of the painted pattern into two zones points to LH IIIA2/B1, because in LH IIIB2 the ridges disappear and decoration runs continuously from rim to base (Mountjoy 1986, 112, 128, 147; Podzuweit 2007, 124 f.). These ancient features were eclectically combined by the potter with an elaborate running spiral in LH IIIC manner, thus yielding an up-to-date product rooted in ancient tradition. It seems likely that such an object was ordered by the probably aristocratic family who resided in the room with the column rows.

In my view, it is conspicuous that two metal mugs were also the only drinking vessels deposited in the Tiryns hoard (Karo 1930, 130, 131 fig. 3, suppl. 34, 1; Matthäus 1980, 252, 256, pl. 42, 360 pl. 43, 364). One could imagine that this vessel form was especially suited to being passed around when the few heads of elite families in post-palatial times were having a common feast. In this line of thought, the palatial tableware, as that exceptionally preserved in

Pylos (*cf.* Whitelaw 2001, 52–60), can also be interpreted as a reflection of the social system: the bulk of people drank from the same kind of drinking vessels, especially unpainted (carinated) kylikes, whereas the *wanax* himself rose above the rest by using a precious metal drinking vessel (*e.g.* a chalice like the one depicted on the famous golden seal from the Tiryns treasure). Carl Blegen and Marian Rawson (1966, 350) already postulated the usage of metal drinking vessels by the highest-ranking members of society in Pylos (*cf.* also Knappett 2001, 84). Large mugs were not an important vessel type in the tableware at palatial Pylos. Only three mugs were found among the roughly 8540 vessels in the pantries, which represents only 0.035%. As this is the drinking vessel with the largest possible volume, the social importance of this form rose in the context of the small-scale aristocratic feasts of the post-palatial period, where it was handed around among equals. However, the special importance of this particular form might not apply to all LH IIIC mugs. Its elite usage was probably strongly restricted. The fact that the symbolic meaning appears to have been applied to select mugs only may also explain why their number did not increase in LH IIIC Early (Podzuweit 2007, 124).

Like the first settlement phase of the Lower Town, the second phase also shows the symbolic meaning that material culture was capable of acquiring after the end of the palatial system. With regard to the Minoan stirrup jar and the wall bracket, the symbolic revaluation of certain objects in order to legitimize the social position of an elite family has already been demonstrated. In addition, the elaborate mug reflects the change in the relationship between the craftsman – in this case the potter – and the consumer, which took place after the destruction of the palaces and the potters' workshops. As has already been shown, in palatial times, the crucial influence on the shaping of at least the painted fine ware came directly and indirectly from the palaces, but not from the normal household. At the beginning of the post-palatial period, the potters were not only confronted with the ruins of their workshops, but also with a drastically reduced clientele, as many settlements had disappeared together with the palaces after the catastrophes around 1200 BCE. As a result, they had to make a stronger effort to attract customers and take their wishes and demands more seriously into account. Vessels like the splendid mug can be considered the result of this dialogue between producer and consumer, which gathered momentum in the course of LH IIIC Early. However, this change in the relationship between producer and non-palatial consumer might have already started in the last years of LH IIIB.

With the evolution of this dialogue, the necessity of adding antique dishes taken from chamber tombs to one's tableware ceased. The new elites were able to formulate what they expected from the potters, who therefore produced vessels with individual and elaborate shaping and decoration that were far more refined than the standard linear fine ware of the time. Later, the personal relationship between the potter and the high-ranking consumer gave rise to the development of the high-quality, extremely individualistic and quantitatively restricted 'noble wares' of LH IIIC Middle (*cf.* Schachermeyr 1980, 103–63). The Close style and the imaginatively painted pictorial pottery of this time can be considered as the peak of an evolution which already started in LH IIIC Early.

Acknowledgements

I thank Professor Joseph Maran for generously allowing me to use the mostly unpublished documentation from his excavation in the North-eastern Lower Town of Tiryns, and Dr. Christina Sanchez and Dr. Carol Bell for correcting my English translation. I would like to express my deep gratitude towards Dr. Elizabeth B. French, Dr. Spyridon Iakovidis, and Dr. Kim Shelton and Dr. Katie Demakopoulou for giving me insight into the ceramic material found at Mycenae and Midea respectively, and towards Dr. French and Dr. Shelton also for their many helpful comments and suggestions. All illustrated vessels were drawn by Professor Maran and the author.

A NOTE ON THE MATERIAL FROM THE LATE BRONZE AND EARLY IRON AGE CEMETERIES OF TELL EL-FAR'AH SOUTH

Sabine Laemmel

It has long been the tradition in archaeological research in the Levant as well as on Cyprus to link the introduction of new pottery wares, or for that matter of any noticeable change in the local material culture, to various invasion or colonisation processes. This pattern has notably been used in order to explain the appearance on the Levantine coast, sometime in the course of the 12th century BCE, of a new class of monochrome decorated pottery, presenting Aegean affinities and called alternatively 'Mycenaean IIIC', 'Mycenaean IIIC:1b' or 'Philistine Monochrome' (see *e.g.* Dothan 1982, 94–6, 290–5; Dothan 1998a; 1998b; Killebrew 1998a, 381–3, 401–2; 1998b, 162–6; Barako 2000; Dothan 2000; Killebrew 2003; Dothan and Zukerman 2004). However, this conventional view has been challenged on several occasions by scholars who have suggested seeing this phenomenon (and other contemporaneous changes) as a manifestation of wide-ranging modifications in the political and socio-economic structure of the Late Bronze Age eastern Mediterranean, rather than as evidence for large-scale population movements (Sherratt and Sherratt 1991, 373–5; Sherratt 1991; Bauer 1998; Sherratt 1998). In the present paper a few tombs from the site of Tell el-Far'ah (South) will be examined in the framework of this debate. Although Tell el-Far'ah is not normally associated with the earliest Sea Peoples' settlements in Canaan, the following three factors contribute to make it an ideal starting point from which to re-evaluate the transitional period of the Late Bronze and Early Iron Ages in the region as a whole: its proximity to key sites such as Ashdod, Ashkelon and Gaza; the wealth of material and information it has provided; and the fact that the site and the cemeteries cover the period during which the above mentioned events are supposed to have taken place.

My main claim here is that the site of Tell el-Far'ah does not contain undisputable evidence of a change in the population makeup of the site, or indeed in that of the wider region, during the transition from the Bronze to the Iron Age. What I take it to suggest, however, is that contacts and trade were maintained between the different areas of the eastern Mediterranean at that time, although their nature might have changed.

Following a brief introduction to the site and its cemeteries, my argument will be primarily based on a detailed analysis of the contents of ten tombs from the site's cemeteries. These tombs have been selected for this purpose because they exemplify the various trends and influences noticeable at the site over the period concerned. They also allow for parallels with other sites of the region, notably those of the Philistine Pentapolis, and allow alternative suggestions for interpreting their Aegeanizing material culture by placing this particular phenomenon in its wider context. For reasons of clarity the selected tombs have been divided into three groups which represent three different, but partly overlapping chronological phases.

Tell el-Far'ah (South): an introduction to the site and its cemeteries

Much of Tell el-Far'ah's specificity is owed to its strategic geographical position in the southern coastal plain of Israel, near the border of Egypt and along two main trade routes: the Ways of Horus, which broadly follow the coastline from Egypt to Lebanon, and the inland route which used to link Gaza to Beer-Sheva, and beyond that to the Dead Sea and the Jordan valley to the north, and to the Arabah to the south. The Tell also lies on the bank of the Wadi Guzzeh, which reaches its mouth near Tell el-Ajjûl, about 25 km from Tell el-Far'ah.

The area was first excavated by Flinders Petrie and his

collaborators in the years 1927–28 (Petrie 1930; Starkey and Harding 1932). Occupation layers dating from the Middle Bronze Age (MBA) to the Roman period were brought to light, mainly in two unconnected areas of the mound (the first in the south end of the Tell and the other in its north end, where a large building usually interpreted as the residence of the Egyptian governors was identified). Alongside the settlement lies a series of eight cemeteries, with tombs dating from the MBA to the Hellenistic Period, which were also excavated.

Numerous tombs in these cemeteries date to the Late Bronze and Early Iron Ages. They reflect a wide variety of tomb types ranging from rectangular shafts or rounded pit graves, some with jar burials, to chamber tombs with *dromoi*. While the shafts were normally used for single interments, the chamber tombs were typically intended for multiple burials, and were re-opened over the years. Their architecture and layout have been interpreted in the past as a reflection of Aegean and/or Cypriote burial customs (Waldbaum 1966; Loffreda 1968; Stiebing Jr. 1970a; 1970b, 155–62; Dothan 1982, 260–3; Gonen 1992, 23–4, 127–8; Risser and Harvey 1992; Gilmour 1995). However, these tombs were not unique at that time in Palestine as similar structures occur at Gaza (Petrie 1934, pl. 53), at Pella in Jordan (Yassine 1975, 60, n. 11), and further north in Lebanon at Sarepta (Baramki 1959). Three of the bench chamber tombs at Tell el-Far'ah (Tombs 552, 562 and 935) have yielded clay anthropoid sarcophagi similar to those found in the late 13th to early 12th centuries BCE graves from Beth Shan (Oren 1973, 132–50) and Deir el-Balah (Dothan 1972; 1973; 1979, 99–100). Although much has been written on the origin of such anthropoid sarcophagi in Israel/Palestine, it is now clear that they derive from an Egyptian tradition. Indeed, they are widely attested throughout Egypt but they are particularly frequent in the eastern Delta during the late New Kingdom, at sites such as Tanis (Brissaud 1987a, 26, pl. VI:b–c; 1987b, 136 pl. II: a–b), Tell el-Dab'a (Bietak 1984, 139), Qantir/Pi-ramessu (Herold 1998, 144, fig. 13), Tell el-Yehudiyeh (Naville and Griffiths 1890, 47–8) and Tell Basta (Al-Sawi 1979, figs. 121–2; Bakr 1992, 30–3). This is significant because this influence in burial practices suggests that a number of cultural elements transitioned between these two regions, perhaps together with specific commodities along the trade and military routes linking Egypt with the Levant.

The tombs

Ten tombs from the site's cemeteries, dating from the end of the 13th to the later part of the 11th centuries BCE, have been selected for the present paper, and although emphasis lies on the pottery, other classes of artefacts are also taken into consideration. As will be seen below, these assemblages

illustrate the diversity of the influences on the local material culture at the site and the permanence of some forms of Aegeanizing, as well as Cypriote-style, pottery throughout this period, though without any tangible signs of newcomers. This does not mean that the population mix at Tell el-Far'ah and its surroundings remained exactly the same throughout the 200 years or so covered by this study, but rather that there are no archaeological traces of a large-scale and relatively sudden influx of foreigners in the region during the period concerned.

What we have at our disposal is a series of objects, remains of a material culture which on the one hand bears witness to a continuity of local traditions, and on the other hand betrays an undeniable degree of foreign influences. Behind these influences, without doubt, were people – individuals or groups of individuals – because ideas, techniques, styles or 'fashions' do not travel on their own. However, to employ a well-worn but useful formula, pots do not equal people, and the precise identity or ethnic background of those who passed through, traded with or perhaps even settled at Tell el-Far'ah and its environs, whether Aegean, Anatolian, Syrian, Cypriote or Egyptian, cannot be postulated on the basis of a few artefacts. This is especially true when the artefacts in question do not refer to a single cultural tradition, but, as will be shown below, reflect a complex mix of influences.

The tombs to be discussed here can be divided into three main groups, each of them representing successive, though sometimes partly overlapping, typological and chronological phases. The comprehensive description and illustration of the tombs' furnishings can be found elsewhere (Laemmel 2003, vol. II). The main aims of the expository sections below are to show that contacts were maintained at the transition from Bronze to Iron Ages between the different areas of the eastern Mediterranean (though their density and nature might have changed), to illustrate a process of assimilation and integration of foreign styles into the pottery tradition of the southern coastal plain, and to demonstrate how such a process co-existed with, and contributed to, the development of local pottery forms.

Group I: Tombs 902, 920, 936, 939

Tombs of this group were used during the last decades of the Late Bronze Age (LBA) and during the early years of the Iron Age, at a time when Egypt was the dominant political and ideological power in the region. Hand-made wares were dwindling on Cyprus, being progressively replaced by a wheel-made production, and Mycenaean pottery imports to the Levant were dying out (*e.g.* Sherratt 1998, 302–3). The tombs of Group I are in many ways a fine illustration of this period: they are characterised by the recurrent presence of Egyptian scarabs and Egyptian-style faience amulets, and they possess genuine Cypriote handmade imports but lack

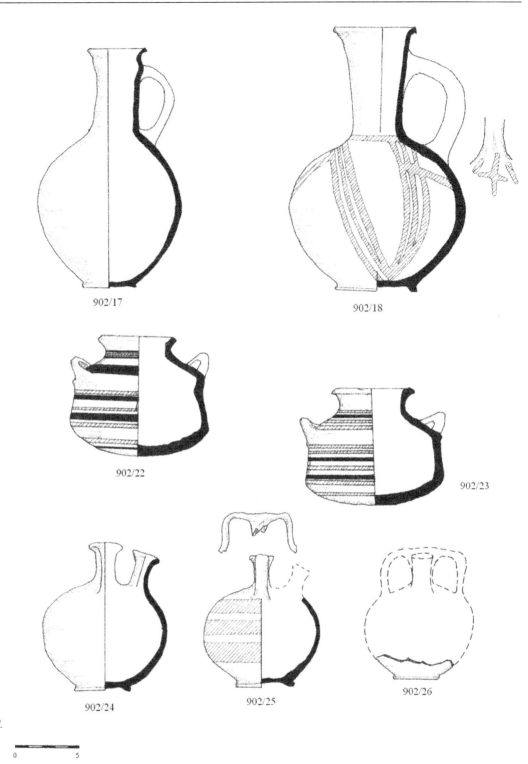

Fig. 20.1: 902/17, 902/18.
902/22, 902/23, 902/24,
902/25, 902/26

Mycenaean ones. However, they also bear witness to two important features which have not often been recognised in past scholarship. First, they show that by the late 13th century BCE hand-made Aegeanizing vessels were being produced both on Cyprus and were being imported to the Levantine coast, an instance of 'import substitution' which can be seen either as having contributed to the decline in real Mycenaean imports to the region, or as a reaction to this decline (see conclusions below). Second, they suggest that foreign wares (both Mycenaean and Cypriote) were not only being reproduced on the eastern Mediterranean coast, but that they had also started undergoing a process of integration

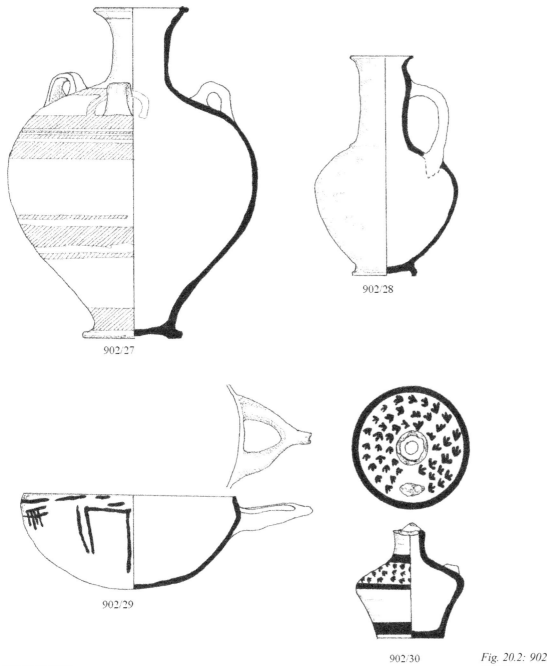

902/27

902/28

902/29

902/30

Fig. 20.2: 902/27, 902/28, 902/29, 902/30

0   5

into regional potting traditions through transformation and assimilation of both shapes and motifs.

Three of the four tombs of Group I are chamber tombs. The first, Tomb 902, was a large single-chamber tomb with side benches onto which the remains of nine individuals were laid, probably over several decades from the later part of the 13th to the early 12th centuries BCE. It contained twenty-six Egyptian scarabs and one plaque, most of them fitting a date between the 18th and the 19th Dynasties. The second, Tomb 920, consisted in a small rectangular chamber tomb

(without benches) which was used for a single deposition only. It was undisturbed at the time of the discovery and, in addition to the pottery, it held four 19th to 20th Dynasty scarabs, copper and silver rings, stone and faience beads and a faience rod. The third, Tomb 936, was a large chamber tomb which housed at least 20 burials. Although it was disturbed, it still contained a rich assemblage of small finds, including pedestal calcite cups, bronze arrowheads and forty-two Egyptian scarabs and plaques. The majority of these date to the 19th or 20th Dynasties, but a few go back to the 13th

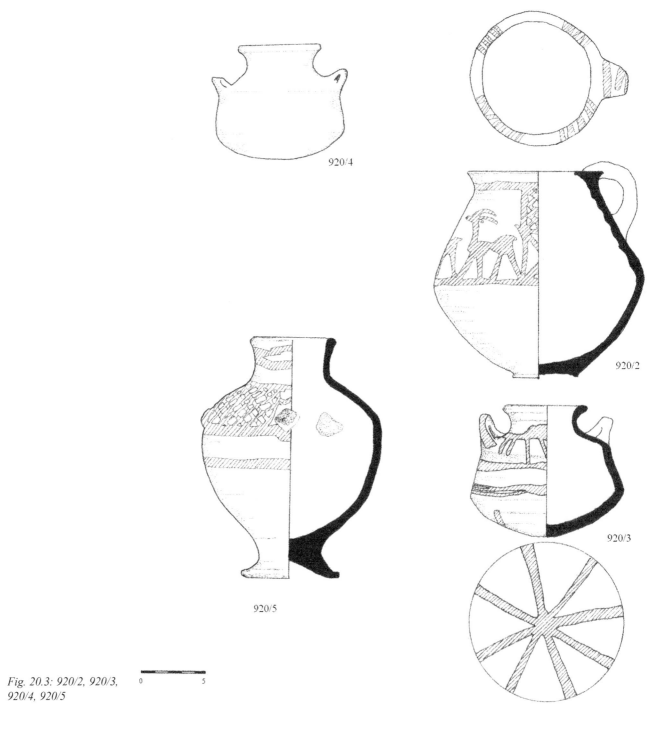

Fig. 20.3: 920/2, 920/3,
920/4, 920/5

to 15th Dynasties. The single shaft grave of this group is
Tomb 939. This undisturbed burial contained the remains of
three children, in all likelihood deposited over a very short
period of time, perhaps even all together. It was relatively
poor in small finds with only four scarabs – the latest of
which dated to Dynasty 19 – and an undetermined number
of faience and bone beads.

A large part of the pottery assemblage in tombs of this
group belongs to the local LBA Canaanite repertoire of
shapes and motifs. Particularly prominent are flat-based
bowls (Tombs 902, 936, 939; Laemmel 2003, pls. 246
[902/1–3], 309 [936/1, 936/4], 320 [939/1–4]), button
base storage jars, one with four handles (Tombs 902, 936;
Laemmel 2003, pls. 247–248 [902/12–14], 310 [936/7–8],
pointed-base juglets (Tombs 902, 936; Laemmel 2003, pls.
248 [902/15–16], 310 [936/9]), small and large carinated

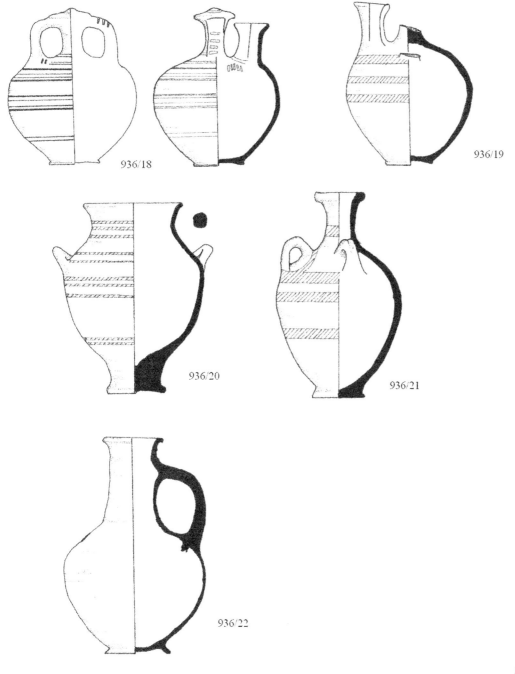

Fig. 20.4: 936/18, 936/19, 936/20, 936/21, 936/22

bowls (Tombs 902, 936; Laemmel 2003, pls. 247 [902/11], 309 [936/5–6]), handled jugs with round or trefoil mouth (Tombs 920, 936, 939; Laemmel 2003, pls. 273 [920/1], 311–12 [936/12–14], 320 [939/5]), and pinched-beak lamps (Tombs 902, 936; Laemmel 2003, pls. 249 [902/20–1], 312 [936/15–17]). Other characteristic, though less frequent, Late Bronze (LB) IIB types include a painted strainer bowl (Tomb 902; Laemmel 2003, pl. 247 [902/10]), biconical

mugs, one with 'gazelle and bird' decoration (Tombs 920, 939; Fig. 20.3, 920/2; Laemmel 2003, pl. 320 [939/6]), a small, fine-ware decorated pilgrim flask (Tomb 902; Laemmel 2003, pl. 248 [902/19]), and a miniature handmade bowl (Tomb 939; Laemmel 2003, pl. 321 [939/10]). All these vessels belong to the traditional repertoire of southern Palestinian pottery. They have been discussed elsewhere and no particular comment need be added here (Laemmel 2003,

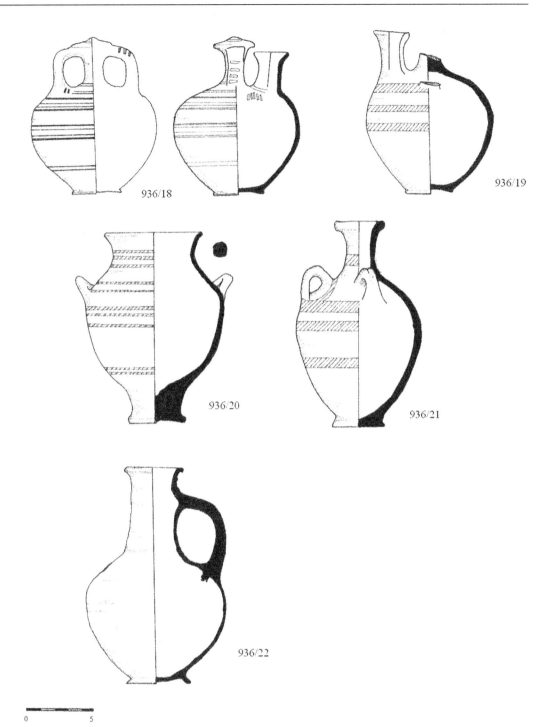

Fig. 20.5: 939/7, 939/8,
939/9

I, types B.1, B.7a, ST.3–4, SD.2a–c, B.8, LB.1, L.1–2, B.13, RJ.2, RJ.6, TJ.1, M.1, PF.1, HM.1).

A small number of shapes, namely the flat-based platters from Tombs 902 and 936 (Laemmel 2003, I, 112–14, pls. 246–7 [902/4–9], 309 [936/2]) and a small rounded base dish from Tomb 936 (Laemmel 2003, I, 114–15, pl. 309 [936/3]) are worthy of notice. They belong to a restricted group of vessels which, though considered part of the local LB IIB repertoire, betray direct Egyptian influences both in terms of shapes and techniques (for the shapes concerned here, see James and McGovern 1993, 78–9; Killebrew 2004, 312, 315–16, forms EG1a, EG4, fig. 1). These Egyptian-type wares are interesting because authentic Egyptian pottery imports, in particular open shapes, are extremely rare at Tell el-Farʿah, and indeed in the surrounding region.

It has been suggested that such wares were made by Egyptians who were part of the personnel of the Ramesside garrisons of the 19th to 20th Dynasties (Killebrew 2004,

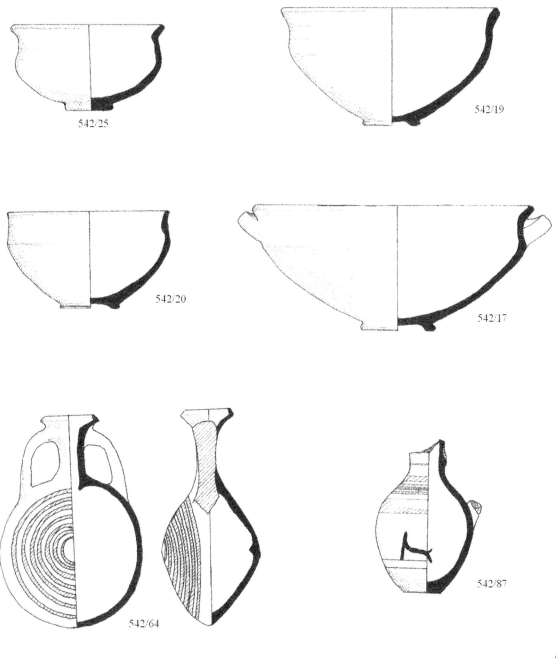

*Fig. 20.6: 542/17,
542/19, 542/20,
542/25, 542/64,
542/87*

341–2). However, they could as well have been made by Egyptianized local potters who were familiar with Egyptian forms and manufacturing techniques. This second explanation would fit better with the very restricted range of shapes represented by such production, which accounts for only a very small fraction of the complete Egyptian contemporary corpus.

Beside the bowls and platters, Egyptian-style pottery is also represented by a beer jar from Tomb 939 (Fig. 20.5, 939/7). This vessel has parallels elsewhere in the Levant, in areas where Egyptian influence was still strong in the late 13th and 12th centuries (see *e.g.* James 1966, figs. 49:6, 51:6, 54:1; Dothan 1971, fig. 81:14, pl. LXXV:3; Pritchard 1980, fig. 7:5; Oren 1984, fig. 7:1; Dothan and Porath 1993, fig. 11:24; James and McGovern 1993, 79–80, figs. 10:7, 17:20; Killebrew 2004, 331–3, fig. 7). Clay analyses carried out on the beer jars found at Deir el-Balah have shown that these were made in the area (Yellin *et al.* 1986) and, on this basis, Levantine beer jars in general tend to be thought of as local products. The example from Tomb 939, however, is made of Nile silt clay and ought to be considered a genuine import.

The tombs of Group I also yielded a fair proportion of vessels showing diverse forms of Aegean and Cypriote influences. A first illustration of this phenomenon is provided by a few ring-base jugs with painted bands on the body, one from Tomb 902 (Fig. 20.1, 902/18) and two from Tomb 936 (Laemmel 2003, pls. 310–11 [936/10–11]). They represent the local adoption of a foreign type and derive ultimately from Cypriote Base Ring vessels. Meanwhile, another juglet from Tomb 902 clearly reproduces the shape of handmade base ring ware (Fig. 20.1, 902/17) and stands much closer to original Cypriote prototypes (Laemmel 2003, I, 158–60).

Vessels directly inspired by Aegean models are more frequent than Cypriote-style ones in the tombs of Group I. A first group is made up by items whose fabric, in both texture and appearance, matches that of the contemporaneous local wares, leaving little doubt as to their local origin. These are pyxides, often decorated in black and/or red-brown paint, from Tombs 902, 920, and 939 (Figs. 20.1, 902/22–3; 20.3, 920/3–4; 20.5, 939/8), stirrup-jars from Tombs 902 and 936 (for parallels see Monchambert 2004a, 225–6, [nos. 1342, 1354], fig. 100), a three-handled piriform jar from Tomb 920 (Fig. 20.3, 920/5) and a two-handled one from Tomb 936 (Fig. 20.4, 936/20), corresponding to a type that is well represented by authentic Mycenaean imports in LB IIB contexts from Kamid el-Loz, in Lebanon, to Lachish (Tufnell 1958, pl. 83:946; Hachmann 1980, 85, 88, [no. 16], pl. 26:4; Metzger and Barthel 1993, 334, 343, pl. 118:2–4; see also Laemmel 2003, I, 204).

A very distinctive, locally-made slender three-handled jar from Tomb 936 (Fig. 20.4, 936/21) bears witness to particularly intricate patterns of influences, involving both the Aegean and Egypt. The three handles placed on the shoulder of this vase are evocative of those found on Mycenaean piriform jars and may derive from such forms which are well known in the Levant. However, the elongated shape of the container itself does not find any parallels, neither in Greece nor on Cyprus. It is very rare in the Levant but it occurs elsewhere at Tell el-Far'ah in Tombs 907 and 532 (Laemmel 2003, I, type PJ.2, Tables 15, 19). In fact, its best parallels are known from Egypt (at Gurob, Tell el-Yehudiyeh and Qantir), as both local silt and marl wares, in contexts dating from Seti II to Ramesses VI (Aston 1996, 62; Aston and Pusch 1999, 48 [no. 42]).

A last category of vessels in the tombs discussed here is made up by a series of genuine imports. Besides the Egyptian beer jar mentioned above there are a few easily recognisable Cypriote handmade wares, such as a white slip milk-bowl from Tomb 902 (Fig. 20.2, 902/29) and Base Ring

II juglets from Tombs 902 and 936 (Figs. 20.2, 902/28; 20.4, 936/22). The other imports, however, are more problematic to identify but their origin can be determined with a fairly good degree of certainty on the basis of their technological and stylistic characteristics

First is a stirrup jar from Tomb 939 decorated with brown-painted horizontal bands on the body and concentric circles under the base. It could be tentatively seen as an Aegean (possibly Mycenaean) import (Fig. 20.5, 939/9). Unlike the rounded stirrup-jars from the other 900-series cemetery tombs, this one is rather squat and the nature of its fine and smooth clay is clearly foreign to the area. Although its matte paint rather points to a Cypriote origin, it finds a good morphological parallel with a Mycenaean imported stirrup-jar from the last levels at Ugarit (Courtois and Courtois 1978, 302, fig. 35:7).

Second is a three-handled piriform jar from Tomb 902 (Fig. 20.2, 902/27). Its clay is smoother and finer than that of the fine local wares and, unlike the latter, it does not contain many visible sand-quartz inclusions. It was certainly not made in the area of Tell el-Far'ah and finds excellent parallels with vases produced on Cyprus (see *e.g.* Karageorghis and Demas 1988, 120, [no. 710], 200, [no. 157], pls. LXI, CLI, CXCI, CCXLIII), or further north along the Levantine coast in the area of Ugarit, where high-quality Aegeanizing wares were presumably manufactured in the late 13th century BCE *(e.g.* Monchambert 1983; Yon *et al.* 2000, 18; van Wijngaarden 2002, 72–3).

Finally comes a small flat-based juglet whose upper part is unfortunately missing (Fig. 20.2, 902/30; Laemmel 2003, I, 213–16). From its fine fabric, its slightly lustrous paint and its stylised floral motif, this small container could be considered as a Mycenaean import, but a lack of parallels for it in the Aegean speaks against this. In fact, it is probably a late 13th or very early 12th century import from Cyprus belonging to the White Painted Wheelmade III pottery class. Its best parallel is a LC IIC bird-jug from Kition-Bamboula which, in a larger version, displays a similar shape and comparable decoration (Yon and Caubet 1985, 135, fig. 65:299), though such motifs are also found on fragments of imported LH IIIA2/IIIB bull-rhytons from Enkomi (Dikaios 1969–71, 248, 330, pls. 67:7, 110:2–3, with reference to a parallel from Ugarit).

Group II: Tombs 542, 562

Only two tombs, both very large and abundantly furnished (especially with pottery), have been included into the second tomb group. They began to be used around the mid-12th century, more or less contemporarily with the latest burials of the 900-series tombs reviewed above, and continued to receive depositions well into the 11th century. This whole period has often been seen as the 'dark ages' of the eastern Mediterranean and is usually associated with the virtual cessation of all forms of inter-polity contacts in the region. The material from the two tombs discussed below, however, shed a rather different light on this period. Although they do not offer any evidence for direct contact with the Aegean, they suggest that trade and exchanges were sustained at that time, at least as far as Cyprus, the Levant and Egypt were concerned.

The major elements which become manifest from the examination of the material from the tombs of Group II are a persistence of the local Canaanite Late Bronze Age traditions, the introduction of a number of new pottery types of the Iron I period, the presence of iron objects, and the survival of Egyptian-type artefacts, though scarabs are significantly fewer than in the earlier tombs. To these features, one should add the emergence of a group of locally-made open shapes evocative of the Aegeanizing pottery production of Cyprus, as well as the appearance of new types of handled cooking pots and jugs relating to Cypriote domestic forms.

Tombs 542 and 562 were both large chamber tombs with side benches. Tomb 562 was disturbed at the time of the discovery, but yielded one of the site's clay anthropoid sarcophagi. Tomb 542 contained ten bodies in two levels of interments, but even with the help of the unpublished tomb cards the original distribution of the material between them could not be fully reconstructed.

As already noted above, both Tombs 542 and 562 were particularly rich in pottery, but had moderate quantities of small finds, relative to their size (see Laemmel 2003, II, 80–98, 111–21). The scarabs from Tomb 542 date from the 18th to the 19th Dynasties and those from 562 from the 19th to the 20th Dynasties. Both tombs also contained a few metal artefacts, and are particularly renowned for representing one of the earliest instances of worked iron – and indeed carburized iron – in the eastern Mediterranean (Stech-Wheeler *et al.* 1981, 258; Bienert and Reinhold 1989, pl. 3; Sherratt 2000).

In tomb 542, there were five iron items: three bracelets, a ring, and an iron dagger blade inserted into a bronze hilt with ivory or bone inlay. There were also bronze bracelets, a bronze ring, bronze tweezers, a bronze dagger with fragments of a bronze chain, beads, and gold lunate earrings of a type also attested in the earlier 900-series tombs, ivory fittings, and an ivory final.

Tomb 562, in addition to a bronze vessel, a bronze dagger, scarabs, stone beads, a bronze toggle pin and ivory inlays, also contained one iron knife with a curved blade and bronze rivets of a type that is attested in the Philistine area in 12th to 11th century contexts at Tell Miqne/Ekron, Tel Dor and Tel Qasile (Mazar 1994, 49; Dothan 2002, 14–22; Ben-Shlomo and Dothan 2006, 25–7), and at Enkomi on Cyprus in LC IIIB–C (Dikaios 1969–71, 761, pls. 135:76, 172:5).

Among the pottery from Tombs 542 and 562 are a few items which would not be out of place in the 900-series

cemetery, such as flat-based bowls and platters (Laemmel 2003, pls. 104 [542/1, 11–12], 139 [562/1–2, 9–10]), large carinated bowls (Laemmel 2003, pls. 107[542/33], 140 [562/13–15]), pointed base juglets (Laemmel 2003, pls. 114 [542/57], 143 [562/25–6]) and pinched-beak lamps (Laemmel 2003, pls. 119–20, [542/80–4], 147 [562/44–8]). However, there are also a number of new shapes, such as ring-base hemispherical bowls (Laemmel 2003, pls. 104 [542/2–10], 139 [562/3–8]) which last throughout the Early Iron Age (Laemmel 2003, I, 110–111), painted chalices (Laemmel 2003, I, 128–9, pl. 107 [542/31–2]), lug-handled large bowls (Laemmel 2003, I, 131–2, pl. 107 [542/34]), ring-based jugs with trefoil mouth (Laemmel 2003, I, 169–70, pls. 114–15 [542/58, 60–1]), and a strainer jar (Laemmel 2003, I, 173–4, pl. 115 [542/63]). Several of the storage-jars from these two tombs are of the same general shape as those of the earlier 900-series tombs, but the typical LB II button base becomes rarer (for the storage jars in these tombs, see Laemmel 2003, I, 142–4). Both tombs also include a range of undecorated bowls with ring-base and high carination – in one case fitted with a pair of horizontal handles (Fig. 20.6, 542/17, 19–20, 25) – which differ in terms of fabric and proportions from the small carinated bowls of the previous period (Laemmel 2003, I, 121–2).

However, the most noticeable change occurring in the tombs of Group II is the emergence of the characteristic Philistine Bichrome wares of the later 12th and early 11th centuries (Laemmel 2003, pls. 106 [542/29], 114 [542/59], 115 [542/62], 144 [562/31]). The striking combination of local tradition with Aegean, Cypriote and Egyptian influences displayed by Philistine Bichrome has already been emphasised by Trude Dothan (*e.g.* 1982, 96). Together with a restricted geographical distribution, this mix of influences leaves little doubt as to the ware's local evolution. At the same time, however, it suggests that contacts and some degree of cultural interaction existed between these different regions, though pottery might not have played an important role in that. With regards to Philistine Bichrome pottery in particular, the suggestion has been made before that many of the motifs (birds, spirals) found on it derived from motifs used on embroidered textiles (*e.g.* Sherratt 1998, 304–5, with further references).

About one-sixth of the total pottery furnishing in both Tombs 542 and 562 is made up by small decorated pilgrim flasks (Fig. 20.6, 542/64). Although the shape was already known in the area in the 13th century, either with a relatively fine clay emulating an Aegean style technology (see Tomb 902; Laemmel 2003, I, 177), or in coarser clays but in much larger size (Amiran 1969, 167, pl. 51:8), its proliferation is fairly representative of the Iron I period in the southern Levant as a whole. They are common, for example, at Ashdod Strata XV–XI, but mainly Stratum XII (Dothan and Porath 1993, figs. 12:12, 32:9–13, 15, 41:11, 43:10, pls. 34:1, 43:4, 6–8), and Tel Qasile Strata XII–X (Mazar

1985, 71–72, figs. 11:23, 15:10, 20:12, 14, 25:20, 37:2–15, 42:12–15, 50:11). They are also found, but to a lesser extent, on Cyprus, where they are usually considered as Levantine imports (*e.g.* Kition Area I, Floor I–II; Karageorghis and Demas 1985, 53, [no. 499], pls. XXIX, LII).

A special feature of Tomb 542 is the presence of a small Midianite pottery juglet (Fig. 20.6, 542/87). It is characterised by a very light buff (almost white) fabric with no core and dark mineral inclusions. It bears a series of painted bands on the shoulder and neck and, according to J. Garrow Duncan's (1930, H3) *Corpus of Dated Palestinian Pottery*, it had a motif painted on the body of which only faint traces remain today. This ware's production centre is usually located in north-west Arabia and it occurs notably in 19th and 20th Dynasty contexts at Timna (Rothenberg 1971, 19, pl. 35; 1972, 162–3, fig. 32, photos 48–54; 1988, 93–4, figs. 6–10, pls. 4, 16–18), in the late 12th to early 11th centuries at Tel Masos (Fritz and Kempinski 1983, pls. 97A, 142:10, 148:11; Kempinski 1993, 988–9), and in earlier (though probably disturbed) contexts at Amman (van der Steen 1996, 56). At Tell el-Far'ah it was found in the area of the 900-series cemetery, and on the Tell in the same layers as Philistine Bichrome (Rothenberg and Glass 1983, 82; Laemmel 2003, I, 39, 219–20).

Finally, Tombs 542 and 562 produced a group of vessels which show some resemblance both with the 'Myc IIIC1b' assemblages from sites like Ashdod or Ekron, and with elements belonging to the Cypriote LC III repertoire. First comes a series of decorated and undecorated bowls some of which can be paralleled, for example, with the pots and sherds found in association with the potter's workshop at Ashdod, Stratum XIIIb (Dothan and Porath 1993, figs. 14:9–23, 16:9–10, pls. 35:14–16, 36:1–9, colour pls. VIII, bottom and IX; Dothan and Zukerman 2004, figs. 5:7–8, 6:1–2, 9, 12–13), or with White Painted Wheelmade III vessels from Cyprus (for parallels see Karageorghis 1974, 68–70, [nos. 114, 122, 145], pls. LXX–LXXII, CLVII; Laemmel 2003, I, 122–3, 125–7). One example from Tomb 562 has a single lug-handle below the rim and painted bands on the inside (Fig. 20.7, 562/12), while other examples are of a deeper bell-shape with or without horizontal handles below the rim (Figs. 20.7, 562/17, 542/18, 22–3, 27). Their decoration consists in red or red-brown matte-painted horizontal bands outside and/or inside. Although it is possible that some of these bowls or even all of them were produced during the Philistine Bichrome phase, their relation to Cypriote shapes and decoration of the LC III period is nonetheless worth underlining.

The bowls 542/13–14 (Fig. 20.7) are of particular interest for the present discussion because they illustrate a syncretism between Cypriote and Levantine traditions in the 12th century BCE. 542/14 is hemispherical with a low ring-base, horizontal grooves below the rim and a small lug handle. It is unslipped, but bears faint remains of a red-brown painted band below

the rim and concentric circles inside the base. Good parallels for it are found on Cyprus, for example at Enkomi in LC III (Dikaios 1969–71, 583, 593, 607, 610, 620, pls. 72:5, 76:6, 79:3, 620, 83:3, 84:10) but also in northern Palestine, for example at Tell Abu Hawam in LBA contexts (Anati 1959, fig. 8:1, pl. XIII:2). In the Iron Age the shape became more frequent in the southern Palestinian repertoire and was produced in the red slip burnish technique throughout the 11th and 10th centuries BCE (e.g. Tufnell 1953, 269–70, pls. 79:24, 99:592–8; Dothan and Porath 1982, fig. 1:4, 7, 17). Bowl 542/13 is relatively shallow with a straightened rim, a single horizontal handle on the side and a red-brown painted band on the exterior. It is an unusual shape in Palestine, and its closest parallel may be a fragmentary bowl from Ashdod, Stratum XII (Dothan and Porath 1993, fig. 26:9). It is, however, reminiscent of Cypriote LC IIIB vessels, for example at Kition Floor I (Karageorghis and Demas 1985, 69, [no. 1151], 75, pls. XXXIII, LV), and Enkomi, French Tomb 5 (Schaeffer 1952, 187, 217, figs. 72:305, 84:1, 18).

In addition to these bowl shapes, Tombs 542 and 562 also had a number of coarse-ware, domestic forms which can be linked to Cypriote (or even Aegean-type Cypriote) vessels. First is a series of two-handled wide-mouth jars with rounded base, made of quartz-rich clay with occasional vegetable tempering (e.g. Fig. 20.8, 562/18). Although these occur with a certain frequency in the EIA tombs at Tell el-Far'ah, they are rather rare in other contemporary sites in the region. Their best parallels are cooking-pots, found on Cyprus in LC III to CG I contexts, for example at Maa-Palaekastro, Floor I (Karageorghis and Demas 1988, 199, [no. 358], pls. CLIII, CCXLV) and Kition, Floor I (Karageorghis and Demas 1985, 69, [no. 659/1], pls. XXXIII, LV). Though not all of the Cypriote examples seem to have been used for cooking, similar two-handled vessels, but with a ring-base, are known as cooking-pots in mainland Greece from LH IIIB1 to the 11th century BCE (French 1967, 173; Tzedakis and Martlew 1999, 131, figs. 112–13). In Iron II, other (and perhaps related) types of rounded-base cooking pots with two handles appear in Transjordan and northern Israel (Green 2003, type TJ3), but they have different rim profiles, proportions and a much stronger body carination than the examples from Tell el-Far'ah.

Second, related in terms of clay to these two-handled pots, are a group of one-handled ring-base jugs with a slightly restricted neck (Fig. 20.8, 542/45; Laemmel 2003, pl. 111 [542/44, 46–7]). As far as morphology is concerned, they compare well with the Aegean-type cooking-pots of the 'Myc IIIC' assemblages of Ashdod and Ekron (Dothan 1998b, 23, pls. 3:14, 6:7–8; Killebrew 1998a, 397, figs. 7:19, 10:13–14, 12:15; 1999, 93–4, fig. 3; Dothan and Zukerman 2004, 28–31, figs. 36:1–4, 37). However, similar shapes also occur elsewhere in transitional Late Bronze/Iron I horizons, for example at Deir Alla (Franken 1992, 38, fig. 4/3:14), and later throughout the Iron I period, for example at Tel Qasile

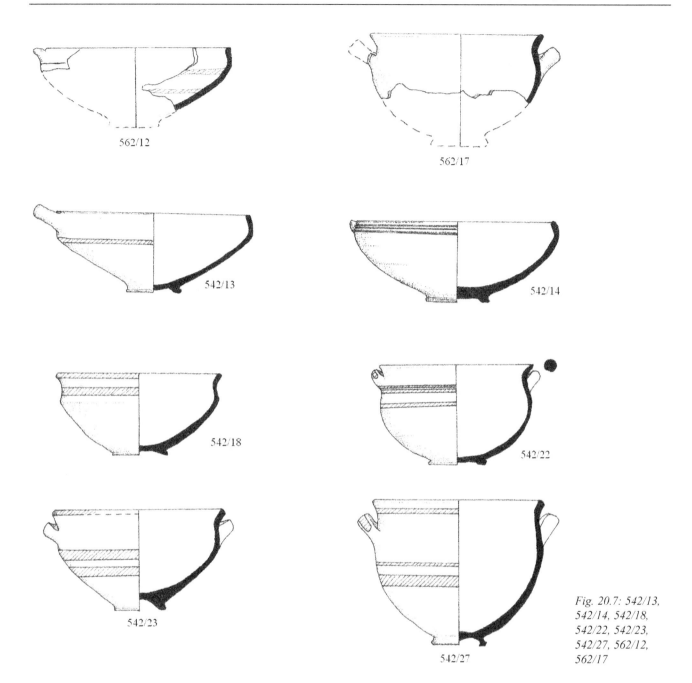

Fig. 20.7: 542/13, 542/14, 542/18, 542/22, 542/23, 542/27, 562/12, 562/17

Strata XI–X (Mazar 1985, figs. 25:17; 49:10, 12–13), and Beth Shemesh Strata III–II (Grant 1929, 211, [no. 337]; Grant and Wright 1938–39, pl. 61:31). At Tell el-Far'ah, these pots are relatively frequent in late 12th to 11th century tombs. Their clay is again particularly rich in sand-quartz inclusions with little vegetable tempering. Of all the examples found in the Tell el-Far'ah tombs, only one (Laemmel 2003, pl. 111 [542/45]) bears clear soot traces on its exterior and was apparently used for heating aliments or liquids.

One way to interpret the Aegeanizing and Cypriote-style bowls from Tombs 542 and 562 is to see them as yet another manifestation of the above-mentioned phenomenon of pottery assimilation which ranges from imitations of foreign styles to their full integration into the local production. In a first stage, foreign-style shapes and decoration were relatively faithfully reproduced by local potters. In a second stage, these foreign characteristics seem to have become inherent in the local production and to have followed a stylistic development of their own.

The handled pots and jugs can also be seen in the same light. However, because they are undecorated domestic vessels, they also call for a parallel with the Egyptian-style flat based bowl of the Late Bronze Age. Like the latter, these jugs and pots are to be seen as a local 'digression' from foreign coarse wares and, like them, they could theoretically have been made either by a foreigner or by local potters exposed to foreign influences. In any case, neither they, nor the finer ware bowls and dishes, are enough to postulate something like a process of Aegean, Cypriote or Philistine acculturation at the site or its environs, just as the Egyptian-style bowls of the LB II period are not enough to support the large-scale presence of Egyptians.

Group III: Tombs 834, 839, 126, 105

The tombs of Group III span the period from the mid to late 12th century to sometime in the second part of the 11th century BCE. They compare to some extent, but on a more modest scale, to the tombs of the 500-series cemetery discussed above, and illustrate further changes that affected pottery technology and style over that time.

Tombs of this group are all undisturbed shaft graves. All but Tomb 105, which contained two bodies, were single burials, and Tomb 126 was a child's grave. In terms of small finds, Tomb 834 was furnished with a bronze bowl, beads and Egyptian-type Pataikoi faience amulets, suggesting that the southern Levant was then, at least to some extent, still under the Egyptian religious/cultural sphere of influence. Tomb 839 had an iron bracelet and an Egyptian faience pilgrim flask of a type known elsewhere in the Levant (*e.g.* Tufnell 1940, 62–3, pl. 22:56), and on Cyprus (Jacobsson 1994, 32–3). A good parallel for this vessel comes from a tomb from Gurob, dating to the reign of Seti II (Petrie and Sayce 1891, 18, pl. 19:14), though the iron bracelet suggests a later date for Tomb 839. Tomb 126 contained at least one Egyptian-type Pataikos faience amulet, but Tomb 105 had no small finds (see Laemmel 2003, II, 7–8, 18–20, 202–3, 205–6).

The pottery of this last tomb group consists mainly in types which are characteristic of the Iron I local repertoire but continue the tradition of the LBA: a painted storage-jar, a pilgrim flask, a rounded base dipper juglet (instead of the pointed-base type of the late 13th to early 12th centuries) and a pinched-beak lamp (Laemmel 2003, pls. 229–30 [834/4–7]). The strainer-jug from Tomb 105 (Laemmel 2003, pl. 36 [105/2]) is again a typical Iron I shape, but bears witness to the emergence of the red slip technique which, in its burnished version, constitutes one of the hallmarks of the Iron IB–II period in the area.

Again associated with these were vessels showing the impact of a foreign, now mainly Cypriote, influence. Some of these are closely related to the Aegeanizing, Cypriote-style pottery of Tombs 542 and 562, but often display a greater degree of integration than the latter. The globular one-handled jug from Tomb 834 (Laemmel 2003, pl. 229 [834/3]) is of the same type as those from tombs 542 and 562 discussed above. Similarly the series of small bowls decorated with painted bands and/or concentric circles inside the base (Fig. 20.9, 834/1–2, 839/2) continue the tradition of the 'Myc

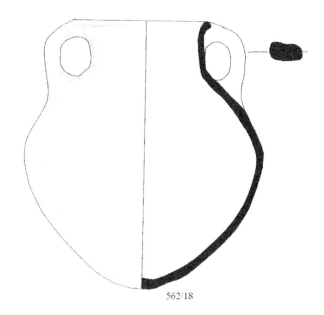

562/18

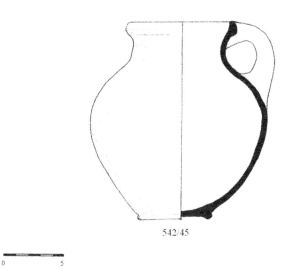

542/45

Fig. 20.8: 542/45, 562/18

IIIC' pottery of the 500-series tombs and, as far as shape is concerned, compare well with Cypriote vessels, such as from Kition Floor I (Karageorghis and Demas 1985, 69, [no. 1151], 75, pls. XXXIII, LV) and Enkomi French Tomb 5 (Schaeffer 1952, 187, 217, figs. 72:305, 84:1, 18). However, two bowls from Tomb 126 are painted with thin red-brown bands, one with diminished horizontal handles (Fig. 20.9, 126/1; Laemmel 2003, pl. 46 [126/1]) that can no longer be paralleled by Cypriote vessels, though it perpetuates the same style and forms. This suggests that by the time these

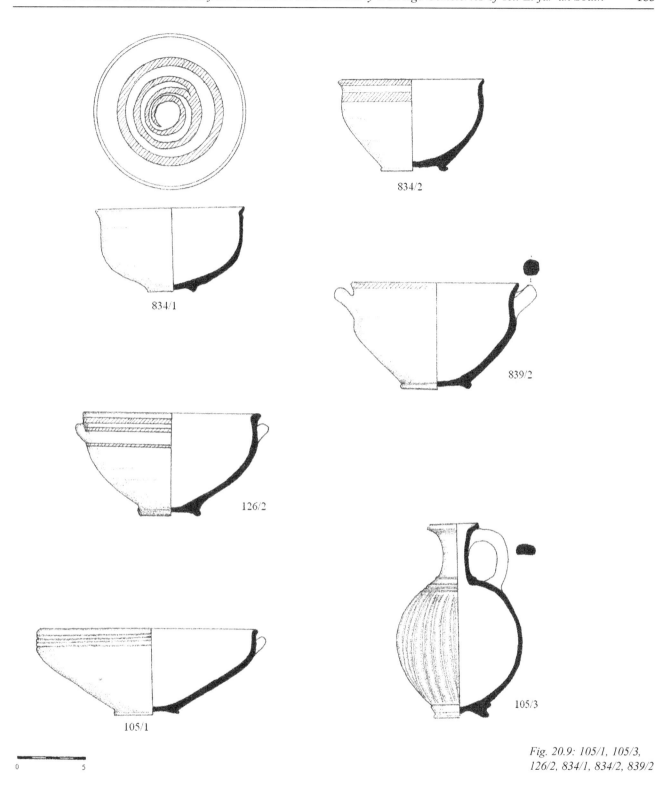

Fig. 20.9: 105/1, 105/3,
126/2, 834/1, 834/2, 839/2

pots were produced, the Aeageanizing two-handled carinated bowl had become inherent in the Levantine repertoire, as it had already become on Cyprus in the late 13th or early 12th centuries BCE. Similarly, the bowl with incised grooves from Tomb 105 (Fig. 20.9, 105/1) is a later version of the one from Tomb 542 that was still comparable to Cypriote forms (Fig.

20.7, 542/14), but it already corresponds to a later version of the shape which remained common throughout the Iron IB–IIA period, especially in the red slip burnish technique (Laemmel 2003, I, 119).

Finally, Tomb 105 produced an imported Bucherro juglet (Fig. 20.9, 105/3) which can be paralleled for example at Enkomi Level IIIC (Dikaios 1969–71, 617, pl. 83:32) or in Kition French Tomb 5 (Schaeffer 1952, 161, fig. 66:7). Although Bucherro Ware has rarely been reported at Levantine sites (Gilboa 1995, 16, fig. 1.10:42; Stern 1995, IA, 271; Gilboa 1998, 418–23, fig. 7:9), it is significant that both genuine Bucchero imports and local imitations of it occur in several of the Tell el-Farʿah tombs (Laemmel 2003, I, 217).

The pottery material from this last group of tombs happens to be less abundant than that from the earlier Groups I and II. However, it is significant because it illustrates the perpetuation and final integration of what were originally foreign characteristics into local pottery production, and points to a continuation of contacts, at least with Cyprus, into that period.

Conclusions

The sample of tombs reviewed here, ranging from within the second half of the 13th to the later part of the 11th centuries BCE, exemplifies the gradual change that affected local material culture during that time. Pottery production is marked by the progressive appearance of Philistine Bichrome (in Tombs 542, 562), followed in the later 11th century by the emergence of the red slip technique (in Tomb 105). As for materials other than pottery, the major innovation of this period was, of course, the introduction of iron.

Change is also apparent in the technology of pottery manufacture, and the nature of the predominant local clay type altered over that period (see Laemmel 2003, I, 87–9). A fair number of bowls, pilgrim flasks or juglets, dating from the mid-12th to the mid-11th centuries, relate to one fabric group, distinguished by a red-brown to light beige or buff clay, and often with a rather gritty surface due to the presence of a large amount of sand-quartz (both in the break and on the pot's surface). This clay differs from that employed for many vessels found in the earlier 900-series grave assemblages, which is often redder in colour and less gritty, though in some cases still relatively coarse because it was tempered with finely chopped straw in the Egyptian manner. The matt reddish paint used for the decoration, on the other hand, looks very similar across all the assemblages.

In other respects, these tombs bear witness to a strong continuity going all the way back to the final stage of the Late Bronze Age. This is demonstrated for example by the survival of the Egyptian influence visible mainly in the small finds assemblages – in particular with scarabs and faience amulets – and in the use of the clay anthropoid sarcophagi. Such continuity is also illustrated by a somewhat persistant taste for Cypriote and Aegeanizing stylistic elements and by a tendency to assimilate these elements into the local production. This can be seen from the imitated Base Ring II juglets and Aegean-type pyxides of LB II style to the

Bucherro juglet of the later part of the 11th century BCE.

The few bell-shaped painted bowls from the Early Iron Age discussed above, which bear some resemblance in shape and decoration to the 'Myc IIIC:1b' of Ashdod Stratum XIIIb, may be part of the same general phenomenon. They bear witness to the role played by Cypriote-style pottery wares in the development of the local ceramic repertoire in 12th century Canaan.

In the Levant, Aegean container shapes that were closely associated with specific products (and thus often placed in tombs or used in cultic contexts) started to be substituted by local variants in LB IIB. On Cyprus, this process of import substitution started slightly earlier in the 13th century BCE with open shapes, such as kraters and bowls which are primarily found in settlement sites. These open shapes were also traded to the Levantine coast, in particular to northern Israel, Lebanon and Syria, and especially to Ugarit, and certainly alongside other products such as the last traditional handmade pottery. In the early 12th century, the progressive emergence of the locally-made 'Myc. IIIC:1b' ware in the Levant, with its dominance of open shapes, mainly at sites located along the coast, may represent nothing but the extension of the same process of import substitution, when local potters started displacing Cypriot-made Aegeanizing ware with their own production. Eventually, these open shapes, like the closed vessels that had already been copied from Aegean models in the 13th century, became fully integrated into the local pottery repertoire and followed a stylistic development of their own, manifest, for example, in the appearance of the Philistine Bichrome of the late 12th to 11th centuries BCE. The obvious problem with this view is the often-mentioned lack of 12th century imports from Cyprus to the southern Levant. However, the material shown here, from the flat-based juglet from Tomb 902 to the small pilgrim flasks from Tombs 542 and 562 and the Bucchero juglet from Tomb 105, suggests that some form of relationship continued between these two areas, perhaps indirectly via the northern coast of Israel, Lebanon and coastal Syria. These are small, individual hints, but they lend further support to theories suggesting the existence of close-knit economic ties between Cyprus and the Levant in the 12th century BCE, based on a trade in metals, recycled metals, textiles and other manufactured commodities (*e.g.* Sherratt 1998, 304–5).

In conclusion, the material from the Tell el-Farʿah cemeteries, taken in its entirety, does not reflect any evidence of major change in the ethnic makeup of the area at the transition from Bronze to Iron Ages. It rather suggests a more subtle network of long-lasting and, perhaps, indirect contacts liking Tell el-Farʿah with Egypt, Cyprus and the northern Levantine coast. Unlike what is often argued, there are hints that trade or other forms of contact actually continued between the different regions of the eastern Mediterranean during the 12th to 11th centuries. Pottery itself might not have played a major role in such exchanges, but because the survival rates of other artefacts and consumable commodities, such as metals or organic materials, are extremely low in the archaeological record, pottery style and technology remain one of the main analytical tools. In the present case, features such as the Midianite juglet from Tomb 542, the Aegeanizing and Cypriote-style painted bowls, together with the Egyptian faience amulets of the Early Iron Age, show that during this time period Tell el-Far'ah was far from isolated, but rather remained a nodal point along some of the main trade routes of the ancient world.

Acknowledgments

I would like to express my thanks to Susan Sherratt for her comments on earlier versions of this paper and to the organisers of the 2006 BANEA conference for their work and their useful suggestions. My thanks also go to Othmar Keel for providing me with a copy of his data-base of Egyptian scarabs in Palestine on which I relied for dating the scarabs from the Tell el-Far'ah tombs.

I am most grateful to the institutions listed below for giving me access to their colections: University College London for Tombs 902, 920, 939, 562, 834, 839, 126, 105; British Museum for Tomb 920; Rockefeller Museum, Jerusalem for Tombs 936, 542, 834; Ashmolean Museum, Oxford for Tomb 839. All the illustrations accompanying the text have been drawn by the author. Whenever it was possible the objects have been drawn after the actual artefacts. When the latter could not be located, drawings were taken from existing publications (Duncan 1930; Petrie 1930; Starkey and Harding 1932), in which case the pottery is only drawn by a contour outline.

THE ORGANIZATION OF CERAMIC PRODUCTION DURING THE TRANSITION FROM THE LATE BRONZE TO THE EARLY IRON AGES: TEL BATASH AS A TEST CASE

Nava Panitz-Cohen

The forces of transformation that swept through the Mediterranean basin and the Levant at the end of the Late Bronze Age affected virtually every aspect of ancient life, from the macro-economic and political spheres to the routine of daily experience. Needless to say, this did not happen all at once or simultaneously in all regions, and the coordination between the *long durée* or international processes and the short term event or local experience is one of the challenges of historical and archaeological reconstruction. Pottery, that workhorse of archaeological investigation, can contribute to our understanding of this interface.

The use of material culture in general, and ceramics in particular, in the analysis of non-material phenomena is based on the assumption that the technological stages of the '*chaîne opératoire*' and the organization of production, as well as distribution and consumption, serve as a viable

window into economic, social, political and ideological aspects of ancient life (Rice 1984; van der Leeuw and Pritchard 1984; Rice 1987; Esse 1989, 77–92; Sinopoli 1991; Lemonnier 1993).

Such an approach was used in a comprehensive study of the rich ceramic assemblages numbering thousands of vessels and sherds uncovered during twelve seasons of excavation at Tel Batash (Biblical Timnah) in the Shephelah region in Israel (Mazar 1997b, 3–194; Panitz-Cohen 2006; see Fig. 21.1). This excavation, under the direction of Amihai Mazar of the Institute of Archaeology of the Hebrew University of Jerusalem, revealed a stratigraphic sequence of twelve strata, spanning the 17th to 6th centuries BCE (Table 21.1; Mazar 1997b). The examination of processes of ceramic change and continuity over this long period, from the Middle Bronze Age IIB (henceforth MB IIB) until the end of the Iron Age I, provided significant information about social, economic, political and ideological processes at the site and beyond. The analysis was conducted on a quantitative basis with variables that included typology, technology, decoration, provenience, capacity and spatial distribution. The results of this detailed examination were interpreted within the context of the geo-political *realia* of each period, adhering to the contextual approach to material culture studies (Hodder 1981, 216; Braun 1995, 125). The relevant geo-political and ethno-historical contexts began with the powerful centralized city-states of MB IIB, continuing with the Egyptian domination of Canaan during the Late Bronze Age (LBA), until the demise of the latter and the rise of the Philistines and other social and ethnic entities in the Iron Age I. The present article spotlights one segment of these developments, namely that of the transition from the Late Bronze to the Iron Ages, the 13th to the 11th centuries BCE in the Shephelah region in Canaan. The focus

Stratum	Period	Proposed Date (BCE)
I	Persian	5th–4th C.
II	Iron Age II	7th C.–end of 6th C.
III	Iron Age II	8th C.
IV	Iron Age II	10th C.
V	Iron Age I	Second half of 12th C.–11th C.
VIa	LB IIB / transitional Iron I	End of 13th C.–early 12th C.
VIb	LB IIB	Latter half of 13th C.
VII	LB IIA	14th C. (Amarna Period)
VIII	LB IB	Second half of 15th C.
IXa–b	LB IA	First half of 15th C.
X	Transitional MB–LB	Mid to late 16th C.
XII–XI	MB IIB	17th–first half of 16th C.

Table 21.1: The stratigraphic sequence at Tel Batash

is on the impact of this transition on ceramic production and how this production expressed cultural, economic and social processes of that time.

Middle Bronze and Late Bronze Age I–IIA organization of ceramic production

In order to more fully understand the forces at the time of the transition from the Late Bronze to Iron Ages, it is necessary to briefly look back at the organization of ceramic production during the preceding Middle and the Late Bronze Ages.

The Middle Bronze Age IIB

The initial settlement at Tel Batash (Stratum XII) at the beginning of the MB IIB was a fortified town in which part of a well-built citadel was uncovered, along with an earthen rampart and a city wall. The limited exposure identified two phases (Strata XII–XI) and yielded a relatively small ceramic assemblage. Though limited in size, typologically the assemblage was indicative of the high level of ceramic production typical of this period. Aside from one hand-made cooking pot type, all vessels were wheel-turned and quite standardized. Most of the pottery was made of two fabric groups, both of which were shown by petrographic analysis to belong to the same source of marl of the Taqiye formation, which is found from Tel Batash eastwards to Beth-Shemesh and northwards to Gezer. A very small number of vessels was made of another clay source, loess, whose origin is further to the south and west of Tel Batash (Panitz-Cohen and Mazar 2006, 12–26; see Fig. 21.1 and below).

The Late Bronze Age I–IIA

The transition to the LBA at Tel Batash is identified in Stratum X, dated to the mid- to late 16th century BCE. The MB IIB citadel and fortifications went out of use, and in their stead a house was built whose outer wall formed the defensive line of the town, which now lacked fortifications. This house contained a rich ceramic assemblage found in a burnt destruction level (Mazar 1997b, 41–5; Panitz-Cohen and Mazar 2006, 123–6). Following the destruction of the Stratum X house, three successive houses were built in Strata IX to VII, the 15th–14th centuries BCE (Mazar 1997b, 45–71; Panitz-Cohen and Mazar 2006, 126–32); the town remained unfortified. Each of these houses was destroyed and contained rich ceramic assemblages, which constitute the main bulk of the ceramic data base for the LBA.

The LBA ceramics

Some of the Stratum X ceramics typologically belonged to the last vestiges of the MB tradition (such as pithoi and molded-rim storage jars), while the rest of the assemblage demonstrated characteristics that would become common throughout the LBA (such as carinated cooking pots with everted triangular rims, the Canaanite storage jar, biconical vessels). It seems that much of the pottery was not wheel-turned at this time, and formation techniques included mainly coiling and turning, or mold and coiling, with slow wheel-finishing. There were a fair number of distorted vessels apparently due to problems in coordinating formation, drying and firing. The same vessel types were found to have sometimes been made by different formation techniques, the cooking pots for example. Storage jars, on the other hand, were all wheel-turned, using somewhat different formation techniques and secondary finishing stages. The capacity of storage jars and cooking pots remained standardized during most of this period, while other vessels showed a greater size and capacity diversity.

Starting with Stratum X, the vast majority of the vessels were of local manufacture (aside from the Cypriot and Mycenaean imports) and there was a wider variety of fabric groups than in MB IIB. This included the continuation of the three fabric groups of the previous stratum (though in different proportions), joined by additional fabrics, making a total of seven main fabric groups. Five of these, constituting the majority of the pottery, were made of marl of the Taqiye formation, while two fabric groups, representing a very small number of vessels, were made of loess. These fabric groups continued virtually unchanged throughout Strata IX–VII as well (LB IB–LB IIA, 15th–14th centuries BCE). Thus, during the course of most of the LBA, there are a number of fabric groups that belong to one major petrographic group, which is the same marl of the Taqiye formation that was used to make pottery in MB IIB Strata XII–XI.

Diversity in the mode of production: household workshops in the LBA

This data indicates a production regime in the LBA that was more diverse and heterogeneous than before, though still on a localized-regional scale. Such diversity of resources and formation techniques indicates that the potters were making differential choices from the available resources and for the most part, did not operate in centralized units of production. The different fabric groups that belonged to the same broad petrographic group represented a variety of tempers and clay mixes that potters used with this same basic clay source. This shift from the few fabrics used to make the MB IIB pottery to the larger numbers and types of fabrics, and the concurrent changes in the typology, were the result of diverse factors, for example: denied access to previous clay sources and the need to seek new clay recipes due to external circumstances such as warfare, destruction or migration, altered marital patterns with women bringing ceramic traditions from other places, new potters working alongside veterans, experienced potters becoming itinerant due to changing technology and consumer needs, among other ethnographically-attested causes that are behind similar production shifts (Feinman *et al.* 1984; Feinman *et al.* 1989; Sinopoli 1991, 153–9; Costin 1996; Schortman and Urban 2004).

It is suggested that as a result of these processes and circumstances, there was a shift from the centralized and redistributive mode of ceramic production in MB IIB (mostly conducted as specialized production attached to the ruling urban elite) to a more dispersed mode of production centered on household workshops in the LBA. These workshops were operated by independent unattached specialists who most likely worked on a seasonal basis, producing pottery on a relatively small-scale level of local distribution and consumption (Rice 1984; Sinopoli 1991, 98–103). Alongside this level of production, it seems that there was some more centralized community-based specialization, particularly for storage jars and perhaps for cooking pots as well, which might have been produced year round. This is inferred based mainly on the capacity analysis, which showed a high degree of standardization and a different type of specialization for these vessel classes. Other types of ceramic production most likely existed as well, such as small specialized workshops attached to temples, as seen in Area C at Hazor (Yadin 1972, 35, 82). However, these were not the mainstream of production, as were the household workshops.

The adoption of such a household workshop mode of production would suit the historical events and geo-political conditions of the 15th–14th centuries BCE under Egyptian domination. Ethno-archaeological analogies demonstrate how political and economic pressure, particularly the loss of agricultural land and its produce, prompts many people to turn to ceramic making as a subsistence measure in lieu of agriculture (Balfet 1965; Nicklin 1971; Arnold 1985, 171–96; Graves 1991, 138–41; Wilson and Blinman 1995; Kramer 1997, 46; Sillar 1997, 6). During the period of their rule, Egyptians exploited Canaan by often confiscating agricultural land and its produce as the property of Egyptian temples. Any tract of land that lay fallow became the '*khato*-land of the Pharaoh' (Na'aman 1988; Redford 1990, 40). The Egyptian practice of burning crops and orchards during military activity must have also affected the ability of the local populace to sustain themselves from agriculture (Hasel 1998, 76–82). During the Late Bronze Age, Egyptian rule was mostly experienced by the average Canaanite in the form of taxes, depopulation, land and manpower confiscation (Bunimovitz 1994). Yet, local government was relatively autonomous, as expressed in the Amarna letters (Moran 1992; Giles 1997). The Egyptian rulers, as well as the local Canaanite elite, were not interested in controlling or monitoring the production and distribution of plain ceramics, leaving the field open for the kind of elementary specialist, household workshop production and exchange proposed here. The majority of the fabric groups

at Tel Batash belong to the same petrographic group (marl of Taqiye formation), whose provenience points to the area defined as the Kingdom of Gezer as the realm in which this production and distribution took place (Goren *et al.* 2004, 271). It seems that the borders of this entity were politically and economically well-defined at this time, since very little pottery from other sources reached our site (Fig. 21.1).

A final point that can be noted concerning the proposed organization of ceramic production during most of the LBA is related to the cognitive or symbolic meaning of the plain and utilitarian Canaanite pottery. It seems that production in dispersed venues of household workshops within a family and/or community framework extended an emblematic role to this pottery. Not only were the function and decoration of this ware shared by Canaanites, but also the organization of its production and the technological style that represented Canaanite identity and promoted its solidarity (van der Leeuw 1993; Gosselain 1998; Stark 1998). Most likely, Egyptian domination and pressure also played a role in making these symbols of Canaanitism such a potent marker of this group's identity, emphasizing the differences between 'them and us'.

The shift in production organization during the transition from LB to Iron I

Stratum VI

Following the violent destruction of the fine domicile of Stratum VII at Tel Batash, no new house was erected on this spot, breaking the chain of architectural and functional continuity that had begun as early as the mid-16th century BCE. If we postulate that there had been a continuation of occupation by the same family, the end of Stratum VII marks the termination of this social sequence as well (Panitz-Cohen and Mazar 2006, 194).

It seems that there was a short gap between the end of Stratum VII and the beginning of Stratum VI, which began sometime during the 13th century and continued into the beginning of the 12th century BCE. The Stratum VI occupation was sparser and had two phases, with the earlier one containing Cypriot imports and the later one lacking them. This latter phase saw the construction of a stone building that continued to be used, with some minor renovation, in the subsequent Iron Age I Stratum V (Mazar 1997b, 72–6). Since this level was not destroyed violently as were its predecessors, the material finds are more fragmentary (Panitz-Cohen and Mazar 2006, 132–34).

The ceramics of Stratum VI

The pottery of Stratum VI demonstrates typological and technological change from the assemblages of the previous

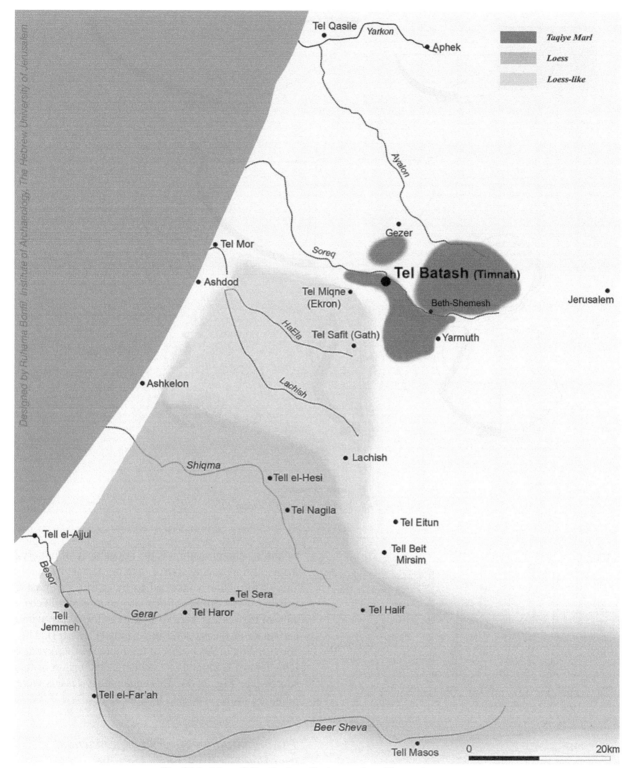

Fig. 21.1: Map of distribution: Taqiye marl and loess clay sources

two centuries. Typologically, a number of key Canaanite types disappear, including the carinated bowl, the Canaanite storage jar and the piriform jug. New types that appear include a narrow bodied storage jar with four handles and a plain rim, as well as small flasks and squat biconical jugs (Fig. 21.2). These are types that will continue into the subsequent Iron Age I Stratum V. On the other hand, cooking pots remain virtually the same, a feature which is considered

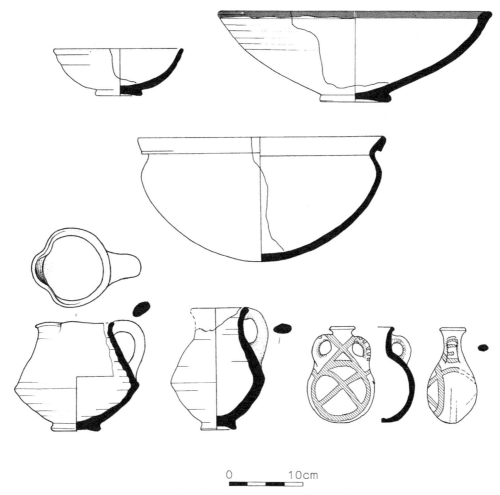

Fig. 21.2: Pottery forms of Stratum VI

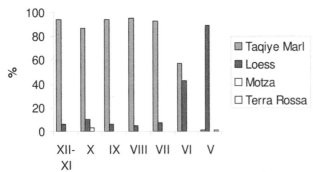

Fig. 21.3: Frequency of Taqiye marl and loess petrographic groups: Strata XII–V

a hallmark of the conservativeness of culinary practices (Killebrew 1999). Technologically, more wheel-turning was identified and there was a higher degree of standardization in a number of vessel classes that were hitherto diverse, such as the open bowls and kraters. Another significant technological innovation is the appearance of pottery made from a different clay source than before; while marl of the Taqiye formation continued to be used (and most of the existing fabric groups of this clay source continued), about 44% of the vessels were now made of loess clay, with either carbonate or quartz sand inclusions (Fig. 21.3). The loess petrographic group points to the more southern zone of the Kingdom of Gath and/or Lachish as the origin of this clay source (see Fig. 21.1). This means that vessels were now imported to the site from another region.

The organization of ceramic production: transitional LBA – Early Iron Age

The changes noted in the typology and technology of the Stratum VI ceramics represent a real innovation (Torrence and van der Leeuw 1989) and are not just a reflection of the formal variation resulting from the dispersed production mode that existed during most of the LBA. While there was a marked degree of continuity in the ceramics from the previous occupation, the changes are significant. The increased use of wheel-turning and standardization point to a more industrialized production mode, while the importation of pottery from a more distant region that was hitherto politically discrete, suggests that there was some economic and/or political force that intervened in the production and distribution of the plain utilitarian Canaanite pottery.

It is suggested that this transformation was the result of the heightened Egyptian presence during the 19th and 20th Dynasties. At this time, direct Egyptian intervention was at its peak, reflected in the governors' residencies built at strategic locations, temples dedicated to Egyptian deities, and a clear increase in Egyptian and Egyptianized objects (Weinstein 1981, 17–22; Oren 1984; Singer 1994, 284; Killebrew 2004, 342; Oren 2006). It should also be considered that at this time the Egyptians were no longer tied to the lucrative import of pottery from Cyprus or that their role changed to a more passive one (Merillees 1968; Gittlen 1981). This would mean a reduction in revenues, which would have required shifts in compensatory production, distribution strategies and market targets. This could have been one of the factors behind the intensified Egyptian intervention in the local Canaanite economy, including pottery making.

Among the many expressions of this amplified presence and increased involvement in the Canaanite economy was the Egyptian-style pottery that was locally made in those towns where Egyptian strongholds were established and that was targeted for the use of Egyptians stationed there (Cohen-Weinberger 1998; Killebrew 2004; Martin 2005). This is particularly true in southern Canaan, where most of the Egyptian centers were concentrated, such as Aphek, Lachish, Jaffa, Gaza, Tel Sher'a and possibly Gezer. This pottery production was conducted in centralized workshops which were most likely controlled by the Egyptian bureaucracy, with Egyptian potters working in them. It is probable that these foreign craftsmen worked side by side with Canaanite potters, who became familiar with the Egyptian forms and also produced Canaanite forms under the influence of Egyptian technology, using the same clay fabrics (Cohen-Weinberger 1998). Egyptian ceramic technology involved wheel-production and kiln-firing, with much standardization of shapes and capacities, as well as a high output of mass production (Martin 2005). This organization of production suggests attached specialization in workshops that were turning out multiple ceramic traditions in the typological and technological sense (London 1999, 59). This is not to say that were many such joint workshops, but that the few that did exist had a significant impact on the organization of local pottery production, particularly in southern Canaan.

This is a departure from the kind of production suggested for most of the LBA, which operated within dispersed household workshops that produced a unified ceramic tradition. At the transition from the LBA to Iron I, the Canaanite potter sitting on the bench next to an Egyptian potter, or working within a nucleated workshop system in or near the Egyptianized town, could certainly have been influenced not so much by the Egyptian vessel shape itself (which was generally not imitated), but by its formation techniques and mode of production. An example of such a workshop is Cave 4034 at Lachish, where evidence was found of wheel-making and mold-making; this workshop turned out both Canaanite and Egyptian-style shapes (Magrill and Middleton 1997; 2004, 2,456–7). It is notable that the only archaeological evidence of pottery making during the LBA, including workshops, wheels and kilns, comes from late 13th or early 12th century BCE contexts, aside from the cultic workshop at Hazor (Wood 1990, 14–38; Killebrew 2005). This increased archaeological visibility is telling for the change in the production mode, as household workshop production is much more archaeologically invisible than a formal industry (Daviau 1993, 41, 46–7).

The Canaanite potters who worked in these centralized workshops under Egyptian jurisdiction created Canaanite-style vessel types that competed with those made in the common dispersed household workshop setting, which of course continued to operate. Competition, and not just centralized bureaucratic control, is a mechanism that can lead to increased specialization and efficiency of production in both spheres (Esse 1989, 91). For example, while production of Egyptian-style vessels in Lachish Workshop 4034 was probably targeted for consumption by the Egyptians at Lachish, certainly a portion of the Canaanite shapes made in that same workshop could have been marketed in other regions, such as the city-state of Gezer. Indeed, while during Strata X–VII at Tel Batash there was virtually no supply of pottery from the region around Lachish or Gath, the competition that was generated at the transition from the LBA to the early Iron Age resulted in the petrographic picture of Stratum VI described above: a mix of loess and Taqiye marl fabrics found in the same vessel types. The economic and political border previously maintained between the city-states of Gezer and Gath was apparently opened for trade. It seems that the strong and centralized 19th and 20th Dynasty Egyptian presence weakened the autonomy of the city-state system, so that ceramic (and other) exchange was able to move more freely across these borders.

The breaking and making of a ceramic tradition

The adoption of the faster wheel for at least some vessels would entail changes in production organization, as well as in ceramic learning and transmission mechanisms, in and of itself a catalyst for change (Schiffer and Skibo 1987, 597). Such a change in formation techniques and motor habits expresses a fundamental social alteration, as this is one part of the *chaîne opératoire* that is usually the most resistant to change and is most indicative of social group identity (Gosselain 1998). Since ceramic learning and transmission in a household workshop setting is mostly conducted within the family and kinship framework, such a change is indicative of a modification in social organization. At the transition from the LBA to the early Iron Age, ceramic learning was being conducted in more formal frameworks and the family or kinship group became less meaningful or effective as a production unit. Above, it was described how Stratum VI saw the termination of a long-lived occupation of superimposed houses most likely belonging to the same family at Tel Batash. This is a disturbance of a very fundamental social institution and not just a technical change. It exemplifies the kind of rift that household workshop production could have suffered at this time that certainly would impact ceramic learning and transmission of the craft.

This is not to say that Egyptian control of at least some pottery production in their administrative centers and the domino effect it created was the only factor that evoked the changes seen in the Stratum VI assemblage. Other functional-economic factors also played a role, such as intensified tax demands and diminished local trade that dictated changes in storage vessels, diminished foreign imports that led to increased import imitation, and so on. The destruction of various Canaanite centers such as Hazor and Ugarit during the course of the latter 13th century BCE impacted this process too, possibly preventing some potters from accessing their traditional clay sources, as well as removing some of the pottery production and exchange venues. This was joined by more and more people leaving the towns for semi-nomadic lifestyles, mostly in the hill country, as well as active deportation, leaving even fewer people in each region (Singer 1994). Immigration of Hittites, Arameans, and Sea Peoples introduced new inhabitants into the depopulated region, but also changed the social composition of the region. No longer were most all neighbours Canaanites, but rather, the chance to mingle with and marry a non-Canaanite increased. Thus, alongside the economic catalyst of Egyptian intervention, a significant mechanism that prompted the changes noted in the Stratum VI pottery was the basic shift in the social fabric of Canaanite society. Social uniformity and an ideology-based shared identity, nurtured by the economic reciprocity of socially-based exchange (Earle 2002), began to crumble at the end of the 13th century BCE. It is possible that long-lived Canaanite shapes that disappear at this time, such as the carinated bowl and piriform jug, are no longer made since they were particularly emblematic of Canaanite identity and were no longer in such demand.

Ultimately, along with the change in the organization of production, there was no longer one single 'correct' pottery tradition that could be equally recognized from Dan to Lachish or from Tel Abu-Hawam to Tel Batash, since there was no longer only one core Canaanite identity. There was a difference now between being a Canaanite and being an inhabitant of Canaan. More choices were opening up to producer and consumer alike. The more diverse the society, the less it acts as one group in initiating, accepting and transmitting cultural innovations and traditions. As a consequence, the material correlates of social cohesion, in our case the pottery, are exposed to fundamental typological and technological change. The influence of such social changes on pottery production is well-attested in the ethnographic literature, often resulting in a breakdown of the traditional 'costumbre' and leading to the production of new shapes with new technology (i.e. Rice 1987, 457). This change was not sudden or drastic, as many LBA types do continue to be made, used and distributed during the transition to the early Iron Age and even later. Those types that were chosen for continued and virtually unmodified production must have had a special symbolic significance (the chalice) or functional role (the cooking pot, the lamp). However, the mechanisms behind their production, as well as the meaning they held for at least some of the population, were altered (London 1989). Thus, while economic and functional reasons were certainly at work, symbolic factors played a crucial role in ceramic change during the transition from the LBA to the early Iron Age.

The processes of ceramic change and continuity described in this study demonstrate a principle that was well formulated by William Y. Adams (1979) for Nubian pottery, but is applicable to many ancient ceramic assemblages. He concluded that the rate and nature of ceramic change is not the direct outcome of historical events, but rather diverse factors impact this process. While in fact the increased Egyptian hold in the south of Canaan in the 13th and early 12th centuries BCE was a politically stabilizing factor, and this was a period of secure relations with the Hittites and of economic stability in general, this was precisely the time of the most acute cultural change at Tel Batash, both in the type and intensity of occupation, as well as in the ceramics and other aspects of material culture. Complex mechanisms, including historical, environmental, socio-economic and cognitive factors are behind the processes of ceramic change and continuity. In-depth quantitative and qualitative analysis of a large body of pottery from secure stratigraphic contexts over a long period of time, such as afforded by Tel Batash, can begin to illuminate such mechanisms.

BIBLIOGRAPHY

Achilara, L. (1996) Mycenaean Events from Psara. In E. de Miro *et al.*, eds., *Atti e memorie del secondo Congresso internazionale di micenologia, Roma-Napoli, 14–20 ottobre 1991* 3, 1,349–53. Rome, Gruppo Editoriale Internazionale

Adamesteanu, D. (1973) Le suddivisioni di terra nel Metapontino. In M. I. Finley, ed., *Problèmes de la terre en Grèce ancienne*, 49–61. Civilisations et sociétés, 33. Paris, Mouton

Adams, W. Y. (1979) On the Argument from Ceramics to History: a challenge based on evidence from medieval Nubia. *Current Anthropology* 20.4, 727–44

Adrimi-Sismani, V. (2006) Η γρίζα ψευδομινύεια και η στιλβωμένη χειροποίητη κεραμική από τον Μυκηναϊκό οικισμό Διμηνίου. *1ο Αρχαιολογικό Έργο Θεσσαλίας & Στερεάς Ελλάδας, Βόλος 27.2–2.3.2003.* Volos

Agelarakis, A., Kanta, A. and Moody, J. (2001) Cremation Burial in LM III C – Sub-Minoan Crete and the Cemetery at Pezoulos Atsipades. In N. C. Stampolidis, ed., *Καύσεις στην Εποχή του Χαλκού και την Πρώιμη Εποχή του Σιδήρου*, 69–82. Athens, Panepistemio tes Kretes

Åkerström, Å. (1968) A Mycenaean Potter's Factory at Berbati near Mycenae. *Atti e memorie del primo congresso internazionale di Micenologia, Roma, 27 Settembre–3 Ottobre 1967* 1. Incunabula Graeca, 25.1. Rome, Ateneo

Åkerström, Å. (1987) *Berbati, vol.2: the pictorial pottery.* Skrifter utgivna av Svenska institutet i Athen, 36.2, 4°. Stockholm, Svenska Institutet i Athen

Al-Sawi, A. (1979) *Excavations at Tell Basta: Report of Seasons 1967–1971 and Catalogue of Finds.* Prague, Univerzita Karlova

Albanese Procelli, R. M. (1997) Le etnie del ferro e le prime fondazioni coloniali. In S. Tusa, ed., *Prima Sicilia: alle origini della società siciliana*, 511–20. Palermo, Giuseppe Maimone Editore

Albanese Procelli, R. M. (2000) Il repertorio vascolare della necropoli di Madonna del Piano presso Grammichele (Catania). *Sicilia Archeologica* 23, 167–80

Albanese Procelli, R. M. (2003) *Sicani, Siculi, Elimi: forme di identità, modi di contatto e processi di trasformazione.* Biblioteca di archeologia, 33. Milan, Longanesi

Alberti, G. (2004) Contributo alla seriazione delle necropoli siracusane. In V. La Rosa, ed., *Le presenze micenee nel territorio siracusano: I Simposio siracusano di preistoria siciliana in memoria di Paolo Orsi, Siracusa, 15–16 dicembre 2003, Palazzo Impellizzeri, Museo archeologico regionale Paolo Orsi*, 97–168. Padua, Bottega d'Erasmo

Alberti, G. (2005) The Earliest Contacts between South-Eastern Sicily and Cyprus in the Late Bronze Age. In R. Laffineur and E. Greco, eds., *Emporia: Aegeans in the Central and Esatern Mediterranean. Proceedings of the 10th International Aegean Conference / 10e Rencontre égéenne internationale. Athens, Italian School of Archaeology, 14–18 April 2004*, 343–51. Aegaeum, 25. Liège, Université de Liège

Alessandri, L. (2007) *L'occupazione costiera protostorica del Lazio centromeridionale.* BAR International Series, 1592. Oxford, Archaeopress

Alexandre, Y. (1995) The 'Hippo' Jar and Other Storage Jars at Hurvat Rosh Zayit. *Tel Aviv* 22, 77–88

Alexiou, S. (1958) I minoikì theà meth'upsomènon cheiròn. *Krètika chronika* 12, 180–299

Amiran, R. B. K. (1969) *Ancient Pottery of the Holy Land: from its beginnings in the Neolithic Period to the end of the Iron Age.* Jerusalem, Masada Press

Ampolo, C. (1980) *La formazione della città nel Lazio: seminario tenuto a Roma, 24–26 giugno 1977.* Dialoghi di Archeologia, 2 (n.s.). Rome, Alpha Print

Ampolo, C. (1997) L'interpretazione storica della più antica iscrizione del Lazio (dalla necropoli di Osteria dell'Osa, tomba 482). In G. Bartoloni, ed., *Le necropoli arcaiche di Veio: giornata di studio in memoria di Massimo Pallottino*, 211–18. Rome, Università degli studi di Roma 'La Sapienza'

Anati, E. (1959) Excavations at the Cemetery of Tell Abu Hawam. *'Atiqot* 2, 89–102

Andreadaki Vlasaki, M. and Papadopoulou, E. (2005) The Habitation at Khamalevri, Rethymnon, during the 12th Century

BCE. In A. L. D'Agata and J. Moody, eds., *Ariadne's Threads: connections between Crete and the Greek mainland in the post-palatial period*, 353–97. Athens, Italian School at Athens

Anthony, D. (1997) Prehistoric Migration as Social Process. In J. Chapman and H. Hamerow, eds., *Migrations and Invasions in Archaeological Explanation*, 21–32. BAR International Series, 664. Oxford, Archaeopress

Aravantinos, V. (2000) Νέα μυκηναϊκά ελεφαντουργήματα από την Καδμεία (Θήβα). In V. Aravantinos, ed., *Επετηρίς της Εταιρείας Βοιωτικών Μελετών, τόμος Γ', τεύχος α', Αρχαιολογία, Γ' Διεθνές Συνέδριο Βοιωτικών Μελετών, Θήβα 4–8 Σεπτ, 1996*, 45–110. Athens

Arnaud, D. (1998) Hazor a la fin de l'age du Bronze d'apres un document meconnu: RS 20.225. *Aula Orientalis* 16, 27–35

Arnold, D. E. (1985) *Ceramic Theory and Cultural Process*. Cambridge, Cambridge University Press

Artzy, M. (1985) Merchandise and Merchantmen: on ships and shipping in the Late Bronze Age Levant. In T. Papadopoullos and S. Chatzestyllis, eds., *Acts of the Second International Cyprological Congress*, 135–40. Nicosia, A. G. Leventis Foundation

Artzy, M. (1988) Development of War/Fighting Boats of the IInd Millennium B.C. in the Eastern Mediterranean. *Report of the Department of Antiquities of Cyprus*, 181–6

Artzy, M. (1994) Incense, Camels and Collard Rim Jars: desert trade routes and maritime outlets in the second millennium. *Oxford Journal of Archaeology* 13.2, 121–47

Artzy, M. (1997) Nomads of the Sea. In S. Swiny *et al.*, eds., *Res Maritimae: Cyprus and the eastern Mediterranean from prehistory to late antiquity*, 1–16. American Schools of Oriental Research Archaeological Reports, 4; Cyprus American Archaeological Research Institute Monograph Series, 1. Atlanta, American School of Oriental Research

Artzy, M. (1998) Routes, Trade, Boats and 'Nomads of the Sea'. In S. Gitin *et al.*, eds., *Mediterranean Peoples in Transition: thirteenth to early tenth centuries BCE*, 439–48. Jerusalem, Israel Exploration Society

Artzy, M. (2006) *The Jatt Metal Hoard in Northern Canaanite/ Phoenician and Cypriote Context*. Cuadernos de arqueología mediterránea, 14. Barcelona, Publicaciones del Laboratorio de Arqueología de la Universidad Pompeu Fabra de Barcelona

Aschenbrenner, S. (1972) A Contemporary Community. In W. A. McDonald and G. R. Rapp, eds., *The Minnesota Messenia Expedition: reconstructing a Bronze Age regional environment*, 47–63. Minneapolis, University of Minnesota Press

Aslan, C. (2002) Ilion Before Alexander: protogeometric, geometric and archaic pottery from D9. *Studia Troica* 12, 81–130

Aslan, C. and Basedow, M. (in final preparation) *The Early Iron Age Sanctuary at Troy*. Stuttgart, Verlag Philipp von Zabern

Aston, D. A. (1996) *Egyptian Pottery of the Late New Kingdom and the Third Intermediate Period (Twelfth–Seventh Centuries BC): tentative footsteps in a forbidden terrain*. Studien zur Archäologie und Geschichte Altägyptens, 13. Heidelberg, Heidelberger Orientverlag

Aston, D. A. and Pusch, E. B. (1999) The Pottery from the Royal Horse Stud and its Stratigraphy: the Pelizaeus Museum excavation at Qantir/Per-Ramesses, Sector Q IV. *Ägypten und Levante* 9, 39–76

Attema, P., ed. (2004) *Centralization, Early Urbanisation and Colonization in First Millennium B.C. Italy and Greece*. Babesch Supplementa, 9. Leuven, Peeters

Aubet, M. E. (2001) *The Phoenicians and the West: politics, colonies and trade. Translated from the Spanish by Mary Turton*. Cambridge, Cambridge University Press

Aubet, M. E., ed. (2003) *The Phoenician cemetery of Tyre-Al Bass: excavations 1997–1999*. Beirut, Minstère de la culture, Direction Générale des Antiquités

Aura-Jorro, F. (1985–93) *Diccionario micénico (D Mic.)*, 2 vols. Diccionario griego-español. Madrid, Consejo Superior de Investigaciones Científicas, Instituto de Filología

Avila, R. (1980) Die Keramischen Befunde. In R. Avila, ed., *Tiryns IX, Grabungen in der Unterburg 1971*, 9–85. Mainz-am-Rhein, Philipp von Zabern

Baboula, E. (2000) 'Buried' Metal in Late Minoan Inheritance Customs. In C. F. E. Pare, ed., *Metals Make the World Go Round: the supply and circulation of metals in Bronze Age Europe*, 70–81. Oxford, Oxbow Books

Bachhuber, C. (2006) Aegean Interest on the Uluburun Ship. *American Journal of Archaeology* 110.3, 345–63

Badre, L. (2003) Handmade Burnished Ware and Contemporary Imported Pottery from Tell Kazel. In N. C. Stampolidis and V. Karageorghis, eds., *Πλόες: Sea Routes. Interconnections in the Mediterranean 16th–6th C. BC*, 83–99. Athens, Museum of Cycladic Art

Bakr, M. I. (1992) *Tell Basta I: tombs and burial customs at Bubastis. The area of the so-called western cemetery*. Cairo, Egyptian Antiquities Organisation Press

Balfet, H. (1965) Ethnographic Observations in North Africa and Archaeological Interpretations: the pottery of the Maghreb. In F. R. Matson, ed., *Ceramics and Man*, 161–77. Chicago, Aldine Pub. Co.

Bankoff, H. A., Meyer, N. and Stefanovich, M. (1996) Handmade Burnished Ware and the Late Bronze Age of the Balkans. *Journal of Mediterranean Archaeology* 9.2, 193–209

Bar-Matthews, M., Ayalon, A., Gilmour, M., Matthews, A. and Hawkesworth, C. J. (2003) Sea–Land Oxygen Isotopic Relationships from Planktonic Foraminifera and Speleothems in the Eastern Mediterranean Region and their Implication for Paleorainfall during Interglacial Intervals. *Geochimica et Cosmochimica Acta* 67.3, 181–99

Barako, T. J. (2000) The Philistine Settlement as Mercantile Phenomenon? *American Journal of Archaeology* 104, 513–30

Baramki, D. C. (1959) A Late Bronze Age Tomb at Sarafend Ancient Sarepta. *Berytus* 12.2, 129–42

Barnett, R. D. (1975) The Sea Peoples. In I. E. S. Edwards *et al.*, eds., *The Cambridge Ancient History, vol. II, part 2*, 359–78. Cambridge, Cambridge University Press

Barth, F. (1969) Introduction. In F. Barth, ed., *Ethnic Groups and Boundaries: the social organization of culture difference*, 9–38. Boston, Little Brown

Bartoloni, G. (2000) Le origini e la diffusione della cultura villanoviana. In M. Torelli, ed., *Gli Etruschi*, 1, 53–71. Milan, Bompiani

Bartoloni, G. and Delpino, F., eds. (2005) *Oriente e Occidente: metodi e discipline a confronto, riflessioni sulla cronologia dell'età del Ferro in Italia. Atti dell'Incontro di studi, Roma, 30–31 ottobre, 2003*. Mediterranea, 1. Pisa, Isittuti editoriali e poligrafici internazionali

Bartoněk, A. (2003) *Handbuch des mykenischen Griechisch.* Indogermanische Bibliothek, Erste Reihe, Lehr- und Handbücher. Heidelberg, Universitätsverlag C. Winter

Basedow, M. (2007) Troy Without Homer, the Bronze Age–Iron Age Transition in the Troad. In R. Laffineur and S. P. Morris, eds., *EPOS: Reconsidering Greek Epic and Aegean Bronze Age Archaeology. Proceedings of the 11th International Aegean Conference, Los Angeles, UCLA – The J. Paul Getty Villa, 20–23 April 2006*, 49–58, pls. III–VII. Aegaeum, 28. Liège, Université de Liège

Basedow, M. (in press) What the Blind Man Saw: new information from the Iron Age at Troy. *Acta of the 16th International Congress on Classical Archaeology, Boston, August 2002.* Boston, Brown

Bass, G. F., ed. (1967) *Cape Gelidonya: a Bronze Age shipwreck.* Transactions of the American Philosophical Society, 57 (n.s.). Philadelphia, American Philosophical Society

Bauer, A. A. (1998) Cities of the Sea: maritime trade and the origin of Philistine settlement in the Early Iron Age southern Levant. *Oxford Journal of Archaeology* 17, 149–68

Bayne, N. (2000) *The Grey Wares of North-West Anatolia.* Bonn, Rudolf Habelt

Beck, P. (1989) Stone Ritual Artifacts and Statues from Areas A and H. In A. Ben-Tor, ed., *Hazor III–IV*. Jerusalem, The Israel Exploration Society

Becks, R., Rigter, W. and Hnila, P. (2006) Das Terrassenhaus im Westlichen Unterstadtviertel von Troia. *Studia Troica* 16, 27–88

Belardelli, C. and Bettelli, M. (1999) La Raum 127 dell'Unterburg di Tirinto: distribuzione della ceramica pseudominia e HMB. In V. La Rosa *et al.*, eds., *Επί πόντον πλαζόμενοι: simposio italiano di studi egei, dedicato a Luigi Bernabò Brea e Giovanni Pugliese Carratelli. Roma, 18–20 febbraio 1998*, 473–4. Rome, Scuola archeologica italiana di Atene

Bell, C. (2005) Wheels Within Wheels? A view of Mycenaean trade from the Levantine emporia. In R. Laffineur and E. Greco, eds., *Emporia: Aegeans in the central and eastern Mediterranean. Proceedings of the 10th international Aegean conference, Athens, Italian School of Archaeology, 14–18 April 2004*, 363–370. Aegaeum, 25. Liège, Université de Liège

Bell, C. (2006) *The Evolution of Long Distance Trading Relationships across the LBA/Iron Age Transition on the Northern Levantine Coast: crisis, continuity and change. A study based on imported ceramics, bronze and its constituent metals.* BAR International Series, 1574. Oxford, Archaeopress

Belli, P. (1997) Architecture as Craftsmanship: LM III Tholoi and their builders. In R. Laffineur and P. P. Betancourt, eds., *Τεξνη: craftsmen, craftswomen and craftsmanship in the Aegean Bronze Age. Proceedings of the 6th International Aegean Conference/6e rencontre égéenne internationale, Philadelphia, Temple University, 18–21 April 1996*, 251–56. Aegaeum, 16. Liège and Austin, Université de Lige and the University of Texas at Austin

Belli, P. (2006) Some Architectural Features of the Thalos Tombs at Kritsà-Lakkoi (Eastern Crete). In *Atti del 9° Congresso Internatzionale*, 271–81. Societa di Studi Storei Cretesi, Iraklion

Ben-Ami, D. (2001) The Iron I at Tel Hazor in light of the Renewed Excavations. *Israel Exploration Journal* 51, 148–70

Ben-Ami, D. (2006) Early Iron Age Cult Places: new evidence from Tel Hazor. *Tel-Aviv* 33, 121–33

Ben-Shlomo, D. and Dothan, T. (2006) Ivories from Philistia: filling the Iron Age I gap. *Israel Exploration Journal* 56.1, 1–38

Ben-Tor, A., ed. (1989) *Hazor III–IV: an account of the third and fourth seasons of excavation, 1957–1958. Text.* Jerusalem, Israel Exploration Society

Ben-Tor, A. (1998) The Fall of Canaanite Hazor: the 'who' and 'when' questions. In S. Gitin *et al.*, eds., *Mediterranean Peoples in Transition: thirteenth to early tenth centuries BCE*, 456–67. Jerusalem, Israel Exploration Society

Ben-Tor, A. (2006) The Sad Fate of Statues and the Mutilated Statues of Hazor. In S. Gitin *et al.*, eds., *Confronting the Past: archaeological and historical essays on Ancient Israel in honor of William G. Dever*, 3–16. Winona Lake, Eisenbrauns

Ben-Tor, A. and Rubiato, M. T. (1999) Excavating Hazor: did the Israelites destroy the Canaanite city? *Biblical Archaeology Review* 25, 22–39

Bennet, J. (1985) The Structure of the Linear B Administration at Knossos. *American Journal of Archaeology* 89, 231–49

Bennett, E. L. (1950) Fractional Quantities in Minoan Bookkeeping. *American Journal of Archaeology* 54, 204–22

Bennett, E. L. (1956) The Landholders of Pylos. *American Journal of Archaeology* 60, 103–33

Bennett, E. L. (1987) To Take the Measure of Mycenaean Measures. In J. T. Killen *et al.*, eds., *Studies in Mycenaean and Classical Greek Presented to John Chadwick*, 89–95. Minos, 20–2. Salamanca, Universidad de Salamanca

Benzi, M. (1982) Tombe Micenee di Rodi riutilizzate nel TE III C. *Studi Micenei ed Egeo Anatolici* 23, 323–35

Benzi, M. (1992) *Rodi e la civiltà micenea*, 2 vols. Rome, Gruppo editoriale internazionale

Benzi, M. (1996) Problems of the Mycenaean expansion in the South-eastern Aegean. In E. de Miro *et al.*, eds., *Atti e memorie del secondo Congresso internazionale di micenologia, Roma-Napoli, 14–20 ottobre 1991* 3, 947–78. Rome, Gruppo Editoriale Internazionale

Bernabò Brea, L. (1990) *Pantalica: ricerche intorno all'anaktoron.* Cahiers du Centre Jean Bérard, 14. Naples, Centre Jean Bérard – Istituto di Studi Acrensi

Bernabò Brea, L. and Albanese Procelli, R. M. (1982) Calascibetta (Enna): la necropoli di Cozzo S. Giuseppe in contrada Realmese. *Notizie e Scavi di antichità*, 425–632

Bernabò Brea, L., Cavalier, M. and Belli, P. (1990) La tholos termale di San Calogero nell'isola di Lipari. *Studi Micenei ed Egeo-Anatolici* 28, 7–84

Bernabò Brea, L., Cavalier, M., Taylour, L. W. and D'Angelo, F. (1980) *Meligunìs-Lipára 4: l'acropoli di Lipari nella preistoria.* Palermo, S. F. Flaccovio

Bernabò Brea, M., Cavalier, M. and Bernabò Brea, L. (2002) *In memoria di Luigi Bernabò Brea.* Palermo, Mario Grispo

Beschi, L. (2005) Libagioni funerarie ctonie. In M. Sapelli Ragni, ed., *Studi di archeologia in memoria di Liliana Mercando*, 33–41. Turin, Soprintendenza per i beni archeologici del Piemonte e del Museo antichità egizie

Bettelli, M. (1997) *Roma: la città prima della città: i tempi di una nascita. La cronologia delle sepolture ad inumazione di Roma e del Lazio nella prima età del ferro.* Rome, 'L'Erma' di Bretschneider

Bettelli, M. (2002) *Italia meridionale e mondo miceneo: ricerche su dinamiche di acculturazione e aspetti archeologici, con particolare riferimento ai versanti adriatico e ionico della penisola italiana*. Grandi contesti e problemi della protostoria italiana, 5. Florence, All'Insegna del Giglio

Bienert, H.-D. and Reinhold, G. G. (1989) *Frühe Eisenfunde in Palästina-Syrien*. Murrhardt/Baden-Württemberg

Bienkowski, P. (1989) Prosperity and Decline in LBA Canaan. *Bulletin of the American Schools of Oriental Research* 275, 59–63

Bietak, M. (1984) Ramsesstadt. In W. Helck and W. Westendorf, eds., *Lexikon der Ägyptologie* V, 128–46. Wiesbaden, Otto Harrassowitz

Bietak, M. (1993) The Sea Peoples at the End of the Egyptian Administration in Canaan. In A. Biran and J. Aviram, eds., *Biblical Archaeology Today, 1990: proceedings of the Second International Congress on Biblical Archaeology*, 292–306. Jerusalem, Israel Exploration Society

Bieti Sestieri, A. M. (1996) *Protostoria – Teoria and Pratica*. Rome, Studi Superiori NIS

Bikai, P. M. (1978) *The Pottery of Tyre*. Warminster, Aris and Phillips

Bikai, P. M. (1983) The Imports from the East. In V. Karageorghis, ed., *Palaepaphos-Skales: an Iron Age cemetery in Cyprus* 1, 396–406. Konstanz, Universitätsverlag Konstanz

Bikai, P. M. (1987) Trade Networks of the Early Iron Age: the Phoenicians at Palaepaphos. In D. W. Rupp, ed., *Western Cyprus Connections: an archaeological symposium held at Brock University, St. Catharines, Ontario, Canada, March 21–22 1986*, 125–128. Studies in Mediterranean Archaeology, 77. Göteborg, Paul Åströms Förlag

Bintliff, J. and Snodgrass, A. M. (1985) The Cambridge/Bradford Boeotian Expedition: the first four years. *Journal of Field Archaeology* 12, 123–61

Biondi, G. (in press) Ricostruire un legame perduto: elementi di tradizione cretese nella cultura funeraria siceliota di età arcaica. *Atti del Convegno di Studi 'Identità culturale, etnicità, processi di trasformazione a Creta fra Dark Age ed Arcaismo' (Atene, 9–12 novembre 2006)*

Birch, S. (1858) *Mémoire sur une Patère égyptienne du Musée du Louvre*, Mémoires de la Société impériale des antiquaires de France [Offprint]

Bisi, A. M. (1988) Modalità e aspetti degli scambi fra oriente ed occidente fenicio in età precoloniale. In E. Acquaro *et al.*, eds., *Momenti precoloniali nel Mediterraneo antico: questioni di metodo, aree d'indagine, evidenze a confronto*, 205–26. Collezione di studi fenici, 28. Rome, Consiglio nazionale delle ricerche

Bjorkman, J. K. (1999) How to Bury a Temple: the case of Nuzi's Ishtar Temple A. In D. I. Owen and G. Wilhelm, eds., *Studies on the Civilization and Culture of Nuzi and the Hurrians*, 103–22. Bethesda, CDL Press

Blegen, C. W., Caskey, J. L. and Rawson, M. (1953) *Troy: excavations conducted by the University of Cincinnati, 1932–1938. Vol. III, the Sixth Settlement*. Princeton, Princeton University Press

Blegen, C. W., Caskey, J. L., Rawson, M. and Boulter, C. G. (1958) *Troy: excavations conducted by the University of Cincinnati, 1932–1938. Vol. IV, Settlements VIIa, VIIb, and VIII*. Princeton, Princeton University Press

Blegen, C. W. and Rawson, M. (1966) *The Palace of Nestor at Pylos in Western Messenia. Vol. 1: the buildings and their contents*. Princeton, University Press (University of Cincinnati)

Blegen, C. W. and Rawson, M. (1973) *The Palace of Nestor at Pylos in Western Messenia. Vol. 3: Acropolois and Lower Town, Tholoi, Grave Circle, and Chamber Tombs, Discoveries Outside the Citadel*. Princeton, University Press (University of Cincinnati)

Bloch-Smith, E. (1992) *Judahite Burial Practices and Beliefs about the Dead*. JSOT/ASOR monograph series, 7. Sheffield, Sheffield Academic Press

Bloedow, E. F. (1985) Handmade Burnished Ware or 'Barbarian' Pottery and Troy VIIB. *La Parola del Passato. Rivista di Studi Antichi* 40, 161–99

Blomberg, M. and Henriksson, G. (2001) Differences in Minoan and Mycenaean Orientations in Crete. In C. L. N. Ruggles *et al.*, eds., *Astronomy, cosmology and landscape: proceedings of the SEAC 98 Meeting, Dublin, Ireland, September 1998*, 72–91. Bognor Regis, Ocarina

Boardman, J. and Hammond, N. G. L., eds. (1982) *The Cambridge Ancient History, 2nd ed., vol. III, part 3: The Expansion of the Greek World, Eighth to Sixth Centuries B.C.* Cambridge, Cambridge University Press

Bond, G., Kromer, B., Beer, J., Muscheler, R., Evans, M. N., Showers, W., Hoffmann, S., Lotti-Bond, R., Hajdas, I. and Bonani, G. (2001) Persistent Solar Influence on North Atlantic Climate During the Holocene. *Science*, 2,130–36

Bondì, S. F. (1988) Problemi della precolonizzazione fenicia nel Mediterraneo centro-occidentale. In E. Acquaro *et al.*, eds., *Momenti precoloniali nel Mediterraneo antico: questioni di metodo, aree d'indagine, evidenze a confronto*, 243–55. Collezione di studi fenici, 28. Rome, Consiglio nazionale delle ricerche

Borgna, E. (1997) Kitchen-Ware from LM III C Phaistos: cooking traditions and ritual activities in LBA Cretan societies. *Studi micenei ed egeo-anatolici* 39.1, 189–217

Borgna, E. (2003) Regional Settlement Patterns, Exchange Systems and Sources of Power in Crete at the End of the Late Bronze Age: establishing a connection. *Studi Micenei ed Egeo-Anatolici* 45, 153–83

Borgna, E. (2004) *Il complesso di ceramica tardominoico III dell'Acropoli mediana di Festòs*. Studi di archeologia cretese, 3. Padua, Bottega d'Erasmo

Boulotis, C. (1990) Villes et Palais dans l'art Egeen du IIe Millenaire AV.J.-C. In P. Darcque and R. Treuil, eds., *L'habitat égéen préhistorique. Actes de la table ronde internationale, Athènes, 23–25 juin 1987, organisés par le Centre National de la Recherche Scientifique, l'Université de Paris et l'École française d'Athènes*, 422–58. Athens, École française d'Athènes

Bounni, A., Lagarce, J. and Lagarce, É. (1998) *Ras Ibn Hani, I: le palais nord du bronze récent: fouilles 1979–1995, synthèse préliminaire*. Beirut, Institute Français d'Archéologie du Proche-Orient

Bourdieu, P. (1987) *Die feinen Unterschiede: Kritik der gesellschaftlichen Urteilskraft*. Frankfurt, Suhrkamp

Bourke, S. J. (2006) The Transition from the Bronze to the Iron

Age in the East Jordan Valley: a view from the margins. Unpublished paper presented at *Forces of Transformation: the end of the Bronze Age in the Mediterranean, St John's College, Oxford, 25–6 March 2006*

Bouzek, J. (1985) *The Aegean, Anatolia and Europe: cultural interrelations in the second millennium B. C.* Studies in Mediterranean Archaeology, 29. Göteborg, Paul Åströms Forlag

Boysal, Y. (1967) New Excavations in Caria. *Anadolu (Anatolia)* 11, 31–56

Braun, D. P. (1995) Style, Selection and Historicity. In C. Carr and J. E. Neitzel, eds., *Style, Society and Person: archaeological and ethnological perspectives*, 123–41. London and New York, Plenum Press

Braunstein, S. L. (1998) *The Dynamics of Power in an Age of Transition: an analysis of the mortuary remains of Tell el-Far'ah (South) in the Late Bronze and Early Iron Ages.* Unpublished PhD thesis, Columbia University

Brissaud, P. (1987a) Les fouilles du secteur de la Nécropole Royale (1984–1986). In P. Brissaud, ed., *Cahiers de Tanis* 1, 7–43. Paris, Recherche sur les Civilisations

Brissaud, P. (1987b) Les prétendus sacrifices humains de Tanis. In P. Brissaud, ed., *Cahiers de Tanis* 1, 129–44. Paris, Recherche sur les Civilisations

Brogan, T. and Barnard, K. (in preparation) Household Archaeology at Mochlos: statistical recipes from the LM I kitchen. In K. Glowacki and N. Vogeikoff-Brogan, eds., *STEGA: the archaeology of houses and households in Ancient Crete from the Neolithic period through the Roman era, 26–28 May 2005, Ierapetra*

Bruins, H. J. and Van Der Plicht, J. (1996) The Exodus Enigma. *Nature* 382, 213–14

Bruno, N., Nicoletti, F. and Tusa, S. (in press) Resoconto preliminare degli scavi dell'insediamento del tardo Bronzo di Mokarta. *Dai Ciclopi agli Ecisti: società e territorio nella Sicilia preistorica e protostorica, XLI Riunione Scientifica dell'I.I.P.P.*

Buccellato, C. and Tusa, S. (in press) Analisi quantitativa e distribuzione funzionale dei reperti dell'insediamento della tarda età del Bronzo di Mokarta. *Dai Ciclopi agli Ecisti: società e territorio nella Sicilia preistorica e protostorica, XLI Riunione Scientifica dell'I.I.P.P.*

Buchholz, H.-G. (1967) The Cylinder Seal. In G. F. Bass, ed., *Cape Gelidonya: a Bronze Age shipwreck*, 148–59. Transactions of the American Philosophical Society, 57 (n.s.). Philadelphia, American Philosophical Society

Bunimovitz, S. (1994) The Problem of Human Resources in Late Bronze Age Palestine and its Socioeconomic Implications. *Ugarit-Forschungen* 26, 1–20

Bunimovitz, S. (1995) On the Edge of Empires: Late Bronze Age (1500–1200 BCE). In T. E. Levy, ed., *The Archaeology of Society in the Holy Land*, 320–31. London, Leicester University Press

Burford, A. (1993) *Land and Labor in the Greek World.* Ancient Society and History. Baltimore and London, Johns Hopkins University Press

Buxeda I Garrigós, J., Jones, R. E., Kilikoglou, V. T. L. S., Maniatis, Y., Mitchell, J., Vagnetti, L., Wardle, K. A. and Andreou, S. (2003) Technology Transfer at the Periphery of the Mycenaean World: the cases of Mycenaean pottery found in central Macedonia (Greece) and the plain of Sybaris (Italy). *Archaeometry* 45.2, 263–84

Cacho, I., Grimalt, J. O., Canals, M., Sbaffi, L., Shackleton, N. J., Schönfeld, J. and Zahn, R. (2001) Variability of the Western Mediterranean Sea Surface Temperatures during the Last 25,000 Years and its Connection with the Northern Hemisphere Climatic Changes. *Paleoceanography* 16, 40–52

Cacho, I., Grimalt, J. O., Pelejero, C., Canals, M., Sierro, F. J., Flores, J. A. and Shackleton, N. J. (1999) Dansgaard-Oeschger and Heinrich Event Imprints in Alboran Sea Paleotemperature. *Paleoceanography* 14, 698–705

Cacho, I., Grimalt, J. O., Sierro, F. J., Shackleton, N. J. and Canals, M. (2000) Evidence of Enhanced Mediterranean Thermohaline Circulation during Rapid Climate Coolings. *Earth and Planetary Science Letters* 183, 417–29

Cadogan, G. (1967) Late Minoan III C Pottery from the Kephala Tholos near Knossos. *Annual of the British School at Athens* 62, 257–65

Cadogan, G. (1992) Karphi. In J. W. Myers *et al.*, eds., *The Aerial Atlas of Ancient Crete*, 116–19. London, Thames and Hudson

Cadogan, G. (2007) Water management in Minoan Crete, Greece: the two cisterns of one Middle Bronze Age settlement. *Water Science and Technology: Water Supply* 7.1, 103–11

Calderone, S. (1968) Terminologia catastale e diritto successorio nel mondo miceneo. *Atti e memorie del 1° Congresso Internazionale di Micenologia, Roma 27 settembre–3 ottobre 1967* 3, 1,109–13. Rome, Ed. dell'Ateneo

Carafa, P. (1996) Roma, II: preistoria e protostoria. *Enciclopedia dell'arte antica, classica e orientale* 6, 790–802. Rome, Istituto della Enciclopedia italiana

Carafa, P. (1997) La 'grande Roma dei Tarquini' e la città romuleo-numana. *Bullettino della Commissione Archeologica Comunale di Roma* 97, 7–34

Carafa, P. (2004) L'Aedes e il Vicus di Vesta. I reperti. *Workshop di Archeologia classica: paesaggi, costruzioni, reperti* 1, 135–43

Carafa, P. (2005) Il Volcanal e il Comizio. *Workshop di Archeologia classica: paesaggi, costruzioni, reperti* 2, 135–49

Carandini, A. (1997) *La nascita di Roma: dei, Lari, eroi e uomini all'alba di una civiltà.* Turin, Einaudi

Carandini, A. (2004) *Palatino, Velia e Sacra Via: paesaggi urbani attraverso il tempo.* Workshop di Archeologia classica, 1. Rome, Edizioni dell'Ateneo

Carandini, A. (2007) *Roma, il primo giorno.* Rome, Editori Laterza

Carandini, A. and Carafa, P., eds. (1995) *Palatium e Sacra Via*, 2 vols. Bollettino di Archeologia, 31–4. Rome, Istituto Poligrafico e Zecca dello Stato

Cardosa, M. (1993) Gli assetti territoriali protovillanoviano e villanoviano alla luce dei modelli dell'archeologia spaziale. In N. Negroni Catacchio, ed., *Preistoria e protostoria in Etruria*, 261–8. Milan, Centro studi sulla preistoria e archeologia

Carpenter, M. (1983) *ki-ti-me-me-na* and *ke-ke-me-na* at Pylos. *Minos* 18, 81–8

Carrier, J. and Heyman, J. M. (1997) Consumption and Political Economy. *Journal of the Royal Anthropological Institute* 3 (n.s.), 355–73

Carter, J. C. (2006) *Discovering the Greek Countryside at*

Metaponto. Jerome Lectures, 23rd series. Ann Arbor, University of Michigan

Casford, J. S. L., Abu-Zied, R., Rohling, E. J., Cooke, S., Boessenkool, K. P., Brinkhuis, H., De Vries, C., Wefer, G., Geraga, M., Papatheodorou, G., Croudace, I., Thomson, J., Wells, N. C. and Lykousis, V. (2001) Mediterranean Climate Variability during the Holocene. *Mediterranean Marine Science* 2, 45–55

Casford, J. S. L., Rohling, E. J., Abu-Zied, R. H., Cooke, S., Fontanier, C., Leng, M. and Lykousis, V. (2002) Circulation Changes and Nutrient Concentrations in the Late Quaternary Aegean Sea: a non-steady state concept for sapropel formation. *Paleoceanography* 17, 1,024–40

Casford, J. S. L., Rohling, E. J., Abu-Zied, R. H., Jorissen, F. J., Leng, M. and Thomson, J. (2003) A Dynamic Concept for Eastern Mediterranean Circulation and Oxygenation during Sapropel Formation. *Palaeogeography, Palaeoclimatology, Palaeoecology* 190, 103–19

Caskey, J. L. (1933–36) *University of Cincinnati Troy Excavations Field Notebooks 1933, 1934, 1935, and 1936*, from the Troy Excavation Archive, University of Cincinnati

Castellana, G. (2000) *La cultura del Medio Bronzo nell'agrigentino ed i rapporti con il mondo miceneo.* Pubblicazione (Istituto 'Luigi Sturzo'), 5. Palermo, Assessorato Regionale Culturali Ambientali e della pubblica Istruzione della Regione Siciliana

Castellana, G., Marazzi, M., Pitrone, A. and Licata, P. (1998) *Il santuario castellucciano di Monte Grande e l'approvvigionamento dello zolfo nel Mediterraneo nell'eta del bronzo.* Quaderni (Museo archeologico nazionale Agrigento), 4. Agrigento, Regione Sicilia

Catling, H. W. (1964) *Cypriot Bronzework in the Mycenaean World.* Oxford Monographs on Classical Archaeology. Oxford, Clarendon Press

Catling, H. W. (1995) Heroes Returned? Subminoan burials from Crete. In J. B. Carter and S. P. Morris, eds., *The Ages of Homer: a tribute to Emily Townsend Vermeule*, 123–36. Austin, University of Texas Press

Catling, R. W. V. (1998) The Typology of the Proto Geometric and Sub Protogeometric Pottery from Troia and its Aegean Context. *Studia Troica* 8, 151–87

Catling, R. W. V. and Lemos, I. S. (1990) *Lefkandi II: the Protogeometric building at Toumba. Part I: the pottery.* British School at Athens Supplement, 22. London, Thames and Hudson

Cavalier, M. (1960) Les cultures préhistoriques des îles Éoliennes et leur rapport avec le monde égéen. *Bulletin de correspondance hellénique* 84, 319–46

Cavanagh, W. G. (1978) A Mycenaean Second Burial Custom? *Bulletin of the Institute for Classical Studies* 25, 171–2

Cavanagh, W. G. and Mee, C. (1978) The Re-use of Earlier Tombs in the LH IIIC Period. *Annual of the British School at Athens* 73, 31–44

Cavanagh, W. G. and Mee, C. (1998) *A Private Place: death in prehistoric Greece.* Studies in Mediterranean Archaeology, 125. Jonsered, Paul Åströms Förlag

Cazzella, A. (2001) Sviluppi verso l'urbanizzazione a Roma alla luce dei recenti scavi nel Giardino Romano. *Bullettino della Commissione Archeologica Comunale di Roma* 102, 265–8

Cazzella, A., Marazzi, M. and Tusa, S. (1991) *Vivara: centro commerciale mediterraneo dell'età del bronzo*, 2 vols. Ricerche di storia, epigrafia e archeologia mediterranea. Rome, Bagatto libri

Chabas, F. J. (1873) *Recherches pour servir a l'histoire de la XIXme dynastie et spécialement a celle des temps de l'Exode.* Chalon-sur-Saône, Imprimerie de J. Dejussieu

Chadwick, J. (1966) The Olive Oil Tablets of Knossos. In J. Chadwick and L. R. Palmer, eds., *Proceedings of the Cambridge Colloquium on Mycenaean Studies*, 26–32. Cambridge, Cambridge University Press

Champollion, J.-F. (1844–89) *Monuments de l'Égypte et de la Nubie: notices descriptives conformes aux manuscrits autographes / rédigés sur les lieux par Champollion le Jeune*, 2 vols. Paris, Firmin Didot frères

Christaller, W. (1933) *Central Places in Southern Germany. Translated from Die zentralen Orte in Suddeutschland by Carlisle W. Baskin (1966).* Englewood Cliffs, Prentice-Hall

Cierny, J., Stöllner, T. and Weisgerber, G. (2001) Ohne Zinn keine Bronzezeit. *Leibnitz* 1, 16–17

Clamer, C. (1986) The Dayan Collection: the stone vessels. *Israel Museum Journal* 5, 19–36

Clavel-Lévêque, M. (1999) Le territoire d'Agde grecque: histoire et structures. In M. Brunet, ed., *Territoires des cités grecques: actes de la table ronde internationale organisée par l'École Française d'Athènes, 31 octobre–3 novembre 1991*, 177–97. Bulletin de correspondance hellénique, supplément 34. Athens, École française d'Athènes

Cline, E. H. (1994) *Sailing the Wine-Dark Sea: international trade and the Late Bronze Age Aegean.* BAR International Series, 591. Oxford, Tempus Reparatum

Cocchi Genick, D. (1995) *Aspetti culturali della media età del bronzo nell'Italia centro-meridionale.* Florence, Octavo

Cocchi Genick, D. (1998) *L'antica età del bronzo nell'Italia centrale: profilo di un'epoca e di un'appropriata strategia metodologica.* Florence, Octavo

Cocchi Genick, D., ed. (2004) *L'età del bronzo recente in Italia: atti del Congresso nazionale di Lido di Camaiore, 26–29 ottobre 2000.* Viareggio, Mauro Baroni Editore

Cochavi-Rainey, Z. and Lilyquist, C. (1999) *Royal Gifts in the Late Bronze Age, Fourteenth to Thirteenth Centuries B.C.E.: selected texts recording gifts to royal personages.* Beer-Sheva, 13. Beer-Sheva, Ben-Guryon University of the Negev Press

Cohen-Weinberger, A. (1998) Petrographic Analysis of the Egyptian Forms from Stratum VI at Tel Beth-Shean. In S. Gitin *et al.*, eds., *Mediterranean Peoples in Transition: thirteenth to early tenth centuries BCE*, 406–12. Jerusalem, Israel Exploration Society

Coldstream, J. N. and Catling, H. W. (1996) Knossos North Cemetery: early Greek Tombs. *Annual of the British School at Athens, supplementary volume* 28

Coldstream, J. N. (1990) The Greek Geometric Imports. In V. Karageorghis, ed., *Tombs at Palaepaphos: 1. Teratsudhia; 2. Eliomylia*, 150–3. Nicosia, A. G. Leventis Foundation

Constantin, S., Bojar, A. V., Lauritzen, S. E. and Lundberg, J. (2007) Holocene and Late Pleistocene Climate in the sub-Mediterranean Continental Environment: a speleothem record from Poleva Cave (Southern Carpathians, Romania). *Palaeogeography, Palaeoclimatology, Palaeoecology* 243, 322–38

Cook, K. (1981) The Purpose of the Stirrup Vase. *Annual of the British School at Athens* 76, 167

Cosmopoulos, M. B. (2006) The Political Landscape of Mycenaean States: *a-pu₂* and the Hither Province of Pylos. *American Journal of Archaeology* 110, 205–28

Costin, C. L. (1996) Craft Production and Mobilization Strategies in the Inka Empire. In B. Wailes, ed., *Craft Specialization and Social Evolution: in memory of V. Gordon Childe*, 211–25. Philadelphia, University of Pennsylvania

Coulson, W. D. E. (1997) The Late Minoan IIIC Period on the Kastro at Kavousi. In J. Driessen and A. Farnoux, eds., *La Crète Mycénienne: actes de la Table Ronde Internationale organisée par l'École française d'Athènes, 26–28 Mars 1991*, 59–72. Bulletin de correspondance hellénique, supplément 30. Athens and Paris, École française d'Athènes

Coulson, W. D. E. and Tsipopoulou, M. (1994) Preliminary Investigations at Chalasmenos, Crete, 1992–93. *Aegean Archaeology* 1, 65–97

Courtois, J.-C. (1984) Les poids de Pyla-Kokkinokremos: étude métrologique. In V. Karageorghis and M. Demas, eds., *Pyla-Kokkinokremos: a late 13th-century B.C. fortified settlement in Cyprus*, 85–6. Nicosia, Department of Antiquities

Courtois, J.-C. (1988) Les poids de Maa-Palaeokastro: étude métrologique. In V. Karageorghis and M. Demas, eds., *Excavations at Maa-Palaeokastro, 1979–1986* 1, 404–14. Nicosia, Department of Antiquities

Courtois, J.-C. (1990) Yabninu et le Palais Sud d'Ougarit. *Syria* 67, 103–42

Courtois, J.-C. and Courtois, L. (1978) Corpus céramique de Ras Shamra-Ugarit: niveaux historiques d'Ugarit, Bronze Moyen et Bronze Récent. In C. F.-A. Schaeffer, ed., *Ugaritica VII*, 191–370. Mission de Ras Shamra Tome XVIII. Leiden, Brill

Cox, D. H. (1932) *University of Cincinnati Troy Excavations Field Notebook 1932*, from the Troy Excavation Archive, University of Cincinnati

Crouwel, J. (1981) *Chariots and Other Means of Land Transport in Bronze Age Greece*. Allard Pierson Series, 3. Amsterdam, Allard Pierson Museum

Crouwel, J. and Morris, C. E. (1996) The Beginnings of Mycenaean Pictorial Vase Painting. *Archäologischer Anzeiger*, 197–219

Cucuzza, N. (2002) Osservazioni sui costumi funerari dell'area di Festòs ed Haghia Triada nel TM III A1–A2 iniziale. *Creta Antica* 3, 133–66

Cultraro, M. (1998) La cultura di Pantalica Nord in Sicilia nei suoi rapporti con il mondo egeo. In N. N. Catacchio, ed., *Protovillanoviani e/o Protoetruschi: ricerche e scavi. Atti del terzo incontro di studi, Manciano-Farnese, 12/14 maggio 1995*, 301–12. Florence, Octavo

Cultraro, M. (2005) Le relazioni tra Sicilia e penisola iberica in età postmicenea: una nota. In S. n. Celestino Pérez and J. Jiménez Ávila, eds., *El periodo orientalizante: actas del III Simposio Internacional de Arqueología de Mérida. Protohistoria del Mediterráneo occidental* 1, 97–106. Anejos de AEspA, 35. Mérida, Consejo Superior de Investigaciones Científicas, Instituto de Arqueología

Cunliffe, B. (2001) *Facing the Ocean: the Atlantic and its peoples, 8000 BC–1500 AD*. Oxford, Oxford University Press

Curtis, J., Weiss, H., Rosenmeir, M., Willis, K. and McCoy, F. (in preparation) Analyses of Two New Cores from Lake Kournas, Crete

D'Agata, A. L. (1986) Considerazioni su alcune spade siciliane della media e tarda età del bronzo. In M. Marazzi *et al.*, eds., *Traffici micenei nel Mediterraneo: problemi storici e documentazione archeologica. Atti del Convegno di Palermo (11–12 maggio e 3–6 dicembre 1984)*, 105–10. Magna Graecia, 3. Taranto, Istituto per la storia e l'archeologia della Magna Grecia

D'Agata, A. L. (1992) Late Minoan Crete and Horns of Consecration: a symbol in action. In R. Laffineur and J. L. Crowley, eds., *EIKON. Aegean Bronze Age Iconography: shaping a methodology. Proceedings of the 4th International Aegean Conference/4ᵉ Rencontre egénne internationale, University of Tasmania, Hobart, Australia 6–9 April 1992*, 247–56. Aegaeaum, 8. Liège, Université de Liège

D'Agata, A. L. (1997–2000) Ritual and Rubbish in Dark Age Crete: the settlement of Thronos/Kephala (ancient Sybrita) and the pre-Classical roots of a Greek city. *Aegean Archaeology* 4, 45–59

D'Agata, A. L. (1999) *Haghia Triada II: statuine minoiche e post-minoiche dai vecchi scavi di Haghia Triada (Creta)*. Monografie della Scuola Archeologica di Atene e delle Missioni Orientali in Oriente, 11. Padua, Bottega d'Erasmo

D'Agata, A. L. (2000) Interactions Between Aegean Groups and Local Communities in Sicily in the Bronze Age: the evidence from pottery. *Studi Micenei ed Egeo Anatolici* 42.1, 61–83

D'Agata, A. L. (2001) Religion, Society and Ethnicity on Crete at the End of the Late Bronze Age: the contextual framework of LM IIIC cult activities. In R. Laffineur and R. Hägg, eds., *Potnia: deities and religion in the Aegean Bronze Age. Proceedings of the 8th International Aegean Conference, Göteborg, Göteborg University, 12–15 April 2000*, 346–54. Aegaeum, 22. Liège, Université de Liège

Dakoronia, F. (1990) Warships on Sherds of LH III C Kraters from Kynos. In H. Tzalas, ed., *2nd International Symposium on Ship Construction in Antiquity, Delphi: proceedings*, 117–22. Tropis, 2. Athens, Hellenic Institute for the Preservation of Nautical Tradition

Dakoronia, F. (1996) Kynos Fleet. In H. Tzalas, ed., *4th International Symposium on Ship Construction in Antiquity, Center for the Acropolis Studies, Athens, 28, 29, 30, 31 August 1991: proceedings*, 159–71. Tropis, 4. Athens, Hellenic Institute for the Preservation of Nautical Tradition

Dakoronia, F. (1999a) Representations of Sea-Battles on Mycenaean Sherds from Kynos. In H. Tzalas, ed., *5th International Symposium on Ship Construction in Antiquity, Nauplia, 26, 27, 28 August 1993: proceedings*, 119–28. Tropis, 5. Athens, Hellenic Institute for the Preservation of Nautical Tradition

Dakoronia, F. (1999b) Νομός Φθιώτιδας: μέρος του μυκηναϊκού κόσμου ή της περιφέρειας του. *Η Περιφέρεια του Μυκηναϊκού Κόσμου*, 181–6. Lamia, Έκδοση ΙΔ Εφορείας Προϊστορικών και Κλασσικών Αρχαιοτήτων

Dakoronia, F. (2002) Further Finds from Kynos. In H. Tzalas, ed., *7th International Symposium on Ship Construction in Antiquity, Pylos, 26, 27, 28, 29 August 1999: proceedings*, 283–90. Tropis, 7. Athens, Hellenic Institute for the Preservation of Nautical Tradition

Dakoronia, F. (2003) The Transition from Late Helladic IIIC to the

Early Iron Age at Kynos. In S. Deger-Jalkotzy and M. Zavadil, eds., *LH IIIC Chronology and Synchronisms*, 37–51. Vienna, Österreichische Akademie der Wissenschaften pilosophisch-historische Klasse Denkscriften

Dakoronia, F., Kotoulas, D., Balta, E., Sithiakaki, V. and Tolias, J. (2002) *Λοκρίδα: ιστορία και πολιτισμός*. Athens, Κτήμα Χατζημιχάλη

Dakouri-Hild, A. (2001) The House of Kadmos in Mycenaean Thebes Reconsidered: architecture, chronology, and context. *The Annual of the British School at Athens* 96, 81–122

Damgaard Andersen, H., Horsnae, H. and Rathje, A., eds. (1997) *Urbanization in the Mediterranean in the 9th to 6th Centuries B.C.* Acta Hyperborea, 7. Copenhagen, Tusculanum Press

Daniilidou, D. (1998) *Η Οκτώσχημη Ασπίδα στο Αιγαίο της 2ης π. Χ. Χιλιετίας*. Athens, Ακαδημία Αθηνών. Κέντρο Ερεύνης Αρχαιότητας

Daux, G. (1960) Chronique des fouilles et découvertes archéologiques en Grèce en 1959. *Bulletin de correspondance hellénique* 84, 617–874

Davaras, C. (1973) Cremations in Minoan and Sub-Minoan Crete. *Antichità cretesi: studi in onore di Doro Levi*, 159–67. Cronache di archeologia, 12. Catania, Università di Catania, Istituto di archeologia

Daviau, P. M. (1993) *Houses and Their Furnishings in Bronze Age Palestine: domestic activity areas and artefact distribution in the Middle and Late Bronze Ages*. Sheffield, Sheffield Academic Press

Davies, S. (2004) Pylos Regional Archaeological Project, Part VI: administration and settlement in Venetian Navarino. *Hesperia* 73, 59–120

Day, L. (in preparation) Household Assemblages in LM IIIC Crete: the evidence from Karphi. In K. Glowacki and N. Vogeikoff-Brogan, eds., *STEGA: the archaeology of houses and households in Ancient Crete from the Neolithic period through the Roman era, 26–28 May 2005, Ierapetra*

Day, L., Glowacki, K. and Klein, N. C. (2000) Cooking and Dining at LM IIIC Vronda, Kavousi. *Πεπραγμένα Η' Διεθνούς Κρητολογικού Συνεδρίου, Ηράκλειο 9–14 Σεπτεμβρίου 1996*, Herakleion 1996, 115–25

Day, P. M. and Joyner, L. (2005) Coarseware Stirrup Jars from Cannatello, Sicily: new evidence from petrographic analysis. *Studi micenei ed egeo anatolici* 47, 309–14

De Cesare, M. and Gargini, M. (1997) Monte Finestrelle di Gibellina: nota preliminare sulla prima campagna di scavo. *Atti delle seconde giornate internazionali di studi sull'area elima*, 371–4. Pisa, Edizioni della Normale

De Fidio, P. (1977) *I dosmoi pilii a Poseidon: una terra sacra di età micenea*. Incunabula Graeca, 65. Rome, dell'Ateneo & Bizzarri

de Miro, E. (1988) Polizzello, centro della Sicania. *Quaderni di Archeologia dell'Università di Messina* 3, 25–41

de Miro, E. (1996) Recenti ritrovamenti micenei nell'Agrigentino e il villaggio di Cannatello. In E. de Miro et al., eds., *Atti e memorie del secondo Congresso internazionale di micenologia, Roma-Napoli, 14–20 ottobre 1991* 3, 995–1,011. Rome, Gruppo editoriale internazionale

de Miro, E. (1999) Un emporio miceneo sulla costa sud della Sicilia. In V. La Rosa et al., eds., *Επί πόντον πλαζόμενοι: simposio italiano di studi egei, dedicato a Luigi Bernabò Brea e Giovanni Pugliese Carratelli. Roma, 18–20 febbraio 1998*, 439–49. Rome, Scuola archeologica italiana di Atene

De Siena, A. (1986) Termitito. In M. Marazzi et al., eds., *Traffici micenei nel Mediterraneo: problemi storici e documentazione archeologica. Atti del Convegno di Palermo (11–12 maggio e 3–6 dicembre 1984)*, 41–54. Taranto, Istituto per la storia e l'archeologia della Magna Grecia

Deger-Jalkotzy, S. (1977) *Fremde Zuwanderer im spätmykenischen Griechenland. Zu einer Gruppe handgemachter Keramik aus den Mykenischen IIIC Siedlungsschichten von Aigeira*. Philosophisch-historische Klasse. Sitzungsberichte, 326. Vienna, Verlag der Osterreichischen Akademie der Wissenschaften

Deger-Jalkotzy, S. (1983) Das Problem der Handmade Burnished Ware von Mykenischen IIIC. In S. Deger-Jalkotzy, ed., *Griechenland, die Ägäis und die Levante während der 'Dark Ages' vom 12. bis zum 9. Jh. v. Chr.: Akten des Symposions von Stift Zwettl (NÖ) 11.–14. Oktober 1980*, 161–78. Veröffentlichungen der Kommission für mykenische Forschung, 10. Vienna, Verlag der Österreichischen Akademie der Wissenschaften

Deger-Jalkotzy, S. (1991a) Die Erforschung des Zusammenbruchs der sogenannten mykenischen Kultur und der sogenannten dunklen Jahrhunderte. In J. Latacz, ed., *Zweihundert Jahre Homer-Forschung: Rückblick und Ausblick*, 127–54. Colloquium Rauricum, 2. Stuttgart, B.G. Teubner

Deger-Jalkotzy, S. (1991b) Diskontinuität und Kontinuität: Aspekte politischer und sozialer Organisation in mykenischer Zeit und in der Welt der Homerischen Epen. In D. Musti et al., eds., *La transizione dal miceneo all'alto arcaismo: dal palazzo alla città. Atti del Convegno Internazionale, Roma, 14–19 Marzo 1988*, 53–66. Rome, Consiglio nazionale delle ricerche

Deger-Jalkotzy, S. (1995) Mykenische Herrschaftsformen ohne Paläste und die griechische Polis. In R. Laffineur and W.-D. Niemeier, eds., *Politeia I: society and state in the Aegean Bronze Age. Proceedings of the 5th International Aegean Conference, Heidelberg, 10–13 April 1994*, 367–77. Aegaeum, 12. Liège, Université de Liège

Deger-Jalkotzy, S. (1996) "Hier können wir Achäer nicht alle König sein". Zur Geschichte des frühgriechischen Königtums. In W. Leschhorn et al., eds., *Hellas und der griechische Osten: Studien zur Geschichte und Numismatik der griechischen Welt. Festschrift für Peter Robert Franke zum 70 Geburtstag*, 13–30. Saarbrücken, SDV Saarbrücker Druckerei und Verlag

Deger-Jalkotzy, S. (2003) Work in Progress: report on the 'End of the Mycenaean Civilization' project for the years of 1999–2001. In M. Bietak, ed., *The Synchronisation of Civilisations in the Eastern Mediterranean in the 2nd Millenium BCE (II). Proceedings of the SCIEM 2000 Euro-Conference, Schloß Haindorf, May 2–7, 2001*, 455–70. Contributions to the chronology of the Eastern Mediterranean, 4. Vienna, Verlag der Österreichischen Akademie der Wissenschaften

Deger-Jalkotzy, S. and Dakoronia, F. (1992) Elateia, die antike Phokis und das Ausklingen der mykenischen Kultur in Mittelgriechenland. *Archäologie Österreichs* 3, 67–71

Demakopoulou, K. (1968) Μυκηναϊκά αγγεία εκ θαλαμοειδών τάφων περιοχής Αγίου Ιωάννου Μονεμβασίας. *ΑΔ* 23 *Μελέτες*, 145–94

Demakopoulou, K., ed. (1988) *The Mycenaean World: five centuries of early Greek culture, 1600–1100 B. C.* Athens, Ministry of Culture, National Hellenic Committee (ICOM)

Demakopoulou, K., Eluère, C., Jensen, J., Jockenhövel, A. and Mohen, J.-P., eds. (1999) *Gods and Heroes of the European Bronze Age*. London, Thames and Hudson

Demakopoulou, K. and Konsola, D. (1981) *Αρχαιολογικό Μουσείο της Θήβας*. Athens, General Direction of Antiquities and Restoration

DeMarrais, E. (2004) The Materialization of Culture. In E. DeMarrais *et al.*, eds., *Rethinking Materiality: the engagement of mind with the material world*, 11–22. Cambridge, McDonald Institute for Archaeological Research

Deorsola, D. (1996) Il villaggio del Medio Bronzo di Cannatello presso Agrigento. In E. de Miro *et al.*, eds., *Atti e memorie del secondo Congresso internazionale di micenologia, Roma-Napoli, 14–20 ottobre 1991* 3, 1,029–38. Rome, Gruppo editoriale internazionale

Deoudi, M. (1999) *Heroenkulte in homerischer Zeit*. BAR International Series, 806. Oxford, Archaeopress

Deroy, L. and Gérard, M. (1965) *Le cadastre mycénien de Pylos*. Incunabula Graeca, 10. Rome, dell'Ateneo

Desborough, V. R. d'A. (1964) *The Last Mycenaeans and their Successors: an archaeological survey, c. 1200–c. 1000 B.C.* Oxford, Clarendon Press

Desborough, V. R. d'A. (1972) *The Greek Dark Ages*. London, Benn

di Fraia, T. (2000) I dolii di Archi e il problema dei grandi contenitori per derrate nel Bronzo Finale. In N. Negroni Catacchio, ed., *L' Etruria tra Italia, Europa e mondo mediterraneo, ricerche e scavi: atti del quarto incontro di studi, Manciano, Montalto di Castro, Valentano, 12–14 settembre 1997*, 161–70. Milan, Centro studi di preistoria e archeologia

di Gennaro, F. and Guidi, A. (2000) Il bronzo finale dell'Italia centrale. Considerazioni e prospettive di indagine. In M. Harari and M. Pearce, eds., *Il protovillanoviano al di qua e al di là dell'Appennino*, 99–132. Biblioteca di Athenaeum, 38. Como, New Press

Dickinson, O. T. P. K. (2006) *The Aegean from Bronze Age to Iron Age: continuity and change between the twelfth and eighth centuries BC*. London, Routledge

Dietler, M. (1996) Feasts and Commensal Politics in the Political Economy: food, power and status in prehistoric Europe. In P. Wiessner and W. Schiefenhövel, eds., *Food and the Status Quest: an interdisciplinary perspective*, 87–125. Providence, Berghahn Books

Dietler, M. (2001) Theorizing the Feast: rituals of consumption, commensal politics, and power in African contexts. In M. Dietler and B. Hayden, eds., *Feasts: archaeological and ethnographic perspectives on food, politics and power*, 65–114. Washington DC and London, Smithsonian Institution Press

Dietz, S. (1984) *Lindos IV, 1. Excavations and Surveys in Southern Rhodes: the Mycenaean period*. Publications of the National Museum, 22.1. Copenhagen, National Museum of Denmark,

Dikaios, P. (1969–71) *Enkomi: excavations 1948–1958*, 3 vols. Mainz-am-Rhein, Philipp von Zabern

Dixon, C. A. (1999) *Notes on the Ceramic Assemblage*. www.hf.uio.no/iakk/Sicilia [not accessed]

Dixon, C. A. (2004) Notes on the Ceramic Assemblage. In C. Mühlenbock, C. Prescott and C. A. Dixon, eds., *The Scandinavian Sicilian Archaeological Preoject: archaeological excavations at Monte Polizzo, Sicily. Reports 1998–2001, 58–72*. Göteborg, Department of Archaeology, University of Göteborg

Dörpfeld, W. (1902) *Troja und Ilion: Ergebnisse der Ausgrabungen in den vorhistorischen und historischen Schichten von Ilion 1870–1894*. Athens, Beck and Barth

Dorrell, P. G. (1988) Appendix B. Tell es-Sa'idiyeh: the physical background. In J. N. Tubb, ed. *Levant* 22, 80–2

Dothan, M. (1971) *Ashdod II–III: the second and third seasons of excavations, 1963, 1965, soundings in 1967*. 'Atiqot, 9–10. Jerusalem, Dept. of Antiquities and Museums in the Ministry of Education and Culture

Dothan, M. and Porath, Y. (1982) *Ashdod IV: excavations of Area M. The fortification and the Lower City*. 'Atiqot, 7. Jerusalem, Israel Antiquities Authority

Dothan, M. and Porath, Y. (1993) *Ashdod V: excavations of Area G, the fourth – sixth seasons of excavations, 1968–1970*. 'Atiqot, 23. Jerusalem, Israel Antiquities Authority

Dothan, T. (1972) Anthropoid Clay Coffins from a Late Bronze Age Cemetery near Deir el-Balah (Preliminary Report). *Israel Exploration Journal* 22.2–3, 65–72

Dothan, T. (1973) Anthropoid Clay Coffins from a Late Bronze Age Cemetery near Deir el-Balah (Preliminary Report II). *Israel Exploration Journal* 23.3, 129–46

Dothan, T. (1979) *Excavations at the Cemetery of Deir el-Balah*. Qedem, 10. Jerusalem, Institute of Archaeology, Hebrew University

Dothan, T. (1982) *The Philistines and their Material Culture*. Jerusalem, Israel Exploration Society

Dothan, T. (1998a) Initial Philistine Settlement: from migration to coexistence. In S. Gitin *et al.*, eds., *Mediterranean Peoples in Transition: thirteenth to early tenth centuries BCE*, 148–61. Jerusalem, Israel Exploration Society

Dothan, T. (1998b) The Pottery. In N. Bierling, ed., *Report on the 1995–1996 Excavations in Field XNW: areas 77, 78, 79, 89, 90, 101, 102. Iron Age I: text and data base (plates, sections, plans)*, 20–51. Tel Miqne-Ekron Limited Edition Series, 7. Jerusalem, W. F. Albright Institute of Archaeological Research

Dothan, T. (2000) Reflections on the Initial Phase of Philistine Settlement. In E. D. Oren, ed., *The Sea Peoples and their World: a reassessment*, 145–68. University Museum Monograph 108, University Museum Symposium Series, 11. Philadelphia, University Museum, University of Pennsylvania

Dothan, T. (2002) Bronze and Iron Objects with Cultic Connotations from Philistine Temple Building 350 at Ekron. *Israel Exploration Journal* 52.1, 1–27

Dothan, T. and Ben-Tor, A. (1983) *Excavations at Atheniou, Cyprus 1971–1972*. Qedem, 15. Jerusalem, Institute of Archaeology, Hebrew University

Dothan, T. and Dothan, M. (1992) *People of the Sea: the search for the Philistines*. New York, Macmillan

Dothan, T. and Zukerman, A. (2004) A Preliminary Study of the Mycenaean IIIC:1 Pottery Assemblages from Tel Miqne-Ekron and Ashdod. *Bulletin of the American Schools of Oriental Research* 333, 1–54

Doumas, C. (1965) Κορφή τ' Αρωνιού. *Αρχαιολογικό Δελτίο* 20 (α) Μελέται, 41–64

Drennan, R. and Peterson, C. E. (2004) Comparing Archaeological Settlement Systems with Rank-Size Graphs: a measure of shape and statistical confidence. *Journal of Archaeological Science* 31, 533–49

Drews, R. (1993) *The End of the Bronze Age*. Princeton, Princeton University Press

Driessen, J. (1995) 'Crisis architecture': some observations on architectural adaptations as immediate responses to changing socio-cultural conditions. *Topoi* 5, 63–88

Driessen, J. and MacDonald, C. F. (1997) *The Troubled Island: Minoan Crete before and after the Santorini eruption*. Aegaeum, 17. Liège, Université de Liège

Du Boulay, J. (1974) *Portrait of a Greek Mountain Village*. Oxford, Oxford University Press

Du Plat Taylor, J. (1967) The Stone Objects. In G. F. Bass, ed., *Cape Gelidonya: a Bronze Age shipwreck*, 126–30. Philadelphia, American Philosophical Society

Ducke, B. (2006) Unpublished seminar presented within the Summer School for Quantitative Methods and Data Analysis in Archaeology, Campiglia Marittima, 10th–17th September 2006

Dufkova, M. and Pečirka, J. (1970) Excavations of Farms and Farmhouses in the Chora of Chersonesos in the Crimea. *Eirene* 8, 123–60

Duhoux, Y. (1976) *Aspects du vocabulaire économique mycénien: cadastre, artisanat, fiscalité*. Amsterdam, A. M. Hakkert

Dunand, M. (1954) *Fouilles de Byblos II (1933–1938)*. Paris, P. Geuthner

Duncan, J. G. (1930) *Corpus of Dated Palestinian Pottery*. London, British School of Archaeology in Egypt

Dunkel, G. (1981) Mycenaean and Central Greek. *Kadmos* 20.2, 132–42

Durand, J.-M. (2006) Haşor à l'époque d'Ugarit. *Nouvelles Assyriologiques Brèves et Utilitaires* 3 (septembre), 74

Earle, T. K. (2002) *Bronze Age Economics: the beginnings of political economies*. Boulder, Westview Press

Eder, B. (1999) Ancient Elis in the Dark Ages. *Η Περιφέρεια του Μυκηναϊκού Κόσμου*, 263–8. Lamia, Έκδοση ΙΔ Εφορείας Προϊστορικών και Κλασσικών Αρχαιοτήτων

Eder, B. and Jung, R. (2005) On the Character of Social Relations between Greece and Italy in the 12th/11th C. BC. In R. Laffineur and E. Greco, eds., *Emporia: Aegeans in the central and eastern Mediterranean. Proceedings of the 10th International Aegean Conference/10ᵉ Rencontre égéenne internationale. Athens, Italian School of Archaeology, 14–18 April 2004*, 485–95. Aegaeum, 25. Liège, Université de Liège

Eggler, J. and Keel, O. (2006) *Corpus der Siegel-Amulette aus Jordanien: vom Neolithikum bis zur Perserzeit*. Orbis biblicus et orientalis, 25. Friborg, Academic Press

Ehrman, W., Schmiedl, G., Hamann, Y., Kuhnt, T., Hemleben, C. and Siebel, W. (2007) Clay Minerals in Late Glacial and Holocene Sediments of the Northern and Southern Aegean Sea. *Palaeogeography, Palaeoclimatology, Palaeoecology* 249, 36–57

Ekroth, G. (2002) *The Sacrificial Rituals of Greek Hero-Cults in the Archaic to the Early Hellenistic Periods*. Kernos, 12. Liège, Centre international d'étude de la religion grecque antique

Eliopoulos, T. (1998) A Preliminary Report on the Discovery of a Temple Complex of the Dark Age at Kephala Vasilikis. In N. C. Stampolidis *et al.*, eds., *Eastern Mediterranean: Cyprus-Dodecanese-Crete, 16th–6th cent. B.C.: Archaeological Museum of Heraklion, March–August 1998*, 301–13. Heraklion, University of Crete

Enzel, Y., Bookman, R., Sharon, D., Gvirtzman, H., Dayan, U., Ziv, B. and Stein, M. (2003) Late Holocene Climates of the Near East Deduced from Dead Sea Level Variations and Modern Regional Winter Rainfall. *Quaternary Research* 60, 263–73

Epigraphic Survey, the (1930–70) *Medinet Habu*, 8 vols. Oriental Institute Publications. Chicago, University of Chicago Press

Esse, D. L. (1989) Village Potters in Early Bronze Age Palestine: a case study. In A. Leonard and B. B. Williams, eds., *Essays in Ancient Civilization Presented to Helene J. Kantor*, 77–92. Chicago, Oriental Institute of the University of Chicago

Evans, A. J. (1921–35) *The Palace of Minos: a comparative account of the sucessive stages of the early Cretan civilization as illustrated by the discoveries at Knossos*, 4 vols. London, Macmillan

Evely, D., ed. (2006) *Lefkandi IV. The Bronze Age: the Late Helladic IIIC settlement at Xeropolis*. British School at Athens Supplement, 39. London, British School at Athens

Falconer, S. E. and Savage, S. H. (1995) Heartlands and Hinterlands: alternative trajectories of early urbanisation in Mesopotamia and the southern Levant. *American Antiquity* 60.1, 37–58

Falsone, G. (1993) Sulla cronologia del bronzo fenicio di Sciacca alla luce delle nuove scoperte di Huelva e Cadice. *Studi sulla Sicilia occidentale in onore di Vincenzo Tusa*, 45–56. Padua, Bottega d'Erasmo

Farnell, L. R. (1921) *Greek Hero Cults and Ideas of Immortality: the Gifford lectures delivered in the University of St. Andrews in the year 1920*. Oxford, Clarendon

Farrington (2002) *Trading Places: the East India Company and Asia 1600–1834*. London, The British Library

Faust, A. (2002) Burnished Pottery and Gender Hierarchy in Iron Age Israelite Society. *Journal of Mediterranean Archaeology* 15.1, 53–73

Faust, A. (2004) Mortuary Practices, Society and Ideology: the lack of Iron Age I burials in the highlands in context. *Israel Exploration Journal* 54.2, 174–90

Feinman, G. M., Banker, S., Cooper, R. F., Cook, G. B. and Nicholas, L. M. (1989) A Technological Perspective on Changes in the Ancient Oaxacan Grayware Ceramic Tradition: preliminary results. *Journal of Field Archaeology* 16, 331–43

Feinman, G. M., Kowalewski, S. and Blanton, R. (1984) Modelling Ceramic Production and Organizational Change in the Pre-Hispanic Valley of Oaxaca, Mexico. In S. E. van der Leeuw and A. C. Pritchard, eds., *The Many Dimensions of Pottery: cramics in archaeology and anthropology*, 295–338. Amsterdam, University of Amsterdam

Feldman, M. H. (2006) *Diplomacy by Design: luxury arts and an 'International Style' in the Ancient Near East, 1400–1200 BCE*. Chicago, University of Chicago Press

Felsch, R. C. S. (1980) Apollon und Artemis oder Artemis und Apollon: Bericht von den Grabungen im neu entdeckten Heiligtum bei Kalapodi 1973–7. *Archäologischer Anzeiger*, 38–122

Felsch, R. C. S. (1987) Kalapodi: Bericht Obre die Grabungen im Heiligtum der Artemis Elaphebolos und des Apollon von Hyampolis 1978–82. *Archäologischer Anzeiger*, 1–99

Ferrara, S. (2005) *An Interdisciplinary Approach to the Cypro-*

Minoan Script. Unpublished PhD thesis, University College London

Ferrarese Ceruti, M. L., Vagnetti, L. and Lo Schiavo, F. (1987) Minoans, Mycenaeans and Cypriots in Sardinia in the Light of Recent Research. In M. S. Balmuth, ed., *Studies in Sardinian Archaeology III: Nuragic Sardinia and the Mycenaean world*, 35–7. BAR International Series, 387. Oxford, Archaeopress

Filippi, D. (2005) Il Velabro e le origini del Foro. *Workshop di Archeologia classica: paesaggi, costruzioni, reperti* 2, 93–115

Finkelstein, I. (1998) Philistine Chronology: high, middle or low? In S. Gitin *et al.*, eds., *Mediterranean Peoples in Transition: thirteenth to early tenth centuries BCE*, 140–7. Jerusalem, Israel Exploration Society

Finkelstein, I. (2002) The Campaign of Shoshenq I to Palestine: a guide to the 10th century BCE polity. *Zeitschrift des Deutschen Palästina-Vereins* 118.2, 109–35

Finley, M. I., Caskey, J. L., Kirk, G. S. and Page, D. L. (1964) The Trojan War. *Journal of Hellenic Studies* 84, 1–20

Fiorentino, G. (1995) Primi dati archeobotanici dall'insediamento dell'età del bronzo di Piazza Palmieri (Monopoli – BA). In F. Radina, ed., *L'età del bronzo lungo la fascia adriatica pugliese. Atti del seminario di studi, Bari S. Teresa dei Maschi, 26–28 maggio 1995, Taras XV* 2, 335–73. Bari, Schena Editore

Fiorentino, G. (2002) Paleo-ambiente e paleo-economia nel Golfo di Taranto durante l'Età del Bronzo. In M. Gorgoglione, ed., *Strutture e modelli di abitati del Bronzo tardo da Torre Castelluccia a Roca Vecchia: rapporti ed interrelazioni sull'arco ionico da Taranto al canale d'Otranto e sul versante adriatico. Atti del Convegno di studio, 28–29 novembre 1996, Pulsano (Ta), Castello De Falconibus*, 141–53. Manduria, Filo Editore

Fischer, P. M. (2001) The Iron Age at Tell Abū al-Kharaz, Jordan Valley. *Studies in the History and Archaeology of Transjordan* 7, 305–16

Forbes, H. A. (1989) Of Grandfathers and Grand Theories: the hierarchised ordering of responses to hazard in a Greek rural community. In P. Halstead and J. O'Shea, eds., *Bad Year Economics: cultural responses to risk and uncertainty*, 87–97. New Directions in Archaeology. Cambridge, Cambridge University Press

Foster, K. P. (1979) *Aegean Faience of the Bronze Age*. New Haven, Yale University Press

Foxhall, L. (1995) Bronze to Iron: agricultural systems and political structures in Late Bronze Age and Early Iron Age Greece. *Annual of the British School at Athens* 90, 239–50

Franken, H. J. (1969) *Excavations at Tell Deir 'Alla I*. Leiden, Brill

Franken, H. J. (1992) *Excavations at Tell Deir 'Alla: the Late Bronze Age sanctuary*. Louvain, Peeters Press

Frankenstein, S. (1979) The Phoenicians in the Far West: a function of Neo-Assyrian imperialism. In M. T. Larsen, ed., *Power and Propaganda: a symposium on ancient empires*, 263–94. Mesopotamia, 7. Copenhagen, Akademisk Forlag

French, E. B. (1965) Late Helladic III A2 Pottery from Mycenae. *The Annual of the British School at Athens* 60, 159–202

French, E. B. (1967) Pottery from Late Helladic IIIB 1 Destruction Contexts at Mycenae. *Annual of the British School at Athens* 62, 149–93

French, E. B. (1971) The Development of Mycenaean Terracotta Figurines. *Annual of the British School at Athens* 66, 101–84

French, E. B. (1989) Possible Northern Intrusion at Mycenae. In J. G. P. Best and N. M. W. de Vries, eds., *Thracians and Mycenaeans: proceedings of the 4th international congress of Thracology, Rotterdam, 24–26 September 1984*, 39–51. Leiden, Brill

French, E. B. (in press-a) Town Planning in Palatial Mycenae. In S. Owen and L. Preston, eds., *Conference on Urbanism, Cambridge 2004*. Oxford, Oxbow Books

French, E. B. (in press-b) Well Built Mycenae, Fascicule 16/17, The Post-Palatial Levels

Friedland, R. and Robertson, A. F. (1990) Beyond the Marketplace. In R. Friedland and A. F. Robertson, eds., *Beyond the Marketplace: rethinking economy and society*, 3–49. Sociology and Economics: controversy and integration. New York, Walter de Gruyter

Frigola, J., Moreno, A., Cacho, I., Canals, M., Sierro, F. J., Flores, J. A., Grimalt, J. O., Hodell, D. A. and Curtis, J. H. (2007) Holocene Climate Variability in the Western Mediterranean Region from a Deepwater Sediment Record. *Paleoceanography* 22, PA2209, doi:10.1029/2006PA001307

Fritz, V. and Kempinski, A. (1983) *Ergebnisse der Ausgrabungen auf der Hirbet el-Mšaš (Tel Masos), 1972–1975*, 3 vols. Abhandlungen des Deutschen Palastinavereins. Wiesbaden, Otto Harrassowitz

Frizell, B. S. (1986) *Asine II: results of the excavations east of the Acropolis 1970–1974. Fasc. 3: the late and final Mycenaean periods*. Skrifter utgivna av Svenska institutet i Athen, 24.3, 4°. Stockholm, Svenska institutet i Athen

Frödin, O. and Persson, A. W. (1938) *Asine: results of the Swedish excavations 1922–1930*. Stockholm, Generalstabens litografiska anstalt

Fukuyama, F. (1999) *The Great Disruption*. New York, The Free Press

Fulminante, F. (2003) *Le sepolture principesche nel Latium Vetus: tra la fine della prima età del Ferro e l'inizio dell'età Orientalizzante*. Rome, 'L'Erma' di Bretschneider

Fulminante, F. (2007) Environment and Settlement Analysis: investigating Bronze Age and Iron Age *Latium vetus*' physical and political landscape. In B. Ooghe and G. Verhoeven, eds., *Broadening Horizons: multidisciplinary approaches to landscape study*, 152–83. Newcastle, Cambridge Scholar Publishing

Furumark, A. (1941) *Mycenaean Pottery: analysis and classification*. Stockholm, Victor Pettersons Bokindustriaktiebolag

Gal, Z. (1995) The Diffusion of Phoenician Cultural Influence in Light of the Excavations at Hurvat Rosh Zayit. *Tel Aviv* 22, 89–93

Galaty, M. L. (1999) Wealth Ceramics, Staple Ceramics: pots and the Mycenaean palaces. In M. L. Galaty and W. A. Parkinson, eds., *Rethinking Mycenaean Palaces: new interpretations of an old idea*, 49–59. Los Angeles, The Cotsen Institute of Archaeology

Gallet de Shaunter, H. and Tréheux, J. (1947–48) Depôt égéen et géometrique de l'Artémission à Délos. *Bulletin de correspondance hellénique* 71–2, 148–206

Gallou, C. (2005) *The Mycenaean Cult of the Dead*. BAR International Series, 1372. Oxford, Archaeopress

Gallou, C. and Georgiadis, M. (in press) The Cemeteries of the Argolid and the South-Eastern Aegean during the Mycenaean Period: a landscape assessment. *Opuscula Atheniensia*

Gardiner, A. H. (1940) Adoption Extraordinary. *Journal of Egyptian Archaeology* 26, 23–29

Gardiner, A. H. (1941) Ramesside Texts Relating to the Taxation and Transport of Corn. *Journal of Egyptian Archaeology* 27, 19–73

Gardiner, A. H. (1941–52) *The Wilbour Papyrus*, 4 vols (vol. 4 by R. O. Faulkner). London, Oxford University Press for the Brooklyn Museum

Gardiner, A. H. (1947) *Ancient Egyptian Onomastica*, 3 vols. Oxford, Clarendon Press

Gardiner, A. H. (1948) *Ramesside Administrative Documents*. London, Published on behalf of the Griffith Institute, Ashmolean Museum, Oxford by the Oxford University Press

Gates, C. (1995) Defining Boundaries of a State: the Mycenaeans and their Anatolian frontier. In R. Laffineur and W.-D. Niemeier, eds., *Politeia: Society and State in the Aegean Bronze Age*, 289–97. Aegaeum, 12. Liège, Université de Liège

Gauthier, H. (1925–31) *Dictionnaire des noms géographiques contenus dans les textes hiéroglyphiques*, 7 vols. Caire, Imprimerie de l'Institut Français d'Archéologie Orientale for Société Royale de Géographie d'Égypte

Genz, H. (1997) Northern Slaves and the Origin of Handmade Burnished Ware: a comment on Bankoff *et al.* (*JMA* 9 [1996] 193–209). *Journal of Mediterranean Archaeology* 10.1, 109–11

Georgiadis, M. (2003) *The South-Eastern Aegean in the Mycenaean Period: islands, landscape, death and ancestors*. BAR International Series, 1196. Oxford, Archaeopress

Gesell, G. C. (1985) *Town, Palace and House Cult in Minoan Crete*. Studies in Mediterranean Archaeology, 67. Göteborg, Paul Åmströms Förlag

Geva, A. (1995) *The Interaction of Climate, Culture, and Building Type on Built Form: a computerized simulation study of energy performance of historic buildings*. Unpublished PhD thesis, Texas A & M University

Giannitrapani, E. (1997) Rapporti tra la Sicilia e Malta durante l'età del Bronzo. In S. Tusa, ed., *Prima Sicilia: alle origini della società siciliana*, 429–43. Palermo, Giuseppe Maimone Editore

Giardino, C. (1995) *Il Mediterraneo Occidentale fra XIV ed VIII secolo a.C.: cerchie minerarie e metallurgiche*. BAR International Series, 612. Oxford, Tempus Reparatum

Gilboa, A. (1995) The Typology and Chronology of the Iron Age Pottery and the Chronology of Iron Age Assemblages. In E. Stern, ed., *Excavations at Dor, Final Report* 1B, 1–49. Areas A and C: the Finds. Qedem Reports, 2. Jerusalem, Israel Exploration Society

Gilboa, A. (1998) Iron I–IIA Pottery Evolution at Dor: regional context and the Cypriot connection. In S. Gitin *et al.*, eds., *Mediterranean Peoples in Transition: thirteenth to early tenth centuries BCE*, 413–25. Jerusalem, Israel Exploration Society

Gilboa, A. (1999) The View from the East – Tel Dan and the Earliest Cypro-Geometric Exports to the Levant. In M. Iacovou and D. Michaelides, eds., *Cyprus, the Historicity of the Geometric Horizon: proceedings of an archaeological workshop, University of Cyprus, Nicosia, 11th October 1998,* 119–40. Nicosia, Archaeological Research Unit, University of Cyprus

Gilboa, A. (2005) Sea Peoples and Phoenicians along the Southern Phoenician Coast – a Reconciliation: an interpretation of Šikila (SKL) material culture. *Bulletin of the American Schools of Oriental Research* 337, 47–78

Gilboa, A. and Sharon, I. (2003) An Archaeological Contribution to the Early Iron Age Chronological Debate: alternative chronologies for Phoenicia and their effects on the Levant, Cyprus, and Greece. *Bulletin of the American School of Oriental Research* 323, 7–80

Giles, F. J. (1997) *The Amarna Age: Western Asia*. Warminster, Aris and Philips

Gilmour, G. (1995) Aegean Influence in Late Bronze Age Funerary Practices in the Southern Levant. In S. Campbell and A. Green, eds., *The Archaeology of Death and Burial in the Ancient Near East*, 155–70. Oxford, Oxbow Books

Gilmour, G. (2002) Foreign Burials in Late Bronze Age Palestine. *Near Eastern Archaeology* 65.2, 112–19

Gitin, S., Mazar, A. and Stern, E., eds. (1998) *Mediterranean Peoples in Transition: thirteenth to early tenth centuries BCE*. Jerusalem, Israel Exploration Society

Gittlen, B. (1981) The Cultural and Chronological Implications of the Cypro-Palestinian Trade During the Late Bronze Age. *Bulletin of the American Schools of Oriental Research* 241, 49–59

Givoni, B. (1969) *Man, Climate and Architecture*. Amsterdam, Elseveir Publishing Company Limited

Glowacki, K. T. (2004) Household Analysis in Dark Age Crete. In L. Day *et al.*, eds., *Crete beyond the Palaces: proceedings of the Crete 2000 conference*, 125–36. Prehistory Monographs, 10. Philadelphia, INSTAP Academic Press

Godart, L. (1968) Le grain à Cnossos. *Studi Micenei ed Egeo-Anatolici* 5, 56–63

Goldman, H. (1940) The Acropolis of Halae. *Hesperia* 9, 381–514. Athens, American School of Classical Studies at Athens

Gonen, R. (1992) *Burial Patterns and Cultural Diversity in Late Bronze Age Canaan*. ASOR Dissertation Series, 7. Winona Lake, Eisenbrauns

Goren, Y., Finkelstein, I. and Na'aman, N. (2004) *Inscribed in Clay: provenance study of the Amarna tablets and other Ancient Near Eastern texts*. Tel Aviv, Emery and Claire Yass Publications in Archaeology

Gosselain, O. P. (1998) Social and Technical Identity in a Clay Crystal Ball. In M. T. Stark, ed., *The Archaeology of Social Boundaries*, 78–106. Washington and London, Smithsonian Institution Press

Graham, A. J. (1971) Patterns in Early Greek Colonisation. *Journal of Hellenic Studies* 91, 35–47

Graham, A. J. (1989) Pre-Colonial Contacts: questions and problems. *Greek Colonists and Native Populations* 91, 45–60

Graham, J. W. (1987) *The Palaces of Crete*. Princeton, Princeton University Press

Grandet, P. (1999) *Le Papyrus Harris I (BM 9999)*, 3 vols. Bibliothèque d'Etude, 109. Cairo, Institut Français d'Archéologie Orientale

Grant, E. (1929) *Beth Shemesh (Palestine): progress of the Haverford Archaeological Expedition*. Haverford, Biblical and Kindred Studies

Grant, E. and Wright, G. E. (1938–39) *Ain Shems Excavations (Palestine)*. Parts IV–V (Pottery). Haverford, Haverford College

Graves, M. W. (1991) Pottery Production and Distribution Among the Kalinga: a study of household and regional organization and differentiation. In W. A. Longacre, ed., *Ceramic Ethnoarchaeology*, 112–43. Tucson, University of Arizona Press

Green, J. D. M. (2003) *Death, Ritual and Society in Late Bronze and Early Iron Age Southern Levant*. Unpublished thesis, University College London

Green, J. D. M. (2006) *Ritual and Social Structure in the Late Bronze and Early Iron Age Southern Levant: the cemetery at Tell es-Sa'idiyeh, Jordan*. Unpublished PhD thesis, University College London

Green, J. D. M. (2007) Anklets and the Social Construction of Gender and Age in the Late Bronze and Early Iron Age Southern Levant. In S. Hamilton *et al.*, eds., *Archaeology and Women: ancient and modern issues*, 283–311. Walnut Creek, Left Coast Press

Greenhalgh, P. A. L. (1973) *Early Greek Warfare: horsemen and chariots in the Homeric and Archaic Ages*. Cambridge, Cambridge University Press

Guglielmino, R. (2005) Rocavecchia: nuove testimonianze di relazioni con l'Egeo e il Mediterraneo orientale nell'età del bronzo. In R. Laffineur and E. Greco, eds., *Emporia: Aegeans in the central and eastern Mediterranean. Proceedings of the 10th International Aegean Conference/10ᵉ Rencontre égéenne internationale. Athens, Italian School of Archaeology, 14–18 April 2004*, 637–51. Aegaeum, 25. Liège, Université de Liège

Guidi, A. (1982) Sulle prime fasi dell'urbanizzazione nel Lazio protostorico. *Opus* 1, 279–89

Guidi, A. (1985) An Application of the Rank-Size Rule to Proto-Historic Settlement in the Middle Thyrrenian Area. In C. Malone and S. Stoddart, eds., *Papers in Italian Archaeology* 3, 217–42. BAR International Series, 243–6. Oxford, Archaeopress

Guidi, A. (in press) The Archaeology of Early State in Italy. *Social Evolution and History*

Güntner, W. (2000) *Tiryns: Figürlich Bemalte Mykenische Keramik aus Tiryns*. Forschungen und Berichte 12. Mainz, Philipp von Zabern

Gusberti, E. (2005) La cronologia della ceramica di VIII sec. a.C. *Workshop di Archeologia classica: paesaggi, costruzioni, reperti* 2, 157–67

Guzowska, A. and Yasur-Landau, A. (2003) Before the Aeolians: prolegomena to the study of the interactions with the North-East Aegean islands in the 13th and 12th centuries B.C. In N. Kyparissi-Apostolika and M. Papakonstantinou, eds., *Β Διεθνές Διεπιστημονικό Συμπόσιο: Η Περιφέρεια του Μυκηναϊκού Κόσμου*, 471–86. Athens, Έκδοση ΙΔ Εφορείας Προϊστορικών και Κλασσικών Αρχαιοτήτων

Guzowska, M., Kuleff, I., Pernicka, E. and Satir, M. (2002) On the Origin of Coarse Wares of Troia VII. In G. Wagner *et al.*, eds., *Troia and the Troad: scientific approaches*, 233–50. Natural Science in Archaeology. Berlin and London, Springer

Hachmann, R. (1980) *Bericht über die Ergebnisse der Ausgrabungen in Kamid el-Lôz in den Jahren 1968 bis 1970*. Saarbrücker Beiträge zur Altertumskunde, 22. Bonn, Rudolf Habelt Verlag

Hadjicosti, M. (1988) 'Canaanite' Jars from Maa-Palaeokastro. In V. Karageorghis and M. Demas, eds., *Excavations at Maa-Palaeokastro, 1979–1986* 1, 340–85. Nicosia, Department of Antiquities

Hadjisavvas, S. (2003) The Production and Diffusion of Olive Oil in the Mediterranean, ca. 1500–500 BC. In N. C. Stampolidis and V. Karageorghis, eds., *Πλόες: Sea Routes. Interconnections in the Mediterranean 16th–6th C. BC*, 53–61. Athens, Museum of Cycladic Art

Hafford, W. B. (2001) *Merchants in the Late Bronze Age Eastern Mediterranean: tools, texts and trade*. Unpublished PhD thesis, University of Michigan

Hägg, R. (1983) Funerary Meals in the Geometric Necropolis at Asine? In R. Hägg, ed., *The Greek Renaissance of the Eighth Century B.C.*, 189–93. Stockholm and Lund, Paul Åströms Förlag

Haggis, D. C. (1993) Intensive Survey, Traditional Settlement Patterns, and Dark Age Crete: the case of Early Iron Age Kavousi. *Journal of Mediterranean Archaeology* 6.2, 131–74

Halbherr, F. (1901) Three Cretan Necropoleis: report on the researches at Erganos, Panaghia and Courtes. *American Journal of Archaeology* 5, 259–93

Hall, D. (1982) *Medieval Fields*. Risborough, Shire Publications

Hall, E. (1914) *Excavations in Eastern Crete: Vrokastro*. University of Pennsylvania Museum Anthropological Publications, 3.3. Philadelphia, University Museum

Hall, H. R. (1901–02) *Keftiu and the Peoples of the Sea*. Annual of the British School at Athens. [Offprint]. London, British School at Athens

Hall, J. M. (1997) *Ethnic Identity in Greek Antiquity*. Cambridge, Cambridge University Press

Hallager, E. (1990) Upper floors in LM I Houses. In P. Darcque and R. Treuil, eds., *L'habitat égéen préhistorique. Actes de la table ronde internationale, Athènes, 23–25 juin 1987, organisés par le Centre National de la Recherche Scientifique, l'Université de Paris et l'École française d'Athènes*, 281–92. Athens, École française d'Athènes

Hallager, E. and Pålsson Hallager, B., eds. (2000) *The Greek-Swedish Excavations at the Agia Aikaterini Square, Kastelli, Khania, 1970–1987: results of the excavations under the direction of Yannis Tzedakis and Carl-Gustaf Styrenius. Vol. 2: the Late Minoan IIIC settlement*. Skrifter utgivna av Svenska Institutet i Athen, 47.2, 4°. Stockholm, Paul Åmströms Förlag

Hallager, E. and Pålsson Hallager, B., eds. (2003) *The Greek-Swedish excavations at the Agia Aikaterini Square, Kastelli, Khania, 1970–1987 and 2001: results of the excavations under the direction of Yannis Tzedakis and Carl-Gustaf Styrenius. Vol.3: the Late Minoan IIIB:2 settlement, 1 (text)*. Skrifter utgivna av Svenska Institutet i Athen, 47.3.1, 4°. Stockholm, Paul Åmströms Förlag

Halstead, P. (1987) Traditional and Ancient Rural Economy in Mediterranean Europe: plus ça change? *Journal of Hellenic Studies* 107, 77–87

Halstead, P. (1989) The Economy has a Normal Surplus: economic stability and social change among early farming communities of Thessaly, Greece. In P. Halstead and J. O'Shea, eds., *Bad Year Economics: cultural responses to risk and uncertainty*, 68–80. New Directions in Archaeology. Cambridge, Cambridge University Press

Halstead, P. (1992a) Agriculture in the Bronze Age Aegean: towards a model of palatial economy. In B. Wells, ed., *Agriculture in Ancient Greece: proceedings of the Seventh International Symposium at the Swedish Institute at Athens, 16–17 May, 1990*, 105–17. Stockholm, Svenska institutet i Athen

Halstead, P. (1992b) The Mycenaean Palatial Economy: making the most of the gaps in the evidence. *Proceedings of the Cambridge Philological Society* 38, 57–86

Halstead, P. (1995a) Late Bronze Age Grain Crops and Linear B Ideograms *65, *120, and *121. *Annual of the British School at Athens* 90, 229–34

Halstead, P. (1995b) Plough and Power: the economic and social significance of cultivation of the ox-drawn ard in the Mediterranean. *Bulletin on Sumerian Agriculture* 8, 11–22

Halstead, P. (1999) Surplus and Share-Croppers: the grain production strategies of Mycenaean palaces. In P. P. Betancourt, ed., *Meletemata: studies in Aegean archaeology presented to Malcolm H. Wiener as he enters his 65th year*, 319–26. Aegaeum, 20. Liège, Université de Liège

Hankey, V. (1974) A Late Bronze Age Temple at Amman. 1: the Aegean pottery. *Levant* 6, 131–59

Härke, H. (1997) The Nature of Burial Data. In C. K. Jensen and K. H. Nielsen, eds., *Burial and Society: the chronological and social analysis of archaeological burial data*, 19–27. Aarhus, Aarhus University Press

Harrison, T. P. (2004) *Megiddo 3: final report on the Stratum VI excavations*. Chicago, Oriental Institute of the University of Chicago

Hasel, M. G. (1998) *Domination and Resistance: Egyptian military activity in the southern Levant, ca. 1300–1185 B.C.* Probleme der Ägyptologie, 11. Leiden and Boston, Brill

Haskell, H. W. (1981) Coarse-ware Stirrup-jars at Mycenae. *The Annual of the British School at Athens* 76, 225–38

Hassan, F. A. (2002) Palaeoclimate, Food, and Culture Change in Africa: an overview. In F. A. Hassan, ed., *Droughts, Food and Culture: ecological change and food security in Africa's later prehistory*, 11–26. New York and London, Kluwer Academic and Plenum Publishers

Hawkins, J. D. and Çambel, H. (1999–2000) *Corpus of Hieroglyphic Luwian Inscriptions*, 4 vols. Untersuchungen zur indogermanischen Sprach- und Kulturwissenschaft. Berlin, Walter de Gruyter

Hawkins, J. D. and Easton, D. F. (1996) A Hieroglyphic Seal from Troia. *Studia Troica* 6, 111–18

Hayden, B. (2001) Fabulous Feasts: a prolegomenon to the importance of feasting. In M. Dietler and B. Hayden, eds., *Feasts: archaeological and ethnographic perspectives on food, politics and power*, 23–64. Washington DC and London, Smithsonian Institution Press

Hayden, B. J. (1981) *The Development of Cretan Architecture from the LM IIIA through Geometric Periods*. Unpublished PhD thesis, University of Pennsylvania

Hayden, B. J. (1983) New Plans of the Early Iron Age Settlement of Vrokastro. *Hesperia* 52.4, 367–87

Hayden, B. J. (1987) Crete in Transition: LM IIIA–IIIB architecture. A preliminary study. *Studi Micenei ed Egeo Anatolici* 26, 199–234

Hayden, B. J. (1990) Aspects of Village Architecture in the Cretan Postpalatial Period. In P. Darcque and R. Treuil,

eds., *L'habitat égéen préhistorique. Actes de la table ronde internationale, Athènes, 23–25 juin 1987, organisés par le Centre National de la Recherche Scientifique, l'Université de Paris et l'École française d'Athènes*, 204–13. Athens, École française d'Athènes

Hayes, A., Kucera, M., Kallel, N., Sbaffi, L. and Rohling, E. J. (2005) Glacial Mediterranean Sea Surface Temperatures Reconstructed from Planktonic Foraminiferal Assemblages. *Quaternary Science Reviews* 24, 999–1,016

Helck, W. (1977) Die Seevölker in den ägyptischen Quellen. *Jahresbericht des Frankfurter Instituts für Vorgeschichte*, 7–21

Held, W. (1993) Milet-Heiligtum und Wohnhaus. *Istanbuler Mitteilungen* 43, 371–80

Heltzer, M. (1971) Soziale Aspekte des Heereswesens in Ugarit. In H. Klengel, ed., *Beiträge zur sozialen Struktur des alten Vorderasiens*, 125–31. Berlin, Akademie Verlag

Heltzer, M. (1978) *Goods, Prices and the Organization of Trade in Ugarit: marketing and transportation in the Eastern Mediterranean in the second half of the II Millennium B.C.E.* Wiesbaden, Dr. Ludwig Reichert Verlag

Heltzer, M. (1979) Some Questions Concerning the Sherdana in Ugarit. *Israel Oriental Studies* 9, 9–16

Heltzer, M. (1982) *The Internal Organization of the Kingdom of Ugarit: royal service-system, taxes, royal economy, army and administration*. Wiesbaden, Dr. Ludwig Reichert

Hencken, H. (1968) *Tarquinia, Villanovans and Early Etruscans*. Cambridge, Peabody Museum

Herold, A. (1998) Piramesses – The Northern Capital: chariots, horses and foreign gods. In J. G. Westenholz, ed., *Capital Cities: urban planning and spiritual dimensions. Proceedings of the symposium held on May 27–29, 1996, Jerusalem, Israel*, 129–46. Jerusalem, Bible Lands Museum Jerusalem

Hertel, D. (1991) Schliemanns These vom Fortleben Troias in den 'Dark Ages' im Lichte neuer Forschungsergebnisse. *Studia Troica* 1, 131–44

Hertel, D. (1992) Über die Vielschichtigkeit des Troianischen Krieges. Die Archäologie von Troia VI, VII und VIII. In J. Cobet and B. Patzak, eds., *Archäologie und historische Erinnerung: Nach 100 Jahren Heinrich Schliemann*, 73–104. Essen, Klartext

Hertel, D. (2003a) *Die Mauern von Troja: Mythos und Geschichte im antiken Ilion*. Munich, C. H. Beck

Hertel, D. (2003b) Protogeometrische, subgeometrische und geometrische Keramik Troias aus den Grabungen Scliemanns und Dörpfelds. In B. Rückert and F. Kolb, eds., *Probleme der Keramikchronologie des südlichen und weslichen Kleinasiens in geometrischer und archaischer Zeit: internationales Kolloquium, Tübingen 24.3.–16.3.1998*, 91–138. Bonn, Habelt

Herzog, Z. (1997) *Archaeology of the City: urban planning in ancient Israel and its social implications*. Sonia and Marco Nadler Institute of Archaeology Monograph Series, 13. Tel Aviv, Emery and Claire Yass Archaeology Press

Higginbotham, C. R. (2000) *Egyptianization and Elite Emulation in Ramesside Palestine: governance and accommodation on the imperial periphery*. Culture and History of the Ancient Near East, 2. Leiden, Brill

Hirschfeld, N. (2000) Marked Late Bronze Age Pottery from the Kingdom of Ugarit. In M. Yon *et al.*, eds., *Céramiques mycéniennes d'Ougarit*, 163–200. Ras Shamra-Ougarit, 13. Paris and Nicosia, Éditions Recherche sur les Civilisations and A. G. Leventis Fondation

Hnila, P. (2006) Das Terrassenhaus während der Troia VIIb–Zeiten. *Studia Troica* 16, 69–79

Hochstetter, A. (1984) *Kastanas: Ausgrabungen in einem Siedlungshügel der Bronze- und Eisenzeit Makedoniens 1975–1979, III. Die Handgemachte Keramik. Schichten 19 bis 1.* Prähistorische Archäologie in Südosteuropa, 3. Berlin, Spiess

Hodder, I. (1979) Simulating the Growth of Hierarchy. In A. C. Renfrew and K. L. Cooke, eds., *Transformations: mathematical approaches to cultural change*, 117–44. New York, Academic Press

Hodder, I. (1981) Pottery, Production and Use: a theoretical discussion. In H. Howard and E. L. Morris, eds., *Production and Distribution: a ceramic viewpoint*. BAR International Series, 120. Oxford, Archaeopress

Hodder, I. (1991) *Reading the Past: current approaches to interpretation in archaeology*. Cambridge, Cambridge University Press

Hoftijzer, J. and Van Soldt, W. H. (1998) Texts from Ugarit Pertaining to Seafaring. In S. Wachsmann, ed., *Seagoing Ships and Seamanship in the Bronze Age Levant*, 333–44. College Station, Texas A&M University Press

Holladay, J. S. (2001) Toward a New Paradigmatic Understanding of Long-Distance Trade in the Ancient Near East: from the Middle Bronze II to Early Iron II – a sketch. In P. M. Michèle Daviau *et al.*, eds., *The World of the Aramaeans II: studies in history and archaeology in honour of Paul-Eugène Dion*, 136–98. Sheffield, Sheffield Academic Press

Hood, M. S. F. (1953) A Mycenaean Cavalryman. *Annual of the British School at Athens* 48, 84–93

Hood, M. S. F. (1967) Buckelkeramik at Mycenae? In W. C. Brice, ed., *Europa: Studien zur Geschichte und Epigraphik der Frühen Aegaeis. Festschrift für Ernst Grumach*, 120–31. Berlin, Walter de Gruyter

Hood, M. S. F. (1981–82) *Excavations in Chios 1938–1955: prehistoric Emporio and Ayio Gala*, 2 vols. Oxford, The British School of Archaeology at Athens, supplementary vols. 15–16

Hood, M. S. F. (1995) The Bronze Age Context of Homer. In J. B. Carter and S. P. Morris, eds., *The Ages of Homer: a tribute to Emily Townsend Vermeule*, 25–32. Austin, University of Texas Press

Hope Simpson, R. (2003) The Dodecanese and the Ahhiyawa Question. *Annual of the British School at Athens* 98, 203–37

Horejs, B. (2005) *Die handgemachte Keramik der Toumba von Olynth/Agios Mamas, Chalkidike (Griechenland), Schichten 9–1*. Unpublished PhD thesis, Freie Universität Berlin

Iacovou, M. (2006) 'Greeks', 'Phoenicians' and 'Eteocypriots': ethnic identities in the Cypriot kingdoms. In J. Chrysostomides and C. Dendrinos, eds., *'Sweet Land...': lectures on the history and culture of Cyprus*, 27–59. Camberley, Porphyrogenitus

Iakovides, S. E. (1969–70) *Peratē: to nekrotapheion*. Bibliothēkē tēs en Athēnais Archaiologikēs Hetaireias, 67. Athens, Archaiologike Hetaireia

Iakovidis, S. E. (1969) *Περατή: Το Νεκροταφείο. Α, Β, Γ.* Αρχαιολογική Εταιρεία εν Αθήναις

Iakovidis, S. E. (1970) *Περατή: Το Νεκροταφείον.* Athens, Πρακτικά της Αρχαιολογικής Εταιρείας

Iakovidis, S. E. (1995) Οι Αχαιοί στην Κύπρο μαρτυρίες και θεωρίες. *Κύπρος: Από την Προϊστορία στους Νεότερους Χρόνους*, 209–22. Πολιτιστικό Ίδρυμα Τραπέζης Κύπρου. Nicosia

Immerwahr, S. A. (1990) *Aegean Painting in the Bronze Age*. University Park, Pennsylvania State University Press

Jacob-Felsch, M. (1996) Die Spätmykenische bis Frühprotogeometrische Keramik. Mit einem Beitrag von Richard E. Jones. In R. C. S. Felsch, ed., *Kalapodi: Ergebnisse der Ausgrabungen im Heiligtum der Artemis und des Apollon von Hyampolis in der antiken Phokis*, 1–105. Mainz-am-Rhein, Philipp von Zabern

Jacobsson, I. (1994) *Aegyptiaca from Late Bronze Age Cyprus*. Studies in Mediterranean archaeology, 112. Jonsered, Paul Åströms Förlag

James, W. F. (1966) *The Iron Age at Beth Shan: a study of levels VI–IV*. Philadelphia, University of Pennsylvania University Museum

James, W. F. and McGovern, P. E. (1993) *The Late Bronze Egyptian Garrison at Beth Shan: a study of levels VII and VIII*. University Museum Monograph, 85. Philadelphia, The University Museum, University of Pennsylvania

Jameson, M. H., Runnels, C. N., Munn, M. H. and Van Andel, T. H. (1994) *A Greek Countryside: the southern Argolid from prehistory to the present day*. Stanford, Stanford University Press

Jean-Marie, M. (1999) *Tombes et Nécropoli de Mari*. Mission Archéologique de Mari, 5. Beirut, Institute Français d'Archéologie du Proche-Orient

Jenness, J. (2004) *Weighted Mean of Points (v. 1.2c)*. http://www.jennessent.com/arcview/weighted_mean.htm (accessed 14 December 2007)

Johnson, G. A. (1977) Aspects of Regional Analysis in Archaeology. *Annual Review of Anthropology* 6, 479–508

Johnson, G. A. (1980) Rank-Size Convexity and System Integration: a view from archaeology. *Economic Geography* 56, 234–47

Johnson, G. A. (1981) Monitoring Complex System Integration and Boundary Phenomena with Settlement Size Data. In S. E. van der Leeuw, ed., *Archaeological Approaches to the Study of Complexity*, 144–88. Cingula, 6. Amsterdam, Universiteit von Amsterdam

Jones, D. (1988) *A Glossary of Ancient Egyptian Nautical Titles and Terms*. Studies in Egyptology. London and New York, Kegan Paul International

Jones, G. (1987) Agricultural Practice in Greek Prehistory. *Annual of the British School at Athens* 82, 115–23

Jones, G. (1995) Charred Grain from Late Bronze Age Gla, Boiotia. *Annual of the British School at Athens* 90, 235–8

Jones, R. and Vaughan, S. (1988) A Study of Some 'Canaanite' Jar Fragments from Maa-Palaeokastro. In V. Karageorghis and M. Demas, eds., *Excavations at Maa-Palaeokastro, 1979–1986* 1, 386–96. Nicosia, Department of Antiquities

Jones, R. E. (1986) *Greek and Cypriot Pottery: a review of scientific studies*. Athens, The British School at Athens

Jones, R. E. and Day, P. M. (1987) Late Bronze Age and Cypriot-type Pottery on Sardinia: identification of imports and local imitations by physico-chemical analysis. In M. S. Balmuth, ed., *Studies in Sardinian Archaeology III: Nuragic Sardinia and the Mycenaean world*, 257–69. BAR International Series, 387. Oxford, Archaeopress

Jones, R. E., Levi, S. T. and Vanzetti, A. (in press) Cannatello (AG): seriazione cronologica e caratterizzazione delle materie prime. *Dai Ciclopi agli Ecisti. Società e territorio nella Sicilia preistorica e protostorica, XLI Riunione Scientifica dell'I. I.P.P.*

Jones, R. E., Levi, S. T. and Vagnetti, L. (2002) Connections between the Aegean and Italy in the Later Bronze Age: the ceramic evidence. In V. Kilikoglou *et al.*, eds., *Modern Trends in Scientific Studies on Ancient Ceramics: papers presented at the 5th European Meeting on Ancient Ceramics, Athens 1999*, 171–84. BAR International Series, 1011. Oxford, Archaeopress

Jones, R. E. and Mee, C. (1978) Spectrographic Analyses of Mycenaean Pottery from Ialysos on Rhodes: results and implications. *Journal of Field Archaeology* 5, 461–70

Jones, R. E. and Vagnetti, L. (1991) Traders and Craftsmen in the Central Mediterranean: archaeological evidence and archaeometric research. In N. H. Gale, ed., *Bronze Age Trade in the Mediterranean*, 127–47. Jonsered, Paul Åström

Jones, S. (1997) *The Archaeology of Ethnicity: constructing identities in the past and present*. London and New York, Routledge

Jørgensen, L. (1987) Family Burial Practices and Inheritance Systems: the development of an Iron Age society from 500 BC to AD 1000 on Bornholm, Denmark. *Acta Archaeologica* 58, 17–53

Jung, R. (2005) Πότε? Quando? Wann? Quand? When? Translating Italo-Aegean Synchronisms. In R. Laffineur and E. Greco, eds., *Emporia: Aegeans in the Central and Esatern Mediterranean. Proceedings of the 10th International Aegean Conference/10e Rencontre égéenne internationale. Athens, Italian School of Archaeology, 14–18 April 2004*, 473–84. Aegaeum, 25. Liège, Université de Liège

Jung, R. (2006) *Χρονολογία comparata. Vergleichende Chronologie von Südgrechenland und Süditalien von ca. 1700/1600 bis 1000 v. u. Z.* Vienna, Verlag der Österreichischen Akademie der Wissenschaften

Jung, R. (in press) LH IIIC Middle Synchronisms Across the Adriatic. In S. Deger-Jalkotzy and M. Zavadil, eds., *LH IIIC Chronology and Synchronisms: LH IIIC Middle. Proceedings of the International Workshop held at the Austrian Academy of Sciences at Vienna, October 29th and 30th, 2004*

Jung, R., Badre, L., Boileau, M.-C. and Mommsen, H. (2005) The Provenance of Aegean- and Syrian-type Pottery Found at Tell Kazel (Syria). *Ägypten und Levante* 15, 15–47

Kanta, A. (1980) *The Late Minoan III Period in Crete: a survey of sites, pottery and their distribution*. Göteborg, Paul Astöms Förlag

Kanta, A. (1997) Late Bronze Age Tholos Tombs, Origins and Evolution: the missing links. In J. Driessen and A. Farnoux, eds., *La Crète Mycénienne: actes de la Table Ronde Internationale organisée par l'École française d'Athènes, 26–28 Mars 1991*, 229–47. Bulletin de correspondance hellénique, supplément 30. Athens and Paris, École française d'Athènes

Kanta, A. (1998) Introduction: 16th–11th cent. B.C. In N. C. Stampolidis *et al.*, eds., *Eastern Mediterranean: Cyprus-Dodecanese-Crete, 16th–6th cent. B.C.: Archaeological Museum of Heraklion, March–August 1998*, 30–66. Heraklion, University of Crete

Kanta, A. (2001) The Cremations of Olous and the Custom of Cremation in Bronze Age Crete. In N. C. Stampolidis, ed., *Καύσεις στην Εποχή του Χαλκού και την Πρώιμη Εποχή του Σιδήρου*, 59–68. Athens, Panepistemio tes Kretes

Kanta, A. (in press) Tylisos Towards the End of the Bronze Age and during the Dark Ages: elements of history for central Crete from the archaeological evidence. *Atti del Convegno di Studi 'Identità culturale, etnicità, processi di trasformazione a Creta fra Dark Age ed Arcaismo' (Atene, 9–12 novembre 2006)*

Karageorghis, V. (1974) *Excavations at Kition I: the tombs.* Nicosia, Department of Antiquities

Karageorghis, V., ed. (1983) *Palaepaphos-Skales: an Iron Age cemetery in Cyprus.* Konstanz, Universitätsverlag Konstanz

Karageorghis, V. (1992) The Crisis Years: Cyprus. In W. A. Ward and M. S. Joukowsky, eds., *The Crisis Years: the 12th century B.C. from beyond the Danube to the Tigris*, 79–86. Dubuque, Kendall/Hunt Publishing Co.

Karageorghis, V. and Demas, M. (1984) *Pyla-Kokkinokremos: a late 13th-century B.C. fortified settlement in Cyprus.* Nicosia, Department of Antiquities

Karageorghis, V. and Demas, M. (1985) *Excavations at Kition V: the pre-Phoenician levels.* Nicosia, Department of Antiquities

Karageorghis, V. and Demas, M. (1988) *Excavations at Maa-Palaeokastro, 1979–1986*, 3 vols. Nicosia, Department of Antiquities

Karantzali, E. (2001) *The Mycenaean Cemetery at Pylona on Rhodes.* BAR International Series, 988. Oxford, Archaeopress

Karantzali, E. and Ponting, M. J. (2000) ICP-AES Analysis of some Mycenaean Vases from the Cemetery at Pylona, Rhodes. *Annual of the British School at Athens* 95, 219–38

Karatzali, E. (2003) Η Μυκηναϊκή Εγκατάσταση στα Δωδεκάνησα: Η Περίπτωση της Ρόδου. In N. Kyparissē-Apostolika and M. Papakonstantinou, eds., *The Periphery of the Mycenaean World: proceedings of the 2nd International Interdisciplinary Colloquium, Lamia 1999*, 513–34. Athens, Ministry of Culture and 14th Ephorate of Prehistoric and Classical Antiquities

Kardara, C. (1977) *Απλώματα Νάξου: Κινητά Ευρήματα Τάφων Α και Β.* Athens, Βιβλιοθήκη της εν Αθήναις Αρχαιολογικής Εταιρείας, 88

Karo, G. (1930) Schatz von Tiryns. *Mitteilungen des Deutschen Archäologischen Instituts, Athenische Abteilung* 55, 119–40

Kempinski, A. (1979) Hittites in the Bible: what does the archaeology say? *Biblical Archaeology Review* 5.5, 20–44

Kempinski, A. (1993) Masos, Tel. In E. Stern, ed., *The New Encyclopedia of Archaeological Excavation in the Holy Land*, 986–89. Jerusalem, Israel Exploration Society and Carta

Keramopoullos, A. D. (1909) Η Οίκα τού Καδμον, *Άρχαιλογική Εφημερίς*, 57–122

Khalifeh, I. A. (1988) *Sarepta II: the Late Bronze and Iron Age periods of area II, X. The University Museum of the University of Pennsylvania excavations at Sarafand, Lebanon.* Beirut, Département des Publications de l'Université Libanaise

Kienast, H. J. (1992) Topolgraphische Studien im Heraion von Samos. *Archäologischer Anzeiger*, 171–214

Kilian, K. (1978a) Ausgrabungen in Tiryns 1976: Bericht zu den Grabungen. *Archäologischer Anzeiger*, 449–70

Kilian, K. (1978b) Nordwestgriechische Keramik aus der Argolis und ihre Entsprechungen in der Subapenninfacies. *Atti della XX riunione scientifica dell'Istituto italiano di preistoria e protostoria in Basilicata 1976*, 311–20

Kilian, K. (1980) Zum Ende der mykenischen Epoche in der Argolis. *Jahrbuch des Römisch-Germanischen Zentralmuseums Mainz* 27, 166–95

Kilian, K. (1982) Ausgrabungen in Tiryns 1980. *Archäologischer Anzeiger*, 393–466

Kilian, K. (1988a) Ausgrabungen in Tiryns 1982/83: Bericht zu den Grabungen. *Archäologischer Anzeiger*, 105–211

Kilian, K. (1988b) Mycenaeans up to Date. In E. B. French and K. A. Wardle, eds., *Problems in Greek Pehistory: papers presented at the Centenary Conference of the British School of Archaeology at Athens, Manchester, April 1986*, 115–52. Bristol, Bristol Classical Press

Kilian, K. (1990) Mycenaean Colonization: norm and variety. In J.-P. Descœudres, ed., *Greek Colonists and Native Populations: proceedings of the First Australian Congress of Classical Archaeology held in honour of Emeritus Professor A. D. Trendall*, 445–67. Oxford, Clarendon Press

Killebrew, A. E. (1998a) Ceramic Typology and Technology of Late Bronze II and Iron I Assemblages from Tel Miqne-Ekron: the transition from Canaanite to Philistine culture. In S. Gitin *et al.*, eds., *Mediterranean Peoples in Transition: thirteenth to early tenth centuries BCE*, 379–405. Jerusalem, Israel Exploration Society

Killebrew, A. E. (1998b) Mycenaean and Aegean-Style Pottery in Canaan During the 14th–12th Centuries BC. In E. Cline and D. Harris-Cline, eds., *The Aegean and the Orient in the Second Millennium: proceedings of the 50th anniversary symposium, Cincinnati, 18–20 April 1997*, 159–70. Aegaeum, 18. Liège, Université de Liège

Killebrew, A. E. (1999) Late Bronze and Iron I Cooking Pots in Canaan: a typological, technological, and functional study. In T. Kapitan, ed., *Archaeology, History and Culture in Palestine and the Near East: essays in memory of Albert E. Glock*, 83–126. Atlanta, Scholars Press

Killebrew, A. E. (2003) The Southern Levant During the 13th–12th Centuries BCE: the archaeology of social boundaries. In B. Fischer *et al.*, eds., *Identifying Changes: the transition from Bronze to Iron Ages in Anatolia and its neighbouring regions. Proceedings of the International Workshop, Istanbul, November 8–9, 2002*, 117–24. Istanbul, Türk Eskiaçag Bilimleri Enstitüsü

Killebrew, A. E. (2004) New Kingdom Egyptian-Style and Egyptian Pottery in Canaan: implications for Egyptian rule in Canaan during the 19th and 20th Dynasties. In G. N. Knoppers and A. Hirsch, eds., *Egypt, Israel and the Ancient Mediterranean World: studies in honor of Donald B. Redford*, 309–43. Leiden, Brill

Killebrew, A. E. (2005) *Biblical Peoples and Ethnicity: an archaeological study of Egyptians, Canaanites, Philistines, and early Israel, 1300–1100 B.C.E.* Atlanta, Society of Biblical Literature

Killen, J. T. (1992–93) The Oxen's Names on the Knossos Ch tablets. *Minos* 27–8, 101–7

Killen, J. T. (1994–95) A-ma e-pi-ke-re. *Minos* 29–30, 329–33

Kitchen, K. A. (1975–83) *Ramesside Inscriptions: historical and biographical*, 6 vols. Oxford, B. H. Blackwell

Knapp, A. B. (1983) An Alashiyan Merchant at Ugarit. *Tel Aviv* 10, 38–45

Knapp, A. B. (1996) Power and Ideology on Prehistoric Cyprus. In P. Hellström and B. Alroth, eds., *Religion and Power in the Ancient Greek World*, 9–25. Boreas – Uppsala Studies in Ancient Mediterranean and Near Eastern Civilizations, 24. Uppsala, Acta Universitatis Upsaliensis

Knapp, A. B. and Cherry, J. (1994) *Provenience Studies and Bronze Age Cyprus: production, exchange and politico-economic change.* Madison, Prehistory Press

Knapp, A. B., Muhly, J. D. and Muhly, P. M. (1988) To Hoard is Human: the metal deposits of LCIIC–LCIII. *Report of the Department of Antiquities of Cyprus*, 233–62

Knappett, C. (2001) Overseen or Overlooked? Ceramic production in a Mycenaean palatial system. In S. Voutsaki and J. Killen, eds., *Economy and Politics in the Mycenaean Palace States: proceedings of a conference held on 1–3 July 1999 in the Faculty of Classics, Cambridge*, 80–95. Cambridge, Cambridge Philological Society

Knauss, J. (1996) Arkadian and Boiotian Orchomenos: centres of Mycenaean hydraulic engineering. In E. de Miro *et al.*, eds., *Atti e memorie del secondo Congresso internazionale di micenologia, Roma-Napoli, 14–20 ottobre 1991* 3, 1,211–19. Incunabula Graeca, 98. Rome, Gruppo Editoriale Internazionale

Knudtzon, J. A. (1915) *Die El-Amarna-Tafeln: mit Einleitung und Erläuterungen*, 2 vols. Vorderasiatische Bibliothek. Leipzig, J. C. Hinrichs

Koehl, R. B. (1985) *Sarepta III: the imported Bronze and Iron Age wares from area II, X. The University Museum of the University of Pennsylvania excavations at Sarafand.* Publications de l'Université libanaise, 2. Beirut, Université libanaise

Konsolaki-Yannopoulou, E. (1999) A Group of New Mycenaean Horsemen from Methana. In P. P. Betancourt *et al.*, eds., *Meletemata: Studies in Aegean Archaeology Presented to Malcolm H. Wiener as He Enters His 65th Year*, 427–33. Liège, Université de Liège, Histoire de l'art et archéologie de la Grèce antique

Kontorli-Papadopoulou, L. (1987) Some Aspects Concerning Local Peculiarities of the Mycenaean Chamber Tombs. In R. Laffineur, ed., *Thanatos: les coutumes funéraires en Égée à l'âge du bronze. Actes du colloque de Liège, 21–23 avril 1986*, 145–60. Aegaeum, 1. Liège, Université de l'Etat, Histoire de l'art et archéologie de la Grèce antique

Koppenhöfer, D. (1997) Troia VII: Versuch einer Zusammenschau einschließlich der Ergebnisse des Jahres 1995. *Studia Troica* 7, 295–354

Korfmann, M. (1995) Troia – Ausgrabungen 1994. *Studia Troica* 5, 1–38

Korfmann, M. (1997) Troia – Ausgrabungen 1996. *Studia Troica* 7, 1–72

Korfmann, M. (1998) Troia – Ausgrabungen 1997. *Studia Troica* 8, 1–70

Korfmann, M. (2003) Die Arbeiten in Troia/Wilusa 2002. *Studia Troica* 13, 3–26

Korfmann, M. (2004) Die Arbeiten in Troia/Wilusa 2003. *Studia Troica* 14, 3–32

Korou, N. and Karetsou, A. (1994) To ierò tou Ermoù Kranaìou stin Pàtso Amariou. In L. Rocchetti, ed., *Sybrita: la valle di Amari fra bronzo e ferro*, 81–164. ncunabula graeca, 96. Rome, Gruppo Editoriale Internazionale

Kourou, N. (2001) Tenos-Xombourgo: a new defensive site in the Cyclades. In V. Karageorghis and C. Morris, eds., *Defensive*

Settlements of the Aegean and the Eastern Mediterranean after c. 1200 B.C., 171–89. Dublin, Trinity College and the Anastasios G. Leventis Foundation

Kraiker, W. and Kübler, K. (1939) *Die Nekropolen des 12. bis 10. Jahrhunderts.* Kerameikos, 1. Berlin, Walter de Gruyter

Kramer, C. (1997) *Pottery in Rajasthan: ethnoarchaeology in two Indian cities.* Washington and London, Smithsonian Institution Press

Krzyszkowska, O. (1991) The Enkomi Warrior Head Reconsidered. *Annual of the British School at Athens* 86, 107–120

Kuentz, C. (1928) *La bataille de Qadech: les textes ('Poème de Pentaour' et 'Bulletin de Qadech) et les bas-reliefs.* Mémoires publiés par les membres de l'Institut français d'archéologie orientale du Caire, 55. Cairo, l'Institut français d'archéologie orientale

Kumwenda, W. F. (1999) Design and Manufacture of a Withers Yoke for Zebu, Oxen and Cows. In P. Starkey and P. Kaumbutho, eds., *Meeting the Challenges of Animal Traction: a resource book for the Animal Traction Network for Eastern and Southern Africa (ATNESA), Harare, Zimbabwe*, 140–2. London, Intermediate Technology

Kuniholm, P. I., Kromer, B., Manning, S. W., Newton, M., Latini, C. E. and Bruce, M. J. (1996) Anatolian Tree Rings and the Absolute Chronology of the Eastern Mediterranean. *Nature* 381, 780–3

La Rocca, E. (1976) Ceramica d'importazione a Roma. In G. Colonna, ed., *Cviltà del Lazio primitivo*, 367–71. Exhibition catalogue. Rome

La Rosa, V. (2000) Riconsiderazioni sulla media e tarda età del Bronzo nella media valle del Platani. *Quaderni di Archeologia dell'Università di Messina* 1 (n.s.), 125–38

La Rosa, V. (2005) Pour une réflexion sur le problème de la première présence égéenne en Sicile. In R. Laffineur and E. Greco, eds., *Emporia: Aegeans in the Central and Esatern Mediterranean. Proceedings of the 10th International Aegean Conference/10ᵉ Rencontre égéenne internationale. Athens, Italian School of Archaeology, 14–18 April 2004*, 571–83. Aegaeum, 25. Liège, Université de Liège

La Rosa, V. (2007) Di tradizione cretese alcune tombe protostoriche dell'area etnae? *Creta Antica* 8, 315–24

La Rosa, V., Mazzoleni, P. and Pezzino, A. (2002) Doppie corna di tipo cretese in una collezione siciliana. *Creta Antica* 3, 247–53

Lackenbacher, S. (2000) Between Egypt and Hatti. *Near Eastern Archaeology* 63.4, 194

Laemmel, S. (2003) *A Case Study of the Late Bronze and Early Iron Age Cemeteries from Tell el-Far'ah (South).* Unpublished DPhil thesis, University of Oxford

Lagarce, J. and Lagarce, É. (1997) Les lingots 'en peau de boeuf'. Objets de commerce et symboles idélogues dans le monde Méditerranéen. *Revue des études Phéniciennes-Puniques* 10, 73–97

Lamb, W. (1921–23) The Pithos Area: the frescoes. *Annual of the British School at Athens* 25, 162–72

Lamb, W. (1932) Grey Wares from Lesbos. *Journal of Hellenic Studies* 52, 1–12

Lambrinoudakis, V. and Philaniotou-Hadjianastasiou, O. (2001) The Town of Naxos at the End of the Late Bronze Age: the Mycenaean fortification wall. In V. Karageorghis and C. Morris, eds., *Defensive Settlements of the Aegean and the Eastern Mediterranean after c. 1200 B.C.*, 157–69. Dublin, Trinity College and the Anastasios G. Leventis Foundation

Lamprinoudakis, V. (1975) Ιερόν Μαλεάτου Απόλλωνος εις Επίδαυρον. *Πρακτικά της εν Αθήναις Αρχαιολογικής Εταιρείας* 130, 162–75

Lan, M. (2004) Polygon Characterisation with the Multiplicatively Weighted Voronoi Diagrams. *The Professional Geographer* 56.2, 223–39

Lang, M. L. (1964) The Palace of Nestor: excavations of 1963. Part II. *American Journal of Archaeology* 68.2, 99–105

Lang, M. L. (1969) *The Palace of Nestor at Pylos in Western Messenia. Vol. 2: the Frescoes.* Princeton, Princeton University Press

Laxton, R. R. and Cavanagh, W. G. (1995) The Rank-Size Dimension and the History of Site Structure from Survey Data. *Journal of Quantitative Anthropology* 5, 327–58

Leach, S. and Rega, E. (1996) Interim Report on the Human Skeletal Material Recovered from the 1995 Tell es-Sa'idiyeh Excavations, Areas BB & DD. *Palestine Exploration Quarterly* 128, 131–8

Leahy, A. (1995) Ethnic Diversity in Ancient Egypt. In J. M. Sasson *et al.*, eds., *Civilizations of the Ancient Near East* 1, 225–34. New York, Charles Scribner's Sons

Leaman, K. D. and Schott, F. A. (1991) Hydrographic Structure of the Convection Regime in the Gulf of Lions: Winter 1987. *Journal of Physical Oceanography* 21, 575–98

Leighton, R. (1996) From Chiefdom to Tribe? Social organisation and change in later prehistory. In R. Leighton, ed., *Early Societies in Sicily: new developments in archaeological research*, 101–15. London, Accordia Research Centre

Leighton, R. (1998) *Sicily Before History: an archaeological survey from the Palaeolithic to the Iron Age.* London, Duckworth

Lembessi, A. (2002) *Το Ιερό του Ερμή και της Αφροδίτης στη Σύμη Βιάννου III. Τα Χάλκινα Ανθρωπόμορφα Ειδώλια.* Athens, Βιβλιοθήκη της εν Αθήναις Αρχαιολογικής Εταιρείας αρ. 225

Lemonnier, P., ed. (1993) *Technological Choices: transformation in material cultures since the Neolithic.* New York, Routledge

Lemos, I. S. (2002) *The Protogeometric Aegean: the archaeology of the late eleventh and tenth centuries BC.* Oxford Monographs on Classical Archaeology. Oxford, Oxford University Press

Lenz, D., Ruppenstein, F., Baumann, M. and Catling, R. W. V. (1998) Protogeometric Pottery at Troia. *Studia Troica* 8, 189–222

Leonard, A. (1994) *An Index to the Late Bronze Age Pottery from Syria-Palestine.* Studies in Mediterranean Archaeology, 114. Jonsered, Paul Åströms Förlag

Leonard, A. (1995) 'Canaanite Jars' and the Late Bronze Age Aegeo-Levantine Wine Trade. In P. E. McGovern *et al.*, eds., *The Origins and Ancient History of Wine*, 233–54. Luxembourg, Gordon and Breach Publishers

Leonard, A., Hughes, M., Middleton, M. and Schofield, L. (1993) The Making of Aegean Stirrup Jars: technique, tradition and trade. *Annual of the British School at Athens* 88, 105–23

Lerat, L. (1937) Tombes Sub-myceniennes et Geometriques a Delphes. *Bulletin de correspondance hellénique* 61, 44–52

Lev-Tov, J. and Maher, E. F. (2001) Food in Late Bronze Age Funerary Offerings: faunal evidence from Tomb 1 at Tell Dothan. *Palestine Exploration Quarterly* 133, 91–110

Lev-Tov, J. and McGeough, K. (2006) Examining Feasting in Late

Bronze Age Syro-Palestine through Ancient Texts and Bones. In K. Twiss, ed., *The Archaeology of Food and Identity*, 85–111. Center for Archaeological Investigations occasional papers, 34. Carbondale, Southern Illinois University

Levi, S. T. (2004) La Ceramica: circolazione dei prodotti e organizzazione della manifattura. In D. Cocchi Genick, ed., *L'età del bronzo recente in Italia: atti del Congresso nazionale di Lido di Camaiore, 26–29 ottobre 2000*, 233–42. Viareggio, Mauro Baroni

Levy, T. E., Adams, R. B. and Muniz, A. (2004) Archaeology and the Shasu Nomads: recent excavations in the Jabal Hamrat Fidan, Jordan. In W. H. C. Propp and R. E. Freedman, eds., *Le-David Mashid: a birthday tribute for David Noel Freedman*, 63–89. Winona Lake, Eisenbrauns

Levy, T. E., Adams, R. B. and Shafiq, R. (1999) The Jabal Hamrat Fidan Project: excavations at the Wadi Fidan 40 Cemetery, Jordan (1997). *Levant* 31, 293–308

Lewis, D. M. (1973) The Athenian *rationes centesimarum*. In M. I. Finley, ed., *Problèmes de la terre en Grèce ancienne*, 187–212. Paris, Mouton

Liebowitz, H. (1980) Military and Feast Scenes on Late Bronze Palestinian Ivories. *Israel Exploration Journal* 30, 162–9

Lindblom, M. (2001) *Marks and Makers: appearance, distribution and function of middle and late Helladic manufacturers' marks on Aeginetan pottery*. Studies in Mediterranean archaeology, 128. Jonsered, Paul Åmströms Förlag

Linder, E. (1972) A Seafaring Merchant-Smith from Ugarit and the Cape Gelidonya Wreck. *International Journal of Nautical Archaeology* 1, 163–4

Lipiński, E. (1971) Épiphanie de Baal-Haddu, *RS* 24.245. *Ugarit-Forschungen* 3, 81–92

Liu, L. (1996) Settlement Patterns, Chiefdom Variability and the Development of Early States in North China. *Journal of Anthropological Archaeology* 15, 237–88

Liverani, M. (1986) La ceramica e i testi: Commercio Miceneo e politica Orientale. In M. Marazzi *et al.*, eds., *Traffici micenei nel Mediterraneo: problemi storici e documentazione archeologica. Atti del Convegno di Palermo (11–12 maggio e 3–6 dicembre 1984)*, 405–12. Magna Graecia, 3. Taranto, Istituto per la storia e l'archeologia della Magna Grecia

Liverani, M. (1987) The Collapse of the Near Eastern Regional System at the End of the Bronze Age: the case of Syria. In M. Rowlands *et al.*, eds., *Centre and Periphery in the Ancient World*, 66–73. Cambridge, Cambridge University Press

Liverani, M. (1989) Economy of Ugaritic Royal Farms. In C. Zaccagnini, ed., *Production and Consumption in the Ancient Near East*, 127–68. Eötvös Loránd Tudományegyetem ókori történeti tanszékeinek kiadványai. Budapest, Chaire d'Égyptologie de l'Université Loránd Eötvös

Liverani, M. (1990) *Prestige and Interest: international relations in the Near East ca. 1600–1100 B.C.* History of the Ancient Near East, 1. Padua, Sargon

Liverani, M. (2003) The Influence of Political Institutions on Trade in the Ancient Near East (Late Bronze to Early Iron Ages). In C. Zaccagnini, ed., *Mercanti e politica nel Mondo Antico*, 119–37. Rome, 'L'Erma' di Bretschneider

Liverani, M. (2005) The Near East: the Bronze Age. In J. G. Manning and I. Morris, eds., *The Ancient Economy: evidence and models*, 47–57. Stanford, Stanford University Press

Lo Porto, F. G. (1963) Leporano (Taranto): la stazione protostorica di Porto Perone. *Notizie degli scavi di antichità* 17, 280–380

Lo Schiavo, F. (2003) Sardinia between East and West: interconnection in the Mediterranean. In N. C. Stampolidis and V. Karageorghis, eds., *Πλόες: Sea Routes. Interconnections in the Mediterranean 16th–6th C. BC*, 15–34. Athens, Museum of Cycladic Art

Lo Schiavo, F. (2005) Metallhandel im zentralen Mittelmeer. In U. n. Yalçin *et al.*, eds., *Das Schiff von Uluburun: Welthandel vor 3000 Jahren. Katalog der Ausstellung des Deutschen Bergbau-Museums Bochum vom 15. Juli 2005 bis 16. Juli 2006*. Bochum, Deutsches Bergbau-Museum

Lo Schiavo, F., Macnamara, E. and Vagnetti, L. (1985) Late Cypriot Imports to Italy and their Influence on Local Bronzework. *Papers of the British School at Rome* 53, 1–71

Loffreda, S. (1968) Typological Sequence of Iron Age Rock-Cut Tombs in Palestine. *Liber Annuus* 18, 244–87

Lolis, C. J., Bartzokas, A. and Katsoulis, B. D. (2002) Spatial and Temporal 850 hPa Air Temperature and Sea-Surface Temperature Covariances in the Mediterranean Region and their Connection to Atmospheric Circulation. *International Journal of Climatology* 22, 663–76

Lolos, Y. G. (2003) Cypro-Myceneaan Reltions *ca*. 1200 BC: Point Iria in the gulf of Argos and Old Salamis in the Saronic gulf. In N. C. Stampolidis and V. Karageorghis, eds., *Πλόες: Sea Routes. Interconnections in the Mediterranean 16th–6th C. BC*, 101–16. Athens, Museum of Cycladic Art

London, G. A. (1989) A Comparison of Two Contemporaneous Lifestyles of the Late Second Millennium B.C. *Bulletin of the American Schools of Oriental Research* 273, 37–55

London, G. A. (1999) Central Jordanian Ceramic Traditions. In B. MacDonald and R. W. Younkers, eds., *Ancient Ammon*, 57–102. Leiden, Brill

Long, C. R. (1978) The Lasithi Dagger. *American Journal of Archaeology* 82.1, 35–46

Loretz, O. (1996) A Hurrian word (*tkt*) for the Chariot of the Cloud-Rider? (KTU 1.4 v 6–9). In N. Wyatt *et al.*, eds., *Ugarit, Religion and Culture*, 167–78. Münster, Ugarit-Verlag

Luckenbill, D. D. (1914) Jadanan and Javan (Danaans and Ionians). *Zeitschrift für Assyriologie und verwandte Gebiete* 28, 92–9

Maasch, K. A., Mayewski, P. A., Rohling, E. J., Stager, J. C., Karlen, W., Meeker, L. D. and Meyerson, E. A. (2005) A 2000 Year Context for Modern Climate Change. *Geografiska Annaler* 87A, 7–15

Macdonald, C. (1986) Problems of the Twelfth Century BC in the Dodecanese. *Annual of the British School at Athens* 81, 125–51

MacDonald, C. and Driessen, J. (1990) Storm Drains of the East Wing at Knossos. In P. Darcque and R. Treuil, eds., *L'habitat égéen préhistorique. Actes de la table ronde internationale, Athènes, 23–25 juin 1987, organisés par le Centre National de la Recherche Scientifique, l'Université de Paris et l'École française d'Athènes*, 141–46. Athens, École française d'Athènes

Macqueen, J. G. (1996) *The Hittites and their Contemporaries in Asia Minor*. Ancient Peoples and Places, 83. London, Thames and Hudson

Maeir, A. M. (2004) *Bronze and Iron Age Tombs at Tel Gezer, Israel: finds from Raymond-Charles Weill's excavations in 1914 and 1921*. BAR International Series, 1206. Oxford, Archaeopress

Maekawa, K. (1984) Cereal Cultivation in the Ur III Period. *Bulletin on Sumerian Agriculture* 1, 73–96

Maekawa, K. (1986) The Agricultural Texts of Ur III Lagash of the British Museum (III). *Acta Sumerologica* 8, 85–120

Maekawa, K. (1990) Cultivation Methods in the Ur III Period. *Bulletin on Sumerian Agriculture* 5, 115–45

Magill, C. (2006) *Reconstruction of Holocene Climate Variability within the Central Mediterranean using Lake Sediment Cores from the Akrotirí Peninsula, Crete*. Unpublished undergraduate honours thesis, Department of Geology and Planetary Science, University of Pittsburgh

Magrill, P. and Middleton, A. (1997) A Canaanite Potter's Workshop of Lachish, Israel. In I. Freestone and D. Gaimster, eds., *Pottery in the Making: world ceramic traditions*, 68–74. London, British Museum Press

Magrill, P. and Middleton, A. (2004) Studies in Pottery, Petrography, Geology, Environment and Technology. Section A: Late Bronze Age pottery technology – Cave 4034 Revisited. In D. Ussishkin, ed., *Renewed Archaeological Excavations at Lachish*, 2,514–51. University of Tel Aviv Monographs, 22. Tel Aviv, Emery and Claire Yass Publications in Archaeology

Maheras, P., Xoplaki, E., Davies, T., Martin-Vide, J., Bariendos, M. and Alcoforado, M. J. (1999) Warm and Cold Monthly Anomalies across the Mediterranean Basin and their Relationship with Circulation; 1860–1990. *International Journal of Climatology* 19, 1,697–1,715

Maier, F. G. (1999) Palaipaphos and the Transition to the Early Iron Age: continuities, discontinuities and location shifts. In M. Iacovou and D. Michaelides, eds., *Cyprus, the Historicity of the Geometric Horizon: proceedings of an archaeological workshop, University of Cyprus, Nicosia, 11th October 1998*, 79–94. Nicosia, Archaeological Research Unit, University of Cyprus

Maier, F. G. and Karageorghis, V. (1984) *Paphos: history and archaeology*. Nicosia, A. G. Leventis Foundation

Malbran-Labat, F. (2000) Commerce at Ugarit. *Near Eastern Archaeology* 63.4, 195

Malkin, I. (2003) Networks and the Emergence of Greek Identity. *Mediterranean Historical Review* 18, 56–74

Manassa, C. (2003) *The Great Karnak Inscription of Merneptah: grand strategy in the 13th century BC*. Yale Egyptological Studies 5. New Haven, Yale Egyptological Seminar

Mangini, A., Verdes, P., Spötl, C., Scholz, D., Vollweiler, N. and Kromer, B. (2007) Persistent Influence of the North Atlantic Hydrography on Central European Winter Temperature during the Last 9000 Years. *Geophysical Research Letters* 34, L02704, doi:10.1029/2006GL028600

Manning, S. W. and Hulin, L. (2005) Maritime Commerce and Geographies of Mobility in the Late Bronze Age of the Eastern Mediterranean: problematizations. In E. Blake and A. B. Knapp, eds., *The Archaeology of Mediterranean Prehistory*, 270–302. Oxford, Blackwell

Mannino, G. and Spatafora, F. (1995) Mokarta: la necropoli di Cresta di Gallo. *Quaderni del Museo Archeologico Regionale 'A. Salinas'* 1

Maran, J. (2000a) Das Megaron im Megaron: zur Datierung und Funktion des Antenbaus im mykenischen Palast von Tiryns. *Archäologischer Anzeiger*, 1–16

Maran, J. (2000b) Tiryns, Jahresbericht 1999. *Archäologischer Anzeiger*, 574–5

Maran, J. (2001a) Political and Religious Aspects of Architectural Change on the Upper Citadel of Tiryns: the case of Building T. In R. Laffineur and R. Hägg, eds., *Potnia: deities and religion in the Aegean Bronze Age. Proceedings of the 8th International Aegean Conference, Göteborg, Göteborg University, 12–15 April 2000*, 113–22. Aegaeum, 22. Liège, Université de Liège

Maran, J. (2001b) Tiryns, Archaeology in Greece 2000–2001. *Archaeological Reports* 47, 30–1

Maran, J. (2001c) Tiryns, Jahresbericht 2000. *Archäologischer Anzeiger*, 639–40

Maran, J. (2002) Licht auf ein dunkles Jahrhundert. *Ruperto Carola* 2, 4–11

Maran, J. (2004a) Architektonische Innovation im spätmykenischen Tiryns: lokale Bauprogramme und fremde Kultureinflüsse. In H.-G. n. Buchholz, ed., *Der Werkstoff Holz und seine Nutzung im ostmediterranen Altertum: Beiheft zum Tagungsband 'Althellenische Technologie und Technik, Ohlstadt 2003'*, 261–86. Weilheim, Verein zur Förderung der Aufarbeitung der Hellenischen Geschichte e.V.

Maran, J. (2004b) The Spreading of Objects and Ideas in the Late Bronze Age Eastern Mediterranean: two case examples from the Argolid of the 13th and 12th centuries B. C. *Bulletin of the American Schools of Oriental Research* 336, 11–30

Maran, J. (2005) Late Minoan Coarse Ware Stirrup Jars on the Greek Mainland: a postpalatial perspective from the 12th century BC Argolid. In A. L. D'Agata and J. Moody, eds., *Ariadne's Threads: connections between Crete and the Greek mainland in the post-palatial period*, 415–31. Athens, Italian School at Athens

Maran, J. (2006) Coming to Terms with the Past: ideology and power in Late Helladic IIIC. In S. Deger-Jalkotzy and I. S. Lemos, eds., *Ancient Greece: from the Mycenaean palaces to the Age of Homer*, 123–50. Edinburgh, Edinburgh University Press

Maran, J. (in press) Ideentransfer im östlichen Mittelmeerraum während der spätmykenischen Zeit. *Festschrift für H. Todorova*

Maran, J. and Papadimitriou, A. (2006) Bericht zu den Ausgrabungen in Stadt-Nordost. In J. Maran (ed.) 'Forschungen im Stadtgebiet von Tiryns 1999–2002'. *Archäologischer Anzeiger*, 99–133

Marangou, L., ed. (1992) *Minoan and Greek Civilization from the Mitsotakis Collection*. Athens, N. P. Goulandris Foundation; Museum of Cycladic Art

Margueron, J.-C. (1994) Fondations et refondations au Proche Orient au Bronze Recent. In S. Mazzoni, ed., *Nuove Fondazioni nel Vicino Oriente Antico: Realta e Ideologia*, 3–27. Seminari di Orientalistica 4. Pisa, Giardini

Marinatos, S. (1931) Μια Ὑστερομινοικὶ καύσισ αεκρού εκ Τψλίσου. *Mitteilungen des Deutschen Archäologischen Instituts* 56, 112–18

Marketou, T. (1988) Ιαλυσός-Ιξιά. *Αρχαιολογικό Δελτίο* 43 Χρονικά, 611–25

Marketou, T. (1991) Τριάντα. *Αρχαιολογικό Δελτίο* 46 Χρονικά, 481–3

Markoe, G. (1985) *Phoenician Bronze and Silver Bowls from Cyprus and the Mediterranean*. Berkeley, University of California Press

Markoe, G. (1992) In Pursuit of Metal: Phoenicians and Greeks in Italy. In G. Kopcke and I. Tokumaru, eds., *Greece between East and West, 10th–8th centuries BC: papers of the meeting at the Institute of Fine Arts, New York University, March 15–16th, 1990*, 61–84. Mainz-am-Rhein, Philipp von Zabern

Martin, M. A. S. (2004) Egyptian and Egyptianized Pottery in Late Bronze Age Canaan. *Egypt and the Levant* 14, 265–84

Martin, M. A. S. (2005) *Aspects of the Egyptian Involvement in Late Bronze and Early Iron Age Canaan: the Egyptian and Egyptian-style pottery*. Unpublished PhD dissertation, University of Vienna

Matson, F. R. (1972) Ceramic Studies. In W. A. McDonald and G. R. Rapp Jr., eds., *The Minnesota Messenia Expedition: reconstructing a Bronze Age regional environment*, 200–24. Minneapolis, University of Minnesota Press

Matthäus, H. (1980) *Die Bronzegefäße der kretisch-mykenischen Kultur*. Prähistorische Bronzefunde II, 1. Munich, Beck

Mayewski, P. A., Meeker, L. D., Twickler, M. S., Whitlow, S., Yang, Q. and Prentice, M. (1997) Major Features and Forcing of High Latitude Northern Hemisphere Atmospheric Circulation using a 110,000-Year-Long Glaciochemical Series. *Journal of Geophysical Research* 102, 26,345–66

Mayewski, P. A., Rohling, E. J., Stager, J. C., Karlén, W., Maasch, K., Meeker, L. D., Meyerson, E., Gasse, F., Van Kreveld, S., Holmgren, K. J. L.-T., Rosqvist, G., Rack, F., Staubwasser, M., Schneider, R. R. and Steig, E. (2004) Holocene Climate Variability. *Quaternary Research* 62, 243–55

Mazar, A. (1985) *Excavations at Tell Qasile: part two*. Qedem, 20. Jerusalem, The Hebrew University of Jerusalem

Mazar, A. (1994) The 11th Century BC in the Land of Israel. In V. Karageorghis, ed., *Cyprus in the 11th Century B.C: proceedings of the international symposium organized by the Archaeological Research Unit of the University of Cyprus and the Anastasios G. Leventis Foundation, Nicosia, 30–31 October, 1993*, 39–57. Nicosia, A. G. Leventis Foundation and the University of Cyprus

Mazar, A. (1997a) Area P. In A. Ben-Tor and R. Bonfil, eds., *Hazor V: an account of the fifth season of excavation, 1968*, 353–84. Jerusalem, Israel Exploration Society

Mazar, A. (1997b) *Timnah (Tel Batash) I: stratigraphy and architecture*. Qedem, 37. Jerusalem, Hebrew University of Jerusalem

Mazarakis Ainian, A. (1997) *From Rulers' Dwellings to Temples: architecture, religion and society in Early Iron Age Greece (1100–700 B.C.)*. Studies in Mediterranean Archaeology, 121. Jonsered, Paul Åmströms Förlag

McDonald, W. A. and Rapp, G. R., eds. (1972) *The Minnesota Messenia Expedition: reconstructing a bronze age regional environment*. Minneapolis, University of Minnesota Press

McEnroe, J. C. (1982) A Typology of Minoan Houses. *American Journal of Archaeology* 86.1, 3–19

McEnroe, J. C. (1990) The Significance of Local Styles in Minoan Vernacular Architecture. In P. Darcque and R. Treuil, eds., *L'habitat égéen préhistorique. Actes de la table ronde internationale, Athènes, 23–25 juin 1987, organisés par le Centre National de la Recherche Scientifique, l'Université de Paris et l'École française d'Athènes*, 196–202. Athens, École française d'Athènes

McEnroe, J. C. (2001) The Architecture of Pseira. In J. C. McEnroe, ed., *Pseira V: the architecture of Pseira*, 1–78. Philadelphia, University of Pennsylvania Museum of Archaeology and Anthropology

McGeorge, P. J. P. (2001) Anthropological Approach to the Pylona Tombs: the skeletal remains. In E. Karantzali, ed., *The Mycenaean Cemetery at Pylona on Rhodes*, 82–99. BAR International Series, 988. Oxford, Archaeopress

McGovern, P. (1994) Were the Sea Peoples at Beth Shan? In N. P. Lemche and M. Müller, eds. *Fra dybet: festskrift til John Strange i anledning af 60 års fødselsdagen den 20 juli 1994*, 144–56. Forum for bibelsk eksegese, 5. Copenhagen, Museum Tusculanum

McHugh, F. (1999) *Theoretical and Quantitative Approaches to the Study of Mortuary Practice*. BAR International Series, 785. Oxford, Archaeopress

Mee, C. (1978) Aegean Trade and Settlement in Anatolia in the Second Millennium B.C. *Anatolian Studies* 28, 121–56

Mee, C. (1982) *Rhodes in the Bronze Age: an archaeological survey*. Warminster, Aris and Phillips

Mee, C. (1988) The LH IIIB Period in the Dodecanese. In S. Dietz and I. Papachristodoulou, eds., *Archaeology in the Dodecanese*, 56–8. Copenhagen, National Museum of Denmark Department of Near Eastern and Classical Antiquity

Mee, C. (1998) Anatolia and the Aegean in the Late Bronze Age. In E. Cline and D. Harris-Cline, eds., *The Aegean and the Orient in the Second Millennium: proceedings of the 50th anniversary symposium Cincinnati, 18–20 April 1997*, 137–48. Aegaeum, 18. Liège, Histoire de l'art et archéologie de la Grèce antique

Meeker, L. D. and Mayewski, P. A. (2002) A 1400-Year High-Resolution Record of Atmospheric Circulation over the North Atlantic and Asia. *Holocene* 12, 257–66

Meiggs, R. and Lewis, D. (1988) *A Selection of Greek Historical Inscriptions to the End of the Fifth Century B.C.* Oxford, Clarendon Press

Melas, E. M. (1984) The Origins of Aegean Cremation. *Ανθρωπολογικά* 5, 21–36

Melas, E. M. (2001) Καύσεις νεκρών: προς μιά αρχαιολογία του φόβου. In N. C. Stampolidis, ed., *Καύσεις στην Εποχή του Χαλκού και την Πρώιμη Εποχή του Σιδήρου*, 15–29. Athens, Panepistemio tes Kretes

Mellink, M. J. (1986) Postscript. In M. J. Mellink, ed., *Troy and the Trojan War: a symposium held at Bryn Mawr College, October 1984*, 93–101. Bryn Mawr, The Department of Classical and Near Eastern Archaeology, Bryn Mawr College

Menu, B. (1970) *Le regime juridique des terres et du personnel attaché à la terre dans le Papyrus Wilbour*. Lille, P. Geuthner

Meriç, R. (2003) Excavations at Bademgediği Tepe (Puranda) 1999–2002: a preliminary report. *Istanbuler Mitteilungen* 53, 79–98

Merillees, R. S. (1962) Opium Trade in the Bronze Age Levant. *Antiquity* 36, 287–92

Merillees, R. (1968) *The Cypriote Bronze Age Pottery Found in Egypt*. Studies in Mediterranean Archaeology, 18. Lund, Bloms Boktryckeri

Merousis, N. I. (2000) *Οι Εικονογραφικοί Κύκλοι των ΥΜΙΙΙ λαρνάκων: Οι Διαστάσεις της Εικονογραφίας στα Πλαίσια των Ταφικών Πρακτικών*. Thessaloniki, Αριστοτέλειο Πανεπιστήμιο Θεσσαλονίκης, Φιλοσοφική Σχολή

Metzger, M. and Barthel, U.-R. (1993) *Die spätbronzezeitlichen*

Tempelanlagen: die Kleinefunde, 2 vols. Saarbrücker Beiträge zur Altertumskunde, 40. Bonn, Habelt

Michailidou, A. (1990) The Settlement of Akrotiri (Thera): a theoretical approach to the function of the upper story. In P. Darcque and R. Treuil, eds., *L'habitat égéen préhistorique. Actes de la table ronde internationale, Athènes, 23–25 juin 1987, organisés par le Centre National de la Recherche Scientifique, l'Université de Paris et l'École française d'Athènes*, 293–306. Athens, École française d'Athènes

Militello, P. (2004) Commercianti, architetti ed artigiani: riflessioni sulla presenza micenea nell'area iblea. In V. La Rosa, ed., *Le presenze micenee nel territorio siracusano: I Simposio siracusano di preistoria siciliana in memoria di Paolo Orsi, Siracusa, 15–16 dicembre 2003, Palazzo Impellizzeri, Museo archeologico regionale Paolo Orsi*, 293–334. Padua, Bottega d'Erasmo

Militello, P. (2005) Mycenaean Palaces and Western Trade: a problematic relationship. In R. Laffineur and E. Greco, eds., *Emporia: Aegeans in the Central and Esatern Mediterranean. Proceedings of the 10th International Aegean Conference/10e Rencontre égéenne internationale. Athens, Italian School of Archaeology, 14–18 April 2004*, 585–97. Aegaeum, 25. Liège, Université de Liège

Miller, D. (1982) Structures and Strategies: an aspect of the relationship between social hierarchy and cultural change. In I. Hodder, ed., *Symbolic and Structural Archaeology*, 89–98. Cambridge, Cambridge University Press

Miller, D. (1985) *Artefacts as Categories: a study of ceramic variability in central India*. Cambridge, Cambridge University Press

Mock, S. B. (1998) Prelude. In S. B. Mock, ed., *The Sowing and the Dawning: termination, dedication, and transformation in the archaeological and ethnographic record of Mesoamerica*, 3–18. Albuquerque, University of New Mexico Press

Mommsen, H., Andrikou, E., Aravantinos, V. and Maran, J. (2002) Neutron Activation Analysis Results of Bronze Age Pottery from Boeotia, Including Ten Linear B Inscribed Stirrup Jars of Thebes. In J. Erzsébet and K. T. Biró, eds., *Archaeometry 98: proceedings of the 31st Symposium, Budapest, April 26–May 3 1998*, 607–12. BAR International Series, 1043. Oxford, Archaeopress

Mommsen, H. and Maran, J. (2000–01) Production Places of some Mycenaean Pictorial Vessels: the contribution of chemical pottery analysis. *Opuscula Atheniensia* 25–26, 95–106

Monchambert, J.-Y. (1983) La céramique de fabrication locale à Ougarit à la fin du bronze récent: quelques exemples. *Syria* 60, 25–45

Monchambert, J.-Y. (2004a) *La céramique d'Ougarit: campagnes de fouilles 1975 et 1976*. Ras Shamra-Ougarit, 15. Paris, Editions Recherche sur les Civilisations

Monchambert, J.-Y. (2004b) La céramique myénienne d'Ougarit: nouvelles données. In J. Balensi *et al.*, eds., *La céramique mycénienne de l'Égée au Levant: hommage à Vronwy Hankey*, 125–40. Travaux de la Maison de l'Orient et de la Méditerranée, 41. Lyon, Maison de l'Orient et de la Méditerranée – Jean Pouilloux

Monroe, C. M. (2000) *Scales of Fate: trade, tradition and transformation in the eastern Mediterranean ca. 1350–1175 BCE*. Unpublished PhD thesis, University of Michigan

Moody, J. (2005a) 'Drought and the Decline of Mycenae', Updated. In A. Dakouri-Hild and S. Sherratt, eds., *Autochthon: papers presented to O. T. P. K. Dickinson on the occasion of his retirement*, 126–33. Oxford, Archaeopress

Moody, J. (2005b) Unravelling the Threads: environmental change in Late Bronze III. In A. L. D'Agata and J. Moody, eds., *Ariadne's Threads: connections between Crete and the Greek mainland in the post-palatial period*, 443–70. Athens, Italian School at Athens

Moody, J. and Steele, L. (in preparation) Cretan and Cypriot Hinterlands and Hinterseas: resource exploitation and production zones in prehistory and antiquity. *Proceedings of the Parallel Lives Conference, November 30–December 2, 2006, Nicosia, Cyprus*

Mook, M. (1993) *The Northwest Building: houses of the Late Bronze and Early Iron Ages on the Kastro at Kavousi, East Crete*. Unpublished PhD thesis, University of Minnesota

Mook, M. (2000) Traditional Architecture and Archaeological Reconstruction at Kavousi. In J. D. Muhly and E. Sikla, eds., *Crete 2000: a centennial celebration of american archaeological work on Crete (1900–2000)*, 94–100. Athens

Mook, M. and Haggis, D. C. (1994) Aspects of Vernacular Architecture in Postpalatial and Early Iron Age Crete (abstract). *American Journal of Archaeology* 98.2, 307

Moran, W. L. (1992) *The Amarna Letters*. Baltimore and London, Johns Hopkins University Press

Morgan, C. (1999) *Isthmia: excavations by the University of Chicago under the auspices of the American School of Classical Studies at Athens. Vol. 8, the Late Bronze Age settlement and early iron age sanctuary*. Athens, American Shool of Classical Studies at Athens

Morgan, L. (1988) *The Miniature Wall Paintings of Thera: a study in Aegean culture and iconography*. Cambridge, Cambridge University Press

Morricone, L. (1965–66) Eleona e Langada: Sepolcreti della Tarda Età del Bronzo a Coo. *Annuario della Scuola archeologica di Atene e delle missioni italiane in Oriente* 43–4, 5–311

Morricone, L. (1972–73) Coo: scavi e scoperte nel 'Serraglio' E in localita minori (1935–1943). *Annuario della Scuola archeologica di Atene e delle Missioni italiane in Oriente* 50–51, 139–396

Morris, C. E. (1990) In Pursuit of the White Tusked Boar: aspects of hunting on Mycenaean society. In R. Hägg and G. C. Nordquist, eds., *Celebrations of Death and Divinity in the Bronze Age Argolid: proceedings of the Sixth International Symposium at the Swedish Institute at Athens, 11–13 June 1988*, 149–56. Stockholm, Svenska institutet i Athen

Morris, I. (1992) *Death-Ritual and Social Structure in Classical Antiquity*. Key Themes in Ancient History. Cambridge, Cambridge University Press

Morris, S. (2007) Troy Between Bronze and Iron Ages: myth, cult and memory in a sacred landscape. In R. Laffineur and S. P. Morris, eds., *EPOS: Reconsidering Greek epic and Aegean Bronze Age Archaeology. Proceedings of the 11th International Aegean Conference, Los Angeles, UCLA – The J. Paul Getty Villa, 20–23 April 2006*. Aegaeum, 28. Liège, Université de Liège

Mountjoy, P. A. (1986) *Mycenaean Decorated Pottery: a guide to identification*. Studies in Mediterranean Archaeology, 73. Göteborg, Paul Åströms forlag

Mountjoy, P. A. (1998) The East Aegean – West Anatolian Interface in the Late Bronze Age: Mycenaeans and the kingdom of Ahhiyawa. *Anatolian Studies* 48, 33–68

Mountjoy, P. A. (1999a) *Regional Mycenaean Decorated Pottery*, 2 vols. Rahden, Deutsches Archäologisches Institut

Mountjoy, P. A. (1999b) Troia VII Reconsidered. *Studia Troica* 9, 295–346

Mountjoy, P. A. (2005) Mycenaean Connections with the Near East in LH IIIC: ships and Sea Peoples. In R. Laffineur and E. Greco, eds., *Emporia: Aegeans in the central and eastern Mediterranean. Proceedings of the 10th International Aegean Conference/10ᵉ Rencontre égéenne internationale. Athens, Italian School of Archaeology, 14–18 April 2004*, 423–7; pls. XCV–XCVIII. Aegaeum, 25. Liège, Université de Liège

Mu-chou Poo (2005) *Enemies of Civilization: attitudes toward foreigners in ancient Mesopotamia, Egypt, and China*. SUNY Series in Chinese Philosophy and Culture. New York, State University of New York Press

Mudar, K. R. (1999) How Many Dvaravati Kingdoms? Locational analysis of 1st millennium A.D. moated settlement in central Thailand. *Journal of Anthropological Archaeology* 18, 1–28

Mühlenbock, C., Prescott, C. and Dixon, C. (2004) *The Scandinavian Sicilian Archaeological Project: archaeological excavations at Monte Polizzo Sicily. Reports 1998–2001*. Göteborg, Deptartment of Archaeology, University of Göteborg

Mühlenbruch, T. (2005) *Ein dunkles Zeitalter? Untersuchungen zur Siedlungsstruktur der Unterburg von Tiryns in der mykenischen Nachpalastzeit*. Unpublished PhD dissertation, University of Heidelberg

Muhly, J. D. (1982) How Iron Technology Changed the Ancient World – and Gave the Philistines a Military Edge. *Biblical Archaeology Review* 8.6, 42–54

Muhly, J. D., Stech Wheeler, T. and Madin, R. (1977) The Cape Gelidonya Shipwreck and the Bronze Age Metals Trade in the Eastern Mediterranean. *Journal of Field Archaeology* 4.3, 353–62

Muhly, P. M. (1984) Minoan Hearths. *American Journal of Archaeology* 88.2, 107–22

Müller-Karpe, H. (1962) *Zur Stadtwerdung Roms*. Mitteilungen des Deutschen Archaeologischen Instituts 8. Heidelberg, Kerle

Münger, S. (2003) Egyptian Stamp-Seal Amulets and their Implications for the Chronology of the Early Iron Age. *Tel Aviv* 30, 66–82

Na'aman, N. (1988) Pharaonic Lands in the Jezreel Valley in the Late Bronze Age. In M. Heltzer and E. Lipinski, eds., *Society and Economy in the Eastern Mediterranean (c. 1500–1000 B.C.)*, 177–85. Leuven, Uitgeverij Peeters

Naville, E. and Griffiths, F. L. (1890) *The City of Onias and the Mound of the Jews: the antiquities of Tell el-Yaûdiyeh*. London, Paul Kegan, Trench, Trübner & Co.

Negbi, O. (1976) *Canaanite Gods in Metal: an archaeological study of ancient Syro-Palestinian figurines*. Tel Aviv, Tel Aviv University

Negbi, O. (1989) The Metal Figurines. In A. Ben-Tor, ed., *Hazor III–IV*, 359–62. Jerusalem, The Israel Exploration Society

Negbi, O. (1991) Were there Sea Peoples in the Central Jordan Valley at the Transition from the Bronze Age to the Iron Age? *Tel Aviv* 18, 205–43

Negbi, O. (1998) Were there Sea Peoples in the Central Jordan Valley at the Transition from the Bronze Age to the Iron Age? Once Again. *Tel Aviv* 25, 184–207

Nelson, B. (2000) Abandonment: conceptualization, representation, and social change. In M. B. Schiffer, ed., *Social Theory in Archaeology*, 52–62. Salt Lake City, The University of Utah Press

Nelson, H. H. (1943) The Naval Battle Pictured at Medinet Habu. *Journal of Near Eastern Studies* 2, 40–55

Nicklin, K. (1971) Stability and Innovation in Pottery Manufacture. *World Archaeology* 3, 13–48

Niemeier, W.-D. (1985) *Die Palaststilkeramik von Knossos: Stil, Chronologie und historischer Kontext*. Archäologische Forschungen, 13. Berlin, Mann

Niemeier, W.-D. (1998) The Mycenaeans in Western Anatolia and the Problem of the Origins of the Sea Peoples. In S. Gitin *et al.*, eds., *Mediterranean Peoples in Transition: thirteenth to early tenth centuries BCE*, 17–65. Jerusalem, Israel Exploration Society

Niemeier, W.-D. (2002) Μικρά Ασία και Αχαιοί. *Καθημερινή: Επτά Ημέρες, Sunday March 31st*, 18–22. Athens

Nijboer, A. J. (2005) La cronologia assoluta dell'età del Ferro nel Mediterraneo, dibattito sui metodi e sui risultati. In G. Bartoloni and F. Delpino, eds., *Oriente e Occidente: metodi e discipline a confronto, riflessioni sulla cronologia dell'età del Ferro in Italia. Atti dell'Incontro di studi, Roma, 30–31 ottobre, 2003*, 527–56. Mediterranea, 1. Pisa, Isittuti editoriali e poligrafici internazionali

Nitsche, A. (1987) Protogeometrische und subprotogeometrische Keramik aus dem Heiligtum von Kalapodi. *Archäologischer Anzeiger*, 35–49

Noort, E. (1994) *Die Seevölker in Palästina*. Palaestina Antiqua. Kampen, Kok Pharos

Nougayrol, J. (1955) *Le palais royal d'Ugarit III*, 2 vols. Mission de Ras Shamra, 6. Paris, Klincksieck

Nowicki, K. (1987) The History and Setting of the Town of Karphi. *Studi Micenei ed Egeo-Anatolici* 26, 235–56

Nowicki, K. (2000) *Defensible Sites in Crete, c. 1200–800 B.C. (LM IIIB/IIIC through Early Geometric)*. Liège, Université de Liège

Nowicki, K. (2002) From Late Minoan IIIC Refuge Settlements to Geometric Acropoleis: architecture and social organization of Dark Age villages and towns in Crete. In J.-M. Luce, ed., *Habitat et urbanisme dans le monde grec de la fin des palais mycéniens à la prise de Milet (494 Av. J.-C.)*, 149–174 (English Summary, 362). Toulouse, Presses Universitaires du Mirail

O'Callaghan, R. T. (1949) The Great Phoenician Portal Inscription from Karatepe. *Orientalia* 18, 173–295

O'Connor, D. (2003) Egypt's Views of 'Others'. In J. Tait, ed., *'Never Had the Like Occurred': Egypt's view of its past*, 155–186. Encounters with Ancient Egypt. London, UCL Press

O'Brien, S. R., Mayewski, P. A., Meeker, L. D., Meese, D. A., Twickler, M. S. and Whitlow, S. I. (1995) Complexity of Holocene Climate as Reconstructed from a Greenland Ice Core. *Science* 270, 1,962–64

Oktay, D. (2002) Design with the Climate in Housing Environments: an analysis in northern Cyprus. *Building and Environment* 37, 1,003–12

Oren, E. D. (1973) *The Northern Cemetery of Beth Shan*. Leiden, Brill

Oren, E. D. (1984) 'Governors' Residencies' in Canaan under the New Kingdom: a case study in Egyptian administration. *Journal for the Society of the Study of Egyptian Antiquities* 14, 37–56

Oren, E. D. (2006) The Establishment of Egyptian Imperial Administration on the 'Ways of Horus': an archaeological perspective from north Sinai. In E. Czerny *et al.*, eds., *Timelines: studies in honor of Manfred Bietak*, 279–92. Orentalia Lovaniensia Analecta, 149. Leuven, Uitgeverij Peeters en Departement Oosterse Studies

Oren, E. D., ed. (2000) *The Sea Peoples and Their World: A Reassessment*. Philadelphia, University of Pennsylvania Museum.

Orsi, P. (1889) Contributi all'archeologia preellenica sicula. *Bollettino di Paletnologia* 15, 173–88

Orsi, P. (1895) Thapsos. *Monumenti Antichi dei Lincei* 6, 89–150

Orsi, P. (1899) Pantalica e Cassibile. *Monumenti Antichi dei Lincei* 9, 33–146

Orsi, P. (1912) Le necropoli sicule di Pantalica e Monte Dessueri. *Monumenti Antichi dei Lincei* 21, 301–406

Osborne, R. and Cunliffe, B., eds. (2005) *Mediterranean Urbanization, 800–600 B.C.* Proceedings of the British Academy, 126. Oxford, Oxford University Press

Owen, D. I. (1981) An Akkadian letter from Ugarit at Tel Aphek. *Tel Aviv* 8, 1–17

Özdogan, M. (1987) Taslicabayir: a Late Bronze Age burial in eastern Thrace. *Anatolica* 14, 5–39

Pacciarelli, M. (2001) *Dal villaggio alla città: la svolta protourbana del 1000 a.C. nell'Italia tirrenica*. Florence, All'Insegna del Giglio

Page, D. L. (1959) *History and the Homeric Iliad*. Berkeley, University of California Press

Pagliara, C. (2005) Roca Vecchia (Lecce) il sito, le fortificazioni e l'abitato dell'età del bronzo. In R. Laffineur and E. Greco, eds., *Emporia: Aegeans in the central and eastern Mediterranean. Proceedings of the 10th International Aegean Conference/10ᵉ Rencontre égéenne internationale. Athens, Italian School of Archaeology, 14–18 April 2004*, 629–37. Aegaeum, 25. Liège, Université de Liège

Palaima, T. G. (1989) Perspectives on the Pylos Oxen Tablets: textual (and archaeological) evidence for the use and management of oxen in Late Bronze Age Messenia (and Crete). In T. G. Palaima *et al.*, eds., *Studia Mycenaea 1988*, 85–124. Živa Antika Monograph, 7. Skopje, Macedonian Academy of Sciences and Arts

Palaima, T. G. (1991) Maritime Matters in the Linear B Tablets. In R. Laffineur and L. Basch, eds., *Thalassa: l'Égée préhistorique et la mer. Actes de la troisième Rencontre égéenne internationale de l'Université deLiège, Station de recherches sousmarines et océanographiques (StaReSO), Calvi, Corse (23–25 avril 1990)*, 273–310. Liège, Université de Liège

Palaima, T. G. (1997) Potter and Fuller: the royal craftsmen. In R. Laffineur and P. P. Betancourt, eds., *Τεχνη· craftsmen, craftswomen and craftsmanship in the Aegean Bronze Age. Proceedings of the 6th International Aegean Conference/ 6ᵉ rencontre égéenne internationale, Philadelphia, Temple University, 18–21 April 1996*, 407–12. Aegaeum, 16. Liège and Austin, Université de Liège and the University of Texas at Austin

Palermo, D. (1981) Contributi alla conoscenza dell'età del ferro in Sicilia: Polizzello. *Cronache di Archeologia* 20, 103–48

Palermo, D. (1996) Tradizione indigena e apporti greci nelle culture della Sicilia centro-meridionale: il caso di Sant'Angelo Muxaro. In R. Leighton, ed., *Early Societies in Sicily: new developments in archaeological research*, 147–54. London, Accordia Research Centre

Palermo, D. (1997) I modellini di edifici a pianta circolare da Polizzello e la tradizione cretese nei santuari dell'area sicana. *Cronache di Archeologia* 36, 35–45

Palermo, D. (1999) Il deposito votivo sul margine orientale della Patela di Priniàs. In V. La Rosa *et al.*, eds., *Επί πόντον πλαζόμενοι: simposio italiano di studi egei, dedicato a Luigi Bernabò Brea e Giovanni Pugliese Carratelli. Roma, 18–20 febbraio 1998*, 207–13. Rome, Scuola archeologica italiana di Atene

Palermo, D. (2003) La ripresa degli scavi sulla Montagna di Polizzello. *Orizzonti* 4, 95–9

Palermo, D. and Tanasi, D. (2006) Diodoro Siculo a Polizzello. In C. Miccichè *et al.*, eds., *Diodoro Siculo e la Sicilia indigena: atti del convegno di studi*, 89–102. Caltanissetta, Regione Siciliana

Palmer, L. R. (1963) *The Interpretation of Mycenaean Greek Texts*. Oxford, Clarendon Press

Palmer, R. (1989) Subsistence Rations at Pylos and Knossos. *Minos* 24, 89–124

Panitz-Cohen, N. (2006) *Processes of Ceramic Change and Continuity: Tel Batash in the second millennium BCE as a test case*. Unpublished PhD dissertation. Hebrew University of Jerusalem

Panitz-Cohen, N. and Mazar, A., eds. (2006) *Timnah (Tel Batash) III: the finds from the second millennium BCE*. Qedem, 45. Monographs of the Institute of Archaeology. Jerusalem, Hebrew University of Jerusalem

Panvini, R. (1986) La necropoli preistorica di contrada Anguilla di Ribera. In M. Marazzi *et al.*, eds., *Traffici micenei nel Mediterraneo: problemi storici e documentazione archeologica. Atti del Convegno di Palermo (11–12 maggio e 3–6 dicembre 1984)*, 113–22. Magna Graecia, 3. Taranto, Istituto per la storia e l'archeologia della Magna Grecia

Panvini, R. (1993–44) L'attività della Soprintendenza di Caltanissetta negli anni 1992–93. *Kokalos* 39–40, 783–823

Panvini, R. (1997) Osservazioni sulle dinamiche formative socioculturali a Dessueri. In S. Tusa, ed., *Prima Sicilia: alle origini della società siciliana*, 493–501. Palermo, Giuseppe Maimone Editore

Papadimitriou, A. (1988) Bericht zur Früheizenzeitlichen Keramik aus der Unterburg von Tiryns: Ausgrabungen in Tiryns 1982/83. *Archäologischer Anzeiger*, 227–43

Papadimitriou, I. and Petsas, P. (1950) Ἀνασκαράί εν Μυκήναις, *Πρακτικά τή εν Ἀηναί Ἀρχαιολογική Εταιρεία* 203–33

Papadopoulos, A. (2006) Cities Under Siege? A Look at Bronze Age Iconography. In J. Day *et al.*, eds., *SOMA 2004. Symposium on Mediterranean Archaeology*, 131–7. BAR International Series, 1514. Oxford, Archaeopress

Papasavvas, G. (2003) Cypriot Casting Technology I: the stands. *Report of the Department of Antiquities Cyprus*, 23–52

Papazoglou-Manioudaki, L. (1982) Ανασκαφή του Μινωικού οικισμού στα Τριάντα της Ρόδου. *ΑΔ* 37 *Μελέτες*, 139–90

Parker-Pearson, M. and Richards, C. (1994) Ordering the World: perceptions of architecture, space and time. In M. Parker-

Pearson and C. Richards, eds., *Architecture and Order: approaches to social space*, 1–37. London, Routledge

Parker Pearson, M. (1999) *The Archaeology of Death and Burial.* Stroud, Sutton

Pearce, M. (2000) Metals Make the World Go Round: the copper supply at Frattesina. In C. F. E. Pare, ed., *Metals Make the World Go Round: the supply and circulation of metals in Bronze Age Europe*, 108–15. Oxford, Oxbow Books

Pendlebury, J. D. S., Pendlebury, H. W. and Money-Coutts, M. B. (1937–38) Excavations in the Plain of Lasithi III. Karphi: a city of refuge of the Early Iron Age in Crete. *Annual of the British School at Athens* 38, 57–148

Peregrine, P. N. (1999) Legitimation Crises in Prehistoric Worlds. In P. N. Kardulias, ed., *World Systems Theory in Practice: leadership, production and exchange*, 37–52. Lanham, Rowman and Littlefield Publishers

Perna, K. (2001) Rituali funerari e rappresentazione del potere nella Creta del TM III A2/B. *Creta Antica* 2, 113–25

Perna, K. (2003) Between Mycenaean Culture and Minoan Tradition: social dynamics in Crete at the end of the Bronze Age. *Mediterranean Archaeology and Archaeometry* 3.2, 17–34

Perna, K. (2004) Karfì: soltanto un sito di rifugio? *Creta Antica* 5, 155–79

Perna, K. (2006) *Nuovi dati sull'occupazione TM III C della Patela di Priniàs.* Unpublished paper presented to the 10th Cretological Congress (Chania, October 4–11 2006)

Perna, K. (in press) Aspetti rituali e implicazioni sociali dell'offerta e della consumazione di cibo nel culto della Dea dalle braccia levate. *Atti della Conferenza Internazionale 'Cibo per gli uomini, cibo per gli dei' (Piazza Armerina, May 4–8, 2005)*

Peroni, R. (1989) *Protostoria dell'Italia continentale: la penisola Italiana nelle età del bronzo e del ferro.* Popoli e civiltà dell'Italia antica, 9. Rome, Spazio Tre

Peroni, R. (1994) *Introduzione alla protostoria italiana.* Manuali Laterza, 47. Rome, Laterza

Peroni, R. (1996) *L'Italia alle soglie della storia.* Collezione storica. Rome, Laterza

Peroni, R. (2000) Formazione e sviluppi dei centri protourbani medio-tirrenici. In A. Carandini and R. Cappelli, eds., *Roma, Romolo, Remo e la fondazione della città*, 26–30. Milan, Electa

Peroni, R. (2004) *L'Italia alle soglie della storia.* Bari, Laterza

Peroni, R., Vanzetti, A. and Bagella, S. (1998) *Broglio di Trebisacce, 1990–1994: elementi e problemi nuovi dalle recenti campagne di scavo.* Soveria Mannelli (Catanzaro), Rubbettino

Petrie, W. M. F. (1905) *Ehnasya.* London, Trübner

Petrie, W. M. F. (1930) *Beth Pelet I (Tell Fara).* London, British School of Archaeology in Egypt

Petrie, W. M. F. (1934) *Ancient Gaza IV. Tell el-Ajjûl.* London, British School of Archaeology in Egypt

Petrie, W. M. F. and Sayce, A. H. (1891) *Illahun, Kahun and Gurob.* London, David Nutt

Petruso, K. (1984) Prolegomena to Late Cypriot Weight Metrology. *American Journal of Archaeology* 88, 293–304

Pilides, D. (1994) *Handmade Burnished Wares of the Late Bronze Age in Cyprus.* Studies in Mediterranean Archaeology, 105. Jonsered, Paul Åmströms Förlag

Pini, I. (1989) Zur 'richtigen' ansight Minoisch-Mykenischer siegel und ringdarstellungen. In W. Müller, ed., *Fragen und Probleme der bronzezeitlichen ägäischen Glyptic: Beiträge zum 3. Internationalen Marburger Siegel-Symposium 5–7 September 1985*, 201–17. Corpus der minoischen und mykenischen Siegel. Beiheft, 3. Berlin, Mann

Pintér, F. (2005) *Provenance Study of the Early Iron Age Knobbed Ware in Troia, N-W Turkey and the Balkans: petrographic and geochemical evidence.* Unpublished thesis, University of Tübingen

Pintér, F. (2006) *Petrographic Analysis of Troian VI, VIIb2, Protogeometric and Archaic Pottery.* Unpublished report for the Scientific Laboratory, State Center for Restoration and Conservation of Historic Monuments, Budapest

Plana-Mallart, R. (1999) Cadastre et chôra ampuritaine. In M. Brunet, ed., *Territoires des cités grecques: actes de la table ronde internationale organisée par l'École Française d'Athènes, 31 octobre–3 novembre 1991*, 199–215. Bulletin de correspondance hellénique, supplément 34. Athens, École française d'Athènes

Platon, N. (1951) I archaiologhikì kínisis en Kríti katá to étos 1951. *Krètika Chronika* 5, 438–49

Platon, N. (1952) Excavations in the Area of Sitia. *Praktikà*, 639–43

Platon, N. (1959) I archaiologhikí kínisis en Kríti katá to étos 1959. *Krètika Chronika* 13, 359–93

Platon, N. (1960) Anaskaphaì periochîs Praisoū. *Praktikà*, 303–5

Platon, N. (1962) Anaskafi Chondrou Viannou. *Praktikà*, 136–47

Podzuweit, C. (2007) *Studien zur spätmykenischen Keramik. Tiryns* XIV. Wiesbaden, Reichert

Polanyi, K. (1964) *The Great Transformation.* New York, Rhineheart

Pologhiorghi, M. (1981) Δύο ταπηέσ τισ ΨΜ III περιόδου στο χηοριό Βολιόνεσ, επαρχηίασ Αμαρίου. *Αρχαιολογικὸν Δελτίον* 36, 82–105

Ponting, M. J. and Karantzali, E. (2001) Appendix I: ICP-AES analysis of some Mycenaean vases from the Pylona cemetery. In E. Karantzali, ed., *The Mycenaean Cemetery on Rhodes.* BAR International Series, 988. Oxford, Archaeopress

Popham, M. R. (1991) Pylos: reflections on the date of its destruction and on its Iron Age reoccupation. *Oxford Journal of Archaeology* 10, 315–324

Popham, M. R. and Milburn, E. (1971) The Late Helladic IIIC Pottery of Xeropolis (Lefkandi): a summary. *Annual of the British School at Athens* 66, 333–6

Popham, M. R. and Sackett, L. H. (1968) *Excavations at Lefkandi, Euboea, 1964–66: a preliminary report.* London, The British School of Archaeology at Athens

Poulos, S. E., Drakopoulos, P. G. and Collins, M. B. (1997) Seasonal Variability in Sea Surface Oceanographic Conditions in the Aegean Sea (Eastern Mediterranean): an overview. *Journal of Marine Systems* 13, 225–44

Prent, M. (2003) Glories of the Past in the Past: ritual activities at palatial ruins in Early Iron Age Crete. In R. M. Van Dyke and S. E. Alcock, eds., *Archaeologies of Memory*, 81–103. Malden, Blackwell

Prent, M. (2005) *Cretan Sanctuaries and Cults.* Religions in the Graeco-Roman world, 154. Leiden, Brill

Preston Day, L. (1997) The Late Minoan IIIC Period at Vronda,

Kavousi. In J. Driessen and A. Farnoux, eds., *La Crète Mycénienne: actes de la Table Ronde Internationale organisée par l'École française d'Athènes, 26–28 Mars 1991*, 394–406. Bulletin de correspondance hellénique, supplément 30. Athens and Paris, École française d'Athènes

Pritchard, J. B. (1968) New Evidence on the Role of the Sea Peoples in Canaan at the Beginning of the Iron Age. In W. A. Ward, ed., *The Role of the Phoenicians in the Interaction of Mediterranean Civilizations*, 99–112. Beirut, The American University of Beirut

Pritchard, J. B. (1975) *Sarepta: a preliminary report on the Iron Age. Excavations of the University of Pennsylvania, 1970–72.* Philadelphia, The University Museum of the University of Pennsylvania

Pritchard, J. B. (1978) *Recovering Sarepta, a Phoenician City: excavations at Sarafund, 1969–1974, by the University Museum of the University of Pennsylvania.* Princeton, Princeton University Press

Pritchard, J. B. (1980) *The Cemetery at Tell es-Sa'idiyeh, Jordan.* University Monograph, 41. Philadelphia, The University Museum of the University of Pennsylvania

Prokopiou, N. (1997) LM III Pottery from the Greek-Italian Excavations at Syvritos Amariou. In E. Hallager and B. Pålsson Hallager, eds., *Late Minoan III Pottery: chronology and terminology. Acts of a meeting held at the Danish Institute at Athens, August 12–14, 1994*, 371–94. Monographs of the Danish Institute at Athens, 1. Athens, Danish Institute at Athens

Psychoghios, D. K. (1995) *Προίκες, φόροι, σταφίδα και ψωμί: οικονομία και οικογένεια στην αγροτική Ελλάδα του 19ου αιώνα.* Athens, Εθνικό Κέντρο Κοινωνικών Ερευνών

Pulak, C. (1997) The Uluburun Shipwreck. In S. Swiny *et al.*, eds., *Res Maritimae: Cyprus and the eastern Mediterranean from prehistory to late antiquity. Proceedings of the Second International Symposium 'Cities on the Sea', Nicosia, Cyprus, October 18–22, 1994*, 233–62. American Schools of Oriental Research Archaeological Reports 4; Cyprus American Archaeological Research Institute Monograph Series, 1. Atlanta, Scholars Press

Pulak, C. (2000) The Copper and Tin Ingots from the Late Bronze Age Shipwreck at Uluburun. *Anatolian Metal I*, 137–57. Der Anschnitt: Zeitschrift für Kunst und Kultur im Bergbau, 13. Bochum, Deutsches Bergbau-Museum

Pulak, C. (2005) Who Were the Mycenaeans Aboard the Uluburun Ship? In R. Laffineur and E. Greco, eds., *Emporia: Aegeans in the Central and Esatern Mediterranean. Proceedings of the 10th International Aegean Conference/10ᵉ Rencontre égéenne internationale. Athens, Italian School of Archaeology, 14–18 April 2004*, 295–310. Aegaeum, 25. Liège, Université de Liège

Pyle, D. M. (1997) The Global Impact of the Minoan Eruption of Santorini, Greece. *Environmental Geology* 30, 59–61

Quagliati, Q. (1900) Prodotti industriali micenei sullo Scoglio del Tonno in Taranto. *Bullettino di Paletnologia Italiana* 26, 285–8

Rackham, O. and Moody, J. (1996) *The Making of the Cretan Landscape.* Manchester, Manchester University Press

Rahmstorf, L. (2001) *Kleinfunde aus Tiryns aus Terrakotta, Stein, Bein und Glas/Fayence vornehmlich spätbronzezeitlicher*

Zeitstellung. Unpublished PhD dissertation, University of Heidelberg

Rahmstorf, L. (2003) Kleinfunde aus Tiryns aus Terrakotta, Stein, Bein und Glas/Fayence vornehmlich spätbronzezeitlicher Zeitstellung. *Archäologisches Nachrichtenblatt* 8, 63–7

Rahmstorf, L. (2005) Ethnicity and Changes in Weaving Technology in Cyprus and the Eastern Mediterranean in the 12th Century BCE. In V. Karageorghis *et al.*, eds., *Cyprus: religion and society from the Late Bronze Age to the end of the Archaic period. Proceedings of the International Symposium on Cypriote Archaeology, Erlangen 23–24 July 2004*, 143–69. Möhnesee, Bibliopolis

Raison, J. (1968) *Les vases à inscriptions peintes de l'Âge Mycénien et leur contexte archéologique.* Incunabula Graeca, 19. Rome, Ateneo

Rajala, U. (2005) From a Settlement to an Early State? The role of Nepi in the local and regional settlement patterns of the Faliscan area and inner Etruria during the Iron Age. In P. Attema *et al.*, eds., *Papers in Italian Archaeology VI: communities and settlements from the Neolithic to the early Medieval period. Proceedings of the 6th Conference of Italian archaeology held at the University of Groningen, Groningen Institute of Archaeology, The Netherlands, April 15–17, 2003*, 706–12. BAR International Series, 1452. Oxford, Archaeopress

Rawson, D. (1936–8) *University of Cincinnati Troy Excavations Field Notebooks 1936–1937 and 1937–1938*, from the Troy Excavation Archive, University of Cincinnati

Reber, K. (1991) *Untersuchungen zur Handgemachten Keramik Griechenlands in der Submykenischen, Protogeometrischen und der Geometrischen Zeit.* Jonsered, Paul Åströms Forlag

Redford, D. B. (1984) *Akhenaten: the heretic king.* Princeton, Princeton University Press

Redford, D. B. (1990) *Egypt and Canaan in the New Kingdom.* Beer-Sheva, Ben-Gurion University of the Negev Press

Redford, D. B. (1992) *Egypt, Canaan, and Israel in Ancient Times.* Princeton, Princeton University Press

Redford, D. B. (2000) Egypt and Western Asia in the Late New Kingdom: an overview. In E. D. Oren, ed., *The Sea Peoples and Their World: a reassessment*, 1–20. Philadelphia, University Museum, University of Pennsylvania

Rega, E. (1996) Age, Gender and Biological Reality in the Early Bronze Age Cemetery at Mokrin. In J. Moore and E. Scott, eds., *Invisible People and Processes: writing gender and childhood into European archaeology*, 229–47. London and New York, Leicester University Press

Renfrew, A. C. (1979) Systems Collapse as Social Transformation: catastrophe and anastrophe in early state societies. In A. C. Renfrew and K. L. Cooke, eds., *Transformations: mathematical approaches to cultural change*, 481–500. New York, Academic Press

Renfrew, A. C. (1981) Questions of Minoan and Mycenaean Cult. In R. Hägg and N. Marinatos, eds., *Sanctuaries and Cults in the Aegean Bronze Age: proceedings of the first international symposium at the Swedish Institute in Athens, 12–13 May, 1980*, 27–33. Stockholm, Svenska institutet i Athen

Renfrew, A. C. (1985) *The Archaeology of Cult: the sanctuary at Phylakopi.* British School at Athens Supplement, 18. London, Thames and Hudson

Renfrew, A. C. (2004) *Future Strategies for Aegean Prehistory –*

Coping with the Unique: the explanatory dilemma. Unpublished paper given at the Mycenaean Seminar, 12 May 2004

Renfrew, C. and Level, E. V. (1979) Exploring Dominance: predicting polities from centers. In K. C. Cooke and C. Renfrew, eds., *Transformations: mathematical approaches to culture change*, 145–67. New York, Academic Press

Ribar, J. W. (1973) *Death Cult Practices in Ancient Palestine*. Unpublished PhD thesis, University of Michigan

Rice, P. M. (1984) The Archaeological Study of Specialized Pottery Production. In P. M. Rice, ed., *Pots and Potters: current approaches in ceramic archaeology*, 45–54. Los Angeles, University of California Press

Rice, P. M. (1987) *Pottery Analysis: a sourcebook*. Chicago, University of Chicago Press

Ridgway, D. (2000) The First Western Greeks Revisited. In D. Ridgway *et al.*, eds., *Ancient Italy in its Mediterranean Setting: studies in honour of Ellen Macnamara*, 179–91. Accordia specialist studies on the Mediterranean, 4. London, Accordia Research Institute

Risser, M. K. and Harvey, S. (1992) A Reexamination of Chamber Tombs at Tell el-Farʻah (South) (Abstract of a paper presented at the 93rd Annual Meeting of the Archaeological Institute of America). *American Journal of Archaeology* 96, 344

Rizza, G. (1962) Siculi e Greci sui colli di Leontinoi. *Cronache di Archeologia* 1, 3–27

Rizza, G. (1996) Priniàs in età micenea. In E. de Miro *et al.*, eds., *Atti e memorie del secondo Congresso internazionale di micenologia, Roma-Napoli, 14–20 ottobre 1991* 3. Rome, Gruppo Editoriale Internazionale

Rizza, G. (in press) Identità, etnicità, processi di trasformazione a Priniàs. *Atti del Convegno di Studi 'Identità culturale, etnicità, processi di trasformazione a Creta fra Dark Age ed Arcaismo' (Atene, 9–12 novembre 2006)*

Rodenwaldt, G. (1911) Fragmente mykenischer Wandgemälde. *Mitteilungen des deutschen Archäologischen Instituts (Athenische Abteilung)* 36, 221–50

Rodenwaldt, G. (1912) *Die Fresken des Palastes*. Tiryns, 2. Athens, Eleutheroudakis und Barth

Rodwell, M. J. and Hoskins, B. J. (1996) Monsoons and the Dynamics of Desserts. *Quarterly Journal of the Royal Meteorological Society* 122, 1,385–1,404

Rohling, E. J., Casford, J. S. L., Abu-Zied, R. H., Cooke, S., Mercone, D., Thomson, J., Croudace, I., Jorissen, F. J., Brinkhuis, H., Kallmeyer, J. and Wefer, G. (2002a) Rapid Holocene Climate Changes in the Eastern Mediterranean. In F. A. Hassan, ed., *Droughts, Food and Culture: ecological change and food security in Africa's later prehistory*, 35–46. New York and London, Kluwer Academic and Plenum Publishers

Rohling, E. J., Jorissen, F. J. and De Stigter, H. C. (1997) 200 Year Interruption of Holocene Sapropel Formation in the Adriatic Sea. *Journal of Micropalaeontology* 16, 97–108

Rohling, E. J., Mayewski, P. A., Hayes, A., Abu-Zied, R. H. and Casford, J. S. L. (2002b) Holocene Atmosphere-Ocean Interactions: records from Greenland and the Aegean Sea. *Climate Dynamics* 18, 587–93

Rose, C. B. (1995) The 1994 Post-Bronze Age Research and Excavations at Troia. *Studia Troica* 5, 81–106

Rose, C. B. (1997) The 1996 Post-Bronze Age Excavations at Troia. *Studia Troica* 7, 73–110

Rose, C. B. (1998) The 1997 Post-Bronze Age Excavations at Troia. *Studia Troica* 8, 71–114

Rose, C. B. (2008) Separating Fact and Fiction in the Aeolian Migration. *Hesperia* 77.3, 399–430

Rothenberg, B. (1971) *Midianite Timna, Valley of the Biblical Copper Mines. an archaeological exhibition from the excavations in the Timna Valley (Israel) at the British Museum*. London and New York, Thames & Hudson

Rothenberg, B. (1972) *Timna, Valley of the Biblical Copper Mines*. London and New York, Thames & Hudson

Rothenberg, B. (1988) *The Egyptian Mining Temple at Timna: researches in the Arabah 1959–1984*. London, Institute for Archaeo-Metallurgical Studies, University College London

Rothenberg, B. and Glass, J. (1983) The Midianite Pottery. In J. F. A. Sawyer and D. J. A. Clines, eds., *Midian, Moab, and Edom: the history and archaeology of Late Bronze and Iron Age Jordan and north-west Arabia*, 65–124. Journal for the Study of the Old Testament, Supplement series, 24. Sheffield, Sheffield University Press

Routledge, B. (2004) *Moab in the Iron Age: hegemony, polity, archaeology*. Philadelphia, University of Pennsylvania Press

Rowe, I. (2002) The King's Men in Ugarit and Society in Late Bronze Age Syria. *Journal of the Economic and Social History of the Orient* 45.1, 1–19

Rowlands, M. (1987) Centre and Periphery: a review of a concept. In M. Rowlands *et al.*, eds., *Centre and Periphery in the Ancient World*, 1–11. Cambridge, Cambridge University Press

Rowlands, M. (1998) The Archaeology of Colonialism. In K. Kristiansen and M. Rowlands, eds., *Social Transformations in Archaeology: global and local perspectives*, 327–33. London, Routledge

Rowlands, M., Larsen, M. T., Kristiansen, K. eds., (1987). *Centre and Periphery in the Ancient World*. Cambridge, Cambridge University Press

Ruijgh, C. J. (1967) *Études sur la grammaire et le vocabulaire du grec mycénien*. Amsterdam, M. Hakkert

Rutter, J. B. (1975) Ceramic Evidence for Northern Intruders in Southern Greece at the Beginning of Late Helladic IIIC Period. *American Journal of Archaeology* 79, 17–32

Rutter, J. B. (1976) 'Non-Mycenaean' Pottery: a reply to Gisela Walberg. *American Journal of Archaeology* 80, 187–88

Rutter, J. B. (1979) The Last Mycenaeans at Corinth. *Hesperia* 48, 348–92

Rutter, J. B. (1990) Some Comments on Interpreting the Dark-Surfaced Handmade Burnished Pottery of the 13th and 12th cent. B. C. Aegean. *Journal of Mediterranean Archaeology* 3.1, 29–49

Rutter, J. B. (1992) Cultural Novelties in the Post-Palatial Aegean World: indices of vitality or decline? In W. A. Ward and M. S. Joukowsky, eds., *The Crisis Years: the 12th Century B.C. from beyond the Danube to the Tigris*, 61–78. Dubuque, Kendall/Hunt Publishing Co.

Rutter, J. B. (2006) Southwestern Anatolian Pottery from Late Minoan Crete: evidence for direct contacts between Arzawa and Keftiu? In M. H. Wiener, ed., *Pottery and Society: the impact of recent studies in Minoan pottery. Gold Meal Colloquium in honor of Philip P. Betancourt, 104th annual meeting of the Archaeological Institute of America, New Orleans, LA, 5 January 2003*, 138–53. Boston, Archaeological Institute of America

Rutter, J. B. (in press) How Different is LH IIIC Middle at Mitrou? An initial comparison with Kalapodi, Kynos and Lefkandi. In S. Deger-Jalkotzy and M. Zavadil, eds., *LH IIIC Chronology and Synchronisms: LH IIIC Middle. Proceedings of the International Workshop held at the Austrian Academy of Sciences at Vienna, October 29th and 30th, 2004*

Saaroni, H., Bitan, A., Alpert, P. and Ziv, B. (1996) Continental Polar Outbreaks into the Levant and Eastern Mediterranean. *International Journal of Climatology* 16, 1,175–91

Sakellarakis, J. A. (1992) *The Mycenaean Pictorial Style in the National Archaeological Museum of Athens*. Athens, Kapon Editions

Sakellarakis, J. A. and Sapouna-Sakellaraki, E. (1997) *Archanes: Minoan Crete in a new light*, 2 vols. [Athens], Ammos Publications

Sakellariou, A., ed. (1964) *Die minoische und mykenischen Siegel des Nationalmuseums in Athen*. Berlin, Mann

Sakellariou, A. (1971) Scène de bataille sur un vase Mycénien en pierre? *Revue archéologique* 1, 3–14

Sams, G. K. (1994) *The Early Phrygian Pottery*. Philadelphia, University Museum, University of Pennsylvania

Sandars, N. K. (1978) *The Sea Peoples: warriors of the ancient Mediterranean*. London, Thames & Hudson

Sandars, N. K. (1985) *The Sea Peoples: warriors of the ancient Mediterranean*. London, Thames & Hudson

Sapouna-Sakellarakis, E. (1990) Archanès à l'époque mycénienne. *Bulletin de correspondance hellénique* 114, 67–102

Saprykin, S. J. (1994) *Ancient Farms and Land-Plots on the Khora of Khersonesos Taurike: research in the Herakleian Peninsula, 1974–1990*. McGill University Monographs in Classical Archaeology and History, 16. Amsterdam, J. C. Gieben

Sasson, J. M. (1966) Canaanite Maritime Involvement in the Second Millennium BC. *Journal of the American Oriental Society* 86, 126–38

Savage, S. H. and Falconer, S. E. (2003) Spatial and Statistical Inference of Late Bronze Age Polities in the Southern Levant. *Bulletin of the American Schools of Oriental Research* 330, 31–45

Savignoni, L. (1904) Scavi e scoperte nella necropoli di Phaestòs. *Monumenti Antichi dei Lincei* 14, 500–666

Schachermeyr, F. (1980) *Die ägäische Frühzeit IV: Griechenland im Zeitalter der Wanderungen vom Ende der mykenischen Ära bis auf die Dorier*. Sitzungsberichte der Österreichischen Akademie der Wissenschaften, 372. Vienna, Österreichische Akademie der Wissenschaften pilosophisch-historische Klasse Denkschriften

Schaeffer, C. F.-A. (1952) *Enkomi-Alasia I: nouvelles missions en Chypre 1946–1950*. Paris, Klinscksieck

Schiffer, M. B. (1990) Technological Change in Water-Storage and Cooking Pots: some predictions from experiment. In W. D. Kingery, ed., *The Changing Roles of Ceramics in Society: 26,000 B.P. to the present*, 119–36. Westerville, American Ceramic Society

Schiffer, M. B. and Skibo, J. M. (1987) Theory and Experiment in the Study of Technological Change. *Current Anthropology* 28, 595–622

Schilardi, D. U. (1992) Paros and the Cyclades after the Fall of the Mycenaean Palaces. In J.-P. Olivier, ed., *Mykenaika: actes du 9e colloque international sur les textes mycéniens et egéens*

organisé par le Centre de l'antiquité grecque et romaine de la Fondation hellénique des recherches scientifiques et l'École française d'Athènes (Athènes, 2–6 octobre 1990), 621–39. Bulletin de correspondence hellénique, supplément 25. Paris, École française d'Athènes

Schlipphak, R. (2001) *Wandappliken der Spätbronze- und Eisenzeit im östlichen Mittelmeerraum*. Abhandlungen des Deutschen Palästinavereins, 28. Wiesbaden, Harrassowitz

Schloen, J. D. (2001) *The House of the Father as Fact and Symbol: patrimonialism in Ugarit and the Ancient Near East*. Studies in the Archaeology and History of the Levant, 2. Winona Lake, Eisenbrauns

Schmandt-Besserat, D. (2001) Feasting in the Ancient Near East. In M. Dietler and B. Hayden, eds., *Feasts: archaeological and ethnographic perspectives on food, politics, and power*, 391–403. Washington DC and London, Smithsonian Institution Press

Schmidt, H. (1902) Die Keramik der verschiedenen Schichten. In W. Dörpfeld, ed., *Troja und Ilion: Ergebnisse der Ausgrabungen in den vorhistorischen und historischen Schichten von Ilion 1870–1894*. Athens, Beck and Barth

Schoep, I. (2004) Assessing the Role of Architecture in Conspicuous Consumption in the Middle Minoan I–II Periods. *Oxford Journal of Archaeology* 23.3, 243–69

Schofield, E. (1983) The Minoan Emigrant. In O. Krzyszkowska and L. Nixon, eds., *Minoan Society: proceedings of the Cambridge Colloquium 1981*, 293–301. Bristol, Bristol Academic Press

Schortman, E. M. and Urban, P. A. (2004) Modeling the Roles of Craft Production in Ancient Political Economies. *Journal of Archaeological Research* 12.2, 185–226

Schwartz, G. M. and Nichols, J. M. (2006) *After Collapse: the regeneration of complex societies*. Tucson, University of Arizona Press

Seager, R. B. (1906–07) Report of Excavations at Vasiliki, Crete in 1906. *University of Pennsylvania Transactions of the Department of Archaeology, Free Museum of Science and Art* 2

Shanks, M. and Tilley, C. (1987) *Social Theory and Archaeology*. Cambridge, Polity Press

Shaw, J. W. and Shaw, M. C., eds. (2000) *Kommos 4: the Greek sanctuary*, 2 vols. Princeton and Oxford, Princeton University Press

Shaw, J. W. and Shaw, M. C., eds. (2006) *Kommos 5: the monumental Minoan buildings at Kommos*. Princeton and Oxford, Princeton University Press

Shaw, M. C. (1990) Late Minoan Hearths and Ovens at Kommos, Crete. In P. Darcque and R. Treuil, eds., *L'habitat égéen préhistorique. Actes de la table ronde internationale, Athènes, 23–25 juin 1987, organisés par le Centre National de la Recherche Scientifique, l'Université de Paris et l'École française d'Athènes*, 231–54. Athens, École française d'Athènes

Shaw, M. C. (1996a) The North House and Peripheral Areas. In J. W. Shaw and M. C. Shaw, eds., *Kommos: an Excavation on the South Coast of Crete. Vol. 1: the Kommos region and houses of the Minoan town. Part 2: the Minoan hilltop and hillside houses*, 15–59. Princeton and Oxford, Princeton University Press

Shaw, M. C. (1996b) Town Arrangement and Domestic Architecture. In J. W. Shaw and M. C. Shaw, eds., *Kommos: an Excavation on the South Coast of Crete. Vol. 1: the Kommos region and houses of the Minoan town. Part 2: the Minoan hilltop and hillside houses*, 345–77. Princeton and Oxford, Princeton University Press

Shaw, M. C. (2001) Symbols of Naval Power at the Palace at Pylos: the evidence from the frescoes. In S. Böhm and K.-V. von Eickstedt, eds., *Ithaki: Festschrift für Jörg Schäfer zum 75. Geburtstag am 25. April 2001*, 37–43. Würzburg, Ergon

Shelmerdine, C. W. (1985) *The Perfume Industry of Mycenaean Pylos*. Studies in Mediterranean Archaeology Pocket-book, 34. Göteborg, Paul Åströms Förlag

Shelmerdine, C. W. (1997) Review of Aegean Prehistory VI: the palatial Bronze Age of the southern and central Greek mainland. *American Journal of Archaeology* 101, 537–85

Shelmerdine, C. W. (1998) Where Do We Go From Here? And can the Linear B Tablets help us get there? In E. Cline and D. Harris-Cline, eds., *The Aegean and the Orient in the Second Millennium: proceedings of the 50th anniversary symposium, Cincinnati, 18–20 April 1997*, 292–98. Aegaeum, 18. Liège, Université de Liège

Shelmerdine, S. (1987) Architectural Change and Economic Decline at Pylos. In J. T. Killen *et al.*, eds., *Studies in Mycenaean and Classical Greek Presented to John Chadwick*, 557–68. Minos, 20–22. Salamanca, Universidad de Salamanca

Sherratt, A. and Sherratt, S. (1991) From Luxuries to Commodities: the nature of Mediterranean Bronze Age trading systems. In N. H. Gale, ed., *Bronze Age Trade in the Mediterranean: papers presented at the conference held at Rewley House, Oxford, in December 1989*, 351–86. Studies in Mediterranean Archaeology, 90. Jonsered, Paul Åström

Sherratt, A. and Sherratt, S. (1998) Small Worlds: Interaction and identity in the ancient Mediterranean. In E. Cline and D. Harris-Cline, eds., *The Aegean and the Orient in the Second Millennium: proceedings of the 50th anniversary symposium, Cincinnati, 18–20 April 1997*, 329–33. Aegaeum, 18. Liège, Université de Liège

Sherratt, A. and Sherratt, S. (2001) Technological Change in the East Mediterranean Bronze Age: capital, resources and marketing. In A. Shortland, ed., *The Social Context of Technological Change: Egypt and the Near East, 1650–1550 B.C. Proceedings of a conference held at St. Edmund Hall, Oxford, 12–14 September 2000*, 15–38. Oxford, Oxbow Books

Sherratt, S. (1982) Patterns of Contact: manufacture and distribution of Mycenaean pottery, 1400–1100 B. C. In J. G. P. Best and N. M. W. de Vries, eds., *Interaction and Acculturation in the Mediterranean II: proceedings of the Second International Congress of Mediterranean pre- and protohistory, Amsterdam, 19–23 November 1980* 2, 179–95. Amsterdam, B. R. Grüner

Sherratt, S. (1991) Cypriot Pottery of Aegean Type in LC II–III: problems of classification, chronology and interpretation. In J. A. Barlow *et al.*, eds., *Cypriot Ceramics: reading the prehistoric record*, 185–98. University Museum monograph, 74. Philadelphia, The University Museum of the University of Pennsylvania

Sherratt, S. (1994a) Commerce, Iron and Ideology: metallurgical innovation in 12th–11th century Cyprus. In V. Karageorghis, ed., *Cyprus in the 11th century B.C.: proceedings of the international symposium, organized by the Archaeological Research Unit of the University of Cyprus and The Anastasios*

G. Leventis Foundation, Nicosia 30–31 October, 1993, 59–106. Nicosia, University of Cyprus

Sherratt, S. (1994b) Patterns of Contact between the Aegean and Cyprus in the 13th and 12th Centuries BC. *Archaeologia Cypria* 3, 35–46

Sherratt, S. (1998) 'Sea Peoples' and the Economic Structure of the Late Second Millennium in the Eastern Mediterranean. In S. Gitin *et al.*, eds., *Mediterranean Peoples in Transition: thirteenth to early tenth centuries BCE*, 292–313. Jerusalem, Israel Exploration Society

Sherratt, S. (1999) *E pur si muove*: pots, markets and values in the Second Millennium Mediterranean. In J. P. Crielaard *et al.*, eds., *The Complex Past of the Pottery: production, circulation and consumption of Mycenaean and Greek Pottery (sixteenth to early fifth centuries BC). Proceedings of the ARCHON international conference held in Amsterdam, 8–9 November 1996*, 163–211. Amsterdam, J. C. Gieben

Sherratt, S. (2000) Circulation of Metals and the End of the Bronze Age in the Eastern Mediterranean. In C. Pare, ed., *Metals Make the World Go Round: the supply and circulation of metals in Bronze Age Europe*, 82–95. Oxford, Oxbow Books

Sherratt, S. (2001) Potemkin Palaces and Route-Based Economies. In S. Voutsaki and J. T. Killen, eds., *Economy and Politics in the Mycenaean Palace States*, 214–38. Cambridge, Cambridge Philological Society

Sherratt, S. (2003) The Mediterranean Economy: 'globalization' at the end of the Second Millennium B.C.E. In W. G. Dever and S. Gitin, eds., *Symbiosis, Symbolism, and the Power of the Past: Canaan, ancient Israel, and their neighbors from the Late Bronze Age through Roman Palaestina. Proceedings of the Centennial Symposium, W. F. Albright Institute of Archaeological Research and American Schools of Oriental Research, Jerusalem, May 29–31, 2000*, 37–62. Winona Lake, Indiana, Eisenbrauns

Sherratt, S. and Crouwel, J. (1987) Mycenaean Pottery from Cilicia in Oxford. *Oxford Journal of Archaeology* 6, 325–52

Shulman, A. R. (1967) The Scarabs. In G. F. Bass, ed., *Cape Gelidonya: a Bronze Age shipwreck*, 143–7. Philadelphia, American Philosophical Society

Siedentopf, H. B. (1991) *Alt-Ägina IV 2. Mattbemalte Keramik der Mittleren Bronzezeit*. Mainz, Philipp von Zabern

Sillar, B. (1997) Reputable Pots and Disreputable Potters: individual and community choice in present-day pottery production and exchange in the Andes. In C. G. Cumberpatch and P. W. Blinkhorn, eds., *Not So Much a Pot, More a Way of Life*, 1–20. Oxford, Oxbow Monographs, 83

Singer, I. (1983) Takuhlinu and Haya: two governors in the Ugarit letter from Tel Aphek. *Tel Aviv* 10, 3–25

Singer, I. (1994) Egyptians, Canaanites and Philistines in the Period of the Emergence of Israel. In I. Finkelstein and N. Na'aman, eds., *From Nomadism to Monarchy: Archaeological and Historical Aspects of Early Israel*, 282–338. Jerusalem, Israel Exploration Society

Singer, I. (1999) A Political History of Ugarit. In W. G. E. Watson and N. Wyatt, eds., *Handbook of Ugaritic Studies*, 603–733. Leiden, Brill

Sinopoli, C. (1991) *Approaches to Archaeological Ceramics*. London and New York, Plenum Press

Sjöberg, B. (1995) The Mycenaean Economy: theoretical frameworks. In C. Gillis *et al.*, eds., *Trade and Production in Premonetary Greece: aspects of trade*, 19–32. Studies in Mediterranean Archaeology Pocket-book, 134. Jonsered, Paul Åströms Förlag

Skerlou, E. (1996) Περίχωρα της πόλης Κω. *Αρχαιολογικό Δελτίο* 51 Χρονικά, 689–92

Skerlou, E. (1997) Κως – Δυτικός τομέας της πόλης. *Αρχαιολογικό Δελτίο* 52 Χρονικά, 1,110–1

Small, D. B. (1990) Handmade Burnished Ware and Prehistoric Aegean Economics: an argument for indigenous appearance. *Journal of Mediterranean Archaeology* 3.1, 3–28

Small, D. B. (1997) Can We Move Forward? Comments on the current debate over handmade burnished ware. *Journal of Mediterranean Archaeology* 10.2, 223–8

Smithson, E. (1977) 'Submycenaean' and LH IIIC Domestic Deposits in Athens. *American Journal of Archaeology* 81, 78–9

Sommella Mura, A., Cazzella, A., Lugli, F., Rosa, C., Baroni, I., Danti, A. and Albertoni, M. (2001) Notizie preliminari sulle scoperte e sulle indagini archeologiche nel versante orientale del Capitolium. *Bullettino della Commissione Archeologica Comunale di Roma* 102, 263–364

Sparks, R. T. (2001) Palestinian Stone Vessels: the evidence from Pella. *Studies in the Archaeology and History of Jordan* 7, 259–63. Amman, Department of Antiquities

Stager, L. E. (1995) The Impact of the Sea Peoples in Canaan (1185–1050 BCE). In T. E. Levy, ed., *The Archaeology of Society in the Holy Land*, 332–48. London, Leicester University Press

Stager, L. E. (2003) Phoenician Shipwrecks in the Deep Sea. In N. C. Stampolidis and V. Karageorghis, eds., *Πλόες: Sea Routes. Interconnections in the Mediterranean 16th–6th C. BC*, 233–47. Athens, Museum of Cycladic Art

Stampolidis, N. C. and Kotsonas, A. (2006) Phoenicians in Crete. In S. Deger-Jalkotzy and I. S. Lemos, eds., *Ancient Greece: from the Mycenaean palaces to the Age of Homer*, 337–60. Edinburgh, Edinburgh University Press

Stark, M. T. (1998) Technical Choices and Social Boundaries in Material Culture Patterning: an introduction. In M. T. Stark, ed., *The Archaeology of Social Boundaries*, 1–11. Washington and London, Smithsonian Institution Press

Starkey, J. L. and Harding, L. (1932) *Beth Pelet II. Beth Pelet Cemetery*. London, British School of Archaeology in Egypt and Bernard Quaritch

Stech-Wheeler, T., Muhly, J. D., Maxwell-Hyslop, K. R. and Maddin, R. (1981) Iron at Taanach and Early Iron Metallurgy in the Eastern Mediterranean. *American Journal of Archaeology* 85, 245–68

Steel, L. (2002) Consuming Passions: a contextual study of the consumption of Mycenaean pottery at Tell el-'Ajjul. *Journal of Mediterranean Archaeology* 15.1, 25–54

Steel, L. (2004) *Cyprus Before History: from the earliest settlers to the end of the Bronze Age*. London, Duckworth

Steponaitis, V. S. (1978) Location Theory and Complex Chiefdoms: a Mississippian example. In B. D. Smith, ed., *Mississippian Settlement Patterns*, 417–54. New York, Academic Press

Sterling, P. (1966) *Turkish Village*. The Nature of Human Societies Series. New York, Wiley

Stern, E. (1995) *Excavations at Dor, Final Report*, 2 vols. Qedem Reports. Jerusalem, Hebrew University of Jerusalem

Stiebing Jr., W. H. (1970a) Another Look at the Origins of the Philistine Tombs at Tell el-Far'ah (S). *American Journal of Archaeology* 74, 139–43

Stiebing Jr., W. H. (1970b) *Burial Practices in Palestine During the Bronze Age*. Unpublished PhD thesis, University of Pennsylvania

Stieglitz, R. R. (2006) Classical Greek Measures and the Builder's Instruments from the Ma'agan Mikhael Shipwreck. *American Journal of Archaeology* 110, 195–203

Stockfisch, D. (1999) Ugarit – Internationale Handelsmetropole im Schnittpunkt des vererasiatischostmediterranen Verkhersnetzes. In M. Kropp and A. Wagner, eds., *'Schnittpunkt' Ugarit*, 255–270. Nordostafrikanisch Westasiatische Studien, 2. Frankfurt, Peter Lang

Stockhammer, P. (2006) Bericht zur spätmykenischen Keramik aus Stadt-Nordost. In J. Maran (ed.) Forschungen im Stadtgebiet von Tiryns 1999–2002. *Archäologischer Anzeiger*, 139–62

Stoddart, S. (1990) The Political Landscape of Etruria. *Accordia Research Paper* 1, 39–52

Stoddart, S. and Redhouse, D. (2005) Complexity and Landscape: a case study from Etruria. Unpublished paper presented at *Defining Social Complexity: approaches to power and interaction in the archaeological record*, 11–13 March 2005, University of Cambridge

Stubbings, F. H. (1947) The Mycenaean Pottery in Attica. *Annual of the British School at Athens* 42, 1–75

Tanasi, D. (2003) Mycenaean Influences on the Pottery of North Pantalica Culture (Sicily). In N. Kyparissi-Apostolika and M. Papakonstantinou, eds., *Β Διεθνές Διεπιστημονικό Συμπόσιο: Η Περιφέρεια του Μυκηναϊκού Κόσμου*, 599–611. Athens, Έκδοση ΙΔ Εφορείας Προϊστορικών και Κλασσικών Αρχαιοτήτων

Tanasi, D. (2004a) Per un riesame degli elementi di tipo miceneo nella cultura di Pantalica Nord. In V. La Rosa, ed., *Le presenze micenee nel territorio siracusano: I Simposio siracusano di preistoria siciliana in memoria di Paolo Orsi, Siracusa, 15–16 dicembre 2003, Palazzo Impellizzeri, Museo archeologico regionale Paolo Orsi*, 337–83. Padua, Bottega d'Erasmo

Tanasi, D. (2004b) Per una rilettura delle necropoli sulla Montagna di Caltagirone. In V. La Rosa, ed., *Le presenze micenee nel territorio siracusano: I Simposio siracusano di preistoria siciliana in memoria di Paolo Orsi, Siracusa, 15–16 dicembre 2003, Palazzo Impellizzeri, Museo archeologico regionale Paolo Orsi*, 399–447. Padua, Bottega d'Erasmo

Tanasi, D. (2004c) Tre modellini fittili dalla necropoli di Thapsos. *Sicilia Antiqua* 1, 21–7

Tanasi, D. (2005) Mycenaean Pottery Imports and Local Imitations: Sicily vs. southern Italy. In R. Laffineur and E. Greco, eds., *Emporia: Aegeans in the Central and Esatern Mediterranean. Proceedings of the 10th International Aegean Conference / 10e Rencontre égéenne internationale. Athens, Italian School of Archaeology, 14–18 April 2004*, 561–9. Aegaeum, 25. Liège, Université de Liège

Tanasi, D. (2007) A Late Bronze Age Upland Sanctuary in the Core of Sikania? In M. Fitzjohn, ed., *Uplands of Ancient Sicily and Calabria: the archaeology of landscape revisited*, 157–70. London, Accordia

Tanasi, D. (in press-a) La Montagna di Polizzello alla fine dell'Età del Bronzo: il caso dell'Edificio Nord sull'acropoli, Atti della XLI Riunione Scientifica dell'I.I.P.P. *Dai Ciclopi agli Ecisti. Società e territorio nella Sicilia preistorica e protostorica*

Tanasi, D. (in press-b) Nuove evidenze ceramiche del periodo Bronzo/Ferro dall'acropoli della Montagna di Polizzello, Atti della XLI Riunione Scientifica dell'I.I.P.P. *Dai Ciclopi agli Ecisti. Società e territorio nella Sicilia preistorica e protostorica*

Taramelli, A. (1899) Ricerche archeologiche cretesi. *Monumenti Antichi dei Lincei* 9, 297–446

Tegou, E. (2001) Τηολοτόσ ταπηόσ τισ πρόιμισ εποχηίσ του Σιδίρου στιν Παντάνασσα Αμαρίου Ν. Ρετηγύμνισ. In N. C. Stampolidis, ed., *Καύσεις στην Εποχή του Χαλκού και την Πρώιμη Εποχή του Σιδήρου*, 121–53. Athens, Panepistemio tes Kretes

Taylour, W. D. (1964) *The Mycenaeans.* Ancient Peoples and Places, 39. London, Thames and Hudson

Televantou, C. A. (1990) New Light on the West House Wall-Paintings. In D. A. Hardy *et al.*, eds., *Thera and the Aegean World III: proceedings of the Third International Congress, Santorini, Greece, 3–9 September 1989* 1 (Archaeology), 309–26. London, The Thera Foundation

Televantou, C. A. (1994) *Ακρωτήρι Θήρας. Οι Τοιχογραφίες της Δυτικής Οικίας.* Athens, Η εν Αθήναις Αρχαιολογική Εταιρεία

Televantou, C. A. (2001) Ayios Andreas on Sifnos: a Late Cycladic III fortified acropolis. In V. Karageorghis and C. Morris, eds., *Defensive Settlements of the Aegean and the Eastern Mediterranean after* c. *1200 B.C.*, 191–213. Dublin, Trinity College and the Anastasios G. Leventis Foundation

Tomasello, F. (2004) L'architettura «micenea» nel Siracusano. In V. La Rosa, ed., *Le presenze micenee nel territorio siracusano: I Simposio siracusano di preistoria siciliana in memoria di Paolo Orsi, Siracusa, 15–16 dicembre 2003, Palazzo Impellizzeri, Museo archeologico regionale Paolo Orsi*, 183–210. Padua, Bottega d'Erasmo

Torelli, M. (2005) *Storia degli Etruschi.* Bari, Laterza

Torrence, R. and van der Leeuw, S. E. (1989) What's New About Innovation? In S. E. van der Leeuw and R. Torrence, eds., *What's New? A Closer Look at the Process of Innovation*, 1–15. London, Unwin Hyman

Touchais, G., Huber, S. and Philippa-Touchais, A. (2000) Chronique des fouilles et découvertes archéologiques en Grèce en 1999. *Bulletin de correspondance hellénique* 124.4, 753–1,023

Touchais, G., Huber, S. and Philippa-Touchais, A. (2001) Chronique des fouilles et découvertes archéologiques en Grèce en 2000. *Bulletin de correspondance hellénique* 125.2, 779–1,063

Tournavitou, I. (1995) *The 'Ivory Houses' at Mycenae.* British School at Athens Supplement 24. [Athens], British School at Athens

Trigo, I. F., Davies, T. D. and Bigg, G. R. (1999) Objective Climatology in the Mediterranean Region. *Journal of Climate* 12, 1,685–96

Trump, D. (2003) Overseas Connections of the Maltese Temples. *Exploring the Maltese Prehistoric Temple Culture (The EMPTC 2003 Conference)*, 1–7

Tsipopoulou, M. (2005) 'Mycenaeans' at the Isthmus of Ierapetra: some (preliminary) thoughts on the foundation of the (Eteo) Cretan cultural identity. In A. L. D'Agata and J. Moody, eds., *Ariadne's Threads: connections between Crete and the Greek mainland in the post-palatial period*, 303–34. Athens, Italian School at Athens

Tsipopoulou, M. and Little, L. (2001) Καύσεισ του τέλουσ τισ εποχηίσ του Χηαλκού στιν Κριτσά Μιραβέλου, Ανατολικί Κρίτι. In N. C. Stampolidis, ed., *Καύσεις στην Εποχή του Χαλκού και την Πρώιμη Εποχή του Σιδήρου*, 83–98. Athens, Panepistemio tes Kretes

Tsipopoulou, M. and Vagnetti, L. (2003) New Evidence for the Dark Ages in Eastern Crete an Unplundered Tholos Tomb at Vasiliki. *Studi Micenei ed Egeo Anatolici* 45.1, 85–124

Tsountas, C. (1896) Γραπτή στήλη εκ Μυκηνών. *Αρχαιολογική Εφημερίς*, 1–22

Tubb, J. N. (1988a) Tell es-Saʿidiyeh: preliminary report on the first three seasons of renewed excavations. *Levant* 20, 23–88

Tubb, J. N. (1988b) The Role of the Sea Peoples in the Bronze Industry of Palestine and Transjordan in the Late Bronze-Early Iron Age Transition. In J. Curtis, ed., *Bronzeworking Centres of Western Asia* c. *1000–539 B.C.*, 99–112. London, British Museum Publications

Tubb, J. N. (1990) Preliminary Report on the Fourth Season of Excavations at Tell es-Saʿidiyeh in the Jordan Valley. *Levant* 22, 21–42

Tubb, J. N. (1995) An Aegean Presence in Egypto-Canaan. In W. V. Davies and L. Schofield, eds., *Egypt, the Aegean and the Levant: interconnections in the second millenium BC*, 136–45. London, British Museum Press

Tubb, J. N. (1998) *Canaanites.* Peoples of the Past. London, British Museum Press

Tubb, J. N. and Dorrell, P. G. (1991) Tell es-Saʿidiyeh: interim report on the fifth (1990) season of excavations. *Levant* 23, 67–86

Tubb, J. N. and Dorrell, P. G. (1993) Tell es-Saʿidiyeh: interim report on the sixth season of excavations. *Palestine Exploration Quarterly* 125, 50–74

Tubb, J. N. and Dorrell, P. G. (1994) Tell es-Saʿidiyeh 1993: interim report on the seventh season of excavations. *Palestine Exploration Quarterly* 126, 52–67

Tubb, J. N., Dorrell, P. G. and Cobbing, F. J. (1996) Interim Report on the Eighth (1995) Season of Excavations at Tell es-Saʿidiyeh. *Palestine Exploration Quarterly* 128, 16–40

Tubb, J. N., Dorrell, P. G. and Cobbing, F. J. (1997) Interim Report on the Ninth Season (1996) of Excavations at Tell es-Saʿidiyeh, Jordan. *Palestine Exploration Quarterly* 129, 54–77

Tuchelt, K. (1984) Didyma: Bericht uber die Arbeiten der Jahre 1980–1983. *Istanbuler Mitteilungen* 34, 193–344

Tufnell, O. (1940) *Lachish II (Tell ed-Duweir): the Fosse temple.* Oxford, Oxford University Press

Tufnell, O. (1953) *Lachish III (Tell ed-Duweir): the Iron Age.* London, Oxford University Press

Tufnell, O. (1958) *Lachish IV (Tell ed-Duweir): the Bronze Age.* London, Oxford University Press

Tusa, S., ed. (1997) *Prima Sicilia: alle origini della società siciliana.* Palermo, Giuseppe Maimone Editore

Tusa, S. (1999) *La Sicilia nella preistoria.* Palermo, Sellerio

Tusa, S. (2004) La Sicilia. Gli insediamenti. In D. Cocchi Genick, ed., *L'età del bronzo recente in Italia: atti del Congresso nazionale di Lido di Camaiore, 26–29 ottobre 2000*, 327–34. Viareggio, Mauro Baroni

Tusa, S. and Nicoletti, F. (2000) L'epilogo sicano nella Sicilia occidentale: il caso Mokarta – Capanna 1. *Atti delle terze giornate internazionali di studi sull'area elima*, 963–77. Pisa, Edizioni della Normale

Tzahou-Aexandri, O. (1989) *Το Πνεύμα και το Σώμα: Οι Αθλητικοί Αγώνες στην Αρχαία Ελλάδα*. Athens, Υπουργείο Πολιτισμού-Ελληνικό Τμήμα I.C.O.M.

Tzedakis, Y. and Martlew, H. (1999) *Minoans and Mycenaeans: flavours of their time*. Athens, Greek Ministry of Culture, General Directorate of Antiquities

Vagnetti, L. (1968) Un vaso miceneo da Pantalica. *Studi micenei ed egeo anatolici* 5, 132–5

Vagnetti, L. (1989) A Sardinian Askos from Crete. *Annual of the British School at Athens* 84, 335–60

Vagnetti, L. (1996) Espansione e diffusione dei Micenei. In S. Settis, ed., *I Greci: storia, cultura, arte, società* 2.1, 133–72. Turin, Einaudi

Vagnetti, L. (1999) I Micenei fra Mediterraneo Orientale ed Occidentale dopo la fine dei Palazzi. *Magna Grecia e oriente mediterraneo prima dell'età ellenistica. Atti del trentanovesimo convegno di studi sulla Magna Grecia, Taranto, 1–5 ottobre 1999*, 63–89. Convegno di studi sulla Magna Grecia. Taranto, Istituto per la storia e l'archeologia della Magna Grecia

Vagnetti, L. (1999) Mycenaean Pottery in the Central Mediterranean: imports and local production in their context. In J. P. Crielaard *et al.*, eds., *The Complex Past of the Pottery: production, circulation and consumption of Mycenaean and Greek Pottery (sixteenth to early fifth centuries BC). Proceedings of the ARCHON international conference held in Amsterdam, 8–9 November 1996*, 137–61. Amsterdam, J. C. Gieben

Vagnetti, L. (2000–01) Preliminary Remarks on Mycenaean Pictorial Pottery from the Central Mediterranean. *Opuscula Atheniensia* 25–6, 107–15

Vagnetti, L. (2001) Some Observations on Late Cypriot Pottery from the Central Mediterranean. In L. Bonfante and V. Karageorghis, eds., *Italy and Cyprus in Antiquity, 1500–450 BC: proceedings of an international symposium held at the Italian Academy for Advanced Studies in America at Columbia University, November 16–18, 2000*, 77–96. Nicosia, Costakis and Leto Severis Foundation

Vagnetti, L. (2003) The Role of Crete in the Exchanges between the Aegean and the Central Mediterranean in the Second Millennium BC. In N. C. Stampolidis and V. Karageorghis, eds., *Πλόες: Sea Routes. Interconnections in the Mediterranean 16th–6th C. BC*, 53–61. Athens, Museum of Cycladic Art

Vallino, F. and Ventura, G. (1984) Dati archeobotanici dal Broglio: semi ed altri reperti. In R. Peroni, ed., *Nuove ricerche sulla protostoria della Sibaritide*, 272–80. Rome, Paleani Editore

van der Kooij, G. and Ibrahim, M. M., eds. (1989) *Picking up the Threads...: a continuing review of excavations at Deir Alla, Jordan*. Leiden, University of Leiden Archaeological Centre

van der Leeuw, S. E. (1993) Giving the Potter a Choice: conceptual aspects of pottery techniques. In P. Lemonnier, ed., *Technological Choices: transformations in material cultures since the Neolithic*, 238–288. London and New York, Routledge

van der Leeuw, S. E. and Pritchard, A. C., eds. (1984) *The Many Dimensions of Pottery: ceramics in archaeology and anthropology*. Amsterdam, University of Amsterdam

van der Steen, E. J. (1996) The Central East Jordan Valley in the Late Bronze and Early Iron Ages. *Bulletin of the American Schools of Oriental Research* 302, 51–74

van der Steen, E. J. (1999) Survival and Adaptation: life east of the Jordan in the transition from the Late Bronze Age to the Early Iron Age. *Palestine Exploration Quarterly* 131, 176–92

van Dommelen, P. (2006) The Orientalizing Phenomenon: hybridity and material culture in the western Mediterranean. In C. Riva and N. C. Vella, eds., *Debating Orientalization: multidisciplinary approaches to change in the ancient Mediterranean*, 135–52. London, Equinox

Van Essche, E. (1989) Quelques réflexions sur l'espace et le récit à Médinet Habou. *Annales d'Histoire de l'Art et d'Archéologie* 11, 7–24

Van Essche-Merchez, E. (1994) Pour une lecture «stratigraphique» des parois du temple de Ramsès III à Médinet Habou. *Revue d'Egyptologie* 45, 87–116

van Wijngaarden, G. J. (1999a) An Archaeological Approach to the Concept of Value: Mycenaean pottery at Ugarit (Syria). *Archaeological Dialogues* 6.1, 2–23

van Wijngaarden, G. J. (1999b) Production, Circulation and Consumption of Mycenaean Pottery (Sixteenth to Twelfth Centuries BC). In J. P. Crielaard *et al.*, eds., *The Complex Past of the Pottery: production, circulation and consumption of Mycenaean and Greek Pottery (sixteenth to early fifth centuries BC). Proceedings of the ARCHON international conference held in Amsterdam, 8–9 November 1996*, 21–47. Amsterdam, J. C. Gieben

van Wijngaarden, G. J. (2002) *Use and Appreciation of Mycenaean Pottery in the Levant, Cyprus and Italy (ca. 1600–1200 BC)*. Amsterdam, Amsterdam University Press

van Wijngaarden, G. J. (2005) Mycenaean Heirlooms, Antiques and Souvenirs in the Levant and Cyprus. In R. Laffineur and E. Greco, eds., *Emporia: Aegeans in the Central and Esatern Mediterranean. Proceedings of the 10th International Aegean Conference/10e Rencontre égéenne internationale. Athens, Italian School of Archaeology, 14–18 April 2004*, 405–13. Aegaeum, 25. Liège, Université de Liège

Vanzetti, A. (2002) Some Current Approaches to Protohistoric Centralization and Urbanization in Italy. In P. Attema, ed., *New Developments in Italian Landscape Archaeology: theory and methodology of field survey land evaluation and landscape perception, pottery production and distribution. Proceedings of a three-day conference held at the University of Groningen, April 13–15, 2000*, 36–51. BAR International Series, 1091. Oxford, Archaeopress

Vanzetti, A. (2004) Risultati e problemi di alcune attuali prospettive di studio della centralizzazione e urbanizzazione di fase protostorica in Italia. In P. Attema, ed., *Centralization, Early Urbanisation and Colonization in First Millennium B.C. Italy and Greece*, 1–28. Babesch Supplementa, 9. Leuven, Peeters

Ventris, M. and Chadwick, J. (1973) *Documents in Mycenaean Greek*. Cambridge, Cambridge University Press

Vermeule, E. (1972) *Greece in the Bronze Age*. Chicago, University of Chicago Press

Vermeule, E. and Karageorghis, V. (1982) *Mycenaean Pictorial Vase Painting*. Cambridge, Mass. and London, Harvard University Press

Vianello, A. (2005) *Late Bronze Age Mycenaean and Italic Products in the West Mediterranean: a social and economic analysis*. BAR International Series, 1439. Oxford, Archaeopress

Vichos, Y. and Lolos, Y. G. (1997) The Cypro–Mycenaean Wreck at Point Iria in the Argolic Gulf: first thoughts on the origin and the nature of the vessel. In S. Swiny *et al.*, eds., *Res Maritimae: Cyprus and the eastern Mediterranean from prehistory to late antiquity. Proceedings of the Second International Symposium 'Cities on the Sea', Nicosia, Cyprus, October 18–22, 1994,* 321–37. American Schools of Oriental Research Archaeological Reports, 4; Cyprus American Archaeological Research Institute Monograph Series, 1. Atlanta, Scholars Press

Vlachopoulos, A. G. (1995) *Η Υστεροελλαδική ΙΙΙ Γ Περίοδος στη Νάξο – Τα Ταφικά Σύνολα και οι Συσχετισμοί τους με το Αιγαίο.* Unpublished PhD thesis, University of Athens, Φιλοσοφική Σχολή, Τομέας Αρχαιολογίας και Ιστορίας της Τέχνης

Vlachopoulos, A. G. (1999a) Η Νάξος κατά την ΥΕ ΙΙΙΓ περίοδο. Η φυσιογνωμία και ο χαρακτήρας ενός ακμαίου νησιωτικού κέντρου. *Η Περιφέρεια του Μυκηναϊκού Κόσμου,* 303–14. Lamia, Έκδοση ΙΔ Εφορείας Προϊστορικών και Κλασσικών Αρχαιοτήτων

Vlachopoulos, A. G. (1999b) Ο κρατήρας της Γρόττας. Συμβολή στη μελέτη της Υστεροελλαδικής ΙΙΙΓ εικονιστικής κεραμεικής της Νάξου. In N. C. Stampolidis, ed., *Φώς Κυκλαδικόν. Τιμητικός Τόμος στη Μνήμη του Νίκου Ζαφειρόπουλου,* 74–95. Athens, Ίδρυμα Ν. Π. Γουλανδρή- Μουσείο Κυκλαδικής Τέχνης

Vlachopoulos, A. G. (2003a) The Late Helladic IIIC 'Grotta Phase' of Naxos: its synchronisms in the Aegean and its non-synchronisms in the Cyclades. In S. Deger-Jalkotzy and M. Zavadil, eds., *LH IIIC Chronology and Synchronisms,* 217–34. Vienna, Österreichische Akademie der Wissenschaften pilosophisch-historische Klasse Denkscriften

Vlachopoulos, A. G. (2003b) Ο Υστεροελλαδικός ΙΙΙΓ Οικισμός της Γρόττας Νάξου Στο Κέντρο ή στην Περιφέρεια του Μυκηναϊκού Αιγαίου. In N. Kyparissē-Apostolika and M. Papakonstantinou, eds., *The Periphery of the Mycenaean World: proceedings of the 2nd International Interdisciplinary Colloquium, Lamia 1999,* 493–511. Athens, Ministry of Culture and 14th Ephorate of Prehistoric and Classical Antiquities

Voutsaki, S. (1993) *Society and Culture in the Mycenaean World: an analysis of mortuary practices in the Argolid, Thessaly and the Dodecanese*. Unpublished PhD thesis, University of Cambridge

Voutsaki, S. (1997) The Creation of Value and Prestige in the Aegean Late Bronze Age. *Journal of European Archaeology* 5.2, 34–52

Voutsaki, S. (1998) Mortuary Evidence, Symbolic Meanings and Social Change: a comparison between Messenia and the Argolid in the Mycenaean Period. In K. Branigan, ed., *Cemetery and Society in the Aegean Bronze Age,* 41–58. Sheffield Studies in Aegean Archaeology, 1. Sheffield, Sheffield Academic Press

Voutsaki, S. (1999) Value Beyond Ugarit. *Archaeological Dialogues* 6.1, 27–31

Voutsaki, S. (2001) Economic Control, Power and Prestige in the Mycenaean World: the archaeological evidence. In S. Voutsaki and J. Killen, eds., *Economy and Politics in the Mycenaean Palace States: proceedings of a conference held on 1–3 July 1999 in the Faculty of Classics, Cambridge,* 195–213. Cambridge, Cambridge Philological Society

Voza, G. (1972) Thapsos: primi risultati della più recenti ricerche. *Atti della XIV Riunione scientifica dell'I.I.P.P.,* 175–205. Florence, Istituto Italiano di Preistoria e Protostoria

Voza, G. (1973) Thapsos: resoconto sulle campagne di scavo del 1970–71. *Atti della XV Riunione scientifica dell'I.I.P.P.,* 133–57. Florence, Istituto Italiano di Preistoria e Protostoria

Voza, G. (1976–77) L'attività della soprintendenza alle antichità della Sicilia orientale. *Kokalos* 22–3, 562– 8

Voza, G. (1978) La necropoli della valle del Marcellino presso Villasmundo. *Cronache di Archeologia* 17, 104–10

Voza, G. (1980–81) L'attività della soprintendenza alle antichità della Sicilia orientale. *Kokalos* 26–7, 674–93

Voza, G. (1984–85) L'attività nel territorio della soprintendenza alle antichità di Siracusa nel quadriennio 1980–1984. *Kokalos* 30–1, 657–77

Wachsmann, S. (2000) To the Sea of the Philistines. In E. D. Oren, ed., *The Sea Peoples and their World: a reassessment,* 130–43. University Museum Monograph, 108; University Museum Symposium Series, 11. Philadelphia, University Museum, University of Pennsylvania

Walberg, G. (1976) Northern Intruders in Mycenaean IIIC? *American Journal of Archaeology* 80, 186–7

Walberg, G. (1995) The Midea Megaron and Changes in Mycenaean Ideology. *Aegean Archaeology* 2, 87–91

Waldbaum, J. C. (1966) The Philistine Tombs at Tell Fara and their Aegean Prototypes. *American Journal of Archaeology* 70, 331–40

Waldbaum, J. C. (1978) *From Bronze to Iron: the transition from the Bronze Age to the Iron Age in the eastern Mediterranean*. Studies in Mediterranean Archaeology, 54. Göteborg, Paul Åmströms Förlag

Wallace, S. (2003) The Changing Role of Herding in the Early Iron Age of Crete: some implications of settlement shift for economy. *American Journal of Archaeology* 107, 601–28

Wallace, S. (in preparation) Housing Zones and Templates before and after 1200 BC in Crete: Karphi (Lasithi) and Other Cases. In K. Glowacki and N. Vogeikoff-Brogan, eds., *STEGA: the archaeology of houses and households in Ancient Crete from the Neolithic period through the Roman era, 26–28 May 2005, Ierapetra*

Wallrodt, S. (2002) Ritual Activity in Late Classical Ilion: the evidence from a fourth century B.C. deposit of loomweights and spindlewhorls. *Studia Troica* 12, 179–196

Ward, W. A. and Joukowsky, M. S., eds. (1992) *The Crisis Years: the 12th Century BC from beyond the Danube to the Tigris*. Dubuque, Kendall/Hunt Publishing Co.

Warren, P. M. (1975) *The Aegean Civilizations*. The Making of the Past. New York, Elsevier-Phaidon Press

Warren, P. M. (1982–83) Knossos: Stratigraphical Museum excavations, 1978–82. Part II. *Archaeological Reports,* 63–87

Warren, P. M. and Hankey, V. (1989) *Aegean Bronze Age Chronology*. Exeter, Bristol Classical Press

Watrous, L. V. (1989) A Preliminary Report on Imported 'Italian'

Wares from the Late Bronze Age site of Kommos on Crete. *Studi micenei ed egeo-anatolici* 27, 68–79

Watrous, L. V. (1993) A Survey of the Western Mesara Plain in Crete: preliminary report of the 1984, 1986, and 1987 field seasons. *Hesperia* 62.2, 191–248

Watrous, L. V., Day, P. and Jones, R. (1998) The Sardinian Pottery from the Late Bronze Age Site of Kommos in Crete: description, chemical and petrographic analysis and historical context. In M. S. Balmuth and R. H. Tykot, eds., *Sardinian and Aegean Chronology: towards the resolution of relative and absolute dating in the Mediterranean. Proceedings of the international colloquium 'Sardinian Stratigraphy and Mediterranean Chronology', Tufts University, Medford, Massachussets, March 17–19, 1995*, 333–45. Oxford, Oxbow Books

Webster, T. B. L. (1954) Pylos E tablets (En–Eo and Ep series). *Bulletin of the Institute of Classical Studies* 1, 13–14

Wedde, M. (2000) *Towards a Hermeneutics of Aegean Bronze Age Ship Imagery*. Peleus: Studien zur Archäologie und Geschichte Griechenlands und Zyperns, 6. Mannheim, Bibliopolis

Weinstein, J. M. (1981) The Egyptian Empire in Palestine: a reassessment. *Bulletin of the American Schools of Oriental Research* 241, 1–28

Weinstein, J. M. (1992) The Collapse of the Egyptian Empire in the Southern Levant. In W. A. Ward and M. S. Joukowsky, eds., *The Crisis Years: the 12th Century BC from beyond the Danube to the Tigris*, 142–50. Dubuque, Kendall/Hunt Publishing Co.

Weisgerber, G. and Cierny, J. (1999) Ist das Zinnrätsel gelöst? *Oxus* 4/99, 44–7

Weissl, M. (2002) Grundzuge der Bau- und Schichtenfolge im Artemesion von Ephesos. *Jahreshefte des Osterreichischen Archaologischen Institutes in Wien* 71, 313–346

Wells, B. (1983) *Asine II: results of the excavations east of the Acropolis 1970–1974*. Fasc. 4, Part 2. Stockholm, Svenska institutet i Athen

Wengrow, D. (1996) Egyptian Taskmasters and Heavy Burdens: highland exploitation and the collared-rim pithos of the Bronze/Iron Age Levant. *Oxford Journal of Archaeology* 15, 307–26

Whitbread, I. (1992) Petrographic Analysis of Barbarian Ware from the Menelaion, Sparta. In J. M. Sanders, ed., *Philolakon: Lakonian studies in honour of Hector Catling*, 297–306. London, The British School at Athens

White, D., Gardner, R. and Hulin, L. (2002) *Marsa Matruh: the University of Pennsylvania Museum of Archaeology and Anthropology's excavations on Bates's Island, Marsa Matruh, Egypt, 1985–1989. Volume 2: the Objects*. Philadelphia, Institute for Aegean Prehistory Academic Press

Whitelaw, T. M. (2001) Reading between the Tablets: assessing Mycenaean palatial involvement in ceramic production and consumption. In S. Voutsaki and J. Killen, eds., *Economy and Politics in the Mycenaean Palace States: proceedings of a conference held on 1–3 July 1999 in the Faculty of Classics, Cambridge*, 51–79. Cambridge, Cambridge Philological Society

Whitley, J. (2004–05) Archaeology in Greece 2004–2005: Lefkandi. *Archaeological Reports* 51, 50–2

Wilson, C. D. and Blinman, E. (1995) Changing Specialization of White Ware Manufacture in the Northern San Juan Region. In B. J. Mills and P. L. Crown, eds., *Ceramic Production in the American Southwest*, 63–87. Tucson, University of Arizona Press

Wiman, I. and Bruun-Lundgren, M. (2003) Industrial Activities and Personal Adornments. In E. Hallager and B. Pålsson Hallager, eds., *The Greek-Swedish excavations at the Agia Aikaterini Square, Kastelli, Khania, 1970–1987 and 2001: results of the excavations under the direction of Yannis Tzedakis and Carl-Gustaf Styrenius. Vol.3: the Late Minoan IIIB:2 settlement, 1 (text)*, 266–9. Skrifter utgivna av Svenska Institutet i Athen, 47.3.1, 4°. Stockholm, Paul Åmströms Förlag

Wolff, S. (2005) *Double Pithos Burials in the Levant: some new evidence and thoughts*. Unpublished paper presented at the American Schools of Oriental Research Annual Meeting, Philadelphia, PA., November 2005

Wolfram, S. (2002) *A New Kind of Science*. Champain, Wolfram Media Inc

Wood, B. G. (1990) *The Sociology of Pottery in Ancient Palestine*. Sheffield, JSOT Press

Wreszinski, W. (1923–35) *Atlas zur altägyptischen Kulturgeschichte II*. Leipzig, J. C. Hinrichs

Wright, J. C. (1984) Changes in Form and Function of the Palace at Pylos. In C. W. Shelmerdine and T. G. Palaima, eds., *Pylos Comes Alive: industry and administartion in a Mycenaean palace*, 19–29. New York, Fordham University Lincoln Center

Xanthoudidis, S. (1904) From Crete. Αρχαιολογικη Έφημερίς, 1–56

Xénaki-Sakellariou, A and Chatziliou, C. (1989) *'Peinture en métal' a l'époque mycénienne: incrustation, damasquinage, niellure*. Athens, Ekdotike Athenon

Yadin, Y. (1972) *Hazor: the head of all those Kingdoms (Joshua 11.10)*. The Schweich Lectures of the British Academy. London, Oxford University Press

Yadin, Y. (1982) Is the Biblical Account of the Israelite Conquest of Canaan Historically Reliable? *Biblical Archaeology Review* 8, 16–23

Yadin, Y., Aharoni, Y., Dunayevski, T., Dothan, T., Amiran, R. B. K. and Perrot, J. (1960) *Hazor II: an account of the second season of excavations, 1956*. Jerusalem, Israel Exploration Society

Yadin, Y., Aharoni, Y., Dunayevski, T., Dothan, T., Amiran, R. B. K. and Perrot, J. (1961) *Hazor III–IV: an account of the third and fourth seasons of excavations, 1957–1958*. Jerusalem, Israel Exploration Society

Yassine, K. N. (1975) Anthropoid Coffins from the Raghdam Royal Palace Tombs in Amman. *Annual of the Department of Antiquities in Jordan* 20, 57–68

Yasur-Landau, A. (2002) *Social Aspects of Aegean Settlement in the Southern Levant in the End of the 2nd Millennium BCE*. Unpublished PhD thesis, Tel Aviv University

Yasur-Landau, A. (2003a) The Many Faces of Colonization: 12th century Aegean settlements in Cyprus and the Levant. *Mediterranean Archaeology and Archaeometry* 3.1, 45–54

Yasur-Landau, A. (2003b) Why Can't We Find the Origin of the Philistines? In search of the source of a peripheral Aegean culture. *Η Περιφέρεια του Μυκηναϊκού Κόσμου Β*, 587–98. Athens, Έκδοση ΙΔ Εφορείας Προϊστορικών και Κλασσικών Αρχαιοτήτων

Yellin, J., Dothan, T. and Gould, B. (1986) The Provenience of

Beer Bottles from Deir el-Balah: a study by neutron activation analysis. *Israel Exploration Journal* 36.1–2, 68–73

Yon, M. (1992) The End of the Kingdom of Ugarit. In W. A. Ward and M. S. Joukowsky, eds., *The Crisis Years: the 12th Century BC from beyond the Danube to the Tigris*, 111–22. Dubuque, Kendall/Hunt Publishing Co.

Yon, M. and Caubet, A. (1985) *Kition Bamboula 3: le sondage L-N 13 (Bronze Récent et Géométrique I)*. Paris, Editions Recherche sur les Civilisations

Yon, M., Karageorghis, V. and Hirschfeld, N. (2000) *Céramiques mycéniennes d'Ougarit*. Ras Shamra-Ougarit, 13. Paris and Nicosia, ERC-ADPF and Leventis Foundation

Yoyotte, J. (1949) Les stèles de Ramsès II a Tanis. *Kêmi* 10, 58–74

Zaccagnini, C. (1970) Note sulla terminologica metallurgica di Ugarit. *Oriens Antiquus* 9, 315–24

Zaccagnini, C. (1979) Notes on the Nuzi Surface Measures. *Ugarit Forschungen* 11, 849–56

Zaccagnini, C. (1987) Aspects of Ceremonial Exchange in the Near East During the Late Second Millennium B.C. In M. Rowlands *et al.*, eds., *Centre and Periphery in the Ancient World*, 57–65. Cambridge, Cambridge University Press

Zaccagnini, C. (1990) Again on the Yield of the Fields at Nuzi. *Bulletin on Sumerian Agriculture* 5, 201–17

Zangger, E., Timpson, M. E., Yazvenko, S. B., Kuhnke, F. and Knauss, J. (1997) The Pylos Regional Archaeological Project II: landscape evolution and site preservation. *Hesperia* 66, 548–641

Zarinebaf, F., Bennet, D. J. and Davis, J. L. (2005) *A Historical and Economic Geography of Ottoman Greece: the southwestern Morea in the early 18th century. Hesperia* Supplement, 34. Princeton, American School of Classical Studies

Ziffer, I. (2005) From Acemhöyük to Megiddo: the banquet scene in the art of the Levant in the second millennium BCE. *Tel-Aviv* 32, 133–67

Zipf, G. K. (1949) *Human Behavior and the Principle of Least Effort: an introduction to human ecology*. Cambridge, Addison-Wesley Press

Zuckerman, S. (2006) Where is the Archive of Hazor Buried? *Biblical Archaeology Review* 32, 28–37

Zuckerman, S. (2007) Anatomy of a Destruction: crisis architecture, termination rituals and the call of Canaanite Hazor. *Journal of Mediterranean Archaeology* 20 (1), 3–32

Printed by Printforce, United Kingdom